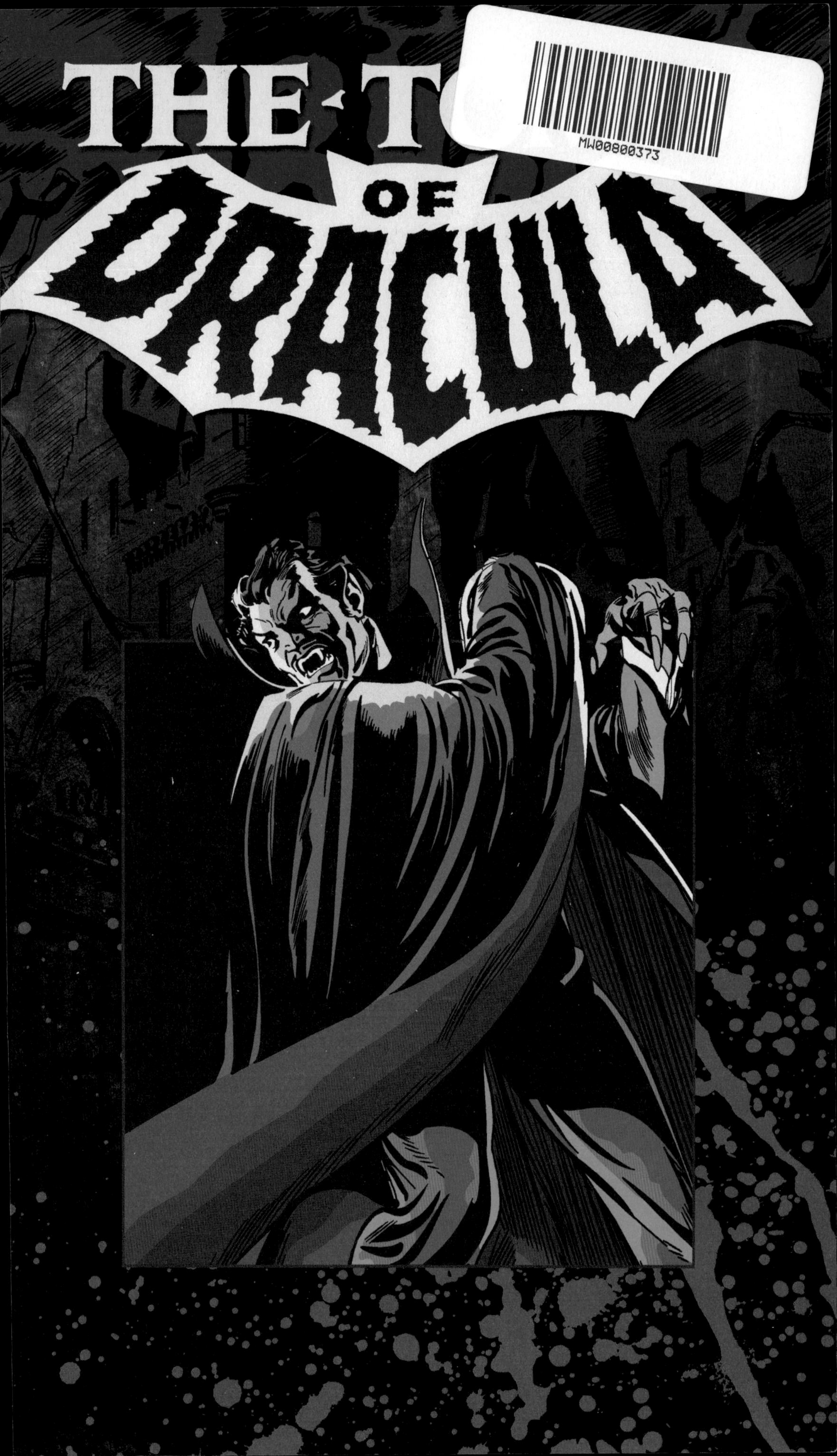
THE T
OF
DRACULA

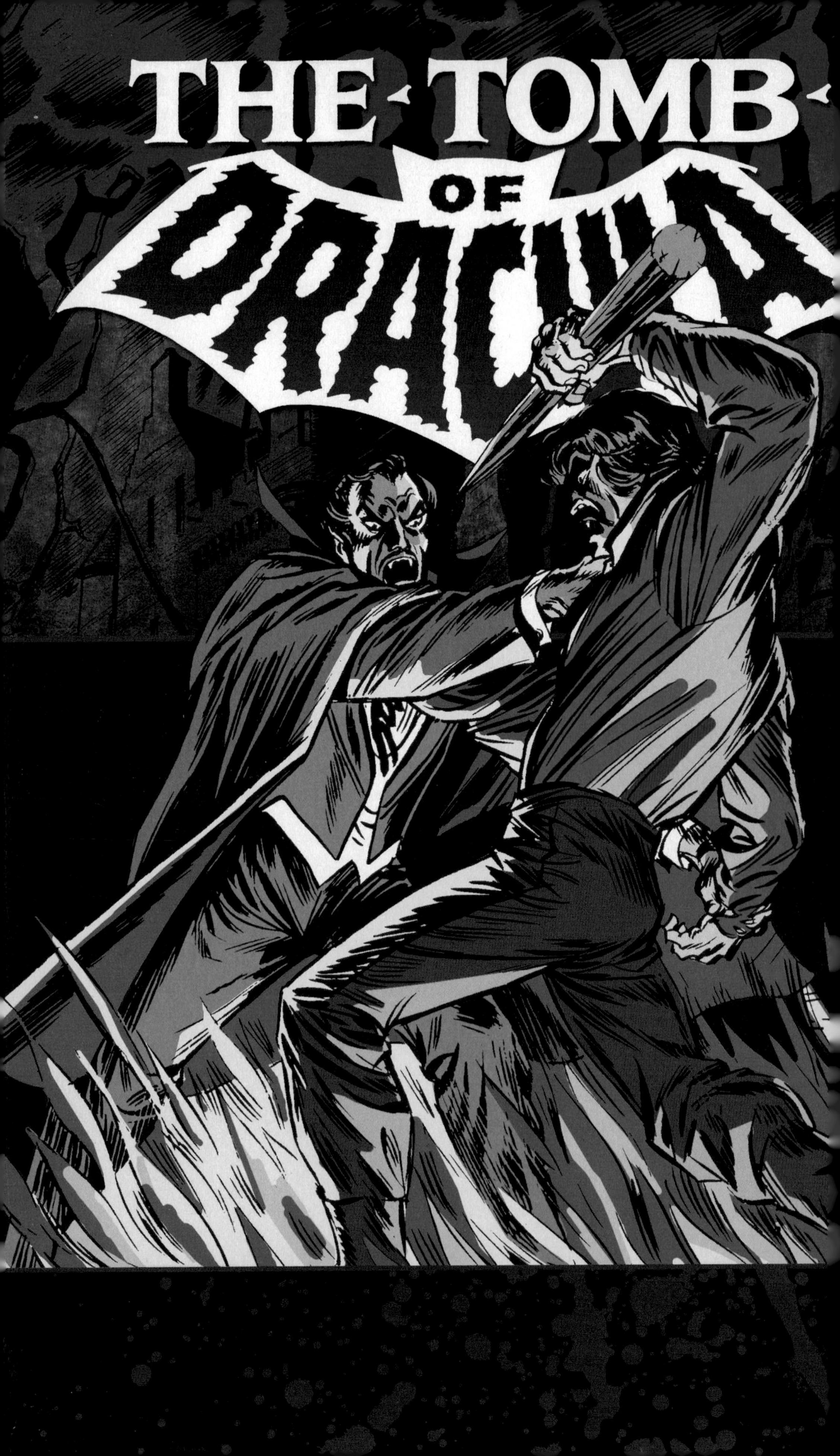
THE TOMB OF DRACULA

writer: **MARV WOLFMAN**
pencilers: **GENE COLAN & MIKE PLOOG**
inkers: **TOM PALMER & FRANK CHIARAMONTE**
colorists: **TOM PALMER, PETRA GOLDBERG,
GLYNIS WEIN & LINDA LESSMAN**
letterers: **JOHN COSTANZA & ART SIMEK**
editor: **ROY THOMAS**

front cover artist: **JOHN ROMITA**
front cover colorist: **CHRIS SOTOMAYOR**
back cover artist: **GIL KANE**
back cover colorist: **AVALON STUDIOS**

collection editor: **MARK D. BEAZLEY**
editorial assistants: **JOE HOCHSTEIN
& JAMES EMMETT**
assistant editors: **NELSON RIBEIRO &
ALEX STARBUCK**
editor, special projects: **JENNIFER GRÜNWALD**
senior editor, special projects: **JEFF YOUNGQUIST**
production: **JERRON QUALITY COLOR**
color reconstruction: **COLORTEK & JASON LEWIS**
select art reconstruction: **TOM ZIUKO & DIGIKORE**
book designer: **ARLENE SO**
senior vice president of sales: **DAVID GABRIEL**

editor in chief: **JOE QUESADA**
publisher: **DAN BUCKLEY**
executive producer: **ALAN FINE**

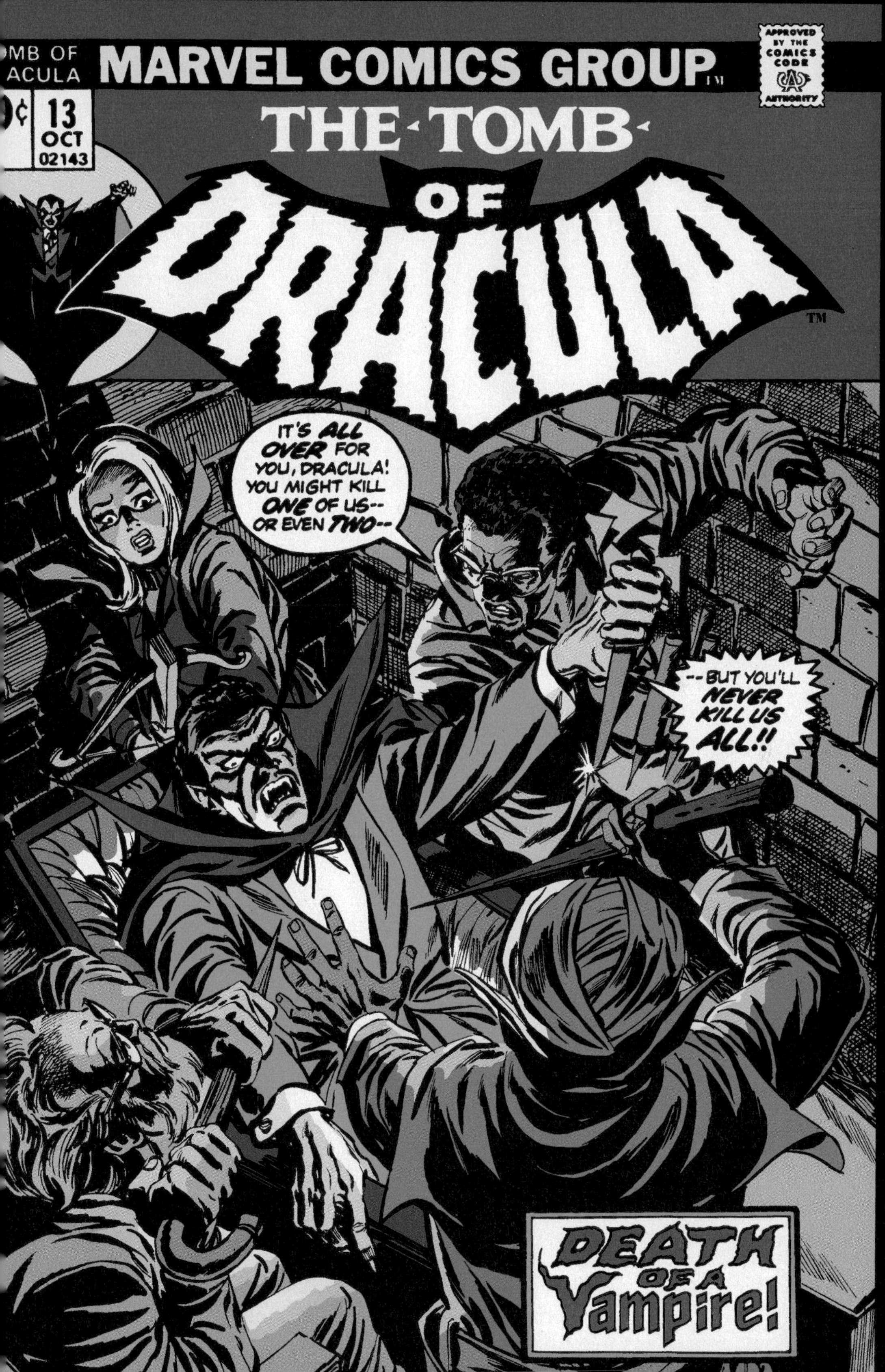

OMB OF
ACULA
MARVEL COMICS GROUP
APPROVED BY THE COMICS CODE AUTHORITY
0¢ 13 OCT 02143
THE TOMB OF DRACULA
IT'S ALL OVER FOR YOU, DRACULA! YOU MIGHT KILL ONE OF US-- OR EVEN TWO--
--BUT YOU'LL NEVER KILL US ALL!!
DEATH OF A Vampire!

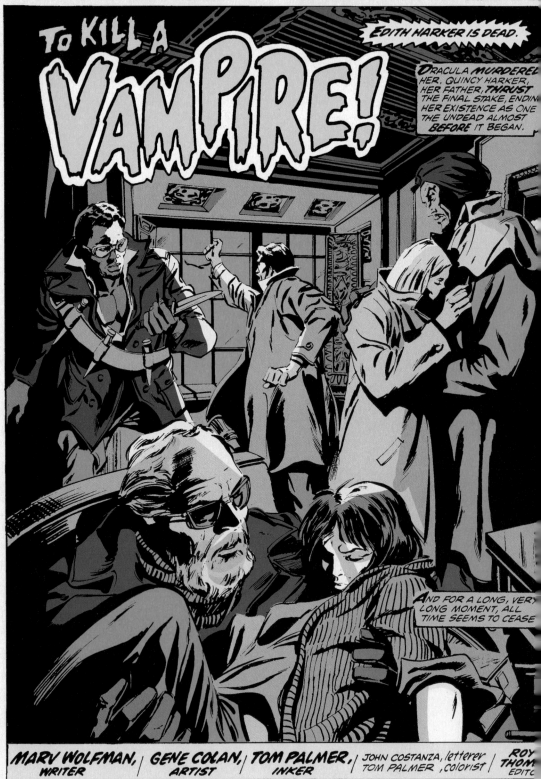

TO KILL A VAMPIRE!

EDITH HARKER IS DEAD.

DRACULA MURDERED HER, QUINCY HARKER, HER FATHER, THRUST THE FINAL STAKE, ENDING HER EXISTENCE AS ONE THE UNDEAD ALMOST BEFORE IT BEGAN.

AND FOR A LONG, VERY LONG MOMENT, ALL TIME SEEMS TO CEASE

MARV WOLFMAN, WRITER | GENE COLAN, ARTIST | TOM PALMER, INKER | JOHN COSTANZA, letterer TOM PALMER, colorist | ROY THOM EDITO

REMEMBER... IT MUST BE BEEN LONG AGO--... SHE ... ONLY ... OR YET KNEW ABOUT WORK--

--SHE SAID "DADDY, I DON'T *EVER* WANT TO BECOME A *VAMPIRE*. PLEASE DON'T LET ME BECOME ONE."

AND I WOULD *LAUGH* AND TELL HER NOT TO *WORRY*, THAT I WOULD *PROTECT* HER ALWAYS.

OH, GOD-- *OH, GOD.*

THERE'S A TIME FOR *MOURNING*, HARKER--AND MAYBE FOR YOU IT'S *NOW*--BUT DRACULA'S *LOOSE*, AND WHO KNOWS WHO *ELSE* HE MIGHT KILL TONIGHT.

NOW, I'M *WILLIN'* TO JOIN YOU PEOPLE, FOR AWHILE-- *IF* WE DO IT *MY* WAY. UNDERSTAND?

JUST WAIT ONE BLASTED MINUTE, BLADE. WHO DO YOU THINK YOU'RE *ORDERING* AROUND? EDITH'S *DEAD!* MAYBE THAT DOESN'T *MEAN* ANYTHING TO YOU--

--BUT I'LL TELL YOU THIS-- SHE WAS IMPORTANT TO US. GET THAT, BLADE--? TO *US!!*

SO IF YOU WANT TO DO *ANYTHING*, YOU DO IT *OUR WAY*-- OR YOU CAN JUST TAKE YOUR STINKING *KNIVES* AND STICK THEM WHERE IT HURTS.

LOOK WHO'S *TALKIN'*, DRAKE-- YOU'RE *DESCENDED* FROM DRACULA, AREN'T YOU? HOW DO WE KNOW YOU'RE NOT *PLAYIN'* BOTH SIDES?

WHY, YOU LOUSY KNIFE-HAPPY *MANIAC*-- I OUGHT TO--

STOP IT, BOTH OF YOU. EDITH'S DEAD--THIS *ISN'T* THE TIME FOR FIGHTING.

LOOK, I *SORRY* ABO[UT] THAT LAST CRA[CK] DRAKE--IT W[AS] *OUTTA* PLAC[E] I KNOW IT[...]

--BUT WH[Y] NOT HAVE ED[ITH'S] *FUNERAL* AND THEN G[ET] *BACK* ON T[HE] TRAIL. DIG[?]

THERE'S TO BE *NO* FUNERAL, MR. BLADE. HER BODY WILL BE *CREMATED* AS IS THE *PROCEDURE*.

BUT YOU ARE *RIGHT*, THERE IS *NO TIME* TO LOSE. ALREADY DRACULA MAY HAVE FOUND...

"...*ANOTHER VICTIM*."

CECILE PARKER'S PARENTS *WARNED* HER NOT TO TAKE HYDE STREET ON HER WAY *HOME* FROM THE UNIVERSITY. IN THE PAST WEEK, *FIVE* OTHER CO-EDS HAD BEEN KILLED IN THE AREA...

...NEEDLESS TO SAY, SHE DID NOT LISTEN.

C'MON, *GIRLEE*--JES A LITTLE *KISS 'LL* DO OLE SKINNEE.

PLEASE, LEAVE ME ALONE.

SURE, HONEY, AFTER YA GIMME A LITTLE *KISS*.

OLE SKINNEE SHORE BEEN *LONELY* THESE DAYS, KNOW WHAT I MEAN, GIRLEE?

GET AWAY-- OR I SWEAR I'LL *SCREAM* TILL SOMEONE COMES.

8

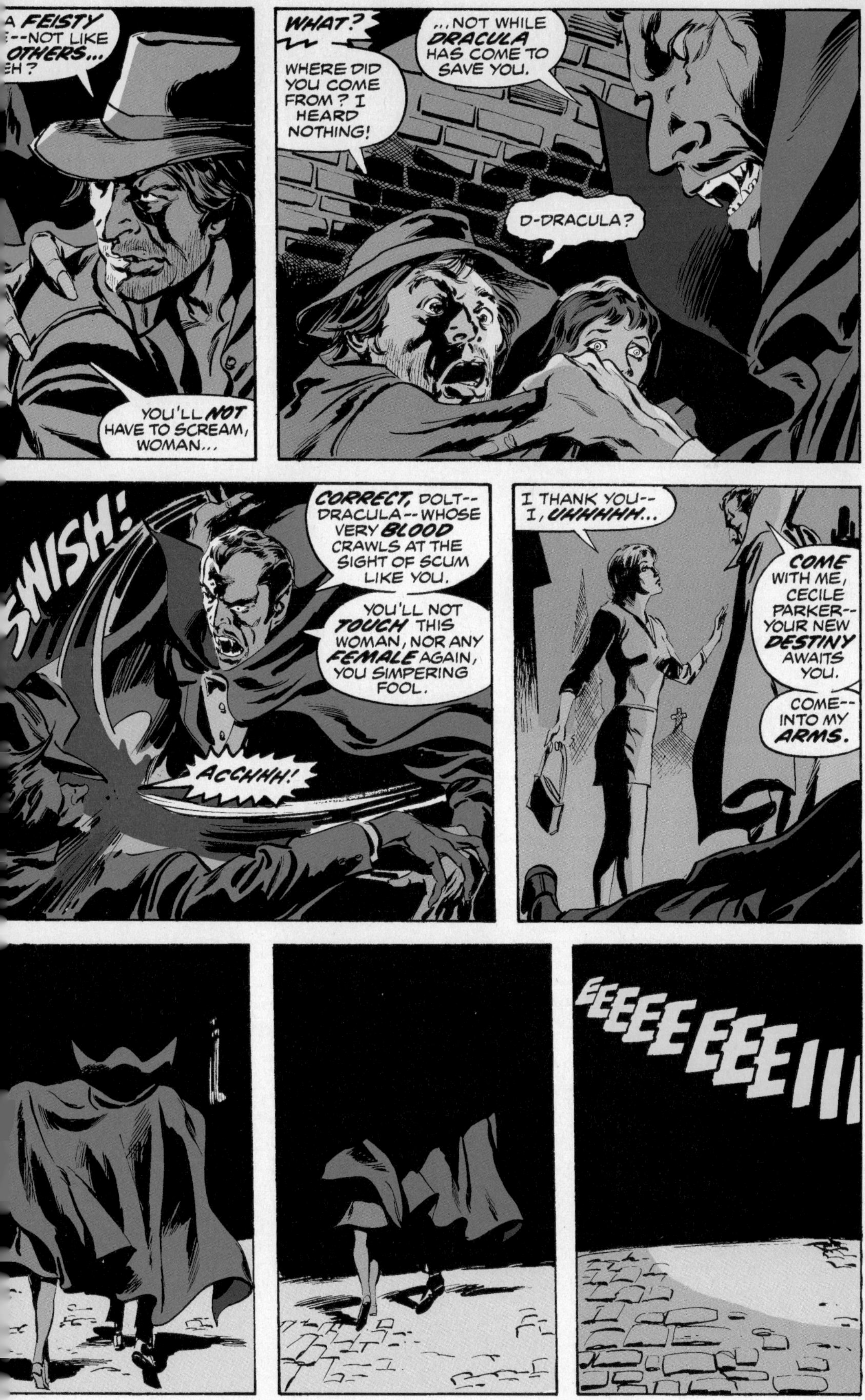
A FEISTY
E--NOT LIKE
OTHERS...
EH?
YOU'LL NOT
HAVE TO SCREAM,
WOMAN...
WHAT?
WHERE DID
YOU COME
FROM? I
HEARD
NOTHING!
...NOT WHILE
DRACULA
HAS COME TO
SAVE YOU.
D-DRACULA?
SWISH!
CORRECT, DOLT--
DRACULA--WHOSE
VERY BLOOD
CRAWLS AT THE
SIGHT OF SCUM
LIKE YOU.
YOU'LL NOT
TOUCH THIS
WOMAN, NOR ANY
FEMALE AGAIN,
YOU SIMPERING
FOOL.
ACCHHH!
I THANK YOU--
I, UHHHHH...
COME
WITH ME,
CECILE
PARKER--
YOUR NEW
DESTINY
AWAITS
YOU.
COME--
INTO MY
ARMS.
EEEEEEEEIII

WORRY NOT, DEAR CECILE--YOU'LL AWAKEN SOON, STILL ALIVE--STILL HUMAN... AND YOU'LL HAVE FORGOTTEN ALL THAT HAS HAPPENED HERE THIS NIGHT...

--BUT THERE WILL BE A TIME... IN THE FUTURE, WHEN YOU WILL HEAR MY MENTAL CALL... AND YOU SHALL COME TO ME AS MY UNFAILING SLAVE.

FOR THE NONCE, YOUR LIFE SHALL BE UNCHANGED, CECILE-- YOU'LL LAUGH, YOU'LL LOVE-- WHATEVER CAN BEFORE SHALL STILL BE YOURS...

AND ALSO YOU WILL BE BUT ANOTHER OF DRACULA'S UNSEEN ARMY, WAITING BUT FOR MY SIGNAL TO RISE INTO ACTION.

FAREWELL, MY SLAVE-- FAREWELL-- HA HA HA HA!

DRACULA RISES HIGH INTO THE WARM JULY SKIES, AND HIS COURSE THIS NIGHT IS ALMOST SKITTISH...

...HE TURNS, HE ARCS, GLIDES THROUGH T[H]E INDIGO DARKNESS, NOT CARING OF A DESTINATION NO[R] PURPOSE IN HIS FL[IGHT]

...AND THEN, ALMOST LIGHTLY, HE LOWERS HIMSELF TO THE GROUND, NOT AS A BAT-- BUT A MAN...

I'VE BEEN TOO LONG AWAY FROM HUMANS-- IF I AM TO EVENTUALLY CONQUER THEM, I MUST KNOW THEIR EVERY WHIM, THEIR EVERY MOOD...

...AND WHERE BEST TO OBSERVE THEM, THAN IN A PLACE WHERE ALL PASSIONS BURST FREE...

SPORTS ARENA

TONIGHT NONE SHALL FALL BENEATH DRACULA'S HAND-- TONIGHT IS A NIGHT FOR STUDY.

AS WE SWITCH OUR SCENE, WHERE A MUGGY HEAT DESCENDS ABOUT THE LONDON *MORGUE*...

LONDON MORGUE
DIVISION OF
SCOTLAND YARD

...WHILE INSIDE, THE SWELTERING HEAT CAN *ALSO* BE FELT...A HEAT THAT MAKES CLOTHING STICK TO A SWEATING, NERVOUS *BODY*...

...A BODY NOT *YET* DECEASED.

MISTER LO, THIS *IS* THE MAN *DOCTOR SUN* SEEKS.

VERY GOOD, CHEN. OUR REPORTS WERE *ACCURATE* THEN.

DR. SUN SHALL BE *VERY* PLEASED.

--YOU *WILL* KEEP OUR, er-- LITTLE BARGAIN A, ER, *SECRET*, LO? I COULD *LOSE* MY BLOODY JOB IF THEY FOUND OUT I WAS SELLIN' YOU THIS STIFF.

ALL IS IN READINESS, CHEN--BUT *FIRST* I WISH ONE LAST LOOK AT--

--AH, *YES*-- THE *PUNCTURE MARKS*. YES, DR. SUN SHALL BE *VERY* PLEASED INDEED.

YOU ASKED FOR OUR *SILENCE,* MR. TOOMY-- BUT YOU WORRY *NEEDLESSLY.* NO ONE SHALL *LEARN* WHAT HAPPENED HERE THIS NIGHT.

LOR' THAT'S A *RELIEF.* WHY, IF EVEN THE MISSUS WAS TO LEARN...

SHE WILL NOT LEARN ANYTHING, MR. TOOMY-- EXCEPT THAT *SOMEHOW* HER HUSBAND WAS *MURDERED* BY PERSONS UNKNOWN...

BAM!

...AND THAT HE DIED WITH ONLY A *FEW* PALTRY POUNDS IN HIS WALLET.

GOODNIG MR. TOO PLEASE R IN PEAC

CHEN, LIN-- *COME*, THE STE OF *DECOMPO ING BODIES* HERE IS *SICKENING*

AGAIN WE *SHIFT* OUR SCENE-- BACK TO THE *LORD OF DARKNESS.*

HUMANS-- THEY CRY OUT FOR *PEACE,* THEN FILL THESE *ARENAS* OF *VIOLENCE* TO THEIR FULLEST CAPACITY.

ISLE 2

INDEED THEY ARE *FASCINATEL* BLOODSHED *MYSTIFIED* BY TH VERY SAME *BRUTAL* THEY CRUSADE SO PIOUSLY AGAINS

NO *LIVES* ARE A STAKE HERE-- *NOT* IS GAINED BY TH *MEANINGLE* SPECTACLE. THER IS NO *PURPOSE* THIS MOCK BATT

--INSTEAD, THIS WANTON WASTE *DISGUSTS* ME-- *REVOLTS* ME.

...ACULA LEAVES, ...NG HIGH INTO ...E FOGGY SKIES ...LONDON, WHILE, ...THE OUT- ...IRTS OF THAT ...RY SAME CITY...

WHAT DO WE DO *NOW,* QUINCY?

WITH EDITH DEAD, HER *ASHES* PRE-SERVED WITHIN THAT *PORCELAIN* URN, WE *MUST* AGAIN BEGIN OUR SEARCH, MR. DRAKE.

TO WAIT ANY LONGER IS *FOOLISH.* TO AVOID ANOTHER CONFLICT WITH THAT FIEND IN THE NAME OF *MOURNING* THE DEAD IS A *MISTAKE* WE CAN *NOT* AFFORD.

AFTER HE IS SLAIN THERE WILL BE TIME ENOUGH FOR US TO *MOURN* THE DEAD.

YOU MAYBE, OLD MAN, ...T IT WON'T BE OVER FOR *ME.*

NOT TILL I FIND THE STINKIN' *BLOODSUCKER* THAT *KILLED* MY MOTHER!

WHAT?

YOU DIDN'T THINK I WAS *CHASIN'* VAMPIRES FOR MY *HEALTH,* DID YOU, DRAKE?

YOU SAID I DIDN'T *KNOW* WHAT IT'S LIKE TO *LOSE* SOMEONE-- MAN --I'M THE *ORIGINAL LOSER!*

...AH, IT BEGAN ...'T BEFORE I ...S *BORN*-- WITH ... MOTHER'S ...IENDS TAKIN' ...RE OF HER AS ...E STARTED ...N' INTA ...BOR...

"SHE WAS *CRYIN'* OUT IN AGONY, 'CAUSE I WAS *PROVIN'* I WAS A TOUGH ONE-- EVEN BACK *THEN.*

"I WASN'T LETTIN' GO--*NO WAY*. I WAS MAKIN' HER *SWEAT* HOT 'N COLD. BLAST IT--I WAS MAKIN' MY *OWN MOTHER DIE!*"

"HER FRIENDS WERE *HELPLESS*, SO THEY CALLED A *DOCTOR*. AND MAN, IT TOOK FOREVER 'FORE THEY GOT ONE WHO'D COME TO *THEM*."

"AN' EVEN THEN IT WAS *HOU* LATER 'FORE HE FINALLY CAME--'FORE THEY FINALLY *HEARD* THE KNOCK ON THE DOOR."

KNOCK KNOCK

"I'LL NEVER *FORGET* WHAT THEY *TOLD* ME HE LOOKED LIKE. HE WAS *TALL*--TALLER 'N MOST OF THE DUDES THEY KNEW, AN' HE HAD *WHITE HAIR*, SLICKED BACK, AND IT WAS *LONG*."

"BUT THE *STRANGEST* PART OF HIM WAS HIS *EYES*...THEY *GLOWED* EVEN IN THE DULLED-DOWN LIGHTING OF THAT PLACE--"

"--AND THEY GLOWE* *RED*...RED AS THE FIRES OF *HELL* ITSELF."

"HE SENT THE *OTHERS* INTO ANOTHER ROOM WHILE HE MOVED CAT-LIKE TOWARDS MY MOTHER'S SHAKING BODY. SHE LOOKED UP AT HIM THROUGH *PAIN-WRACKED* EYES, AN' WHAT SHE SAW *NEARLY* KILLED HER *THEN*."

"SHE SAW HIS *LIPS* PART, HIS TEETH *SPREAD* WIDE, AND SHE SAW TWO LONG, POINTED *FANGS* GLEAMING HUNGRILY IN THE DARK.

"AND SHE KNEW THEN THAT *SCREAMING* WOULD BE USELESS."

"HE SMILED AT HER, SAID SOMETHING *SOFTLY* IN HER EAR...

"HER FRIENDS BURST THROUGH THE LOCKED DOOR TO FIND THAT STINKIN' *CRUD* CROUCHED OVER MY MOTHER'S BODY, *BLOOD* DRIPPING FROM HIS CRIMSON-STAINED TEETH...

"THEY TRIED TO *STOP* HIM, BUT HE LEAPED ACROSS THE ROOM LIKE A *DEMON* POSSESSED, BROKE THROUGH THE GLASS AND *DISAPPEARED* INTO THE NIGHT.

D WHATEVER T *SOMETHING* WAS, MADE HER *BREAK*... AND *SCREAM!*

"...BUT IT WAS *TOO LATE* -- MY MOTHER WAS *DEAD.*

T THERE WAS NO STOPPIN' F FROM BEIN' BORN. AND KNOW SOMETHING--? EY SAY WHEN THEY APPED ME, I *NEVER* IED... AN' THAT I NEVER ED *ONCE* AS A BABY.

YBE I'M ST SAVIN' LL TILL TER I D THAT NKIN' THER LER--

EAH, MAYBE EN I'LL BE LE TO CRY. YBE THEN.

SO *DON'T* HAND ME ANY OF YOUR *BULL* 'BOUT *MOURNIN'* THE DEAD-- 'CAUSE I'VE BEEN THROUGH IT ALL *BEFORE*--

--AN' I'M *STILL* LIVIN' WITH IT, EVERY TIME I LOOK IN THE *MIRROR* AN' REALIZE THAT A WOMAN *DIED* GIVIN' BIRTH TO ME--*ME!*

SO TAKE YOUR HIGH-HAT WORDS AND SHOVE 'EM, 'CAUSE WHEN YOU'VE FINISHED WITH *YOUR* CHASE--I'LL BE *STARTIN'* MINE!

15

BLADE'S WORDS CANNOT BE *HEARD* BY THE LOW-FLYING BAT, YET *SOMETHING* SUDDENLY SENDS AN *ICY* CHILL RACING THROUGH DRACULA'S LEATHERY FORM...

...AND FOR JUST THE *BRIEFEST* OF MOMENTS, THE MANBAT FEELS--*FEAR!*

STILL IT CONTINUES OVER THE LUSH OLIVE COUNTRYSIDE; THE DOTTED *VALLEY* AND LAKES FORMING THE NOW *FAMILIAR* PATHWAY TOWARDS A HIDDEN HILLTOP SANCTUM...

BUT SOMETHING *NEW* HAS BEEN ADDED TO THIS FERTILE VALLEY: A TENT--WITH *HUMANS* MILLING QUIETLY ABOUT.

FOR AN *INSTANT,* THE BAT FORGETS ITS SILENT PROMISE AND SWOOPS DOWNWARDS TOWARDS THE UNSUSPECTING *CROWD...*

THEN, AT THE LAST *MOMENT,* IT REMEMBERS AND SAILS OFF, *UNCARING* OF THE HUMAN WHO *MAY* HAVE SPOTTED IT.

BUT EYES *HAVE* FOLLOWED ITS WINDING COURSE... EYES WHICH HAVE BEEN *SEARCHING* THE HEAVENS FOR JUST SUCH A HELLBORN CREATURE.

FOR THE *LEGIONS* THAT ANSWER TO QUINCY HARKER'S CALL MAY BE *FEW,* BUT THEY ARE *EVER ALERT.*

DARK BEGINS TO *FADE* ’EATH THE EARLY MORNING ...A DAWN WHICH HERALDS ’ONLY THE COMING OF DAY...

’BUT SO OF-- ’ATH!

AN ’ERESTING ’HT... ONE I ’LL *PONDER* ’R MANY ’KS TO ’OME.

MORTUARY

MANKIND HAS CHANGED *LITTLE* THESE PAST FIVE HUNDRED YEARS. STILL THEY ARE SELFISH, ARROGANT-- *MINDLESS.*

INDEED, THEY ARE A *FERTILE* CROP, ONE WHICH AWAITS THE SOWING OF THE *NEW ORDER--*

YES-- THE *SEEDS* OF VAMPIRISM THAT I PLANT THIS NIGHT SHALL *FLOURISH* THE WORLD OVER.

BUT FIRST THERE ARE SOME WHO MUST BE DONE *AWAY* WITH--

-- SUCH AS THAT FOOL *BLADE*-- WHO *DARED* ATTACK ME WITH HIS *DAMNABLE* WOODEN KNIVES.

BUT *ENOUGH* OF SUCH PETTY NUISANCES. *NOW* IS THE TIME FOR *REST.*

DRACULA... NOW *NOT* THE TIME ’R REST... FOR ’Y A SCANT FEW ’OMETERS ’ AWAY...

YOU HAVE ANY IDEA WHERE WE’RE GOIN’, HARKER? I’VE GOT BETTER THINGS TO DO THAN *TRAIPSE* ’ROUND THE COUNTRYSIDE.

SHUT UP, BLADE. I’VE *ALREADY* GOT A HEADACHE.

’SIDES, IF QUINCY SAYS WE DRIVE-- *WE DRIVE!* UNLESS YOU’D RATHER *WALK* BACK TO *LONDON.*

...YES, ’ANK YOU, ’ HASKELL.

THIS *NEWS* MAY HELP US TO *FINALLY* LAY OUR DEAR COUNT AWAY FOREVER.

QUINCY--? DID SCOTLAND YARD GET A *FIX* ON THAT *BAT* THAT WAS SPOTTED?

HALLELUJAH!

17

NO, MR. DRAKE -- ONE OF OUR *OBSERVERS*. HE SPOTTED WHAT *MAY* BE *DRACULA* HEADING THIS WAY.

HE ALSO *LEARNED* THAT THE *BAT* HAS BEEN SEEN HERE *MANY* TIMES IN THE PAST MONTHS.

MR. *BLADE* -- I BELIEVE THE *ACTION* YOU'VE BEEN WAITING FOR IS ABOUT TO *BEGIN*.

GOOD TIMING, HARKER -- I HAD JUST ABOUT FALLEN *ASLEEP!*

AND WE *COULDN'T* ALLOW THAT, COULD WE?

TAJ, TRY THE *POST OFFICE*.

POST OFFICE

SORRY TO *BOTHER* YOU SO *EARLY*, BUT--

DON'T HARDLY SEE NO ONE THESE HOURS, BUT YER *WELCOME*.

NAME'S JASPER O'CONNOR. WHAT CAN I BE *DOIN'* FER YA?

...LOOKIN' FER A *BAT?* WHY, YUH-- I SEEN A LARGE BLACK 'UN FLYIN', WHAT WUZ IT NOW *SOUTH*, I THINK.

YUH, SOUTH IT IS. WHY YOU ASKIN'?

WE'RE *ASKIN'*, THAT'S ALL.

YOU SEE A *STRANGE* DUDE, 'BOUT SIX FOOT, FIVE--*RED EYES*...

...LOOKS SOMETHIN' LIKE *THIS*--

-- LIKE HE JUST STEPPED OUT OF A *DEATH MASK*-- ONLY HE'S STILL WEARIN' IT?

UHHHHHH...

18

UHHHHH...

...FOR A *MOMENT,* JASPER O'CONNER *HESITATES,* UNSURE OF HIS WORDS...HIS THOUGHTS...

THEN...

LOOK AT HIS *EYES*-- THEY'RE *BLANK...* GLAZED...

WE *MUST* BE CLOSE TO DRACULA. THIS MAN'S UNDER SOME SORT OF *HYPNOSIS.*

...IF THAT MEANS WHAT [B]ELIEVE... THE [COU]NT *MUST* BE NEAR...

QUICKLY NOW... EVERY *MOMENT* WE WASTE GIVES DRACULA TIME TO *ESCAPE.*

BUT DRACULA HAS *NO PLANS* FOR LEAVING...

[F]ATHER, DESIRE TO *STAY...* FIGHT...

...AND, AT LONG LAST-- *TO SLAY THE VAMPIRE SLAYERS!*

SO, HARKER AND HIS STALWARTS HAVE *FOUND* ME...

VERY WELL THEN, MY LONG-TIME FOES-- WE SHALL *MEET,* AND BEFORE THIS NIGHT HAS FLED FOREVER--

--YOU SHALL ALL LIE *DEAD* AT THE FEET OF YOUR *MASTER...*

...DRACULA.!!

BUT ALL MUST GO QUICKLY, FOR THE DAWN IS ONLY *MINUTES* AWAY, WHEN AGAIN I MUST REST IN THE SACRED *EARTH* OF MY HOMELAND.

SO COME THIS WAY... BE LED BY THE *INSTINCTS* I PLANT IN YOUR CHILDISH MINDS...

COME... *COME* TO YOUR DEATHS.

THEY APPROACH-- GOOD. FOR A MOMENT I FEARED THE COMING DAY MAY HAVE *DIMIN-ISHED* MY MENTAL POWERS...

BUT, NO, THEY COME LIKE *MOTHS* DRAWN TO THEIR LAST FATAL *FLAME.*

HE'S *INSIDE*-- I FEEL IT. *HURRY* NOW BEFORE HE *VANISHES* AGAIN.

HE *MUSTN'T* LIVE ONE EXTRA MOMENT-- HE'S *GOT* TO DIE NOW-- FOR EDITH--

HE'LL DIE, OLD MAN-- DON'T WORRY-- HE'LL DIE *TONIGHT!*

20

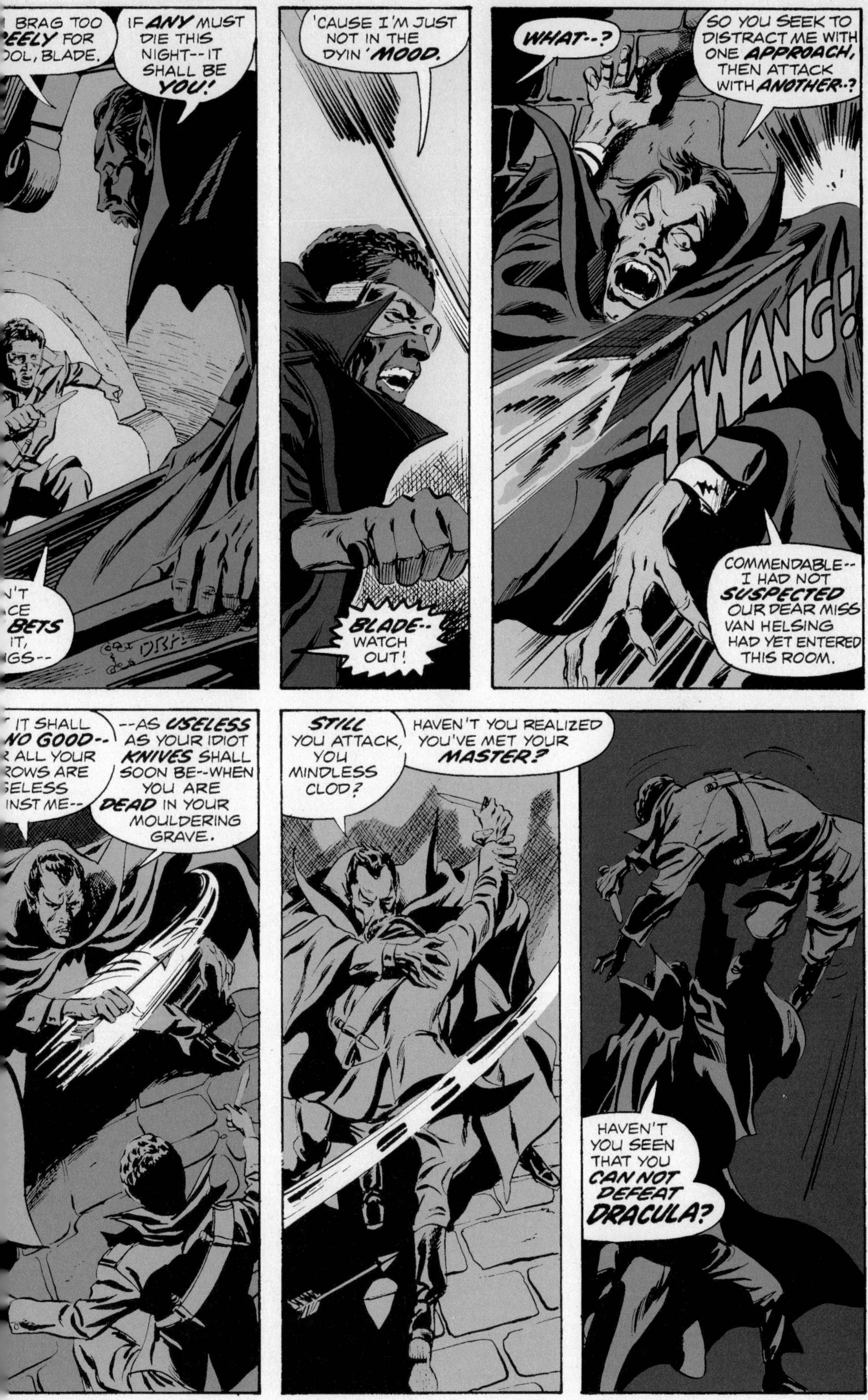
BRAG TOO EELY FOR OOL, BLADE.
IF ANY MUST DIE THIS NIGHT-- IT SHALL BE YOU!
N'T CE BETS IT, GS--
'CAUSE I'M JUST NOT IN THE DYIN' MOOD.
BLADE-- WATCH OUT!
WHAT--?
SO YOU SEEK TO DISTRACT ME WITH ONE APPROACH, THEN ATTACK WITH ANOTHER--?
TWANG!
COMMENDABLE-- I HAD NOT SUSPECTED OUR DEAR MISS VAN HELSING HAD YET ENTERED THIS ROOM.
IT SHALL NO GOOD-- R ALL YOUR ROWS ARE SELESS INST ME--
--AS USELESS AS YOUR IDIOT KNIVES SHALL SOON BE--WHEN YOU ARE DEAD IN YOUR MOULDERING GRAVE.
STILL YOU ATTACK, YOU MINDLESS CLOD?
HAVEN'T YOU REALIZED YOU'VE MET YOUR MASTER?
HAVEN'T YOU SEEN THAT YOU CAN NOT DEFEAT DRACULA?

BUT THEN, WHAT YOU SEE OR BELIEVE MATTERS *LITTLE* IN THE SCHEME OF THINGS, BLADE--

AGHHHH!

ALL THAT IS *IMPORTANT* IS THAT DRACULA HAS LIVED *500 YEARS*-- AND SHALL *NEVER* BE DEFEATED BY ONE SUCH AS *YOU!*

BLADE SINKS *UNCONSCIOUS* AGAINST THE WALL OF THE OLD STONE BUILDING, WHILE SCANT METERS AWAY, *OTHERS* BEGIN A SILENT *MARCH* TOWARDS THAT VERY SAME STRUCTURE...

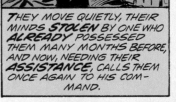

THEY MOVE QUIETLY, THEIR MINDS *STOLEN* BY ONE WHO *ALREADY* POSSESSED THEM MANY MONTHS BEFORE, AND NOW, NEEDING THEIR *ASSISTANCE,* CALLS THEM ONCE AGAIN TO HIS COMMAND.

GUNS COCKED, *KNIVE* BARED, THEY *LUMB* HYPNOTICALLY, TOWAR THEIR MURDEROUS *GO*

WHILE...

LONG HAVE I *WAITED,* VAN HELSING, FOR THE MOMENT WHEN MY FANGS WOULD DRINK DEEPLY OF YOUR WARM, RICH *BLOOD*--

BUT WAIT--! YOUR FOOLISH *PROTECTOR* COMES TO SAVE YOU..!

STRANGE--SINCE *HE* NEEDS SAVING *HIMSELF.*

HA HA HA

HA

PUT HIM *DOWN,* DRACULA-- *PUT HIM DOWN!*

OF COURSE MY DEAR-- TH WAS ALWAY MY *INTENT*

I'LL PUT HIM DOWN--BUT *NOT* ON THIS CONCR FLOOR--

NO, RATHER THE FRIGID ~~TERS~~ THAT ~~RN~~ BENEATH ~~S~~ HILLTOP ~~MORGUE~~.

AND, IF HE HAS LUCK, PERHAPS HE'LL EVEN SURVIVE HIS ORDEAL--

--THOUGH NONE HAVE EVER LIVED THROUGH IT BEFORE.

SPLASH

OUTSIDE, LIKE LIVING ZOMBIES, THE POSSESSED VILLAGERS STALK ON-- MOVING WITH HEAVY, LABORIOUS STEPS TOWARDS THE TENSION-WROUGHT MAUSOLEUM...

THERE IS NO FALTER TO THEIR STEPS, NO REGRET OF THE DEED THEY MUST DO ETCHED UPON THEIR BROWS. FOR THEIR MINDS BELONG NOT TO THEMSELVES...

...BUT TO A DEMON WHO, SOME SAY, WAS BORN WITHOUT A CONSCIENCE... OR A SOUL.

BLADE DOWNED, RACHEL WEAPONLESS, TAJ GONE-- PERHAPS DEAD...

THERE IS NOTHING LEFT FOR ME TO DO.

SO, AT LAST YOU ADMIT YOUR INEVITABLE DEFEAT?

YOU MISUNDER-STAND, DEMON-- I ADMIT NOTHING--

FF FFFFT

--SAVE THE FACT THAT IT SHALL BE MY WOODEN DARTS WHICH END YOUR HELLISH LIFE.

YOUR MIND FAILS YOU, HARKER --OR DID YOU FORGET AFTER SO MANY BATTLES, THAT DRACULA CAN BECOME AS THE MIST ITSELF?

23

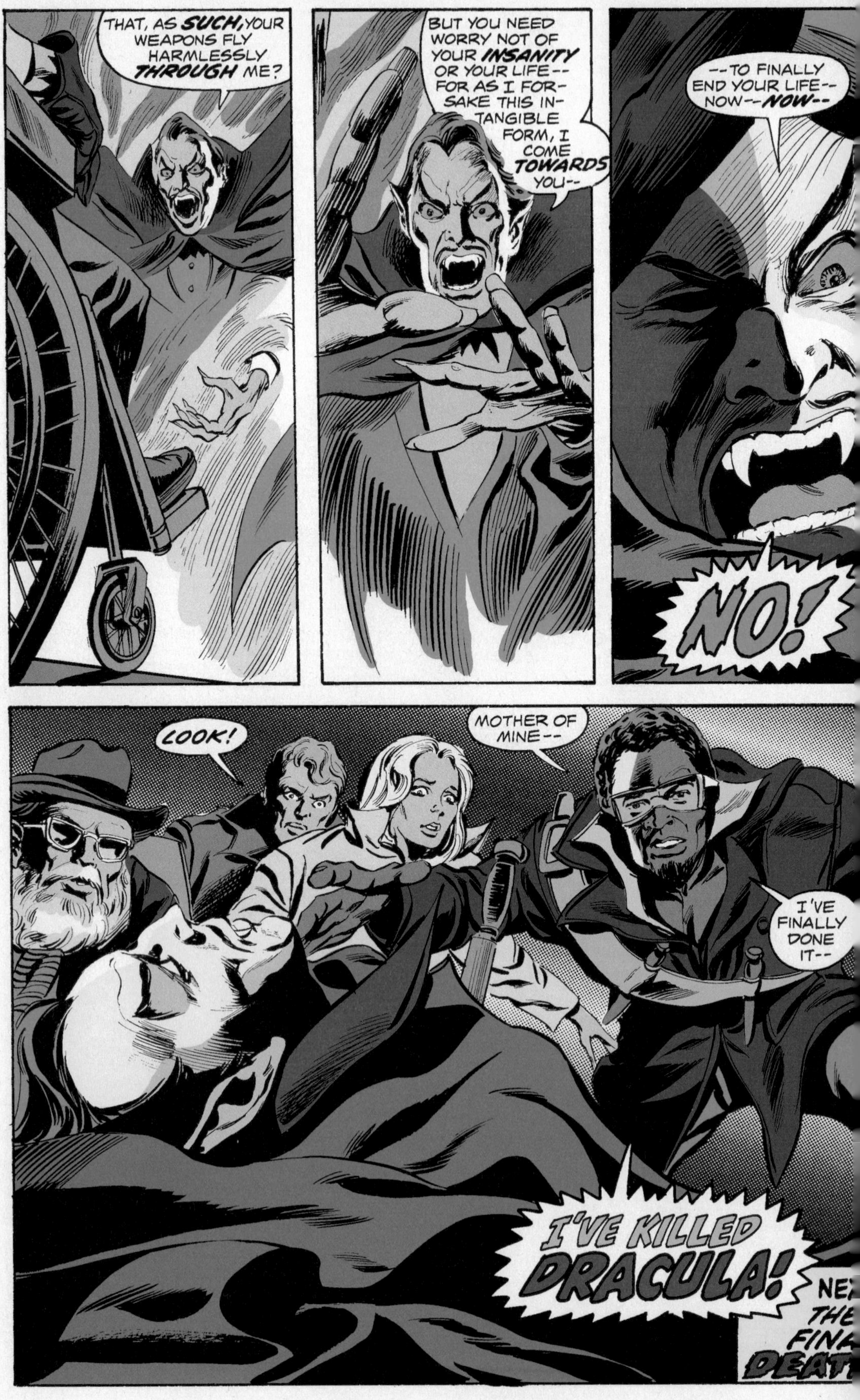
THAT, AS SUCH, YOUR WEAPONS FLY HARMLESSLY THROUGH ME?
BUT YOU NEED WORRY NOT OF YOUR INSANITY OR YOUR LIFE-- FOR AS I FORSAKE THIS INTANGIBLE FORM, I COME TOWARDS YOU--
--TO FINALLY END YOUR LIFE-- NOW--NOW--
NO!
LOOK!
MOTHER OF MINE--
I'VE FINALLY DONE IT--
I'VE KILLED DRACULA!

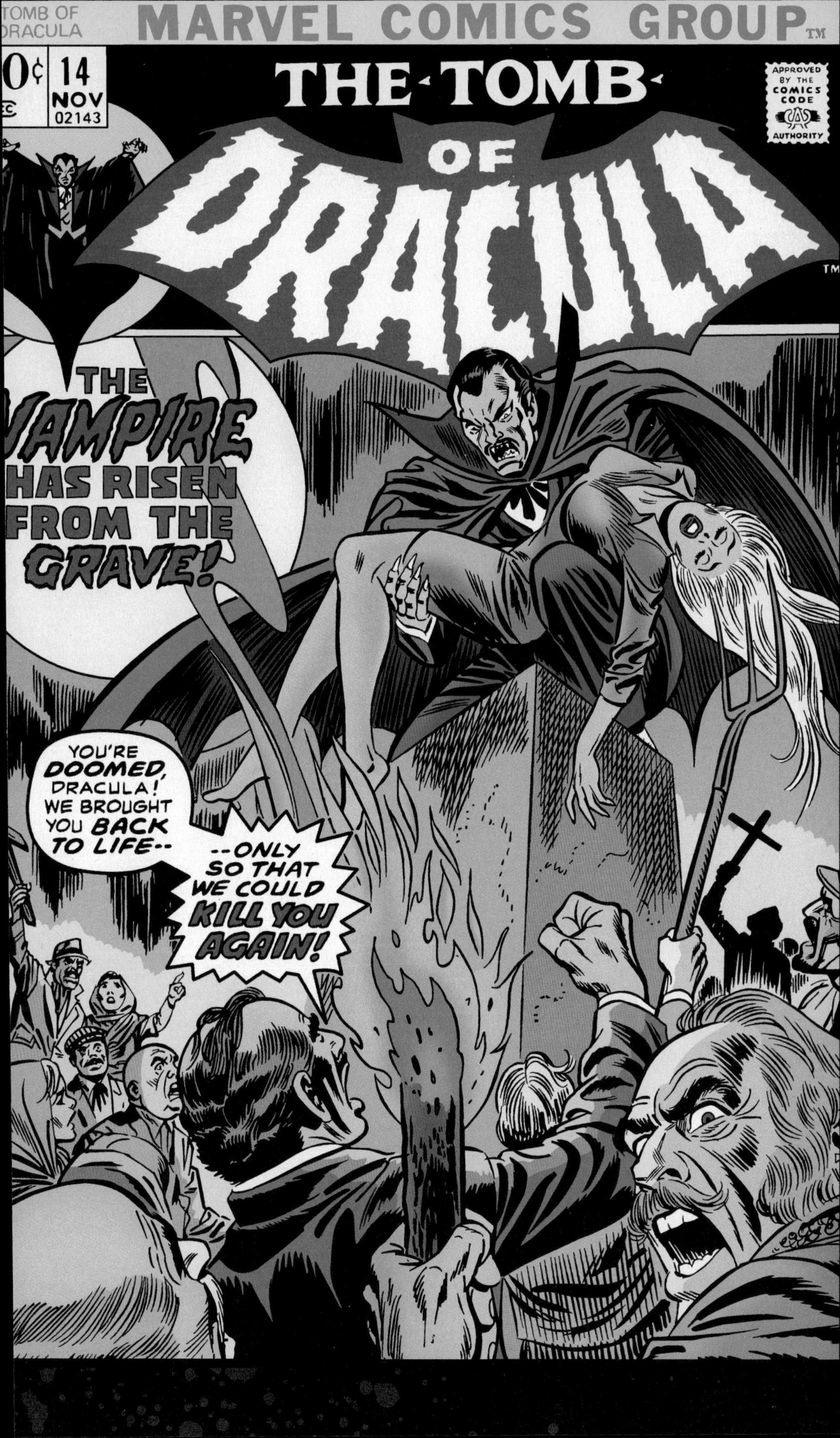
TOMB OF DRACULA
MARVEL COMICS GROUP
20¢ 14 NOV 02143
THE TOMB OF DRACULA
APPROVED BY THE COMICS CODE AUTHORITY
THE VAMPIRE HAS RISEN FROM THE GRAVE!
YOU'RE DOOMED, DRACULA! WE BROUGHT YOU BACK TO LIFE--
--ONLY SO THAT WE COULD KILL YOU AGAIN!

STAN LEE PRESENTS: **TOMB OF DRACULA!**

MARV WOLFMAN, STORY / GENE COLAN, PENCILS / TOM PALMER, INKS / JOHN COSTANZA, LETTERING / TOM PALMER, COLORING / ROY THOMAS, EDITOR

DRACULA IS DEAD!

YET EVEN NOW, FIVE MINUTES *LATER*, THEY STILL STAND *UNBELIEVING*.

THE DEMON *IS DEAD* -- A SHARPLY HEWNED WOODEN *KNIFE* BURIED DEEP WITHIN HIS CHEST--

--A KNIFE THROWN WITH HELLISH *RAGE* BY THE *VAMPIRE-SLAYER* KNOWN AS *BLADE*.

MOTHER OF MINE -- I'VE *FINALLY* DONE IT--

--I'VE KILLED DRACULA!

1591Z

PULSE, AND HIS ...ND FEELS ...ELESS.

...M..ST DEAD-- ...MUST.

I PRAY HE IS, QUINCY... BUT--

WAIT! NOISES, FROM OUTSIDE.

QUINCY, FRANK-- COOK.

IT'S THE VILLAGERS-- THEY'RE COMING THIS WAY-- WITH GUNS.

THE VILLAGERS: THEIR MINDS POSSESSED BY DRACULA MONTHS BEFORE... THEN HELD TILL HE COMMANDED THEIR OBEDIENCE...

...E VILLAGERS: ...O HAD BEEN ...EN A MENTAL ...DER THE MOMENT ...FORE THE ...TAL KNIFE WAS ...UNGED:

"STORM THE HILLTOP MORGUE... RECLAIM THE BODY OF THEIR MASTER...

"...AND, IF NEEDED, KILL ANY WHO GOT IN THEIR WAY."

THEY MOVE ON, MINDLESSLY, TO OBEY THAT LAST COMMAND.

27

QUICKLY, BEFORE THEY *BREAK* IN--

BLADE, SEVER DRACULA'S *HEAD. HE MUST NOT RISE AGAIN!*

AS IF THEY *KNEW* OF THE *THREAT* TO THEIR LIFELESS MASTER, THE VILLAGERS MOVE *FASTER*, SMASHING AT THE OLD OAKEN DOOR...

...PUSHING, BANGING KICKING AT IT TILL IT BEGINS TO *GIVE.*

CAN'T, HARKER-- YOU BETTER DO IT *YOURSELF*, MAN.

I LEAVE GO AN' THOSE LIVIN' *ZOMBIES'LL* BE ALL OVER US.

CAN'T HOLD-- CAN'T...

UGGHHHHHH

SMASH!

BUT, EVEN AS BLADE COMPLETES THAT ILL-SPAWNED SENTENCE...

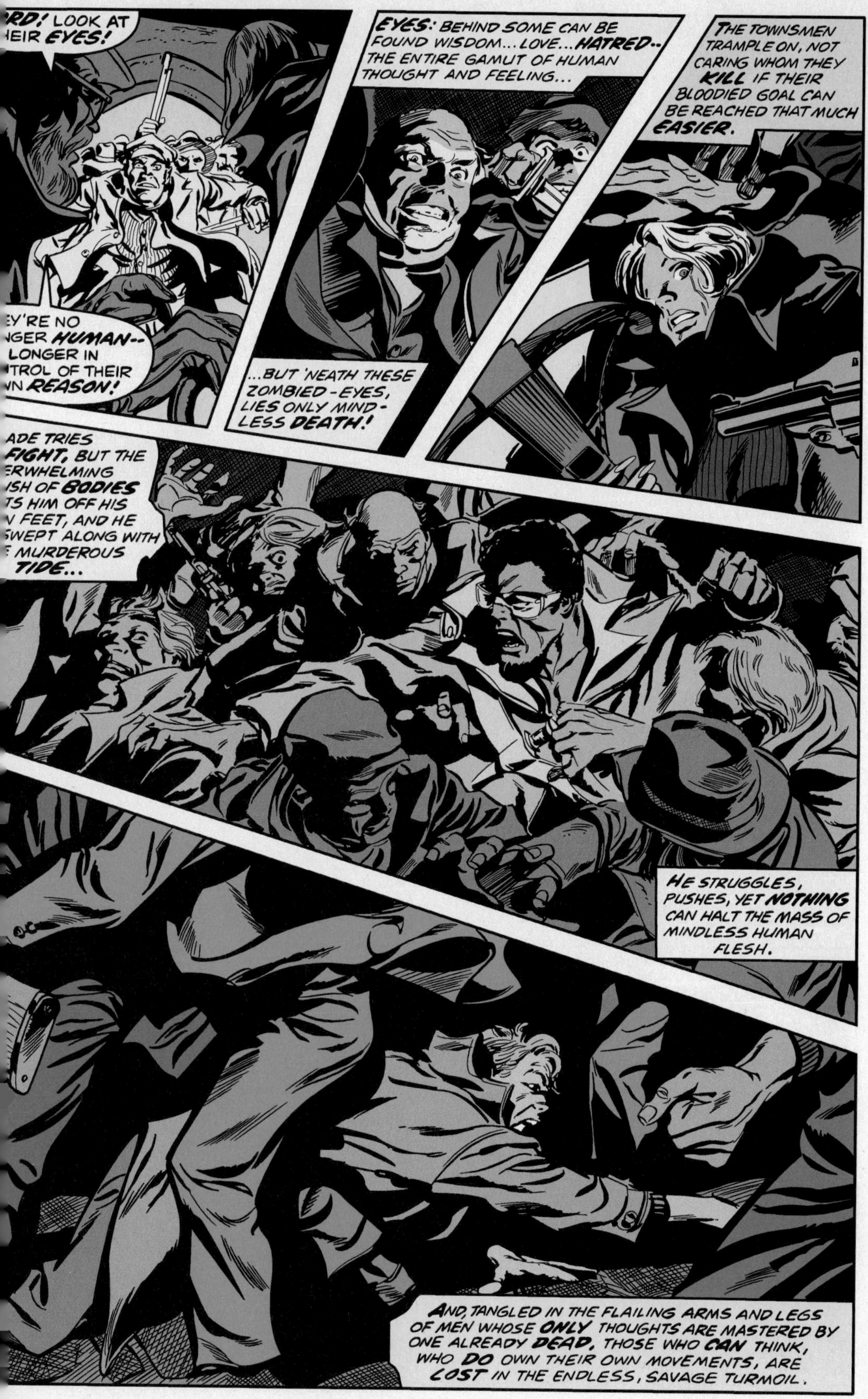
RD! LOOK AT
HEIR EYES!
EY'RE NO
NGER HUMAN--
LONGER IN
NTROL OF THEIR
WN REASON!
EYES: BEHIND SOME CAN BE FOUND WISDOM... LOVE... HATRED.. THE ENTIRE GAMUT OF HUMAN THOUGHT AND FEELING...
...BUT 'NEATH THESE ZOMBIED-EYES, LIES ONLY MINDLESS DEATH!
THE TOWNSMEN TRAMPLE ON, NOT CARING WHOM THEY KILL IF THEIR BLOODIED GOAL CAN BE REACHED THAT MUCH EASIER.
ADE TRIES
FIGHT, BUT THE
ERWHELMING
USH OF BODIES
TS HIM OFF HIS
N FEET, AND HE
SWEPT ALONG WITH
E MURDEROUS
TIDE...
HE STRUGGLES, PUSHES, YET NOTHING CAN HALT THE MASS OF MINDLESS HUMAN FLESH.
AND, TANGLED IN THE FLAILING ARMS AND LEGS OF MEN WHOSE ONLY THOUGHTS ARE MASTERED BY ONE ALREADY DEAD, THOSE WHO CAN THINK, WHO DO OWN THEIR OWN MOVEMENTS, ARE LOST IN THE ENDLESS, SAVAGE TURMOIL.

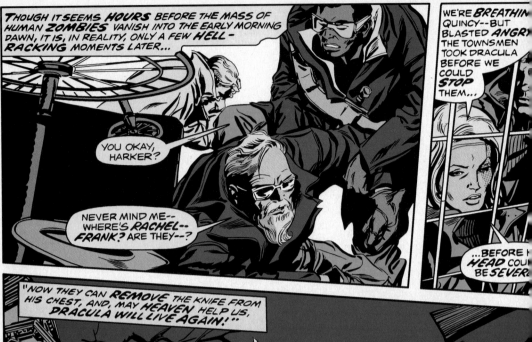

THOUGH IT SEEMS *HOURS* BEFORE THE MASS OF HUMAN *ZOMBIES* VANISH INTO THE EARLY MORNING DAWN, IT IS, IN REALITY, ONLY A FEW *HELL-RACKING* MOMENTS LATER...

YOU OKAY, HARKER?

NEVER MIND ME-- WHERE'S *RACHEL*-- *FRANK?* ARE THEY--?

WE'RE *BREATHIN* QUINCY--BUT BLASTED *ANGRY* THE TOWNSMEN TOOK DRACULA BEFORE WE COULD *STOP* THEM...

...BEFORE H *HEAD* COU BE SEVER...

"NOW THEY CAN *REMOVE* THE KNIFE FROM HIS CHEST, AND, MAY *HEAVEN* HELP US, DRACULA WILL LIVE AGAIN!"

LEAVING THE HILLTOP *MORGUE,* THE HYPNOTIZED MEN LUMBER SILENTLY DOWN THE BLEAK, LONELY HILL...

...CARRYING *BURDEN* THAT MAY VER WELL MEAN *THE DEATH* OF THE *HUMAN RAC*

BUT NOW WE *SWITCH* OUR SCENE TO THE NORTHERN IRISH COASTLINE, WHERE A SMALL PANEL TRUCK PULLS UP TO A GATEWAY OF A LARGE, SPRAWLING *ESTATE...*

AHEAD, CHEN. PROFESSOR MORGO AWAITS US.

YES, MISTER LO.

AH, IS THAT THE ONE *DOCTOR SUN* LOOKS FOR, LO?

AS THE MASTE REQUES OF COUR

THERE WERE *NO* PROBLEM ACQUIRING I

*AS SH LAST ISSUE.

30

EN, TO GIN. LIN, CHEN. REST THE BODY ON THE **TABLE**, PLEASE.

NEED BUT **FIVE** UTES FOR OUR IOROSCOPE TO READY, BUT IN EANTIME--

H, **VERY** OD. ALREADY IRIS TURNS RED.

NO **DETERIORATION** OF CELLS, AH-- GOOD.

BUT ONLY **ONE METHOD** EXISTS TO LEARN IF THIS MAN IS **ALL** THAT DOCTOR SUN NEEDS.

SEN SU, PLEASE TO TURN ON **POWER**.

AH, **VERY GOOD**, SEN SU.

ALL SEEMS IN **READINESS**. NOW TO BEGIN.

CLICK

CLICK

OBSERVE, CHEN: SLOWLY THAT WHICH WE CALL HIS *CANINE TEETH* GROW.

ITS GROWTH, *IMPERCEPTIBLE* TO THE NAKED EYE, YET THROUGH THIS DEVICE, WE MAY *OBSERVE* ITS PROGRESS.

AH, YES, CHEN. ALL MY TESTS ARE *POSITIVE*. THIS MAN *IS* A *VAMPIRE*.

THANK YOU, PROFESSOR MORGO. DOCTOR SUN SHALL BE *PLEASED*.

WHO DOCTOR SUN IS, AND *WHY* HE IS INTERESTED IN VAMPIRES SHALL BE FURTHER UNRAVELLED *SHORTLY*.

...BUT FOR *NOW*, LET US RETURN TO A LESS *MYSTERIOUS* SETTING...

FRANK, QUINCY--*LOOK*. IT'S TAJ! HE'S ALIVE--*HE'S ALIVE*!!

WHEN HE *PLUNGED* THROUGH THAT WINDOW, I THOUGHT FOR *SURE* THAT DRACULA HAD *KILLED* HIM.*

*AGAIN, LAST ISSUE. --R

OH, TAJ--I THANK *GOD* YOU'RE SAFE... THANK *GOD*!

WELCOME BACK, YOU BIG *LUG*.

FOR A MOMENT THE RELENTLESS VAMPIRE HUNTERS CAN *RELAX* AND LET A VERY SMALL TOUCH OF HAPPINESS ENTER THEIR LIVES,...

...HAPPINESS THAT WOULD BE *SHATTERED* IF THEY COULD BUT SEE ONLY A FEW *KILOMETERS* AWAY...

...WHERE A SMALL GROUP OF SHAMBLING MEN WHO POSSESS *NO* WILL OF THEIR OWN, CARRY THE *CORPSE* OF A MAN RAPIDLY *DECOMPOSING*...

...A CORPSE THAT WOULD SOON BE BEYOND *ALL RECOGNITION* TO ALL BUT A VERY TRAINED HUNTERS, UNLESS...

...UNLESS

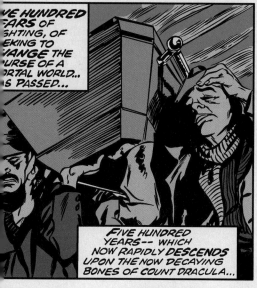

...VE HUNDRED YEARS OF FIGHTING, OF SEEKING TO CHANGE THE COURSE OF A MORTAL WORLD... HAS PASSED...

FIVE HUNDRED YEARS-- WHICH NOW RAPIDLY DESCENDS UPON THE NOW DECAYING BONES OF COUNT DRACULA...

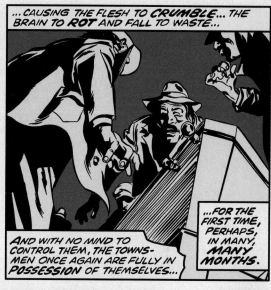

...CAUSING THE FLESH TO CRUMBLE... THE BRAIN TO ROT AND FALL TO WASTE...

AND WITH NO MIND TO CONTROL THEM, THE TOWNSMEN ONCE AGAIN ARE FULLY IN POSSESSION OF THEMSELVES...

...FOR THE FIRST TIME, PERHAPS, IN MANY, MANY MONTHS.

...DDENLY THE TERROR OF THE PAST MOMENTS BURSTS FULL-BLOWN WITHIN THEIR CONSCIOUSNESS...

...AND THE TERROR LEADS TO FRIGHT...

...WHICH LEADS DIRECTLY TO FLIGHT...

A FLIGHT WHICH TAKES THEM DOWN THE SOUTHERN POINT OF THE HILL TO THEIR TINY HAMLET NESTLED NEAR THE SURREY FOREST...

...YET, HAD THEY TAKEN THE NORTHERN ROUTE, THEY MIGHT HAVE FOUND THE SOLACE THEY WOULD BE SEARCHING FOR FOR THE REST OF THEIR LIVES...

...N THE CHURCH OF THE FOREVER RESURRECTED, RESIDED ...ER BY ONE VERY DEJECTED FATHER JOSIAH DAWN...

...A MAN WHOSE FAITH IS ABOUT TO BE SORELY TESTED.

...LORD-- ...Y IS IT EACH ...THE CROWDS ...INISH-- THE ...PLE LEAVE ...LIER AND EARLIER--?

WHY?

WHY?

33

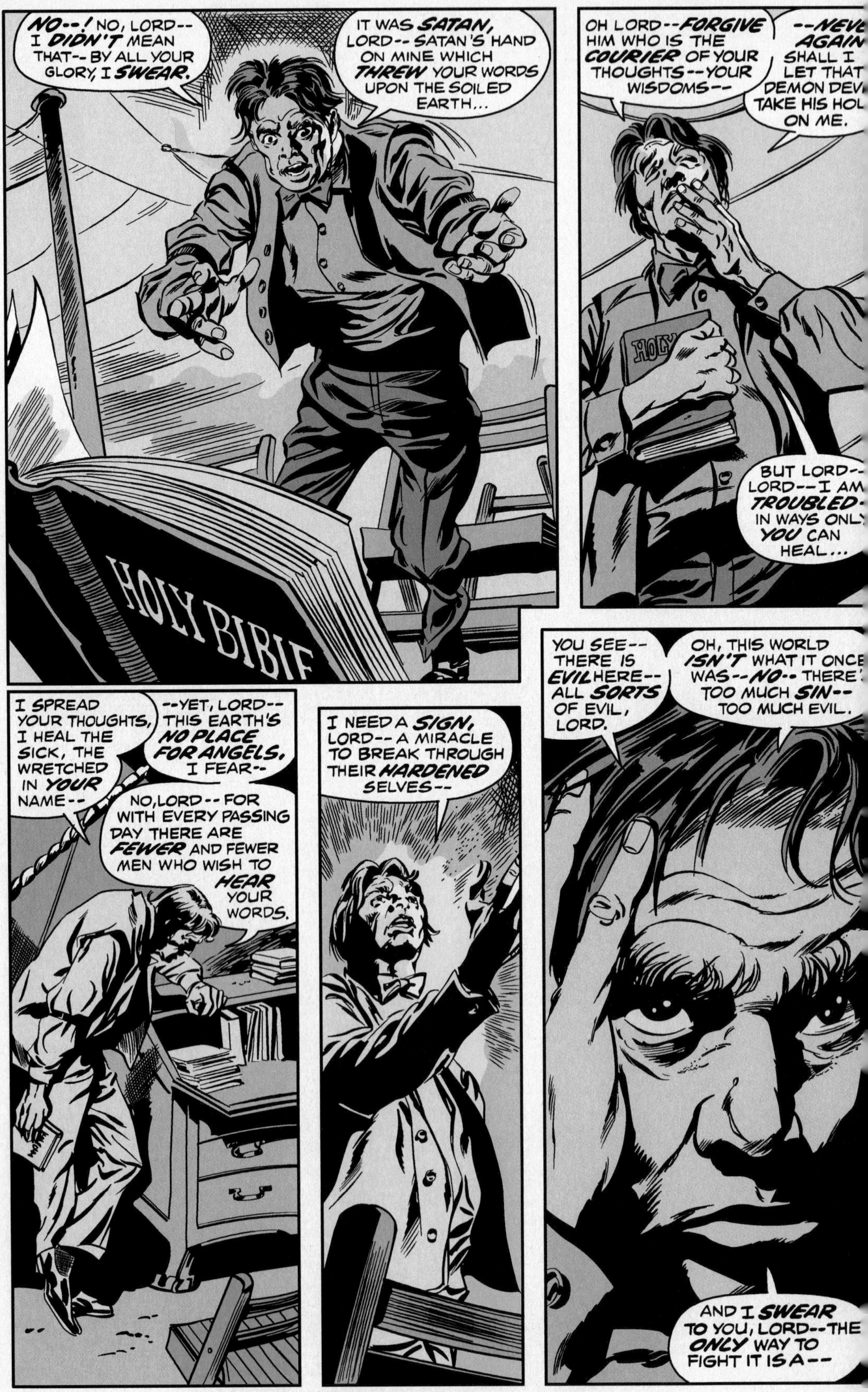
NO--! NO, LORD-- I DIDN'T MEAN THAT-- BY ALL YOUR GLORY, I SWEAR.
IT WAS SATAN, LORD-- SATAN'S HAND ON MINE WHICH THREW YOUR WORDS UPON THE SOILED EARTH...
HOLY BIBLE
OH LORD--FORGIVE HIM WHO IS THE COURIER OF YOUR THOUGHTS--YOUR WISDOMS--
BUT LORD-- LORD--I AM TROUBLED-- IN WAYS ONLY YOU CAN HEAL...
I SPREAD YOUR THOUGHTS, I HEAL THE SICK, THE WRETCHED IN YOUR NAME--
--YET, LORD-- THIS EARTH'S NO PLACE FOR ANGELS. I FEAR--
NO, LORD-- FOR WITH EVERY PASSING DAY THERE ARE FEWER AND FEWER MEN WHO WISH TO HEAR YOUR WORDS.
I NEED A SIGN, LORD-- A MIRACLE TO BREAK THROUGH THEIR HARDENED SELVES--
YOU SEE-- THERE IS EVIL HERE-- ALL SORTS OF EVIL, LORD.
AND I SWEAR TO YOU, LORD--THE ONLY WAY TO FIGHT IT IS A--

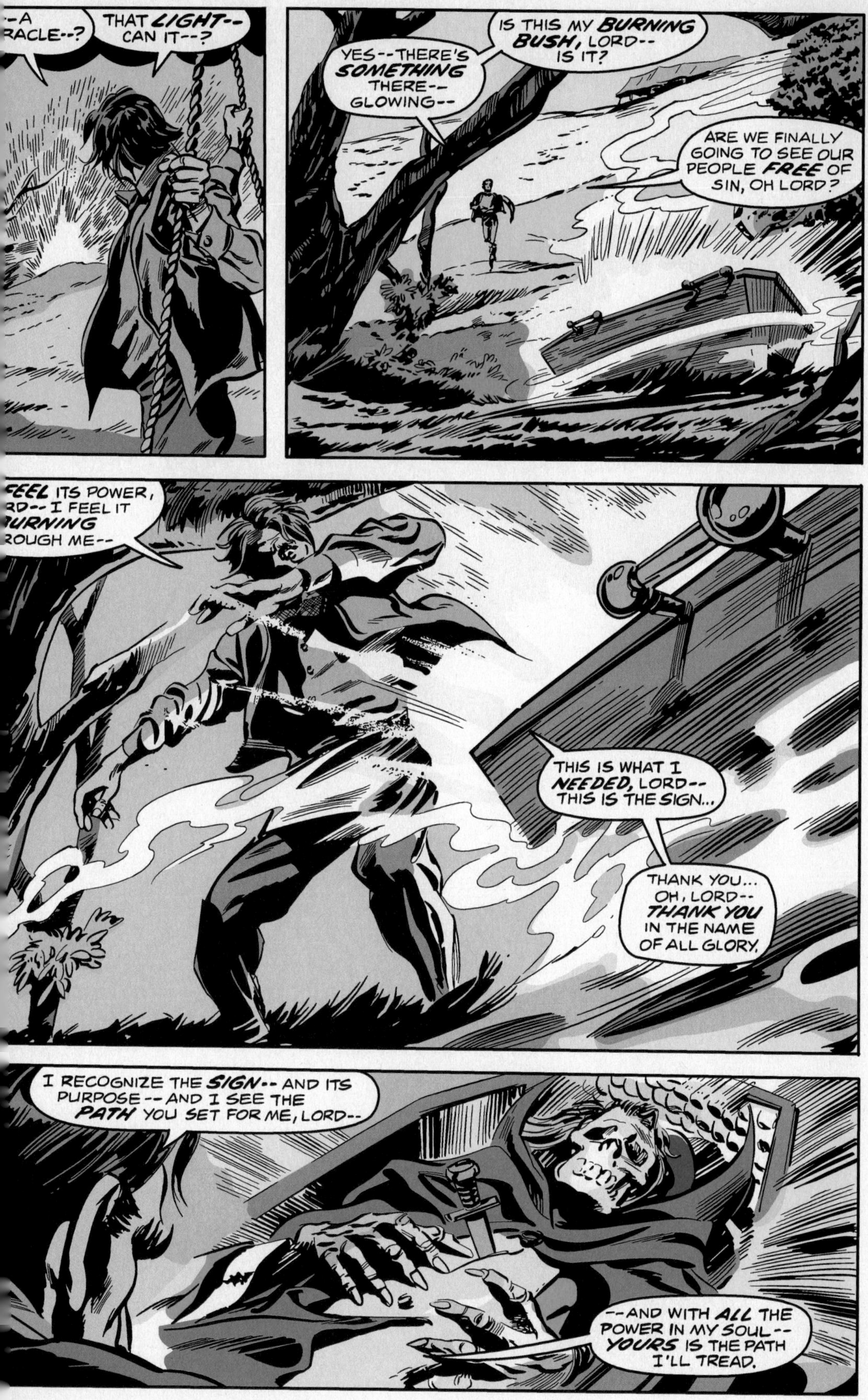
--A RACLE--?
THAT LIGHT-- CAN IT--?
IS THIS MY BURNING BUSH, LORD-- IS IT?
YES--THERE'S SOMETHING THERE-- GLOWING--
ARE WE FINALLY GOING TO SEE OUR PEOPLE FREE OF SIN, OH LORD?
FEEL ITS POWER, RD-- I FEEL IT URNING ROUGH ME--
THIS IS WHAT I NEEDED, LORD-- THIS IS THE SIGN...
THANK YOU... OH, LORD-- THANK YOU IN THE NAME OF ALL GLORY.
I RECOGNIZE THE SIGN-- AND ITS PURPOSE--AND I SEE THE PATH YOU SET FOR ME, LORD--
--AND WITH ALL THE POWER IN MY SOUL-- YOURS IS THE PATH I'LL TREAD.

FATHER JOSIAH DAWN: A MAN WHOSE *FAITH* HAS BEEN TESTED--

--AND HAS NEVER ONCE *QUESTIONED* HIS DESTINY.

IF HE HAD, HE WOULD QUICKLY LEARN-- THE GOD WHOSE "MIRACLE" HE SO READILY *ACCEPTED*--IS A GOD *NOT* HIS OWN--

For *HIS* IS THE GOD OF LOVE AND PEACE-- AND CERTAINLY *NOT* THE GOD OF STYGIAN *DEATH!*

THREE NIGHTS LATER THE WINE-DARK *VALLEY* WHERE JOSIAH DAWN DWEL IS NO LONGER A *CLOISTERED,* QU LAND-- FOR THIS NIGHT IS ALIVE WIT THE *EXCITEMEN* OF PEOPLE AND MIRACLES...

...AS *CONTRASTED* WITH...

YOUR *MOVE,* MY DEAR, AND GOOD LUCK. I HAVE YOU IN *CHECK.*

NO PROBLEM QUINCY--M KNIGHT TAK YOUR ROO AND...

QUINCY, RACHEL, BLADE-- *LOOK--!*

I *FOUND* THESE POSTERS PASTED UP ALL OVER FLEET STREET.

AND SOMETHING TELLS ME, THE *'DEAD'* IN QUESTION IS OUR VERY OWN *COUNT.*

HE DEAD RETURNS TO LIF JOSIAH DAWN-REVIVALIST

ED ME BROTHERS AND SISTERS -- THERE'S *BLOOD* IN ALL OF US, BUT YOU IN LAY DOWN YOUR *SINFUL* OULS -- 'CAUSE TONIGHT'S HE NIGHT FOR *COVE--*

EA, LORD -- TONIGHT'S THE IGHT FOR *COVE OF LIFE*, EA, END YOUR STRIFE, ROTHERS -- TOSS 'WAY OUR EVIL *SINS*.

-ith cometh by believing nd heeding the word of God.

BROTHERS AND SISTERS, TONIGHT'S THE NIGHT FOR THE *TRUTHFUL LIGHT OF OUR LORD*, GOD.

O YOU *WANT* TO SEE AT GOOD LIFE, DON'T U, BROTHERS AND STERS? YOU *WANT* E THE *TRUTH*, E WORDS OF GOD?

Y IT, BROTHERS -- OUT OUT SO AT THE LORD HIM- .F'LL HEAR YOU REAMIN.' EVEN E'S WAY ON THE ER SIDE OF WORLD.

WE WANT THE TRUTH, LORD -- WE WANT THE TRUTH!

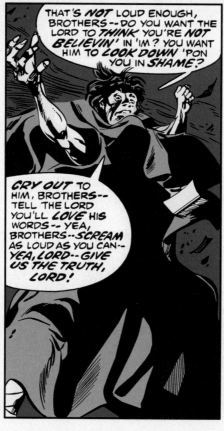

THAT'S *NOT* LOUD ENOUGH, BROTHERS -- DO YOU WANT THE LORD TO *THINK* YOU'RE *NOT BELIEVIN'* IN 'IM? YOU WANT HIM TO *LOOK DOWN* 'PON YOU IN *SHAME?*

CRY OUT TO HIM, BROTHERS -- TELL THE LORD YOU'LL *LOVE* HIS WORDS -- YEA, BROTHERS -- *SCREAM* AS LOUD AS YOU CAN -- YEA, LORD -- GIVE US THE TRUTH, LORD!

YEA, LORD -- GIVE US THE TRUTH, LORD!

37

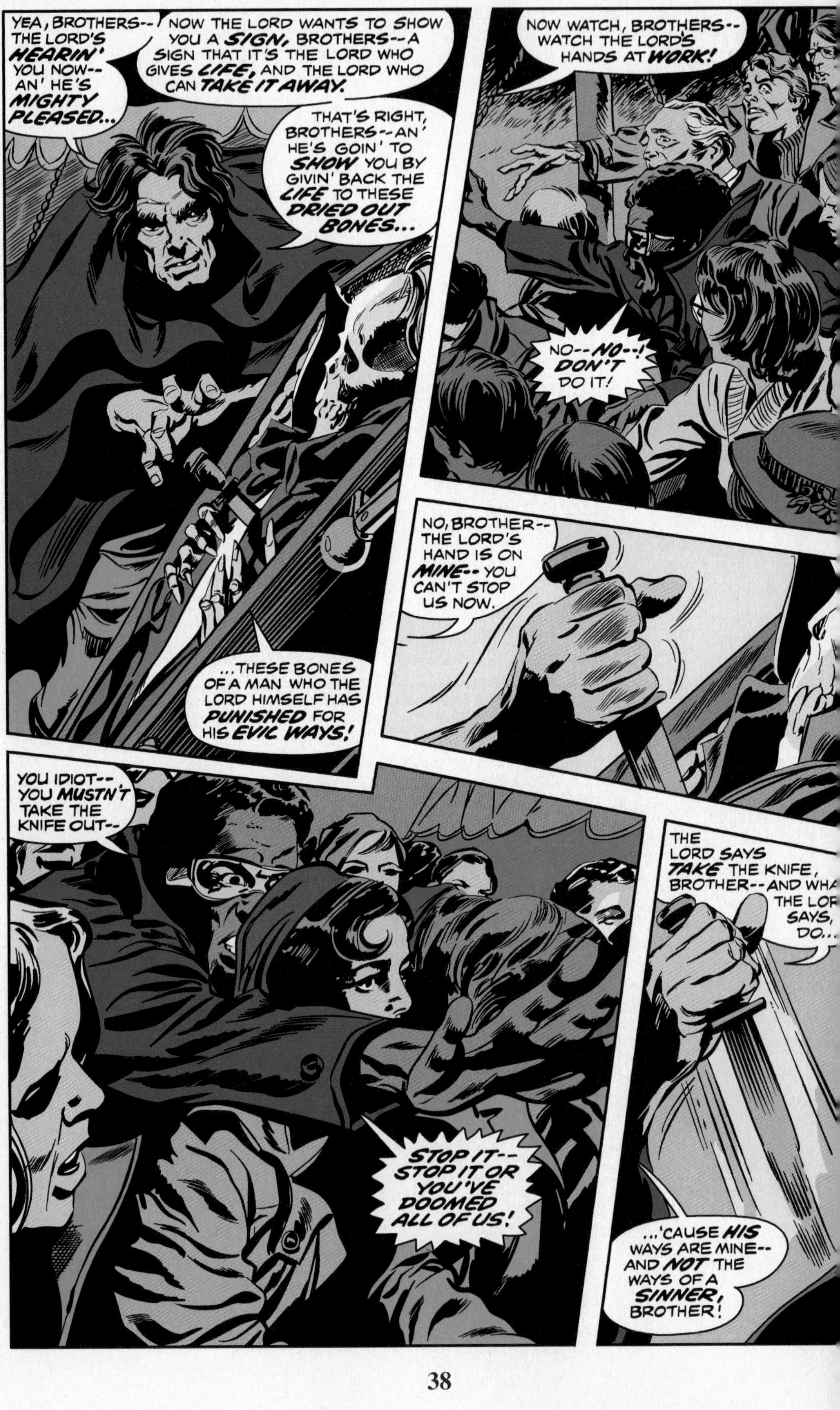
YEA, BROTHERS-- THE LORD'S HEARIN' YOU NOW-- AN' HE'S MIGHTY PLEASED...
NOW THE LORD WANTS TO SHOW YOU A SIGN, BROTHERS--A SIGN THAT IT'S THE LORD WHO GIVES LIFE, AND THE LORD WHO CAN TAKE IT AWAY.
THAT'S RIGHT, BROTHERS--AN' HE'S GOIN' TO SHOW YOU BY GIVIN' BACK THE LIFE TO THESE DRIED OUT BONES...
...THESE BONES OF A MAN WHO THE LORD HIMSELF HAS PUNISHED FOR HIS EVIL WAYS!
NOW WATCH, BROTHERS-- WATCH THE LORD'S HANDS AT WORK!
NO--NO--! DON'T DO IT!
NO, BROTHER-- THE LORD'S HAND IS ON MINE-- YOU CAN'T STOP US NOW.
YOU IDIOT-- YOU MUSTN'T TAKE THE KNIFE OUT--
STOP IT-- STOP IT OR YOU'VE DOOMED ALL OF US!
THE LORD SAYS TAKE THE KNIFE, BROTHER--AND WHA THE LOR SAYS, DO...
...'CAUSE HIS WAYS ARE MINE-- AND NOT THE WAYS OF A SINNER, BROTHER!

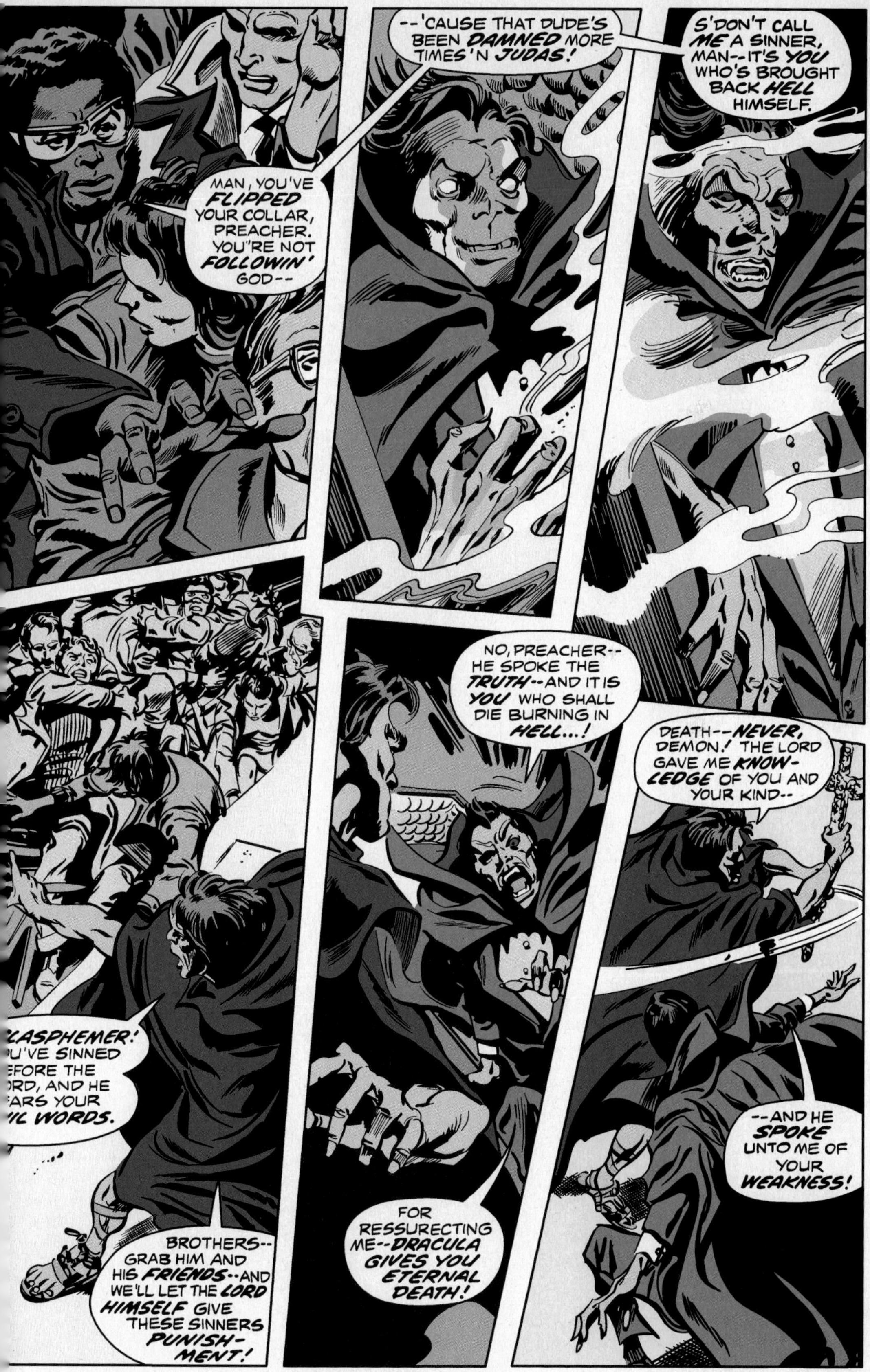
MAN, YOU'VE FLIPPED YOUR COLLAR, PREACHER. YOU'RE NOT FOLLOWIN' GOD--
--'CAUSE THAT DUDE'S BEEN DAMNED MORE TIMES'N JUDAS!
S'DON'T CALL ME A SINNER, MAN--IT'S YOU WHO'S BROUGHT BACK HELL HIMSELF.
BROTHERS--GRAB HIM AND HIS FRIENDS--AND WE'LL LET THE LORD HIMSELF GIVE THESE SINNERS PUNISH-MENT!
NO, PREACHER--HE SPOKE THE TRUTH--AND IT IS YOU WHO SHALL DIE BURNING IN HELL...!
FOR RESSURECTING ME--DRACULA GIVES YOU ETERNAL DEATH!
DEATH--NEVER, DEMON! THE LORD GAVE ME KNOW-LEDGE OF YOU AND YOUR KIND--
--AND HE SPOKE UNTO ME OF YOUR WEAKNESS!

NO! THE **CROSS**! THE **ACCURSED** CROSS!

YES, EVIL ONE-- THE **SIGN** OF THE **LORD HIMSELF**.

AND AS THE LORD **RAISED YOU** FROM THE DEPTHS OF **HELL**-- SO SHALL HE **BANISH** YOU BACK TO ITS **FLAMING PITS**!

YOU'VE **NO CHOICE**, DEMON!

BROTHERS AND SISTERS--**NOW** IS THE TIME TO HEED THE **LORD'S WORD**!

SCREAM IT, BROTHERS --I'M KILLIN' **SATAN'S** DEMON, LORD--I'M KILLIN' **SATAN'S** DEMON!

THE **LORD OF EVIL** TURNS, **REPULSED** BY THE SEARING POWER OF THE **CROSS OF GOD**, YET, HE TURNS **NOT** INTO THE PATH OF **FREEDOM**, RATHER TOWARDS--

MORE CROSSES?!? BUT THEY'LL NOT **TAKE** ME AGAIN-- I WON'T **PERMIT** IT--

--NOT NOW NOT **EVER** AGAIN!

WE'RE KILLING **SATAN'S** DEMON, LORD!

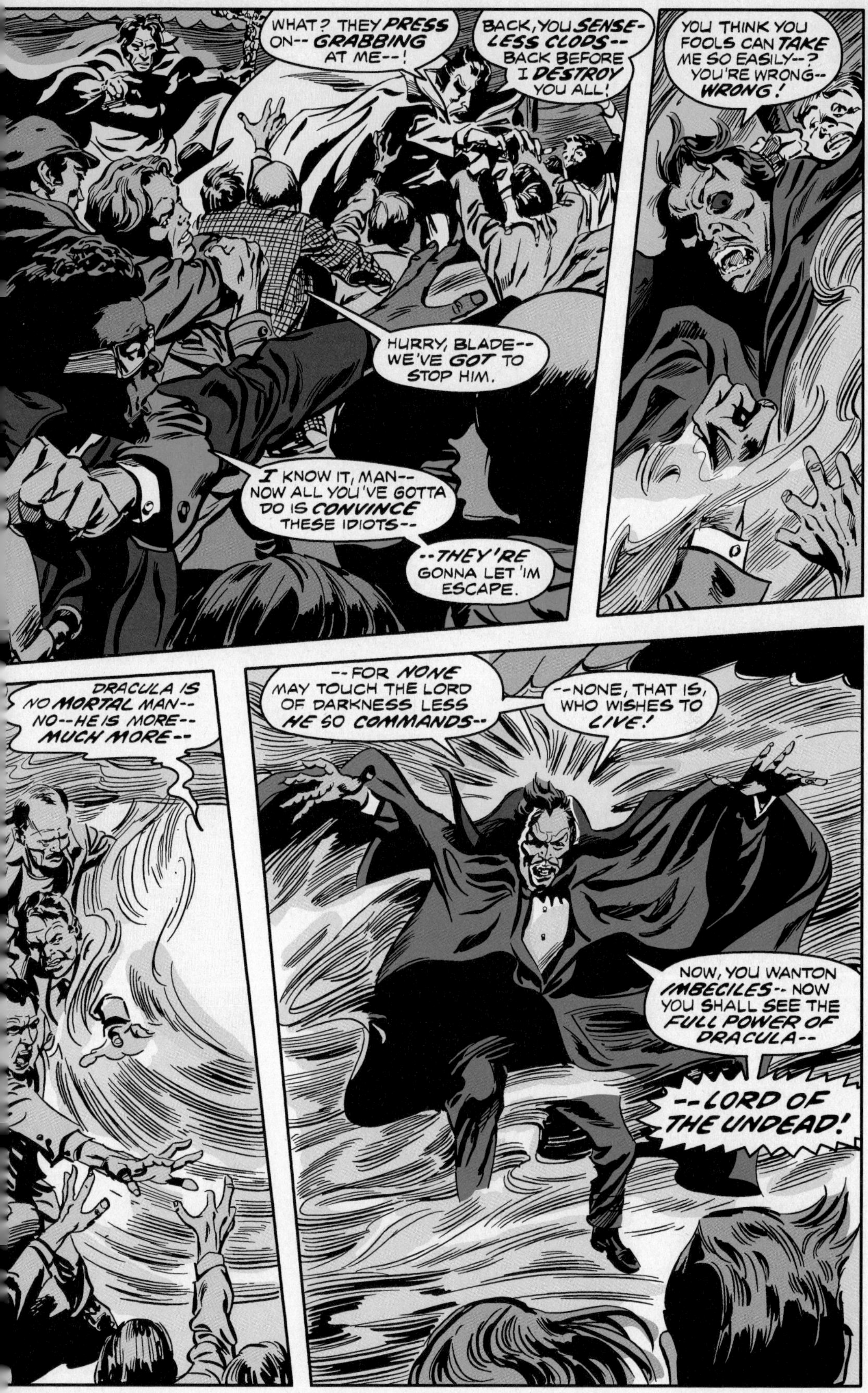
WHAT? THEY PRESS ON-- GRABBING AT ME--!
BACK, YOU SENSE-LESS CLODS-- BACK BEFORE I DESTROY YOU ALL!
HURRY, BLADE-- WE'VE GOT TO STOP HIM.
I KNOW IT, MAN-- NOW ALL YOU'VE GOTTA DO IS CONVINCE THESE IDIOTS--
--THEY'RE GONNA LET 'IM ESCAPE.
YOU THINK YOU FOOLS CAN TAKE ME SO EASILY--? YOU'RE WRONG-- WRONG!
DRACULA IS NO MORTAL MAN-- NO--HE IS MORE-- MUCH MORE--
--FOR NONE MAY TOUCH THE LORD OF DARKNESS LESS HE SO COMMANDS--
--NONE, THAT IS, WHO WISHES TO LIVE!
NOW, YOU WANTON IMBECILES-- NOW YOU SHALL SEE THE FULL POWER OF DRACULA--
--LORD OF THE UNDEAD!

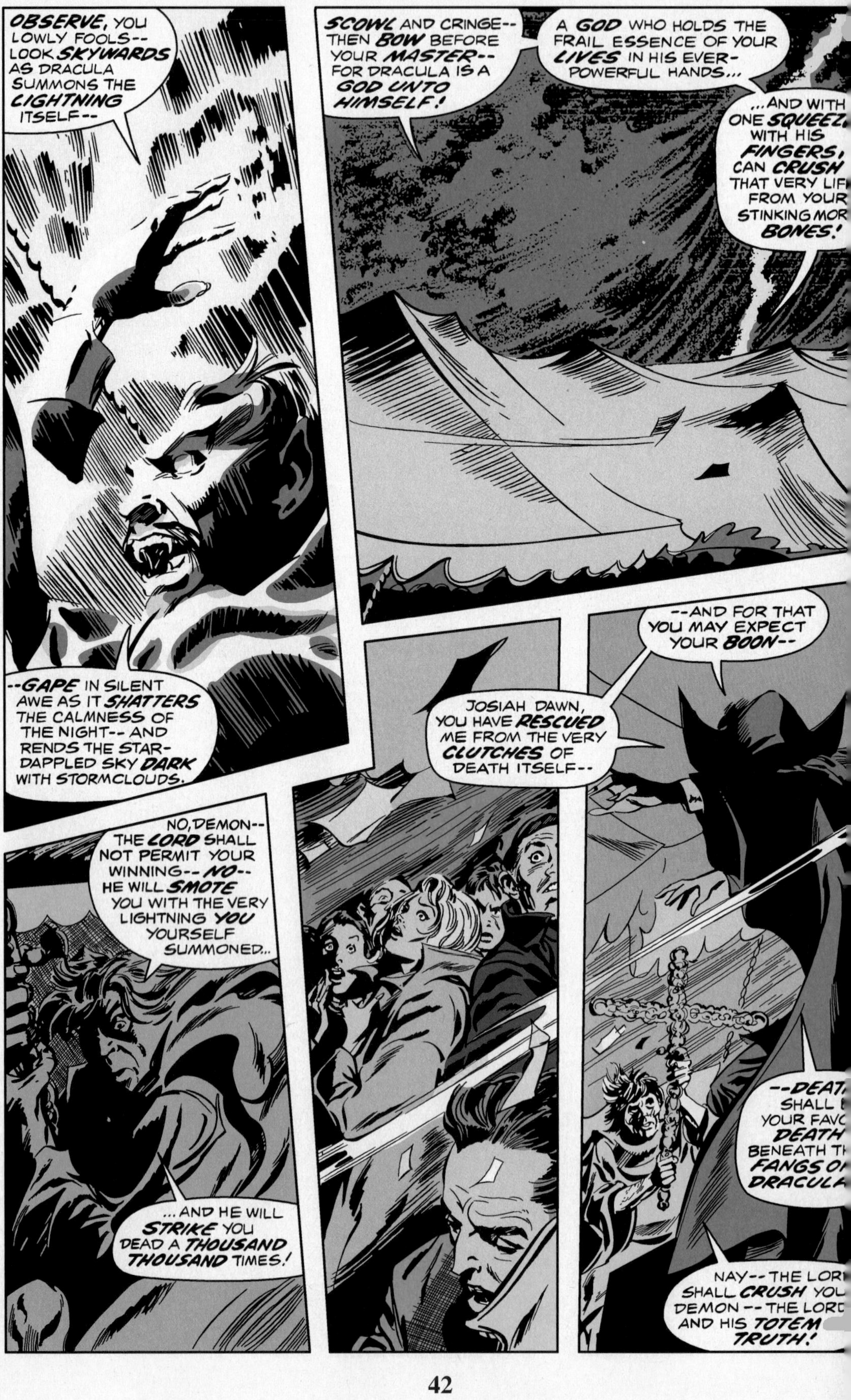
OBSERVE, YOU LOWLY FOOLS-- LOOK SKYWARDS AS DRACULA SUMMONS THE LIGHTNING ITSELF--
--GAPE IN SILENT AWE AS IT SHATTERS THE CALMNESS OF THE NIGHT-- AND RENDS THE STAR-DAPPLED SKY DARK WITH STORMCLOUDS.
SCOWL AND CRINGE-- THEN BOW BEFORE YOUR MASTER-- FOR DRACULA IS A GOD UNTO HIMSELF!
A GOD WHO HOLDS THE FRAIL ESSENCE OF YOUR LIVES IN HIS EVER-POWERFUL HANDS...
NO, DEMON-- THE LORD SHALL NOT PERMIT YOUR WINNING-- NO-- HE WILL SMOTE YOU WITH THE VERY LIGHTNING YOU YOURSELF SUMMONED...
...AND HE WILL STRIKE YOU DEAD A THOUSAND THOUSAND TIMES!
JOSIAH DAWN, YOU HAVE RESCUED ME FROM THE VERY CLUTCHES OF DEATH ITSELF--
--AND FOR THAT YOU MAY EXPECT YOUR BOON--

YOU THINK YOURSELF A *SAVIOR*, DO YOU NOT, JOSIAH DAWN--? BUT *YOU'RE NOT--* **YOU'RE NOT!**

IT ISN'T YOUR *GOD* WHOM YOU FOLLOW, WHOSE WORD YOU *HEED--* *NO!* IT'S YOUR OWN *TWISTED HATE--* YOUR OWN *MINDLESS VENOM!*

YOU CAN *NOT* WITHSTAND THE LORD'S *TOUCH,* DRACULA--

--AND YOU CAN NOT EVEN *HOPE* TO ESCAPE *HIS* BLINDING LIGHT.

UNTOLD TIMES HAVE YOU *DAMNED* OUR LORD'S NAME, AND FOR EACH YOU MUST BE MADE TO *SUFFER.*

AND IT SHALL *NOT* BE DRACULA WHO DIES *EMBALMED* WITH THAT POISONOUS HATE--

--NO-- IT SHALL BE YOU-- *YOU--* **YOU!**

THE SKY SPLITS AND SPILLS FORTH THE *THUNDER...* AND, AS IF *DIRECTED* BY THE HAND OF DRACULA, THE *LIGHTNING* CURLS DOWN-WARDS--*STRIKING THE VERY CRUCIFIX JOSIAH DAWN WIELDS!*

FOR A MOMENT THERE IS ONLY *SILENCE,* AS BONES BEGIN TO BAKE AND FLESH BEGINS TO *SEAR...* BUT THEN, EVEN *OVER* THE SOUND OF THE *TUMULTUOUS* THUNDER, COMES A LONG AND ALMOST *NEVER-ENDING SCREAM...*

43

...WHICH ENDS IN A SLOW, WHINING *RATTLE OF DEATH!*

YOU *SUMMONED* DEATH TO TAKE *ME*, MORTAL--AND SO *YOU* DIED, AS IS ONLY BEFITTING...

WHERE *YOU* LOOKED TO *OTHER* FOR GUIDANCE, DRACULA SEEKS ON *HIMSELF.*

FOR THE *STRENGTH* OF ANY, BE THEY LIVING OR UNDEAD, RESTS *ONLY IN THEMSELVES.*

NO...DEMON... YOU ARE, UHHH, *WRONG...*

I DIE...BUT MY *SOUL*...IS, UHHHH, AT PEACE WITH THE *LORD...*

...WHILE *YOURS*... UHHH, CAN *NEVER* KNOW PEACE--BUT *ONLY* THE...ALL-CONSUMING *HATE.*

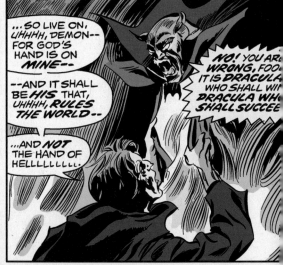

...SO LIVE ON, UHHHH, DEMON-- FOR GOD'S HAND IS ON *MINE*--

--AND IT SHALL BE *HIS* THAT, UHHHH, *RULES THE WORLD*--

...AND *NOT* THE HAND OF HELLLLLLLLL.

NO! YOU AR: *WRONG*, FOO IT IS *DRACULA* WHO SHALL WIN DRACULA WHO SHALL *SUCCEE*

BUT THERE IS NO REPLY... ONLY A SILENT *CORPSE* HOLDING AN UNEARTHLY *CALM* WHI NO MATTER HOW *LONG* HE LIVES, OR HOW *HARD* HE TRIES, DRACULA SHALL *NEVER* KNOW.

AND THE DEMON SEETHES WITHIN THOUGH HE HAS MADE HIS KILL AND HAS PROVEN AT LEAST TO HIM-SELF THAT HE IS *MIGHTIER* THAN THE *GOD* JOSIAH DAWN PRAYED TO--

FOR IS IT NOT *TRUE*, THAT *ALL* SEEK PEACE NO MATTER HOW *EVASIVE* IT MAY BE--

--AND EVEN IF IT CAN *NEVER* BE GRASPED?

NEXT: **BLOODBATH!**

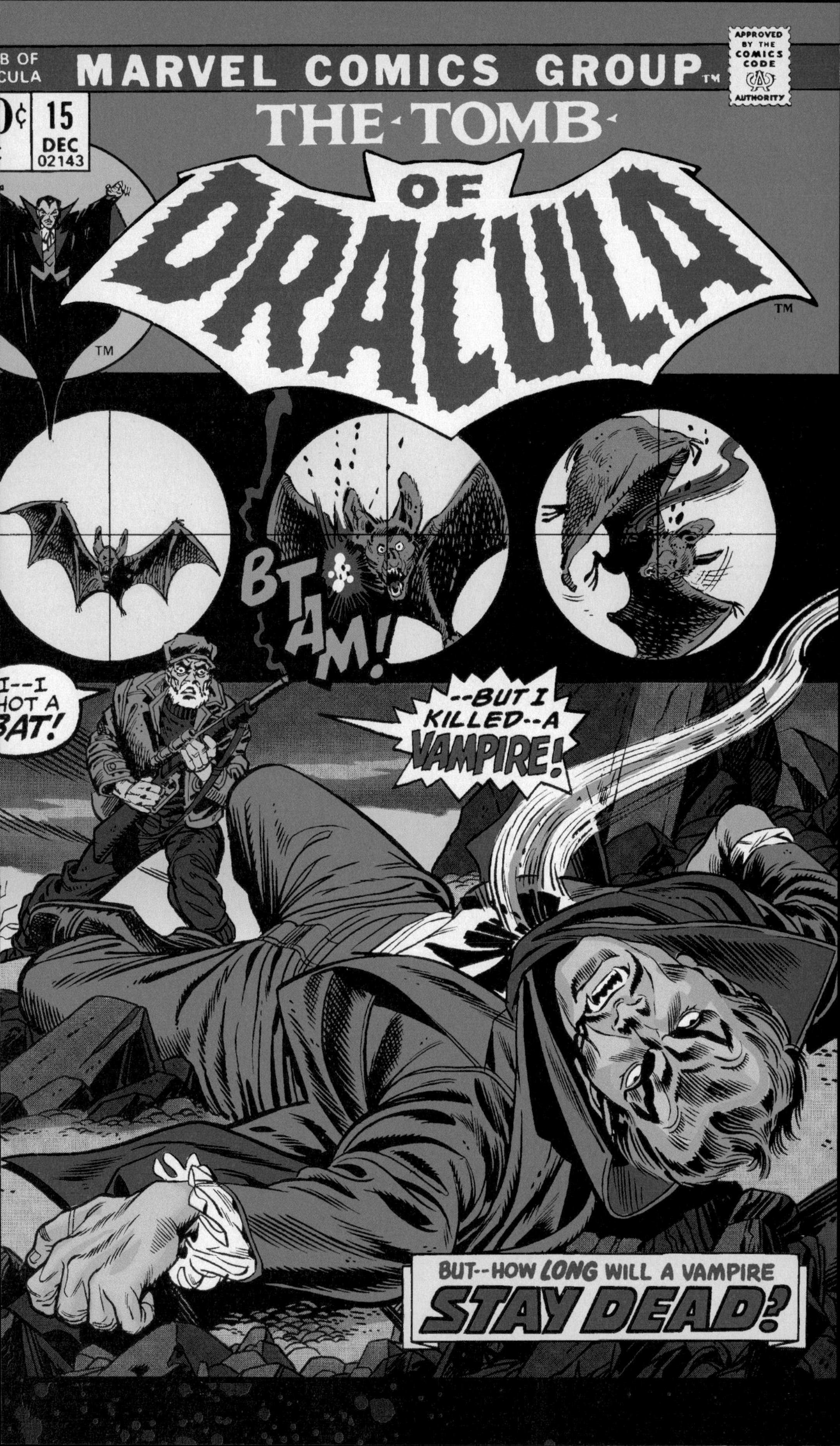
MARVEL COMICS GROUP
APPROVED BY THE COMICS CODE AUTHORITY
15
DEC
02143
THE TOMB OF DRACULA
BTAM!
I--I
HOT A
BAT!
--BUT I KILLED--A VAMPIRE!
BUT--HOW LONG WILL A VAMPIRE
STAY DEAD?

MARV WOLFMAN SCRIPTER / GENE COLAN PENCILER / TOM PALMER INKER / JOHN COSTANZA letterer / TOM PALMER Colorist / ROY THOMAS EDITOR

AUTUMN: THE SEASON FOR THINGS **DECAYING**...

...WHEN CRIMSON LEAVES TUMBLE WISTFULLY TO A ROCK-HARD EARTH, ONLY TO BE **COVERED** BY SOME IVORY WINTER'S SNOW.

AUTUMN: THE SEASON FOR THINGS **DYING**...

AUTUMN: A **FEARFUL** TIME OF YEAR—FOR THE LIVING AND **UNDEAD** ALIKE.

Fear IS THE NAME OF THE GAME

"THERE IS NO PLACE FOR *LIES* HERE IN MY PERSONAL *LEDGER,* AND THOUGH THE VERY *PRECEPTS* OF TRUTH-TELLING SICKENS ME, STILL IT MUST BE *WRITTEN* AS THE FACTS THEM-SELVES WERE PRESENTED.

"THESE NOTES MUST SPEAK WITH NO NEED OF INTERPRETATION. THEY SHOW AT TIMES MY INNATE *GREAT-NESS,* AND ALSO THE STILL-HUMAN FRAILTIES THAT MUST COURSE FOREVER THROUGH MY *BLOOD.*

"OR THOUGH I HAVE BEEN *EBORN* LIKE THE PHOENIX MANY TIMES, STILL THERE IS THE RESIDUE OF MY HUMAN BEGINNINGS.

"AND, PERHAPS, THAT IS *GOOD*-- FOR ALWAYS I MUST KEEP PERSPECTIVE ON BOTH MY *STRENGTHS*-- AND MY *WEAKNESS.*

"I AM *DRACULA,* AND BE ME BORN OF HUMAN *FLESH* OR VAMPIRE *BLOOD,* I AM *STILL* DRACULA...

"--AND THAT IS ALL I *EVER* ASK TO BE."

47

I DIED TWO NIGHTS PAST, AND THE DEATH, THOUGH SHORTLIVED, WAS STILL A DEATH MOST IGNOBLE.

I LEFT THE PRIEST BEHIND; HE WAS NOT MINE TO TAKE CARE OF, NOR EVEN TO MOURN--

BUT, AS ALWAYS BEFORE, I ROSE FROM THE GRAVE, WHILE THE FALSE-PROPHET JOSIAH DAWN PERISHED IN MY PLACE--

--SPRAWLED DEAD ACROSS THE VERY CRUCIFIX INTENDED FOR MY BURIAL MARKER. *

*LAST ISH. --RT.

--LET THE OTHERS--THE MEMBER[S] HIS CONGREGATION GIVE HIM HIS BURIAL, AND PRAY THAT HE NE[VER] RISES FROM HIS UNTIMELY TOMB[E]

FOR ME, I WAS THIRSTING, BUT STILL ABLE TO FEEL THE EXHILARATION OF FLIGHT; THE CRUSH OF CHILLED WIND AS IT RUSHED PAST MY LEATHERY WINGS.

ONLY THOSE WHO KNOW THE ECSTACY OF VAMPIRISM, THE SERENITY OF BEING AN UNDEAD, COULD GRASP MY FEELINGS AT THAT MOMENT...

...AND NOT EVEN THE PREYING EYES OF HIDDEN ASSASSINS COULD STILL THAT JOYOUS CHORD.

BAM

GUNSHOTS-- SOMEONE, SOME HALF-WITTED HUMAN WAS TRYING TO SHOOT ME. I FELT AN UNBRIDLED SURGE OF LAUGHTER FILL MY THROAT AS A DIABOLICALLY CLEVER PLAN ENTERED MY MIND.

AND SO, AS IF SLAIN, I FELL HEAVILY TO THE GROUND...

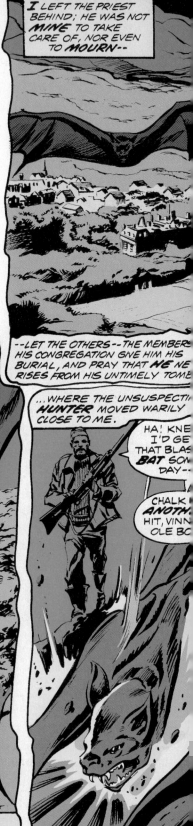

...WHERE THE UNSUSPECTI[NG] HUNTER MOVED WARILY CLOSE TO ME.

HA! KNE[W] I'D GE[T] THAT BLAS[TED] BAT SOM[E] DAY--

CHALK [UP] ANOTH[ER] HIT, VINN[Y] OLE B[OY]

48

YEAH, THIS'S 'IM--HE'S BEEN FLYIN' THESE PARTS FOR *MONTHS* NOW...

...THOUGH I'D *NEVER* SEEN ANYTHIN' LIKE 'IM B'FORE.

SHOULD MAKE ONE BLOODY *TROPHY*.

UHHH...*HEAVY*... HEAVIER 'N IT LOOKS.

YEAH--IT SHOULD MAKE ONE BLOODY TROPHY...

BLAST--IT'S *HEAVY*.

IT'S A [*]RDEN [*]'LL SOON [*] HAVE [*] CARRY, [*]T.

I WISHED TO SEE WHAT SORT OF MAN WOULD *DARE* RAISE A WEAPON TO ME--

--AND WHAT I SEE IS NAUGHT BUT A WEAK, COWARDLY *FOOL!*

[*]THER [*]ARY-- [*]HAT--?

YOU'RE LIKE ALL THE OTHER *HUMANS* WHO PLOD THIS WORLD-- SNIVELING--*DIS-GUSTING*--

--IT *ANGERS* ME TO THINK THAT *MY* LIFE IS DEPENDANT UPON THOSE SUCH AS YOU--

--THOSE WHO HAVE *BLOOD* COURSING THROUGH YOUR VEINS.

UNNNGHH

DON'T KNOW *WHO* YOU ARE, MISTER--

--BUT *BULLETS*'LL KILL *YOU* LIKE ANYONE ELSE.

49

STOP-- YOU'RE SUPPOSED TO-- TO DIE!
HA! HA! HA! I'M ALREADY DEAD, MORTAL-- HOW DID YOU EXPECT TO KILL ME AGAIN--?
-- CERTAINLY NOT WITH THIS PUNY WEAPON OF YOURS.
W-WHAT ARE YOU GOING TO DO--?
SILENCE, HUMAN-- I COULD SLAY YOU WHERE YOU STAND-- BUT NO--
--THERE IS A BETTER WAY--
--ONE FAR MO FITTING FOR SUCH AS YOU
YOU BETT MORT YOUR LIF NOW DEPEND ON YOU AND
WHAT DID HE MEAN BY-- EH--?
NOISES--? GOOD LORD-- RATS-- HE SUMMONED RATS...
...TO CHASE ME.
BUT I KNOW EVERY INCH 'A THIS FOREST... IF I CAN'T ESCAPE 'EM-- NO ONE CAN.
LOOK LIKE HAVE AIN' NON

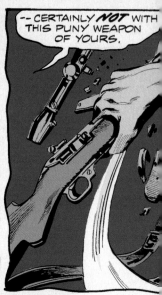

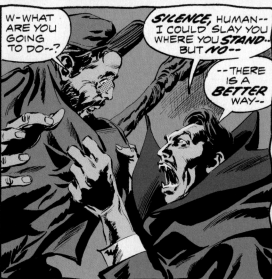

YEAH-- I LOST 'EM BACK IN THE THICKET--

HUH-- *MORE* SOUNDS-- GROWLING-- *NOT* RATS--

--OH GOD, NO!! WOLVES!

NOOOOOOOOOOOOOOOOOOOO

GRRRRRRR

RRRR

WHILE THE FOOL FLED MY RATS, HE HAD NEVER SUSPECTED I COULD ALSO CONTROL THE WILD WOLVES...

S HUNTER-- AME *HUNTED,* DIED AS RIBLY AS HAD LIVED.

AN *IRONY*-- PERHAPS JUST ONE IN A SERIES OF MANY *OTHERS* IN MY LIFE.

SUCH AS THE IRONY OF MY *BIRTH*-- SLAIN AS I WAS ON A TRANSYLVANIAN *BATTLEFIELD* BY LORD TURAC, I WAS TURNED OVER TO A *GYPSY WITCH*--

--ONE WHO TURNED OUT TO BE A *VAMPIRE* HERSELF, THEN TURAC *MURDERED* MARIA, MY DARLING *WIFE*--

--THAT DAMNED *TURK* NEVER KNEW THAT IF IT WERE *NOT* FOR HIS PROWESS *I* WOULD *NOT* HAVE BEEN *REBORN*--

--AND THAT *HE* WOULDN'T HAVE EVER *DIED.**

* *DRACULA LIVES* #2. --R.T.

ARIA-- STILL AFTER 0 YEARS I MOURN OR HER, FOR THOUGH HERS CALLED ME *THE VIL* AND *THE IMPALER,* E CALLED ME HER LOVE, S I DID *HER.*

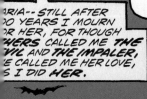

THERE WERE *BONDS* BETWEEN HUSBAND AND WIFE THEN-- BONDS WHICH MEANT *MORE* THAN THE PAPERS ONE SIGNED AT WEDDING.

AND IT SEEMS THAT *THIS* MODERN *ERA* SUFFERS MUCH-- FOR *MARRIAGE* HAS NOT THE *SANCTITY* IT HAD IN *MY* DAY.

I STILL DON'T UNDERSTAND YOU, RICHARD. IT'S OVER--
--WHATEVER THERE WAS BETWEEN US IS GONE NOW.
BESIDES, I'VE ALREADY CALLED MY LAWYER. HE'S WRITING UP THE DIVORCE PAPERS NOW.
I THINK YOU'RE ACTING RATHER RASH, KITTY. WE'VE FOUGHT BEFORE AND THEN MADE UP.
BUT IT ISN'T THE SAME, ANYMORE. I JUST DON'T LOVE YOU. I HAVEN'T FOR AWHILE.
I CAN'T LET YOU DIVORCE ME, DARLING. IT WOULD RUIN ALL MY PLANNING.
PLEASE PUT THAT GUN AWAY, RICH.
IT'S NOT GOING TO SOLVE ANYTHING.
MAYBE THEY'LL CARE FOR YOU.
SORRY, LOVER-- IT ISN'T AS SIMPLE AS THAT.
YOU SEE, I COULDN'T CARE LESS ABOUT YOU--
--IT'S YOUR MONEY I'M INTERESTED IN.
SOME STUPID DIVORCE.

-- RICH -- ... BE I'M ... ONG -- ... BE WE ... STAY ... ETHER.

PLEASE -- I'LL CALL MY LAWYER -- TELL HIM TO FORGET THE PAPERS!

SORRY, HONEY -- BUT I JUST CAN'T TAKE THE *CHANCE.*

SEE YOU SOMEDAY. IT WAS *NICE* KNOWING YOU.

BAM

... MIN I THOUGHT OF ... NY -- FOR AS THE ... LL LITHE *BODY* ... BLED DOWN TO ... CLIFF'S GRAVELED ... TOM, I CONSIDERED ... I MIGHT AFFECT ... E HUMAN'S LIVES.

... EHOW THE HUSBAND ... ST *PAY* FOR HIS ... IMES. BUT HOW -- *HOW?*

I HEARD THE GIRL *MOANING,* SHE WAS STILL ALIVE, IF ONLY *BARELY* SO. THUS I LANDED AT HER SIDE AND SPOKE GENTLY TO HER.

WOMAN, SPEAK TO ME -- DO YOU WISH *REVENGE* -- SWEET REVENGE? *ANSWER?*

... Y... YES...

THEN, MY DEAR -- YOU SHALL *HAVE* IT.

HA! HA! HA!

... HTS HAD ... SSED SINCE ... T FATEFUL ... N-SWEPT ... , BUT I ... S TO SOON ... RN THAT ... ENGE HAD ... ED BEEN ... HAD --

-- IN A MOST-SATISFYING MANNER!

YOU DON'T KNOW HOW *LONG* I'VE WAITED, CINDY. EVERYTHING'S *OURS* NOW -- *EVERYTHING.*

DON'T TALK, RICH... PLEASE DON'T TALK.

I FEEL I *HAVE* TO, CINDY-- IT'S JUST SUCH A *RELIEF* KNOWING I CAN *ALWAYS* BE WITH YOU NOW--

--AND NEVER *FEARING* THAT KITTY MIGHT LEARN OF US OR *CUT* ME OFF WITHOUT A *CENT.*

NO-- DON'T SAY ANYTHING-- I DON'T WANT TO KNOW WHAT *HAPPENED.*

JUST HOLD ME--

WHAT--? WHO IN BLAZES IS IT AT THIS TIME--?

KNOCK KNOCK

DON'T ANSWER IT-- PLEASE. ALL OF A SUDDEN I'M *SCARED.*

DON'T WORRY, LOVE. IT'S PROBABLY JUST SOME COMPLAINING *NEIGHBORS.*

KNOCK

IT'S *ME,* RICHARD. AREN'T YOU GOING TO *WELCOME* YOUR *WIFE* HOME--?

EEYAGGHH

HA

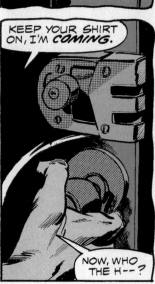

KEEP YOUR SHIRT ON, I'M *COMING.*

NOW, WHO THE H--?

KITTY-- IT CAN'T BE-- NOOOOOOO

cindy stor... most unbeliev... but soon she under... stood-- she understood very well indeed. my followers were many

54

, IRONIES WITHIN
RONIES-- DECEPTIONS
THIN DECEPTIONS.

D WHAT BETTER
RM OF DECEPTION
AN ONE WHICH
ENEFITS ME?

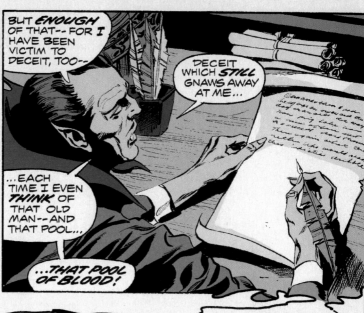

BUT ENOUGH OF THAT-- FOR I HAVE BEEN VICTIM TO DECEIT, TOO--

DECEIT WHICH STILL GNAWS AWAY AT ME...

...EACH TIME I EVEN THINK OF THAT OLD MAN-- AND THAT POOL...

...THAT POOL OF BLOOD!

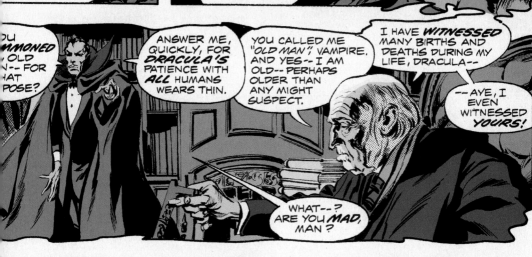

U
MMONED
OLD
N-- FOR
AT
POSE?

ANSWER ME, QUICKLY, FOR DRACULA'S PATIENCE WITH ALL HUMANS WEARS THIN.

YOU CALLED ME "OLD MAN", VAMPIRE. AND YES-- I AM OLD-- PERHAPS OLDER THAN ANY MIGHT SUSPECT.

I HAVE WITNESSED MANY BIRTHS AND DEATHS DURING MY LIFE, DRACULA--

-- AYE, I EVEN WITNESSED YOURS!

WHAT--? ARE YOU MAD, MAN?

HINK,
METIMES,
M-- OR
LEAST
S THAT
FUL

AND THOUGH THERE IS MADNESS IN WHAT I SAY-- THE MADNESS IS NOT MINE.

GAZE AT THIS COCKET, DRACULA -- FORGED PERHAPS IN THE FIRES OF HELL ITSELF.

LOOK CLOSELY-- AND YOU WILL KNOW ALL.

"YOU WILL UNDERSTAND HOW MANY CENTURIES BEFORE, A YOUNG MAN, LOST FROM HIS TROOPS IN ANCIENT BRITAIN, FOUND A POOL.

"YOU WILL KNOW IT WAS NO ORDINARY WATER-FILLED HOLE--NO --IT WAS A POOL OF BLOOD--

"--THE BLOOD OF ALL THOSE WHO HAD EVER DIED IN THE HISTORY OF THIS WORLD.

AN INTERESTING YARN -- YET WHY TELL *ME?*

THE YOUNG MAN'S NAME WAS *ORPHELUS* -- HE LIVED 1700 YEARS AGO, DRACULA.

AND THAT YOUNG MAN -- WAS *ME!*

I AM *ALREADY* IMMORTAL, YET YOUR STOR... INTERESTS... YOU MA... *CONTINU...*

BUT, BE W... I MAY *LOS...* THAT INTERE... AT ANY TIME... ANY MOMEN...

YOU SEE -- I HAD FOUND THE *SECRET OF IMMORTALITY* LOCKED IN THAT CAVE'S HIDDEN POOL.

I HAVE A *BARGAIN* TO MAKE, DRACULA. TAKE ME BACK TO THAT POOL -- FOR ITS *EFFECTS* HAVE ALREADY BEGUN TO *REVERSE* THEMSELVES.

YOU SEE, FOR ME THERE IS *IMMORTAL-ITY* -- BUT FOR YOU -- YOU HAVE AN END-LESS SUPPLY OF *BLOOD* --

-- AND YOU'D NEED *NEVER* HUNT FOR ANY EVER AGAIN.

SO, IMMORTALITY FOR EVERLASTING BLOOD. *FASCINATING.*

YES -- THE IDEA *FANCIES* ME -- LEAD ME TO YOUR *BLOOD-POOL*, HUMAN --

-- AND YOU SHALL *HAVE* WHAT YOU *SEEK.*

ONLY ONE QUESTION REMAINS -- FOR WHAT *REASON* DID YOU NEED *ME?*

COULD YOU *NOT* HAVE DONE THE DEED *ALONE?*

I AM *OLD* AS YOU SAID -- AND I WISHED THAT *NO OTHER* MORTAL KNOW THAT SECRET.

THAT I... WHY I CHO... YOU, VAMPI...

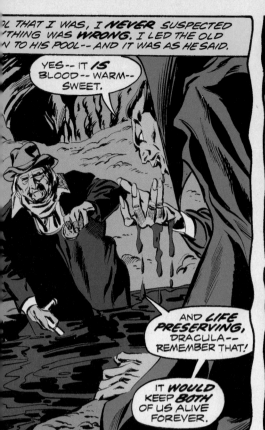

...OL THAT I WAS, I *NEVER* SUSPECTED 'THING WAS *WRONG.* I LED THE OLD N TO HIS POOL-- AND IT WAS AS HE SAID.

YES-- IT *IS* BLOOD-- WARM-- SWEET.

AND *LIFE PRESERVING,* DRACULA-- REMEMBER THAT!

IT *WOULD* KEEP *BOTH* OF US ALIVE FOREVER.

WOULD--? SOME-THING IS *WRONG*-- I SENSE IT!

YOU *LIED* TO ME, HUMAN.

ONLY *PARTIALLY* WHAT I TOLD YOU WAS *TRUE*-- THIS POOL OF BLOOD *CAN* PRESERVE LIFE--

WHAT--? WHAT ARE YOU *DOING?*

--BUT WHAT I DID *NOT* REVEAL WAS THAT I NO LONGER *WISHED* FOR LIFE--

NAY, AFTER *SEVENTEEN* 'UNDRED YEARS OF LIFE--

ALL I WANT IS--

--*DEATH!!*

ENDING THIS *BLASPHEMY* OF MINE, VAMPIRE.

LIFE IS NOT A VIRTUE. TO LIVE AS LONG AS *I* HAVE-- IS A *SIN*.

I KNEW THAT *NONE* SHOULD EVER FALL VICTIM TO *IMMORTALITY* AGAIN, AND THUS, WHEN I SAW MYSELF *AGING* AFTER 17 CENTURIES-- I KNEW I MUST *DESTROY* THE *BLOOD POOL* BEFORE I DIED.

I NEEDED TH[E] ANCIENT *COCK[?]* FOR IT HAD MO[RE] THAN SIMPLY *MYS[TIC]* POWERS-- AYE-- COULD *BURN* [THE] POOL BACK TO [THE] *HELL* FROM WH[ERE] IT CAME.

FAREWELL, DRACULA-- I *DIE* NOW, AT LAST-- AT LONG LAST-- AND I *THANK* YOU FOR YOUR *AID!*

NO! YOU MUSTN'T-- YOU DON'T REALIZE TH--

THE BLOOD-POOL HEAVED AND VOMITED BOILING SCARLET *DEATH*, CONVULSED UPON ITSELF, AND *BURST* FULL BLOWN, WITH SAVAGE *FURY*...

I WAS *THROWN* IN A THOUSAND DIRECTIONS AT ONCE, AND THE *AGONY* I FELT AS THE SIZZLING BLOOD *CANCED* THROUGH ME WOULD HAVE BEEN *MORE* THAN ENOUGH TO KILL ONE HUNDRED THOUSAND HUMANS.

AND WERE IT *NOT* THAT I AM *DRACULA*, SURELY, TOO, *I* WOULD HAVE PERISHED.

BUT HE WAS A *BLIND* FOOL. HA! TO THINK *ANY* COULD FIND *IMMORTALITY* A CURSE.

AH WELL-- IT WOULD HAVE BEEN *GOOD*-- SO SIMPLE TO LIVE IF ALL THAT BLOOD WERE SO ACCESSIBLE.

, PERHAPS, AS NOT *ANT* FOR *GS* TO BE *SIMPLE*.

I AM DRACULA-- A SOLDIER, A *WARRIOR!*

THE BLOOD WOULD HAVE MERELY QUENCHED MY *THIRST*-- IT COULD *NEVER* HAVE SATISFIED MY *SPIRIT*.

I *REQUIRE* THE CONSTANT HUNT --THE INCESSANT *SEARCHING* FOR BLOOD IF *ONLY* TO KEEP MY SPIRIT *ALIVE*.

E--? HOW *BIZARRE* UNREAL IS THAT RESSION TO *ME*-- NE WHO HAS D AGAIN AND AGAIN--

--ONLY TO BE *REBORN* WHOLE AND COMPLETE ONE MORE.

FOR DEATH ITSELF HAS PASSED ITS *MEANING*. THAT FOOL, *BLADE*, THOUGHT HE HAD SLAYED ME--*

--BUT I AM STILL WALKING-- AND I SHALL *ALWAYS* WALK-- EVEN AFTER *HE* HAS ROTTED IN HIS GRAVE.

*ISSUE #13. -- RT.

59

HE WASN'T THE *FIRST* TO TRY TO KILL ME--AND, *TRUTHFULLY,* IT IS DOUBTFUL THAT HE'D BE THE *LAST--.*

ONE SUCH AS MYSELF HAS MANY *ENEMIES,* AND BLADE-- LIKE THE ONE *BEFORE* HIM--ARE *DOOMED* TO FAILURE BEFORE THEY BEGIN.

YES-- THE ONE BEFORE HIM-- THE *SCOTSMAN!*

HAH! YES--HE WAS DOOMED..., TO *DIE!*

IT WAS IN THE YEAR 1969, I REMEMBER-- IN *TRANSYLVANIA--* I ENTERED THE TOWN DISGUISED--TO *OBSERVE* THE ACTIVITIES OF MY HUMAN PUPPETS...

LOOK AT THIS, OTTO-- UNBELIEVABLE--

MAN, WALKING ALIVE-- ON THE *MOON.*

LOOK-- *LOOK.*

UTTER FOOLS-- THEY CARE MORE FOR MEN ON *OTHER* WORLDS-- THAN THE ONES WHO LIVE ON *THIS.*

BUT SOON IT SHALL MATTER *LITTLE* TO ME,

I NEED NO LONGER *STAY* IN TRANSYLVANIA, ALREADY MY *COFFINS* FILLED WITH EARTH HAVE BEEN SENT AHEAD TO ENGLAND--

...AND THAT IS WHERE I MUST GO,

BUT *FIRST,* SOME LAST MOMEN PROVISIONS--

CASTLE DRACULA LOOMED BEFORE ME, AND I THOUGHT OF HOW *LONG* I HAD BEEN *AWAY* FROM IT, AND HOW SOON I WOULD HAVE TO *LEAVE* IT AGAIN.

BUT MY TRAVELS TO THE FAR EAST HAD BEEN A SUCCESS, AND ALREADY MY *LEGIONS* WERE GROWING IN JAPAN, CHINA AND INDONESIA.

...WAS *TIME* I RETURNED TO [...]LAND -- HOME OF MY MOST [...]D *FOE* -- *QUINCY* [...]RKER.

[...]R *SIXTY* [...]ARS WE [...]D BATTLED [...]CH OTHER [...] A *STALE-* [...]ATE: I [...]OK FROM [...]M A *WIFE*, [...]ILE HE [...]BBED A [...]UGHTER [...]OM ME.

[...]IT WAS TIME I HAD [...]URNED...TIME TO EXACT MY *REVENGE*.

BUT MY REVENGE WAS GOING TO HAVE TO WAIT -- *THREE YEARS* -- FOR AS I ENTERED MY *ANCESTRAL* HOME --

WHO--?

I'D BE ADVISIN' YE TO HOLD YE *PLACE*, VAMPIRE -- 'AFORE I RUN YE THROUGH.

I WAN' SOME AWNSWERS TO A QUESTION -- *NOW!*

DO Y' UNNERSTAN' ME -- *NOW!*

MAH **SON**, DRACULA-- HE CAME CHASIN' YE IN CHINA SOME **MONTHS** AGO.

WHAT DID YE' DO WI' HIM?

HE WAS A **FOOL** LIKE YOU, SCOTSMAN-- AND I LET HIM DIE AS HE **DESERVED** TO--

--AS **YOU** DESERVE TO-- AND **SHALL!**

THEN HE'D **NOT** BE A VAMPIRE, DRACULA

NO-- HE DIED CLUTCHING A **CRUCIFIX**, SO I COULD **NOT** APPROACH HIM.

BUT **YOU** HAV NO SUCH **CURSED CROS** AND THEREFOR **WILL** SOON SERVE ME.

NEVER!

QUINCY HARKER SHOWED **ME** TH' WAYS OF BATTLIN' YE, VAMPIRE, AN' I **SWEAR** I'LL BE THE ONE WHO LIVES-- NOT **YE**.

HARKER--? I'M **SICK** OF THAT NAME!

THEN YOU'LL **DIE** WI' IT ON YE **LIPS**...'CAUSE DIE YE SHALL!

62

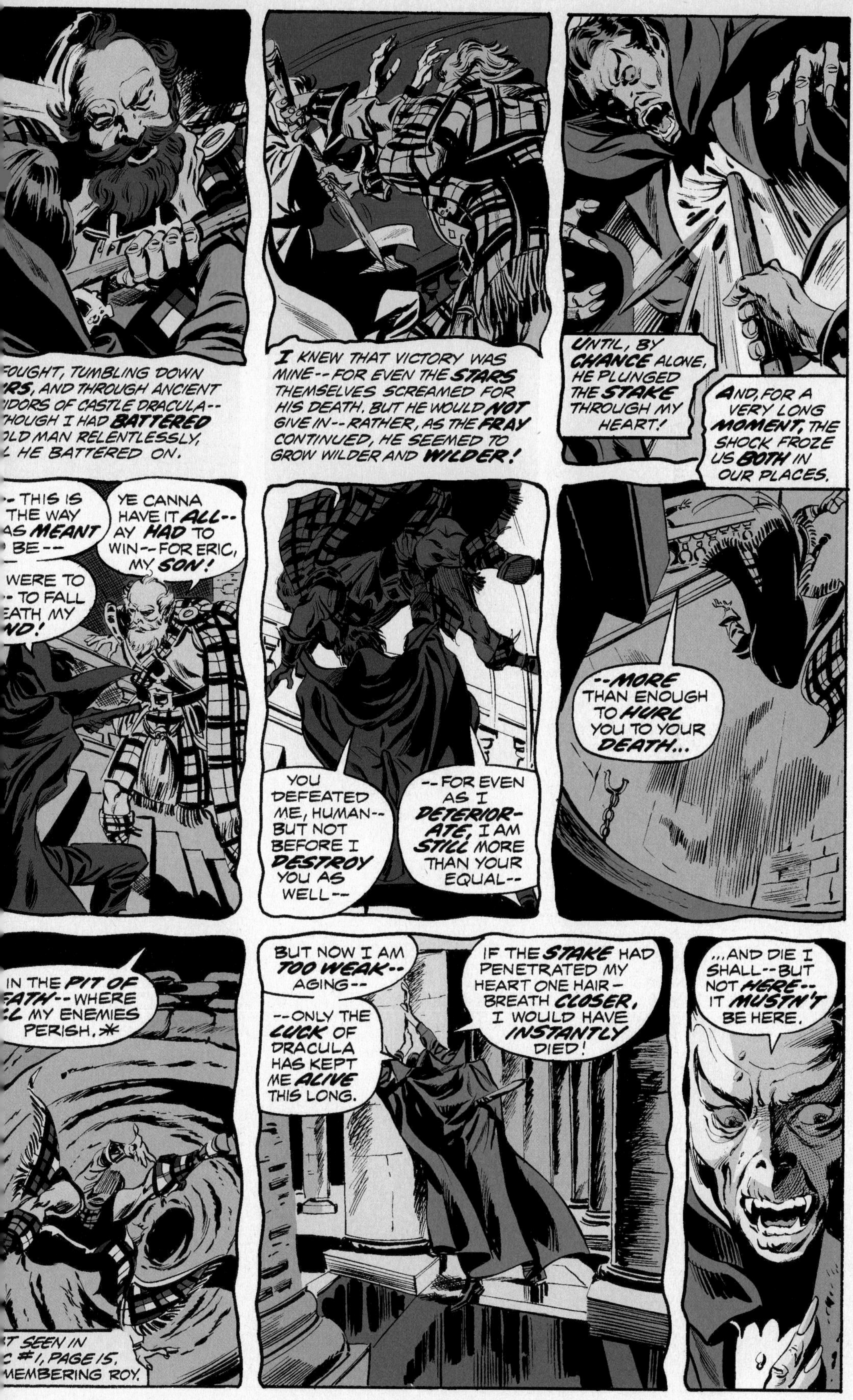
FOUGHT, TUMBLING DOWN
RS, AND THROUGH ANCIENT
RIDORS OF CASTLE DRACULA--
THOUGH I HAD BATTERED
OLD MAN RELENTLESSLY,
L HE BATTERED ON.
I KNEW THAT VICTORY WAS MINE--FOR EVEN THE STARS THEMSELVES SCREAMED FOR HIS DEATH. BUT HE WOULD NOT GIVE IN--RATHER, AS THE FRAY CONTINUED, HE SEEMED TO GROW WILDER AND WILDER!
UNTIL, BY CHANCE ALONE, HE PLUNGED THE STAKE THROUGH MY HEART!
AND, FOR A VERY LONG MOMENT, THE SHOCK FROZE US BOTH IN OUR PLACES.
--THIS IS THE WAY AS MEANT BE--
YE CANNA HAVE IT ALL--AY HAD TO WIN--FOR ERIC, MY SON!
WERE TO --TO FALL EATH MY ND!
YOU DEFEATED ME, HUMAN--BUT NOT BEFORE I DESTROY YOU AS WELL--
--FOR EVEN AS I DETERIOR-ATE, I AM STILL MORE THAN YOUR EQUAL--
--MORE THAN ENOUGH TO HURL YOU TO YOUR DEATH...
IN THE PIT OF EATH--WHERE LL MY ENEMIES PERISH.*
BUT NOW I AM TOO WEAK--AGING--
--ONLY THE LUCK OF DRACULA HAS KEPT ME ALIVE THIS LONG.
IF THE STAKE HAD PENETRATED MY HEART ONE HAIR-BREATH CLOSER, I WOULD HAVE INSTANTLY DIED!
...AND DIE I SHALL--BUT NOT HERE--IT MUSTN'T BE HERE.
ST SEEN IN
C #1, PAGE 15.
MEMBERING ROY.

NO--IT MUST BE IN MY *COFFIN*--RESTING IN THE SACRED SOIL OF TRANSYLVANIA...

...ONLY *THERE* MAY I DIE IN PEACE--

--AND *WAIT* FOR THE DAY THAT--

--DRACU MAY LIV *AGAIN*

MY FLESH *CRUMBLED* AND *WITHERED*, TURNING TO THE EARTH AND ASHES FROM WHENCE IT HAD COME...

...AND FOR THREE LONG YEA I *RESTED* THERE...

YES, UNTIL THE DAY WHEN THAT CLODDISH FOOL *CLIFTON GRAVES* TORE THE STAKE FROM MY HEART.

AND IT WAS *THEN* I MADE MY *VOW*-- NEVER AGAIN WOUL I LET MYSELF *DI*

--NEVER AGAIN WOULD A *COFFIN* BE MY ETERNAL HOME...MY EVER-LASTING *RESTIN* PLACE...

AND, UNTIL *BLADE* SLAYED ME, MY VOW W KEPT UNTOUCHED.

BUT THIS I VOW, ALL *GODS* THAT HEAR ME THIS NIGHT-- BE YOU *SATAN* OR SOME *HEAVENLY FORCE*--

--THOUGH I WALK IN THE SHADOWS OF *HELL* ITSELF--

--THOUGH I MAY DIE *AGAIN AND AGAIN*--

HA HA HA HA HA HA

NOTHING SHALL KEEP ME FROM *RISING FROM MY TOMB*--

NOTHING! NOTHING! NOTHING!

NEXT: *DEATH'S HAND*

64

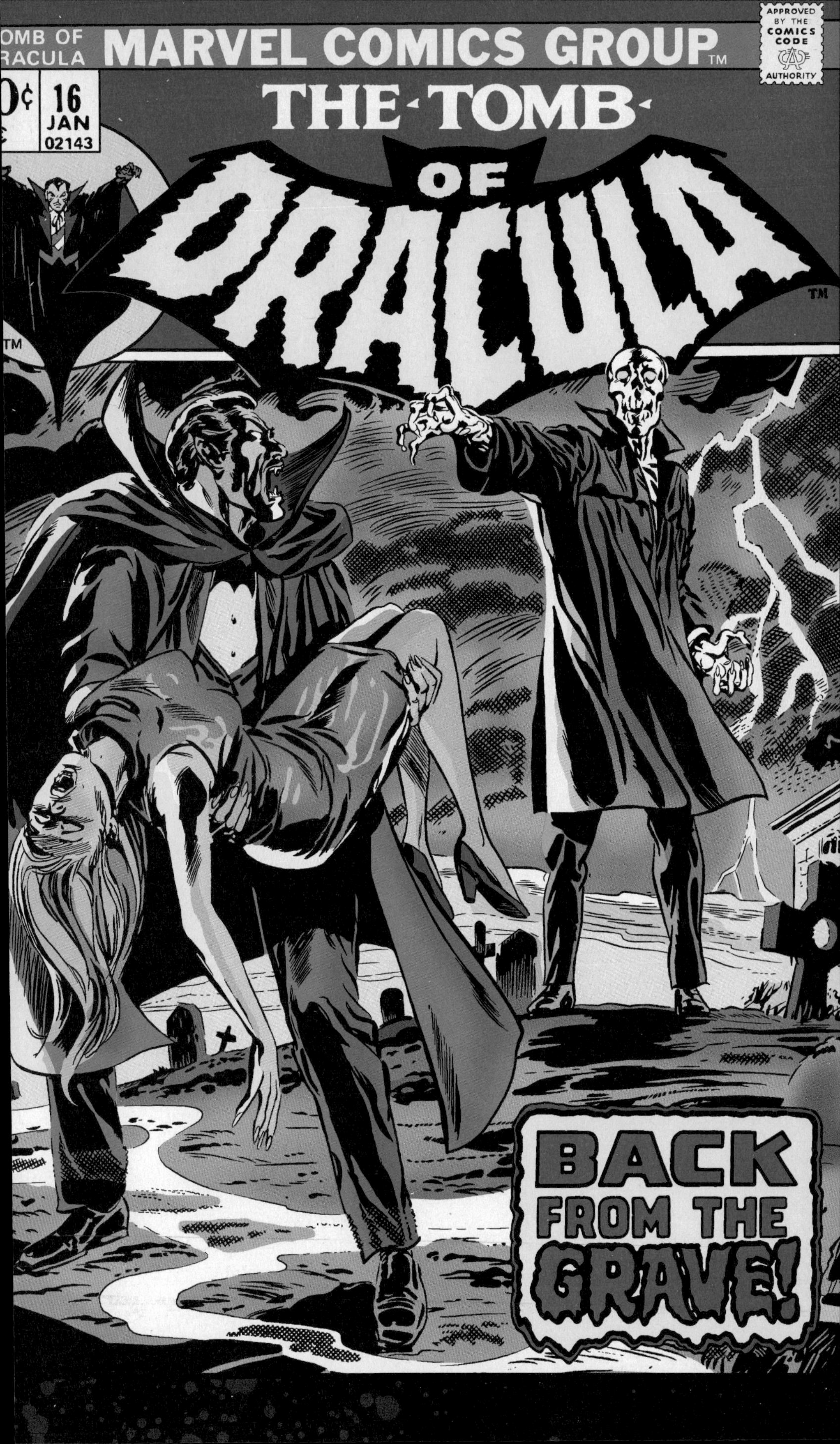

OMB OF
RACULA
MARVEL COMICS GROUP
APPROVED BY THE COMICS CODE AUTHORITY
0¢
16
JAN
02143
THE TOMB
OF
DRACULA
BACK FROM THE GRAVE!

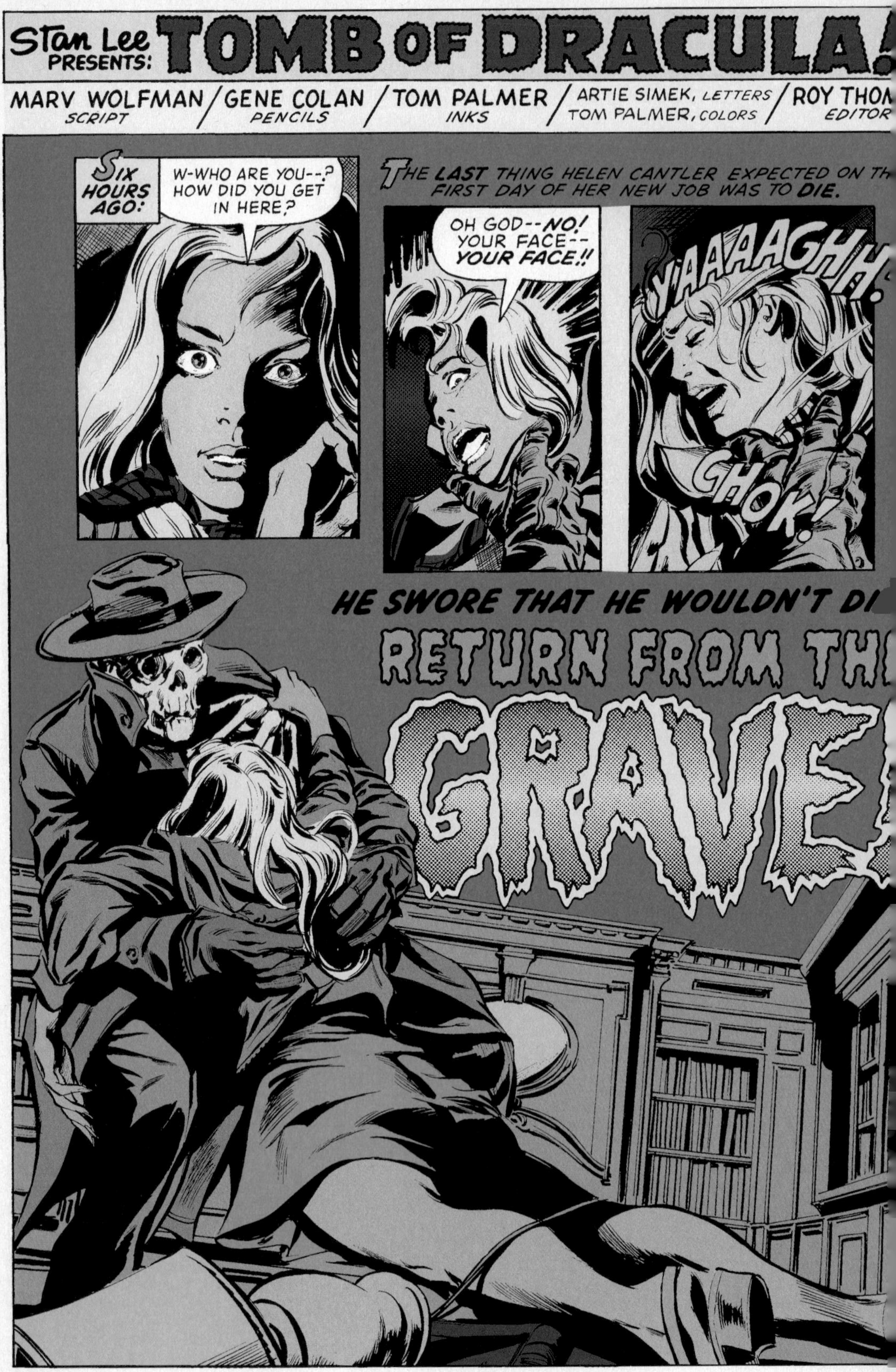

Stan Lee PRESENTS: TOMB OF DRACULA!
MARV WOLFMAN SCRIPT / GENE COLAN PENCILS / TOM PALMER INKS / ARTIE SIMEK, LETTERS TOM PALMER, COLORS / ROY THOM EDITOR
SIX HOURS AGO:
W-WHO ARE YOU--? HOW DID YOU GET IN HERE?
THE LAST THING HELEN CANTLER EXPECTED ON TH FIRST DAY OF HER NEW JOB WAS TO DIE.
OH GOD--NO! YOUR FACE-- YOUR FACE!!
YAAAAGHH!
GHOK!
HE SWORE THAT HE WOULDN'T DI
RETURN FROM TH
GRAVE!

...LEN CANTLER SLUMPED QUIETLY ...HE FLOOR. SHE WAS *DEAD*, AND THE ...ING FORM THAT TOWERED ABOVE HER SEEMED *NOT TO CARE*--

...YET, ...HY ...ULD ...IT?

*A*FTER ALL, WASN'T *IT* DEAD, TOO--?

*A*ND HADN'T *IT* LIFTED ITSELF FROM A *MOULDER-ING GRAVE* TO WALK ONCE MORE AMONGST THE UNSUSPECTING *LIVING?*

*Y*ET, *IT* HAD A REASON TO WALK AGAIN--A *QUEST*-- A *CHALLENGE* TO ITS *EXISTENCE.*

*I*T *HAD* TO BREAK FREE FROM THE BONDS OF ITS CHILL-ING *DEATH.*

*N*OW, FOR A BRIEF *MOMENT*, *IT* STUDIED THE ROOM, TAKING ALL THE MINISCULE *DETAILS* INTO ITS EMPTY EYE SOCKETS--

--AND FINDING WHAT IT WAS *SEARCHING* FOR, IT STARTED FOR ITS GOAL.

...SAFE: TUCKED BEHIND A FRONT ...HONY BOOKS AND WORTHLESS ...KNACKS--*THE SAFE:* FOR *SOME,* AN IMPOSSIBLE *BARRIER*--

...OR IT-- ...ONLY A ...MPORARY ...STRUCTION--

--AND ONE *EASILY* DISPENSED WITH.

*T*HE SAFE WAS FILLED WITH PAPERS; SOME IMPORTANT, SOME ONLY SENTIMENTAL--BUT THERE WAS ONE *OTHER* THING LYING IN THE DARKNESS--

--THE THING *IT* HAD SEARCHED FOR--AND NOW HAD *FOUND.*

67

PLACING ITS **PRIZE** SECURELY IN ITS POCKET, THE SHADOW-SPECKED FORM TURNED TO **LEAVE**--

--BUT FOUND IN ITS WAY, JAMES JACKSON-- SOLICITOR--AND THE **MAN** WHOSE SAFE **IT** JUST ROBBED.

HELEN--? WHAT IN HEAVEN'S NAME DID YOU DO TO HER--?

THE ROOM W DARK, BUT E **THROUGH** DIMNESS SOUGHT OUT FEATURES THE INTRUD FACE--AND OWN BLANC STARK **WH** WITH FE

...FOR JAMES JACKSO KNEW HE HAD SEEN FACE OF--**DEATH**.

DEATH: WHO MOVED WITH SLOW, DELIBERATE **STEPS** TOWARDS THE FRIGHTENED YOUNG **ATTORNEY**.

DEATH: WHOSE BODY REEKED OF FLESH **DECAYING** AND MAGGOTS SQUIRMING.

ARGGHHHHH!!

DEATH: WHO REACHED OUT TO JAMES JACKSON AND--**ATTACKED!**

JACKSON FELL BACK WITH A SICKENING **GROAN**--BUT THING STRUCK **TWICE MORE**, KNOCKING HIM SENSELE TO THE FLOOR.

AND, PERHAPS ONE COULD CALL IT DEVINE **FATE** OR **PROVIDENCE**, BUT BEFORE THE **THIRD BLOW** CAME PLUMMET- ING DOWN ON HIM, JAMES JACKSON WAS ALREADY **UNCONSCIOUS.**

SEEING LIMP F BELOW, TURN ONCE N TO LEA **IT** H WHAT CAME AND WAS THAT IMPORT. FOR N

68

'ER **NECK'S** BEEN SNAPPED, INSPECTOR CHELM--TH' BLOKE WOT DONE IT MUSTA' BEEN BLOODY WELL **STRONG**.

STRONG ENOUGH TO BATTER **ME** ABOUT LIKE A BLINKIN' **SOCCER BALL**. BUT IT WAS HIS **FACE**...

YOU SAID IT LOOKED LIKE A SKULL-- A **SMILING SKULL?**

MORE'N A SKULL, INSPECTOR--'E WAS A BLOODY WALKIN' **HELL**.

I'M NOT COMPLAININ', YOU UNDERSTAND, BUT **WHY** 'E DIDN'T **KILL** ME THEN I DON'T KNOW. BUT I'LL TELL YOU THIS, INSPECTOR--IF 'E HAD A MIND TO, NOT EVEN ALL OF YOUR **SCOTLAND YARD** COULD 'AVE STOPPED 'IM.

...HILE...

I **THIRST**--AND THIS NIGHT IS RIPE FOR **HUNTING!!** SO BEWARE, FOOLISH MORTALS--ONCE MORE, **DRACULA LIVES!!** HA! HA! HA!

HIGHGATE CEMETERY SHIVERS UNDER THE COLD OCTOBER RAINS-- THE GROUND IS HARD, PACKED-- BUT FOR THE BODIES **BURIED** HERE FOR UNTOLD **HUNDREDS** OF YEARS, THE CLIMATE IS OF LITTLE IMPORT--

--RATHER, THERE IS ONLY **ONE** WHO RESIDES THERE WHO COULD **CARE** AT ALL:

DRACULA--LORD OF THE DAMNED!!

"AND WHERE **BEST** TO BEGIN MY PROWLING--THAN **HERE** IN THE CEMETERY I HAVE TAKEN AS **MINE!**

"AND WHOM **BEST** TO MAKE MY **FIRST VICTIMS** THIS NIGHT, THAN THOSE TWO **FOOLS** WHO EVEN NOW TRY STEALING THE **TREASURES** FROM THE SLEEPING **DEAD.**"

TAKE 'ER EASY THERE, MATE. WE GOT TH' **TIME** TO TAKE CARE.

BLOKE BURIED 'ERE WAS A **RICH** ONE, MATE--AN' 'E'S PROB'LY WEARIN' 'IS BEST SUNDAY **JEWELS** T' SHOW IT.

WOTTA **RACKET**, SHIVVEY--TH' **DEAD** DON'T NEED **NOTHIN'**-- SO **WE** TAKES IT FROM 'EM. HAR!

SHIVVEY, IF 'E'S GOT 'IMSELF A *RUBY*, KIN I KEEP IT--?

--SHIVVEY-- *SH-SHIVVEY*-- THE BODY--IT'S *M-MOVIN'*--!

ARE YOU GOIN' BLINKIN' *CRAZY*, MATE? LEMME LOOK FER MYSEL--

*O*NE BRIEF MOMENT--THE SMALLEST *FRACTION* OF A SECOND IS ALL IT TAKES TO *SNUFF* THE CANDLE OF LIFE FROM THE SOULS OF SHIVVEY MARTIN AND GORDO BROWN, GRAVEDIGGERS--

--AND *DURING* THAT FLEETING MOMENT, *ONE THOUGHT* FLICKERS THROUGH *BOTH* THEIR MINDS:

*T*HERE ARE *NONE* WHO WILL *EVER* MOURN FOR THEM.

*A*ND FO THAT, THE DEATHS MOST DOU PAINFU

WHAT--? THAT-- *THING*--HAS ROBBED MY *DINNER*--THE VERY *BLOOD* I NEEDED FOR LIFE--FOR *STRENGTH*--

VERY WELL, DAMNED CREATURE --*ENJOY* YOUR KILLING--

--BUT ENJOY IT WITH *HASTE*--

--FOR *NONE* MAY STEAL WHAT IS DRACULA'S WITHOUT *ANSWERING* TO HIS *VENGEANCE*.

BUT-- *WAIT*-- THE THING... *DISINTEGRATES*--

--AND FALLS AS *ASHES* BACK INTO THE GRAVE.

NO! IT CANNO BE--I MUSTN BE *ROBBED* MY *PREY* SO EASILY.

*B*UT TH IS *NOTH* LEFT BATTLE- LEAS *NOTH* THA *LIVE*

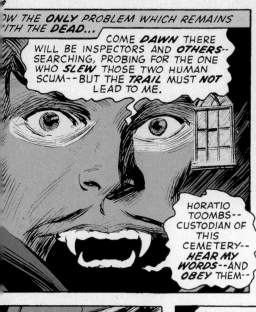

...OW THE **ONLY** PROBLEM WHICH REMAINS ...ITH THE **DEAD**...

COME **DAWN** THERE WILL BE INSPECTORS AND **OTHERS**-- SEARCHING, PROBING FOR THE ONE WHO **SLEW** THOSE TWO HUMAN SCUM--BUT THE **TRAIL** MUST **NOT** LEAD TO ME.

HORATIO TOOMBS-- CUSTODIAN OF THIS CEMETERY-- **HEAR MY WORDS**--AND **OBEY** THEM--

--YOUR **WILL** IS **MINE** TO CONTROL, HORATIO TOOMBS-- NOW **RISE**--RISE FROM YOUR WORK AND HEED MY **COMMANDS.**

IN THE EDGE OF THE DARKLING CEMETERY STANDS THE SMALL STUCCO COTTAGE OF HIGHGATE'S **KEEPER**-- AND WITHIN IT, HORATIO TOOMBS READS HIS DAILY **LEDGER**--

--A LEDGER LISTING ALL THOSE WHO LAY WITHIN ITS BRONZE- METAL GATES...

...ALL BUT ...ONE.

RISE, MY **SLAVE** --RISE NOW-- YOU HAVE **WORK** TO DO--MISCHIEF TO **CONCEAL.**

BRING BOTH YOUR **SHOVEL** AND **SPADE**--BUT BE **QUICK.**

I STILL **THIRST**--AND **YOU** MAY YET BE MY QUARRY.

COME TO ME NOW-- **NOW! NOW!!**

...D **BURY** THOSE DEAD SO **NONE** MAY EVER FIND THEM...

"...WHILE **I** SEEK MY PREY ELSEWHERE."

WESTMINSTER BRIDGE STANDS PROUD AS IT HAS STOOD FOR MANY **DECADES**--FOR EACH DAY **THOUSANDS** OF TOURISTS AND LONDONERS ALIKE CROSS THE MIGHTY BRIDGE ABOVE THE THAMES TOWARDS **PARLIAMENT** AND THE CENTRAL LONDON DISTRICTS...

BUT **THIS** FOUL NIGHT THERE ARE **FEW** WHO PLOD THE RAINSWEPT BRIDGE... AND ALREADY THEY ARE A FEW **TOO MANY.**

MARIE KOMPH HAD PLANNED WELL FOR HER **SUICIDE.** SHE LEFT A CAREFULLY WORDED **NOTE,** PAID ALL HER **BILLS,** AND THEN TOOK THE SLOW WALK TO **WESTMINSTER.**

SHE KNEW SHE COULDN'T FACE HER **PARENTS**--NOT AFTER WHAT HAPPENED-- CERTAINLY NOT AFTER **THAT.**

THEY HAD **WARNED** HER ABOUT HIM-- BUT SHE CHOSE TO **IGNORE** THEIR WORDS AS FOOLISH PARENTAL **CONCERN.**

BUT **THIS** TIME THEY WERE **RIGHT...**

...AND BECAUSE MARIE COULD NOT **ADMIT** IT-- SHE **HAD** TO DIE.

HOLD, WOMA I WISH TO **SPEAK** WIT YOU...

SHE LOOKS C THE EDGE OF STONE RAILI INTO THE BL PITCH **WAT** WHEN THRO THE BLUE-G FOG COME A MAN--

NO--MORE THAN A MAN-- RATHER, A **DEMON**-- THE DEMON CALLED **DRACULA.**

...AND THERE IS **MUCH** TO SPEAK ABOUT INDEED. **HA! HA! HA!**

MARIE KOMPH SUDDENLY **UNDERSTANDS** HOW WASTED DEATH CAN BE-- BUT **TRAGICALLY** THAT UNDER- STANDING COMES MOMENTS TOO LATE.

WHILE...

MR. HARKER--? INSPECTOR CHELM OF SCOTLAND YARD DR. RACHEL VAN HELSING G ME YOUR **NUMBER** TO CAL IN AN **EMERGENCY.**

I BELIEVE THAT YO OLD **NEME DRACUL** ON THE LO

HMMM. INTERESTING, INSPECTOR-- BUT IT **DOESN'T** FIT DRACULA'S PATTERN.

I'M SORRY, BUT I THINK THERE MAY BE **SOME- ONE** ELSE YOU'RE DEAL- ING WITH.

BUT IF I MAY BE OF **ANY** ASSISTANCE--

MINUTES AFTER...

INSPECTOR CHELM--WE'VE JUST RECEIVED A **REPORT**--

"SEEMS TO BE SOME MAJOR **TROUBL** DOWN ON COVENTRY STREET, SIR--BU THINKS IT MAY BE **YOUR** BLOKE, SIR

YE KING PU

SILENT TABLEAU: THOUGH MOST THIRTY PATRONS OF YE GGS PUB LOOK ON, NOT ONE EAKS--AND WORSE--NONE ES TO STOP THE TALL, BONEY FORM...

S IT SHUFFLES ACROSS A BBLESTONE STREET WARDS A TALL, TRACTIVE WOMAN.

INDEED, EVEN THERESA BEARE HERSELF STANDS STARRING-- PERHAPS IN SILENT TERROR, AS THE HAND RIPS THE MARBLE- STONE LOCKET FROM HER...

...AND PLACES ITS NEWEST PRIZE IN ITS POCKET. HOPEFULLY, IT FEELS, THE WOMAN WILL UNDERSTAND.

UT THIS IS NO TIME FOR UNDERSTANDING, FOR-- SHAMED BY THEIR OWN NONACTION--THE CROWD OF PATRONS CLOSES ABOUT THE FIGURE--

N, YOU BLITHERS-- CAN'T LET THIS NG ATTACK OUR WOMEN--

--AND ATTACKS.

IGHT 'IM-- ITH STICKS R BRICKS-- EVEN YOUR ISTS--BUT FIGHT!!

'ENRY'S RIGHT-- GIT THE BLOODY MONSTER--'E'S ONLY ONE--

--ONE TO OUR MANY!

BUT THE THING'S HAND SHOOTS OUT, AND BONE AND CARTILAGE CRUMBLE UNDER ITS GRASP.

HENRY BONNEY **DIES** IN THAT SINGLE MOMENT, HIS **FACE** A MASS OF BLOODIED FLESH AND PULP...

... AND THE **CROWD**, NOW **STRIPPED** OF ITS COURAGE, SLINKS NERVOUSLY FROM THE **THING** THAT MURDERED THEIR FRIEND.

WHILE **ABOVE**, UNSEEN BY THE FRIGHTENED VILLAGERS, DRACULA WATCHES ON--

--AND HAVING **WITNESSED** ALL--PLUMMETS MADDENINGLY TO THE GROUND.

HE STILL SEEKS **REVENGE** AGAINST THIS THING--THIS UNHOLY **CREATURE** WHO DARED ROB HIM OF HIS EVENING'S BLOOD--

--AND HE WILL GAIN THAT VENGEANCE **NOW**.!!

LOR' **NO**--N ANOTHER ONE-- **NO**

LIKE AN AVENGING **DEVIL**, DRACULA CRASHES THE THING BENEATH HIM TO THE ROCK-STREWN GROUND.

FOOL-- DID YOU THINK YOU COULD **STEAL** WHAT WAS DRACULA'S WITHOUT BATTLING FOR YOUR VERY **EXISTENCE**--?

BUT NOW YOU'LL BE MADE TO **SUFFER**-- FOR **NONE** HAVE THAT PRIVILEGE--

THERE YOU ARE **WRONG**, DRACULA-- EVEN AS YOUR BODY **SMOTHERS** THE FALLEN FIGURE, IT **LIFTS** YOU OFF THE GROUND--

--ONLY TO EFFORTLESSLY **HEAVE** YOU THROUGH THE KINGS PUB WINDOW.

...IT THE THING, WITH ITS RBLE NECKLACE SAFELY DEN, LEAVES, VANISHING O THE DARKTIDE *FOG* OF LONDON'S NIGHT...

LEAVING DRACULA ONLY TO RSE THE ILL-SWEPT ATES.

SCUM! HOW DARE YOU MANHANDLE DRACULA, PRINCE OF EVIL--*LORD OF DARKNESS*--?

FOR THAT YOU WILL *PERISH* ONE THOUSAND TIMES OVER--AND YOU WILL *SUFFER* ONE MILLION *HORRID HELLS!*

THAT DRACULA SWEARS, DAMNED ONE-- *THAT DRACULA SWEARS!!*

TRACK YOU OUGH THE RKEST TS--AND D YOU IN ATEVER OLE YOU HIDE--

--FOR *NOTHING* SHALL STAY THE *PAINFUL,* EXCRUCIATING *REVENGE* I'LL HAVE FOR YOU-- *NOTHING!*

BUT WAIT-- *SIRENS*-- THE LOCAL *CONSTABU-LARY*--!

INSPECTOR CHELM--! THERE WERE *TWO* OF THEM. ONE'S GONE--BUT THE *OTHER* ONE--HE'S *TRAPPED* IN THE PUB, SIR.

QUICKLY, MAN-- POINT HIM OUT.

EOOEEOOOOO

R RE IS--! NING R IT.

STAND BACK, MAN--

DRACULA--HOLD. I WISH TO *SPEAK* WITH YOU...

YOU *KNOW* ME--? THEN YOU ALSO KNOW THAT DRACULA WAITS FOR *NO HUMAN.*

THEN I HAVE *NO CHOICE*--

GOD HELP WHAT HAPPENS NEXT-- BUT I *MUST STOP YOU!*

BAM!

HA! HA! HA! HA!

NO--*NO*-- THE BULLETS HAVE NO EFFECT-- NONE AT ALL.

*A*ND EVEN *ABOVE* THE ROAR OF GUNFIRE CAN BE HEARD THE DARK, MOCKING REPLY.

WHILE **FAR** FROM THE MOCKING LAUGHTER, ON A SECLUDED STRETCH OF **LAND** BY THE NORTHERN IRISH COASTLINE, STANDS A **PAGODA**-- NOT AT ALL OF **GAELIC** DESIGN...

AND THOUGH THE STRUCTURE STANDS **PROUD**, NESTLED WITHIN THE OLIVE-GREEN COUNTRYSIDE LIKE A SMALL DAB OF **FANTASY** COME TRUE--

--IT IS, HOWEVER, PAINTED WITH THE DELICATE HAND OF--**HORROR!**

IT HAS BEEN **REPORTED** TO ME, MISTER CHEN, THAT YOU HAVE CARRIED OUT YOUR ASSIGNMENT WELL.

I HAVE ONLY DONE **ALL** YOU ORDERED, DOCTOR SUN.

LET ME SEE THE **SPECIMEN** NOW, PLEASE.

I HAVE BEEN **ASSURE** THAT HE **IS** A **VAMPI** DR. SUN.*

THAT IS **CORRECT**, MISTER CHEN. AND HE IS TOTALLY UNDER MY **CONTROL**.

ISSUE #14. --R

YOU HAVE INDEED COMPLETED YOUR ASSIGNMENT **PROFESSIONALLY**, MR. CHEN, AND YOU HAVE **EARNED** MY GRATITUDE.

NOW **YOU** MAY ASK FOR MY SERVICES--AND WHATEVER YOUR WISH, IT WILL BE GRANTED **IMMEDIATELY**.

TO **SERVE** YOU IS ENO FOR **ME**-- BUT THER SOMETHING FOR **FATHER.**

HE IS **PRISONER** CHINA FOR M THAN **TWEN YEARS**, A ALWAYS UN THE MOS **STRINGE. SECURIT** IF ANYTHI I WOULD W HIM **FRE**

AND SO, MR. CHEN--HE **SHALL BE FREE.**

YOU SHALL SEE HIM AGAIN BEFORE **DAYBREAK.**

LET US LEAVE THE DARK-SHROUDED *MYSTERIES* OF *DR. SUN* FOR *ANOTHER* TIME--FOR NOW THE *ACTION* IS WITH DRACULA...

WHO STRUTS ONCE MORE THE MIST-LADEN GROUNDS OF HIGHGATE CEMETERY.

CURSE ME FOR A *FOOL*--I SEARCH AIMLESSLY FOR THE *SKELETON-BEAST* IN A CITY OF UNTOLD *THOUSANDS*--

WHEN *FIRST* I MET HIM HERE--BURIED DEEP IN DRACULA'S DOMAIN.

PAUL

HERE--THIS WEATHERED *GRAVESTONE* IS HIS--AND UNDER IT...

...I SHOULD FIND MY PREY.

AHHH...YES-- SOMEONE--OR SOME*THING* IS BURIED IN HERE--THE COFFIN HAS *WEIGHT*...

...AND IN MOMENTS I SHALL SEE WHAT ALL MY *SENSES* TELLS ME WAITS WITHIN.

A FEW SECONDS TO *PREPARE* MYSELF IS ALL I NEED--FOR IF INDEED THE *THING* IS STILL ALIVE--

--I MAY NEED *ALL* MY *STRENGTH* TO BATTLE IT...

...AND PAY IT BACK FOR OUR LITTLE *MEETING* EARLIER THIS NIGHT.

AHH--THERE IT LIES IN ALL ITS GRISTLY *RANCOR*...

...WAITING FOR ME TO END ITS *EXISTENCE* FOREVER.

77

WHAT--?

I THOUGHT IT UNCONSCIOUS-- UNLIVING--

--BUT IT MERELY *FEIGNS* ITS RESTIVE POSE.

BUT IT MATTERS NOT--NOT WHILE DRACULA HAS HIS *STRENGTH*--

--FOR *NONE* SHALL EVER DEFEAT HIM AGAIN.

WHAT IS THIS--? FORCEFUL *THRUST* IT *CRUMBLES* TO

THERE IS SOME *FORC* AT WORK HERE THA* DRACULA DOES NOT UNDERSTAN*

AHH--PERHAPS *THIS* EXPLAINS ALL--*PAUL BEARE*--I MET WITH HIM MANY YEARS PAST--

--WHEN HE ASKED ME TO *JOIN* HIM ON SOME *SORCER-OUS* ADVENTURE.

HE WAS A *MYSTIC*-- A SATANIST-- AND I REFUSED HIM, OF COURSE-- BUT...

PAUL BEARE

BORN

...I BELIEVE HE IS THE *MAN* WE'VE BEEN LOOKING FOR, DOOLEY.

IT FITS--THE *CONNECTIONS* --EVEN THE *REASONING.*

RECORDS

IF I MA* SIR--IT SE* A BIT--E* FANTAS*

LISTEN HERE, DOOLEY-- GIVEN THAT THE *FIRST* VICTIM WAS *NOT* MISS CANTLER BUT HER EMPLOYER, ATTORNEY JAMES JACKSON--

--WHO IS EMPLOYED BY MRS. THERESA BEARE, *COINCIDENTALLY,* OUR *SECOND* VICTIM--

--WHOSE HUSBAND *PAUL* PASSED ON RECENTLY-- AND WAS BURIED AT *HIGHGATE*--

--WELL, READ THIS, DOOLEY--CONCERNING THE *ODD CIRCUM-STANCES* OF HIS-- BURIAL.

IT *MAY* BE FANTASTIC AS YOU SAY--BUT I BELIEVE I KNOW NOW WHO OUR *SKELETAL* FRIEND MAY BE.

COME QUICKLY, DOOLEY-- WE MAY HAVE OUR *MYSTERY* WRAPPED AWAY IN A MATTER OF MERE *HOURS.*

AND BRING THE *"SPECIAL"* GUN, FOR THIS CASE. WE MAY *NEED* IT.

BEARE HOUSE: ONCE A PALACE OF *WONDERS* IN THE EARLY 18th CENTURY WHEN THADDEUS BEARE ENTERTAINED DUKES, PRINCES, AND EVEN MIGHTY *KINGS*...

...BUT NOW IT IS A MERE *SHADOW*-- A DECREPIT GROANING BLOT OF CREAKING WOODEN *SHUTTERS* AND SWAYING HALF-EATEN *BEAMS.*

...HAS TREATED THIS [MAN]SION *BADLY.* WHEN LAST [W]AS HERE THE ROOMS WERE [FLO]ODED WITH *MOONLIGHT*...

...AND NOW EVEN THE SHADOWS SEEMS STIFLED IN THE DARKNESS.

BUT--SOMEONE WAITS THERE--AND IF I HAVE *REASONED* CORRECTLY--

"--IT IS PAUL BEARE-- *MASTER* OF THIS [D]ECAYING HOUSE."

Do not bury him again.

YES, THOUGH TIME AND **DEATH** HAVE DECAYED HIS FEATURES--THERE CAN BE NO **DOUBT**--

--THIS MAN **IS** BEARE. AND YET, **HOW** HE CAME HERE AND FOR WHAT **REASON**-- I'VE STILL TO LEARN.

BUT THERE SHALL BE TIME FOR THAT **AFTER** I'VE BURIED HIM ONCE MORE.

S-SIR--LOOK IT'S THE THING THE **THING.**

INSPECTOR CHELM-- THERE'S SOMEONE ON THE **ROAD...**

I SEE HIM, DOOLEY. THE FOOL, HE COULD GET HIMSELF **KILLED** OUT HERE. BLASTED RAIN'S MAKIN' IT BLOODY HARD TO SEE ANYWAY.

SWERVE, MAN-- YOU'RE GOING TO HIT IT-- **SWERVE!**

BUT A FEW SHORT KILOMETERS FROM BEARE HOUSE...

ON TWO WHEELS THE CAR **TURNS**, SKIDDING HEADLONG DIRECTLY INTO THE LARGE, BONEY FORM IT **SWERVED** TO MISS...

...AND SENDING IT SPRAWLING SIDEWAYS INTO A RAIN-COVERED **RUT.**

GET ON THE **PHONE**, DOOLEY AND GET **HELP**. I'LL TRY KEEPING THIS THING HERE.

BUT NOT EVEN THE **SILVER BULLETS**, FORGED AFTER CHELM'S **LAST** INCIDENT WITH DRACULA, COULD STOP THIS NEW DEMON--

BAM BAM

...**W**HO STALKS EVER CLOSER TO THE SCOTLAND YARD INSPECTOR-- THEN

ACCHH

EPPING R CHELM, MOVES TOWARDS E HOUSE OMPLETE MISSION ERE--
--AND NO HUMAN-- NO PUNY INSPECTOR SHALL PREVENT ITS DEADLY CONCLUSION.
BUT--
WHAT--? TWICE I DESTROY YOU-- AND TWICE YOU RETURN FROM THE GRAVE--?
HOW YOU PERFORMED THAT MAGIC I NEITHER KNOW NOR CARE--
--BUT THIS TIME YOU'LL NOT ESCAPE FROM ANYWHERE, MY BONEY FOE.
DDENLY AN ARM--A LETAL FIST OF FLYING TH LASHES OUT--AND ASHES INTO DRACULA--
--SENDING HIM SPRAWLING BACKWARDS IN THE PATH OF THE DRIVING RAIN.
DRACULA'S LIPS SMILE BITTERLY, HIS EYES NARROW INTO HATEFUL, VENGEFUL SLITS--
--AND HE ATTACKS!
HIS OWN STEEL-TENDONED ARM GRABS THAT OF THE SKELETON'S, AND DRACULA YANKS--
--FRACTURING AND SHATTERING THE SKELETAL BONES!

THEN DRACULA ATTACKS FOR A **SECOND** TIME-- SMASHING THE BEAST'S **NECKBONE**-- AND SENDING THE GRINNING SKULL SPIRALLING EARTHWARD.

ONE ARM **SNAPPED** LOOSE, ITS HEAD **TORN** FROM IT, THE SKELETON, STRONGER THAN ANY MAN OR BEAST DRACULA HAS **EVER** FOUGHT BEFORE, BATTLES ON--

--HOLDING **GROUND** AND CLAW... AT THE PRIN... OF EVIL W... ITS ONE EV... POWERF... HAND.

AND AS THE **RAINS** POUND THE RELENTLESS COMBATANTS, THE **THING**-- IN ONE **ALL-POWERFUL** LUNGE, TOPPLES DRACULA INTO THE MUD-SOAKED EARTH BELOW.

NO!

BUT EVEN AS ITS HAND CLOSES TIGHT ON DRACULA'S THROAT--

--FROM WHATEVER HELL-SPAWNED HOLE YOU'RE FROM, FIEND--

--YOU'LL NOT BATTLE DRACULA--

--AND LIVE--

--NEVER! NEVER! NEVER!

CRACK

THE POWERFUL BLOWS ARE DELIVERED WITH AN ANGUISH BORNE WITH 500 YEARS OF LIVING IN HELL--

--AND THEY ARE BLOWS WHICH NOTHING CAN SURVIVE.

ITS BACKBONE CLEAVED IN HALF, THE SKELETON CRUMBLES ONCE MORE--LEAVING ONLY THE CONSTANT RAIN TO WASH AWAY ITS DYING ASHES.

AGAIN IT FALLS-- AND PERHAPS IT SHALL RISE ONCE MORE--

FOR THERE IS A MYSTERY HERE THAT BAFFLES EVEN ME.

YET NOW IS NOT THE TIME TO PONDER SUCH QUESTIONS --FOR THIS CORPSE MUST BE BURIED--

--AND QUICKLY-- BEFORE THE AUTHORITIES CAN TRACE HIM BACK TO HIGH--

DON'T BURY HIM, DRACULA-- YOU MUSTN'T.

EH--?

83

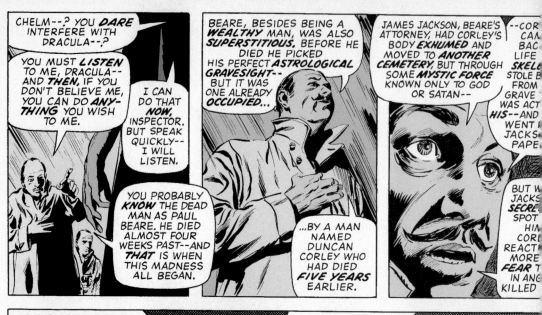

CHELM--? YOU *DARE* INTERFERE WITH DRACULA--?

YOU MUST *LISTEN* TO ME, DRACULA-- AND *THEN*, IF YOU DON'T BELIEVE ME, YOU CAN DO *ANYTHING* YOU WISH TO ME.

I CAN DO THAT *NOW*, INSPECTOR. BUT SPEAK QUICKLY-- I WILL LISTEN.

YOU PROBABLY *KNOW* THE DEAD MAN AS PAUL BEARE. HE DIED ALMOST FOUR WEEKS PAST--AND *THAT* IS WHEN THIS MADNESS ALL BEGAN.

BEARE, BESIDES BEING A *WEALTHY* MAN, WAS ALSO *SUPERSTITIOUS.* BEFORE HE DIED HE PICKED HIS PERFECT *ASTROLOGICAL GRAVESIGHT*-- BUT IT WAS ONE ALREADY *OCCUPIED*...

...BY A MAN NAMED DUNCAN CORLEY WHO HAD DIED *FIVE YEARS* EARLIER.

JAMES JACKSON, BEARE'S ATTORNEY, HAD CORLEY'S BODY *EXHUMED* AND MOVED TO *ANOTHER CEMETERY*, BUT THROUGH SOME *MYSTIC FORCE* KNOWN ONLY TO GOD OR SATAN--

--COR CAM BAC LIFE SKELL STOLE B FROM GRAVE WAS ACT *HIS*--AND WENT JACKS PAPE

BUT W JACKS *SECRE* SPOT HIM COR REACT MORE *FEAR* T IN ANG KILLED

HE THEN FOUND MRS. BEARE, AND IN TRYING TO EXPLAIN HIS *REASONS*, RIPPED HER *MARBLE NECKLESS* FROM HER--

YOU SEE-- IT WAS MADE FROM THE MARBLE OF *CORLEY'S ORIGINAL* TOMBSTONE.

BUT, OF COURSE-- HE WAS *NOT* UNDERSTOOD.

DO YOU EXPECT ME *BELIEVE* SUCH DRIVEL, INSPECTOR?

TWO YEARS AGO I REFUSED TO BELIEVE IN *VAMPIRES*, DRACULA.

I *STILL* DON'T UNDERSTAND, INSPECTOR CHELM-- *WHY* DID IT ALL HAPPEN-- *WHY?*

IT WAS ALMOST *ELEMENTARY*, DOOLEY--CORLEY WANTED HIS *OWN* GRAVE--HE SIMPLY WANTED TO BE LEFT TO DIE-- *IN PEACE.*

A *SMILE* CROSSES BOTH T LIPS OF DRACULA AND CHE ALIKE AS THE LORD OF EVI SCOOPS UP THE BROKEN BO OF THE MAN HE HAD *BATT* ONLY MINUTES BEFORE--A TAKES THEM TO BE *BURIE* THEIR RIGHTFUL *HOME.*

F OR DRACU *UNDERSTAN* THE PEACEFE NESS OF ETER REST--EVE HE CAN *NE* TOUCH IT F HIMSELF

NEXT

RAILROA TO HELL

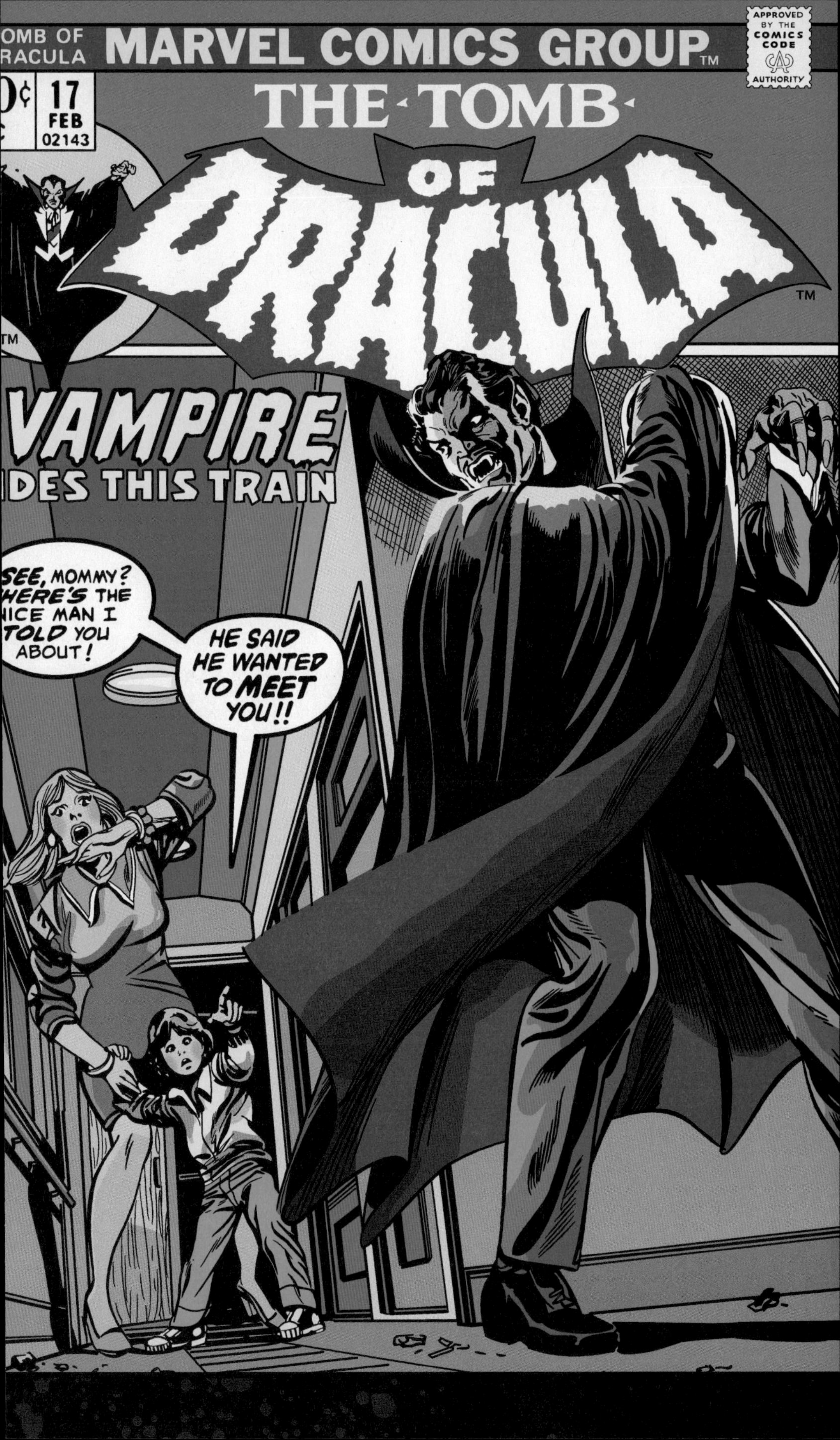
OMB OF
RACULA
MARVEL COMICS GROUP
APPROVED BY THE COMICS CODE AUTHORITY
17
FEB
02143
THE TOMB
OF
DRACULA
VAMPIRE
IDES THIS TRAIN
SEE, MOMMY? HERE'S THE NICE MAN I TOLD YOU ABOUT!
HE SAID HE WANTED TO MEET YOU!!

PARIS, FRANCE. NOVEMBER 3, 1973. 4:37 A.M.

AN EBONY NIGHTWINGED FORM GLIDES GRACEFULLY TOWARDS THE PLACE DENFERT-ROUCHEREAU, AND THEN *ARCS* ITS WAY DOWNWARDS THROUGH THE EARLY MORNING SKIES...

...AND INTO THE DARKENED TUNNELS WHICH *HONEYCOMB* THE PARISIAN *UNDERGROUND.*

FOR IN THIS *ONE-TIME* CEMETERY LURKS A GRIM SPECTER WHOSE EVERY MOCKING *LAUGH* SPELLS--

--*DEATH!*

FURTHER ON LIES MY *PRIZE*-- WAITING FOR ME TO *CLAIM IT!*

BUT--*NO!* IT CAN NOT BE-- NOT HERE--THEY MUSTN'T HAVE FOUND *THIS* COFFIN AS WELL!

DAWN APPROACHES *RAPIDLY*-- AND IF I FAIL TO FIND IT SOON-- *DRACULA WILL DIE!*

DEATH
RIDES THE RAILS

PIN THE TAIL ON THE *DONKEY*, FANG-FACE 'CAUSE THAT'S *EXACTLY* WHAT'S COMIN' OFF *TONIGHT!*

MARV WOLFMAN SCRIPT / **GENE COLAN** PENCILS / **TOM PALMER** INKS / JOHN COSTANZA, *letters* TOM PALMER, *colors* / **ROY THOMAS** EDITS

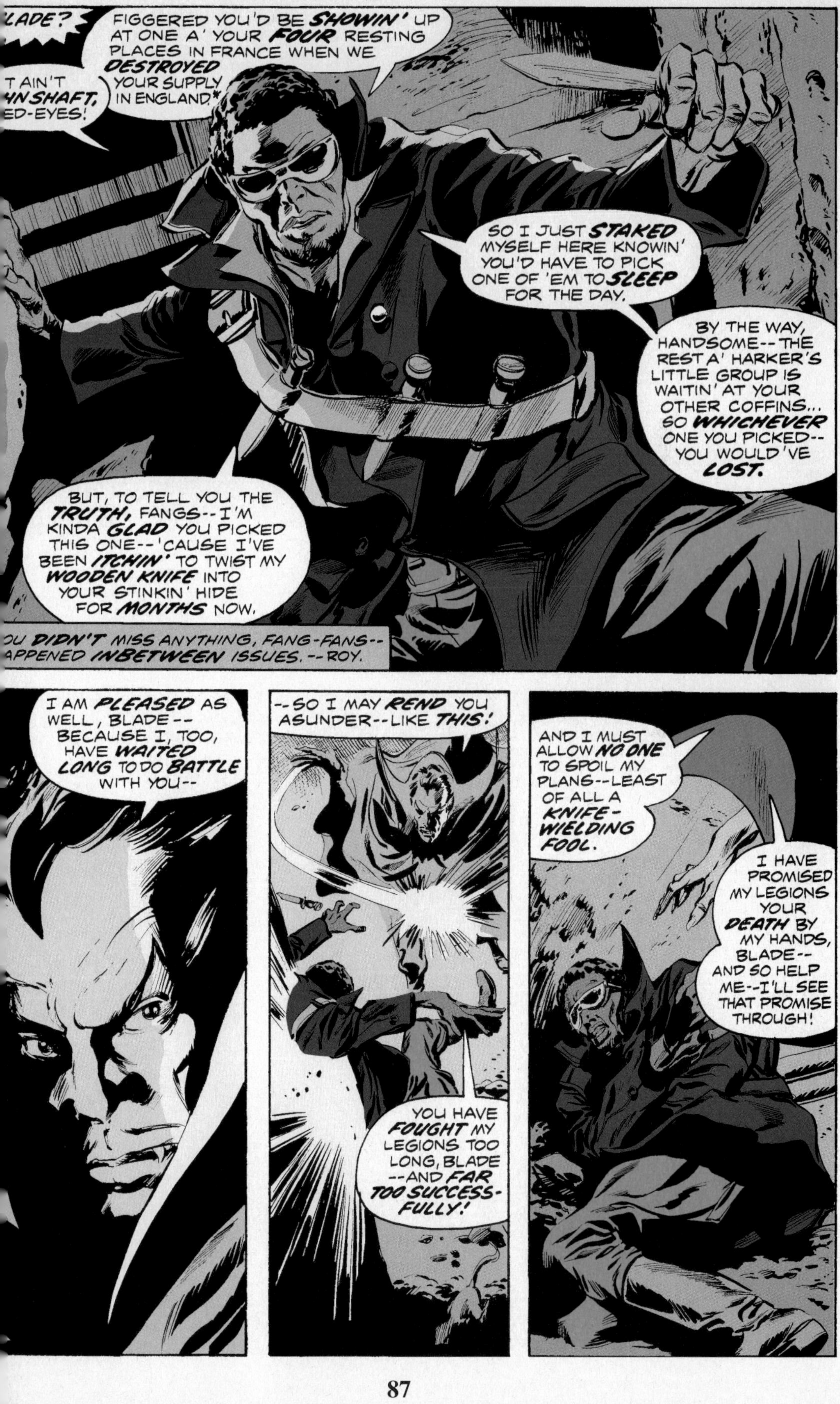
LADE?
T AIN'T NSHAFT, ED-EYES!
FIGGERED YOU'D BE SHOWIN' UP AT ONE A' YOUR FOUR RESTING PLACES IN FRANCE WHEN WE DESTROYED YOUR SUPPLY IN ENGLAND.*
SO I JUST STAKED MYSELF HERE KNOWIN' YOU'D HAVE TO PICK ONE OF 'EM TO SLEEP FOR THE DAY.
BY THE WAY, HANDSOME-- THE REST A' HARKER'S LITTLE GROUP IS WAITIN' AT YOUR OTHER COFFINS... SO WHICHEVER ONE YOU PICKED-- YOU WOULD'VE LOST.
BUT, TO TELL YOU THE TRUTH, FANGS-- I'M KINDA GLAD YOU PICKED THIS ONE-- 'CAUSE I'VE BEEN ITCHIN' TO TWIST MY WOODEN KNIFE INTO YOUR STINKIN' HIDE FOR MONTHS NOW.
OU DIDN'T MISS ANYTHING, FANG-FANS-- APPENED INBETWEEN ISSUES. --ROY.
I AM PLEASED AS WELL, BLADE-- BECAUSE I, TOO, HAVE WAITED LONG TO DO BATTLE WITH YOU--
--SO I MAY REND YOU ASUNDER--LIKE THIS!
YOU HAVE FOUGHT MY LEGIONS TOO LONG, BLADE --AND FAR TOO SUCCESS-FULLY!
AND I MUST ALLOW NO ONE TO SPOIL MY PLANS--LEAST OF ALL A KNIFE-WIELDING FOOL.
I HAVE PROMISED MY LEGIONS YOUR DEATH BY MY HANDS, BLADE-- AND SO HELP ME--I'LL SEE THAT PROMISE THROUGH!

HAH! YOU KICK--? DID YOU *TRULY* BELIEVE SUCH A *PRIMITIVE* SHOW OF FORCE COULD POSSIBLY TAKE DRACULA *UNAWARES*--?

DRACULA--WHO ONCE WAS THE *MIGHTIEST SOLDIER* IN ALL TRANSYLVANIA--

--WHO LED *ARMIES* OF THOUSANDS INTO BATTLE--WHO *TAUGHT* THEM EVERY FORM OF *WARFARE*?

HERE IS YOUR KICK, BLADE! AND LEARN YOUR LESSON WELL.

YOU MAY HAVE *DEFEATED* MY UNDEAD, BUT DRACULA SHALL *NEVER* BE VANQUISHED AGAIN!

UNGHHHHH!

YOU SOUGHT *MY* DEATH, MY RAVEN-FLESHED FOE--

NOOOOO....!

--BUT IT SHALL BE *YOUR BLOOD* WHICH STAINS THESE MUSTY GROUNDS.

FAREWELL, BLADE--YOUR BATTLE HAS ENDED... *FOREVER...*

...WHILE MINE HAS YET TO BEGIN.

IF I FIND NO **RESTING PLACE** THIS MORN, VICTORY SHALL BE YOURS,

CURSE ME FOR A **FLEDGING** VAMPIRE--! I'LL NOT DIE THIS NIGHT AFTER ALL--

OU SAID YOU ESTROYED ALL OUR OF MY OFFINS, BLADE--

--BUT THERE IS A **FIFTH**, MY FOOLISH FRIEND-- THERE IS A **FIFTH**--!

IN NEARBY **VERSAILLES**, THERE HIDES ONE THAT **ALL** YOUR SNOOPING COULD NOT HAVE FOUND.

SOUTH AND WEST, THE BAT FLIES --FASTER, EVER **FASTER** AS THE NIGHT GROWS LIGHT WITH THE COMING RAYS OF **DAWN**...

...THE **CLEANSING** RAYS OF A **SUN** WHICH WOULD **BURN** THE VERY LIFE FROM THE MAN-BAT DRACULA.

TIL, ON THE SOUTHERN TIP OF SAILLES, HE SOARS **ABOVE** DAIRY FARMLAND OF HENRI NÉ.

ERNÉ HAS ED IN THIS ERTILE LAND R MORE AN **SIXTY** EARS...

ND HE HAS N DRACULA'S TIM FOR OST THIRTY--

R ON VERNÉ'S **WEDDING NIGHT** DRACULA ADDED **ONE** E LIVING SOUL TO HIS EVER-GROWING **LEGION.**

HENRI VERNÉ-- HEED THE WORD OF YOUR **MASTER!**

HENRI--? WHAT IS **WRONG**--? YOUR **EYES**-- THEY ARE **GLOWING!**

GERTA VERNÉ SPEAKS ONCE THEN IS SILENT. SHE HAS SEEN HER DEAR *HUSBAND* IN THIS 'TRANCE' MANY TIMES BEFORE--

--AND AFTER NEARLY THIRTY YEARS, SHE KNOWS THAT SOON IT WILL *PASS.*

PREPARE MY COFFIN, HENRI VERNÉ.

TWO BARNS REST ON THE VER- FARM: ONE IS FILLED WITH *LIVESTOCK* WAITING HUNG- TO BE FED -- WHILE THE O- --THE *OTHER*-- IS CLOAKE DARKNESS-- TO BE USED ONLY ON 'SPECIAL' OCCA- SIONS...

...WHEN *SLEEP* IS REQUIRED FOR ONE NOT ALIVE--AND YET NOT TRULY *DEAD.*

VERY GOOD, HENRI-- YOU HAVE *SERVED* YOUR MASTER WELL THESE MANY YEARS--

--AND, IN TURN, I HAVE *SPARED* YOU THE EVER- LASTING *LIFE* OF A VAMPIRE.

BUT *NOW,* OLD ONE-- GUARD THIS COFFIN-- FOR I MUST *REST* THIS DAY--

--REST FOR MY COMING VOYAGE--

--TO *TRANSYLVANIA!*

GERTA VERNÉ SAYS *NOTHING* THE NEXT MORNIN(WHEN HENRI, DAZED AND UNREMEMBERING, STAG BACK TO THE WOODEN FRAME FARMHOUSE. AFTER IF HER *HUSBAND* WISHES NOT TO SPEAK OF THE PREVIOUS DAY--IS IT *HER* PLACE TO QUESTION HI

MUNICH, GERMANY. NOVEMBER 5, 1973. 1:47 A.M.

TRANSYLVANIA IS A MERE *500* MILES AWAY.

90

R DRACULA, EVERY-K ALL HT?

I DO NOT *SEE* YOU AT ALL DURING DINNER.

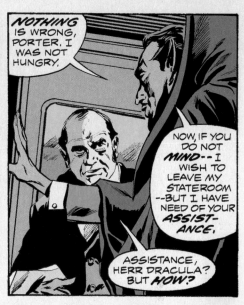

NOTHING IS WRONG, PORTER, I WAS NOT HUNGRY.

NOW, IF YOU DO NOT *MIND*-- I WISH TO LEAVE MY STATEROOM --BUT I HAVE NEED OF YOUR *ASSIST-ANCE.*

ASSISTANCE, HERR DRACULA? BUT *HOW?*

VE MUST ER THIS ROOM, TER--NEITHER NOR THE AFF WHO ANS THESE CABINS.

YOU WILL *GUARD* AGAINST SUCH ENTRY, WILL YOU *NOT,* PORTER?

...OF COURSE, HERR DRACULA..., I VILL ALLOW *NO ONE* TO ENTER...NO..., ONE...

3:35 A.M. MOST ABOARD THE SPEEDING *RAIL-ROAD* ARE ASLEEP. MOST, BUT NOT ALL.

AND BEFORE THIS *NIGHT* IS OVER, MANY MORE WILL WISH THEY WERE *TUCKED* BENEATH THE SAFETY OF THEIR CABIN BEDSHEETS...

MONSIEUR GRUBER--ARE YOU COMFOR-TABLE? EEF NOT, I WEEL GET YOU PEELOW,

ACH, I AM *SAFE,* HERR *GRANÉT,* THAT IS *ALL* VUN COULD ASK FOR VHEN YOU FLEE AS I DO FOR YOUR *LIFE.*

BUT, IF POSSIBLE --I WOULD LIKE SOMETHING TO-- *DRINK.*

DO NOT BE LONG, HERR *GRANÉT*-- ACH! I *FEAR* THE ENEMY HAS *ALREADY* BOARDED DIS RAILROAD.

YOU WEEL BE *SAFE*, MONSIEUR? I WOULD NEVAIR *LEAVE* YOU OTHERWISE!

ACH! THERE IS *NO* SUCH THING AS *SAFETY*, MEIN FREUND. BUT ASH LONG AS *YOU* ARE NEAR AND I HOLD THIS *CASE--NOTHING* VILL BEFALL ME.

ELSEWHERE ON THIS SPEEDING *RAILROAD* IN THE DINING CAR--TWO *FAMILIAR* MEN OF OUR CAST PAUSE IN THEIR TRAVELS, IF (FOR A MOMENT.

I STILL DON'T FOLLOW, RACHEL. WHY A *RAILROAD?* WE COULD'VE BEEN TO *TRANSYLVANIA* AND BACK ALREADY...!

BECAUSE, FRANK, DEAR--DRACULA WOULDN'T *DARE* TAKE A JET--IT'S TOO SMALL--TOO *OPEN!*

RAILROADS OFFER *PRIVATE COMPARTMENTS*-- AND A VERY *CONVENIENT* PLACE TO HIDE IN.

AND, SINCE *THIS* IS THE ONLY RAILROAD HEADING ANYWHERE EVEN *NEAR* TRANSYLVANIA-- MY GUESS IS HE'S ON BOARD!

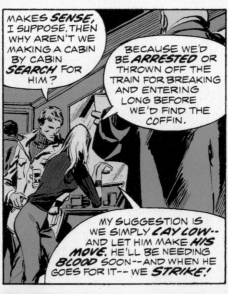

MAKES *SENSE*, I SUPPOSE, THEN WHY AREN'T WE MAKING A CABIN BY CABIN *SEARCH* FOR HIM?

BECAUSE WE'D BE *ARRESTED* OR THROWN OFF THE TRAIN FOR BREAKING AND ENTERING LONG BEFORE WE'D FIND THE COFFIN.

MY SUGGESTION IS WE SIMPLY *LAY LOW*-- AND LET HIM MAKE *HIS MOVE*. HE'LL BE NEEDING *BLOOD* SOON--AND WHEN HE GOES FOR IT-- WE *STRIKE!*

OHHHHH--PARDON, MADAMOISELLE-- I AM SORRY, PLEASE *FORGIVE* ME.

I'M F BUT YO BETTE CLEAN T *COFFE STA*

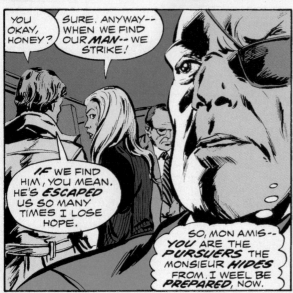

YOU *OKAY*, HONEY?

SURE. ANYWAY-- WHEN WE FIND OUR *MAN*-- WE STRIKE!

IF WE FIND HIM, YOU MEAN. HE'S *ESCAPED* US SO MANY TIMES I LOSE HOPE.

SO, MON AMIS-- *YOU* ARE THE *PURSUERS* THE MONSIEUR *HIDES* FROM. I WEEL BE *PREPARED*, NOW.

TWO CARS AWAY, HOWEVER, THE TARGET OF FRANK DRAKE AND RACHEL VAN HELSING'S SEARCH SAUNTERS CONFIDENTLY THROUGH NARROW STEEL CORRIDORS.

HIS FACE IS FIX LIKE A DEATH MASK--BUT CONTINENCE ALMOST SURPRIS

FOR THOUGH HIS THIRS FOR BLOOD IS GREAT-- T ARE OTHER THOUGHTS DESIRES WHICH TAKE PROMINENCE THIS NIGH

2 A.M. IN SIX HOURS 'CULA SHALL ONCE 'IN BE ON THE LAND OF **BIRTHPLACE** MORE 'N FIVE HUNDRED YEARS 'ORE...AND HE YEARNS 'HIS RETURN...

*BUT IF HIS MIND IS **LOST** ON PAST REMEMBRANCES, ITS **CALM** IS SUDDENLY SHATTERED--*

--BY THE ON RUSHING FIGURE OF A **YOUTH**-- -- A YOUTH NAMED **JACK RUSSELL.** *

* WHOM WE'LL BE SEEING **MORE** OF NEXT ISSUE, WEREWOLF FANS.--ROY.

WHILE... I HAVE FOUND YOUR HUNTER, MONSIEUR GRUBER--A YOUNG MAN AND A WOMAN-- WITH A **SCARRED**, YET STILL-VERY **LOVELY** FACE.

NO--! YOU ARE **MISTAKEN,** HERR GRANÉT-- I HAVE SEEN THE **ENEMY** WITH MY OWN EYES--

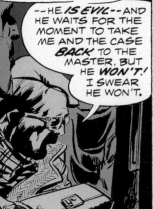

'K--THERE HE IS NOW-- 'UTTING LIKE A SELF-'HTEOUS **CAT,** I SAW HIS 'S, MEIN FREUND-- AND 'RE CAN BE **NO DOUBT**--

--HE **IS EVIL**--AND HE WAITS FOR THE MOMENT TO TAKE ME AND THE CASE **BACK** TO THE MASTER, BUT HE **WON'T!** I SWEAR HE WON'T.

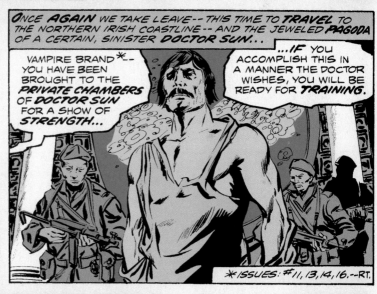

*ONCE **AGAIN** WE TAKE LEAVE -- THIS TIME TO **TRAVEL** TO THE NORTHERN IRISH COASTLINE -- AND THE JEWELED **PAGODA** OF A CERTAIN, SINISTER **DOCTOR SUN**...*

VAMPIRE BRAND *-- YOU HAVE BEEN BROUGHT TO THE **PRIVATE CHAMBERS** OF **DOCTOR SUN** FOR A SHOW OF **STRENGTH**...

...IF YOU ACCOMPLISH THIS IN A MANNER THE DOCTOR WISHES, YOU WILL BE READY FOR **TRAINING.**

*ISSUES: #11, 13, 14, 16.--RT.

'HOULD YOU **FAIL,** 'U WILL BE PUT TO **INSTANTANEOUS** 'D FINAL **DEATH**-- 'D LAID TO REST 'TH THE PREVIOUS 'WELVE VAMPIRE EXPERIMENTS,

NOW, BRAND-- TURN ON YOUR GUARDS, AND--**DESTROY THEM!**

DOCTOR SUN COMMANDS IT!

THE GUARDS DO NOT **PANIC**-- THEY HAVE **TRAINED** TWO YEARS FOR THIS MISSION--

--AND BEFORE THIS **NEW** VAMPIRE CAME--THEY HAD **MURDERED** THE TWELVE BEFORE HIM--

--AND BRAND, THEY THOUGHT --WOULD BE **NO DIFFERENT.**

THEY FIRE THEIR LEADEN BULLETS AT BRAND--THEY **KNOW** BULLETS CAN NOT HURT THE VAMPIRE--BUT THEY MERELY **TEST** IT FOR ITS QUOTIENT OF **FEAR.**

BRAND, HUNCHED OVER TO **KILL**-- TRAMPLES CLOSER TO THEM.

NOW, **THIS** IS THE MOMENT OTHERS DIED -- THIS IS THE MOMENT THEY EXPECTED BRAND TO TURN AND FLEE-- ONLY TO BE **KILLED** BY THE **OTHER** GUARDS WAITING HIDING WITH **STAKES** AND **CROSSES**

BUT BRAND IS **NOT** LIKE THE OTHERS. HE MOVES **UNFLINCHING**--AND THE HE **STRIKES!**

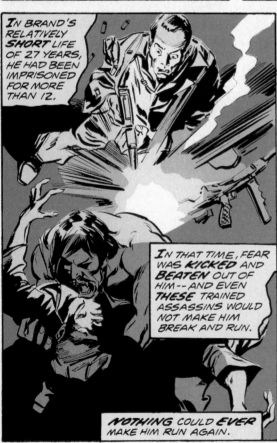

IN BRAND'S RELATIVELY **SHORT** LIFE OF 27 YEARS, HE HAD BEEN IMPRISONED FOR MORE THAN 12.

IN THAT TIME, FEAR WAS **KICKED** AND **BEATEN** OUT OF HIM -- AND EVEN **THESE** TRAINED ASSASSINS WOULD NOT MAKE HIM BREAK AND RUN.

NOTHING COULD **EVER** MAKE HIM RUN AGAIN.

HIS FANGS SPLIT THE FIRST GUARD'S **NECK** AND FRESH BLOOD DRAINS THROUGH BRAND THROAT. THIS IS A **NEW** SENSATION--AND BRAND IS **PLEASED** WITH IT.

ENOUGH, VAMPIRE BRAND, BEFORE THE GUARD DIES-- **CEASE!**

YOU HAVE **PROVEN** YOUR IN THE EYES **DOCTOR S**

RAZ, AUSTRIA.
3:45 A.M.

AUSTRIA'S SECOND LARGEST CITY IS BUT A *BLUR* TO THE FEW STILL AWAKE ABOARD THE SPEEDING RAIL--

--FOR *THEIR* MINDS ARE ON THEIR UPCOMING TOURS, OR MEETINGS, OR FAMILY REUNIONS--

SO, YOU TWO HAVE *FOLLOWED* ME FROM *ENGLAND*-- UNDOUBTEDLY TO SLAY ME, YOU BELIEVE--

--BUT, YOU'LL *NOT* GET THAT CHANCE, MY FRIENDS--

--FOR DRACULA *THIRSTS*-- AND IT SHALL BE YOU WHO ARE *HIS* VICTIMS --

AND IT SHALL BE *YOU* WHO DIES AS DID THAT FOOL, BLADE.

PUT UP YOUR *HANDS*, MISTER, AN' NO FUNNY STUFF.

WHAT..?

RICKY! OH, GOD-- I WAS WORRIED *SICK*. WHERE WERE YOU? YOU WERE *SUPPOSED* TO BE IN BED.

I WASN'T TIRED, MOM-- SO I CAME OUT AN' SHOT THIS *FUNNY-LOOKING* MAN. DIDYA SEES HIS *EARS*? HE LOOKS LIKE *MR. SPOCK!*

RICKY! APOLOGIZE TO THE MAN --THAT *ISN'T NICE* TO SAY.

OH LORD, I'M *SORRY*, MISTER, BUT EVER SINCE JACK DIED, IT'S BEEN *IM-POSSIBLE* TO CONTROL RICKY BY MYSELF.

YES, CHILD-REN *CAN* BE A NUISANCE AT TIMES.

YOU HAVE... CHILDREN?

A LONG TIME AGO--A *BOY* AND A *GIRL*. BUT ENOUGH OF THEM.

LET ME *ESCORT* YOU BACK TO YOUR ROOM,

OHHH-- OF COURSE, MR... MISTER--?

DRACULA!

DRACULA?!

EEEEEEEEEEEE...

THAT SCREAM--?

GOOD LORD-- DRACULA'S STRUCK! C'MON.

CLOSE THE D[OOR] MON AMIS--QU[ICK] WHATEVER HAP[PENS] OUT THERE-- Y[OU] MUST NOT [BE] HARMED.

KEEP THE DOOR LOCKED WHILE I INVESTIGATE.

WHAT HAPPENED, KID? IS THIS YOUR MOTHER?

IT WAS THE MAN WITH THE POINTED EARS-- HE DID SOME- THING TO MY MOTHER.

PLEASE HELP HER, MISTER-- SHE'S NOT MOVING.

SHE'S NOT DEAD-- HIS FANGS JUST DREW A LITTLE BLOOD-- NOT ENOUGH TO CHANGE HER.

BUT WE'RE NOW SURE OF ONE THING-- DRACULA'S HERE-- AND WE'VE GOT TO FIND HIM BEFORE HE STRIKES AGAIN!

YOU STAY WITH HER UNTIL WE GET A DOCTOR-- I'LL TAKE A LOOKSEE FOR OUR TOOTHSOME PLAYMATE.

TAKE C[ARE] HON[EY] PLEA[SE]

BUT DRACULA IS ALREADY GONE-- SPREAD THROUGH THE RAILROAD AS A GOSSAMER-THIN WISP OF SMOKY MIST--

--SLITHERING PAST THE METAL CORRIDORS, UNTIL HE ARRIVES AT ONE CERTAIN STATEROOM...

I'M A FOOL TO HAVE LET HER SCREAM-- AND A DOUBLY- DAMNED FOOL TO HAVE ATTACKED HER--

NOW VAN HELSING AND THAT HAPLESS DESCENDANT OF MINE SHALL KNOW I AM HERE...

...BUT NOW I AM ALSO PREPARED-- AND SHOULD THERE BE A BATTLE, THERE SHALL ALSO BE A VICTOR--

--DRA[CULA] --DRA[CULA] DRA[CULA]

YOU WERE *CORRECT*, MONSIEUR-- THE *PORTER* SAYS THE TALL CLOAKED MAN ATTACKED THE WOMAN,

HE IS ALSO *UNDOUBTEDLY* THE MAN WHO CHASES YOU. BUT *WHY* WOULD HE MAKE SUCH A FOOLISH MOVE?

WHO KNOWS, HERR GRANET? PERHAPS AN *ERROR!* BUT WE'D *BEST* TAKE NO CHANCES NOW.

KILL HIM-- AND THE OTHER TWO YOU *SUSPECT! KILL THEM ALL!*

THE DOOR IS LOCKED ONCE GRANET LEAVES, AND THE SMALL METAL BOX IS ONCE AGAIN GRASPED *TIGHTLY* BY THE TINY TREMBLING GERMAN.

...ING GRUBER HAS LIVED WITH *FEAR* ...ING AWAY HIS SOUL FOR MANY YEARS-- ... WHAT IS *INSIDE* THIS PRECIOUS ...E WILL *FREE* HIM FROM FEAR FOR-- ...R--IF HE IS *LUCKY...*

...OR FREE HIM FROM HIS *LIFE* IF HE IS NOT.

...E...

KNOCK!

PARDON ME, MONSIEUR. I MUST *TALK* WEETH YOU.

HAVE THEY TRACED ME TO THIS *STATEROOM* SO QUICKLY?...

NO! THERE IS ONLY *ONE* MAN OUTSIDE-- PERHAPS A *PORTER?*

IT IS *LATE*-- WHO WISHES TO SPEAK WITH ME AT THIS HOUR?

...EE NIGHT PORTER, ...ONSIEUR. IT IS ...RGENT I TALK TO YOU--

...R VERY ...CETY ... DEPEND ...EET.

VERY WELL THEN, PORTER-- *COME IN.*

MERCI--YOU WERE *SMART* TO OPEN ZEE DOOR, MONSIEUR--

I WOULD NOT HAVE LIKED TO *SHOOT* YOUR LOCK OFF--

--BEFORE I KEELED YOU, THAT IS.

97

DURING WORLD WAR TWO, JACQUE GRANÉT FOUGHT ALONGSIDE THE *UNDERGROUND.*

HE LEARNED, OVER THOSE YEARS, TO *KILL*-- AND TO KILL CALMLY-- COOLY.

AND EVEN NOW AS HE *PRESSE* THE TRIGGER THIS COLD NOVEMBER NIGHT, HIS FACE SHOWS *NO EMOTION.*

IT IS ONLY AFTER THE *FOURTH* BULLET SLA THROUGH A STILL-STANDING DRACULA DOES HIS COLD FACE *CRACK*--

--AND *THIRTY YEARS* OF TRAINING *ABANDONS* HIM.

BAM

SO, HARKER HAS YET *ANOTHER* AGENT ABOARD THIS RAILROAD-- AND ONE I KNEW NOTHING OF--

VERY WELL THEN, MY FRENCH FOOL-- YOU'LL BE *TREATED* TO THE SAME AGONIZING *DEATH* ALL HIS OTHER LEGIONS WILL SUFFER.

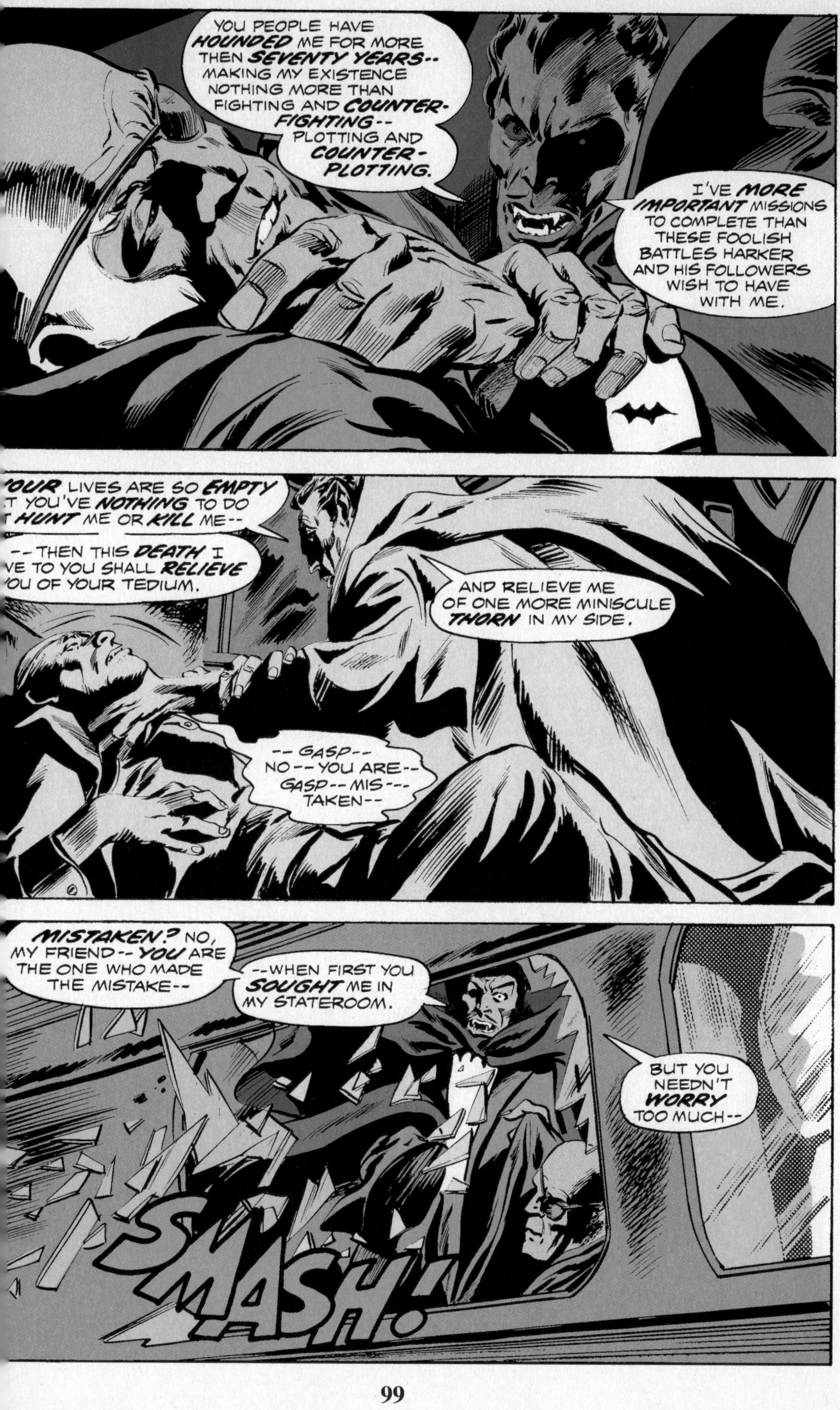
YOU PEOPLE HAVE HOUNDED ME FOR MORE THEN SEVENTY YEARS-- MAKING MY EXISTENCE NOTHING MORE THAN FIGHTING AND COUNTER-FIGHTING-- PLOTTING AND COUNTER-PLOTTING.
I'VE MORE IMPORTANT MISSIONS TO COMPLETE THAN THESE FOOLISH BATTLES HARKER AND HIS FOLLOWERS WISH TO HAVE WITH ME.
YOUR LIVES ARE SO EMPTY YOU'VE NOTHING TO DO HUNT ME OR KILL ME--
--THEN THIS DEATH I TO YOU SHALL RELIEVE OF YOUR TEDIUM.
AND RELIEVE ME OF ONE MORE MINISCULE THORN IN MY SIDE.
--GASP-- NO--YOU ARE-- GASP--MIS--- TAKEN--
MISTAKEN? NO, MY FRIEND--YOU ARE THE ONE WHO MADE THE MISTAKE--
--WHEN FIRST YOU SOUGHT ME IN MY STATEROOM.
BUT YOU NEEDN'T WORRY TOO MUCH--
SMASH!

--FOR IT'S THE LAST MISTAKE YOU'LL EVER MAKE AGAIN! HA! HA! HA! HA!

JACQUE GRANÉT IS *THROWN* FROM THE SPEEDING TRAIN, AND EVEN BEFORE HIS FLESH AND BONE ARE *RIPPED* TO A THOUSAND PULSING *SHREDS* ACROSS THE JAGGED METAL TRACKS-- HE IS *DEAD*.

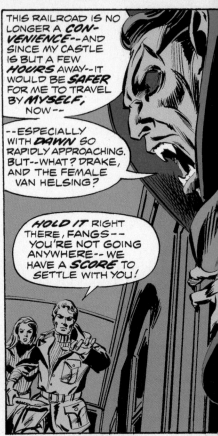

THIS RAILROAD IS NO LONGER A *CON-VENIENCE*--AND SINCE MY CASTLE IS BUT A FEW *HOURS* AWAY--IT WOULD BE *SAFER* FOR ME TO TRAVEL BY *MYSELF*, NOW--

--ESPECIALLY WITH *DAWN* SO RAPIDLY APPROACHING. BUT--WHAT? DRAKE, AND THE FEMALE VAN HELSING?

HOLD IT RIGHT THERE, FANGS-- YOU'RE NOT GOING ANYWHERE-- WE HAVE A *SCORE* TO SETTLE WITH YOU!

YOU KNOW OF YOUR OTHER AGENT'S *DEATH* ALREADY? VERY WELL, THEN-- YOU MAY NOW *JOIN HIM*-- --SPLASHED ACROSS THE RAILS LIKE THE USELESS *CORPSE* HE IS!

FRANK-- WATCH FOR HIS *CLAWS*--

I DON'T KNOW WHO YOU'RE *TALKIN'* ABOUT, BATS--BUT WE *OWE* YOU FOR EDITH'S DEATH--*

--AND FOR WHAT YOU DID TO RACHEL'S *FACE*--*

*ISSUE #12, --RT.

AND SO HE ME--YOU GOING T PAY

100

BAT TURNS TO AVOID **SLASHING STAKE...**

...**D THOUGH IT TURNS** ...**ME** -- STILL THE ...**DEN SPEAR PENE-** ...**TES** A VITAL WING...

--AND BAT AGAIN BECOMES A HELL-MADDENED **MAN.**

YOU'VE SIGNED YOUR **CERTIFICATE OF DEATH** WITH THAT THRUST, MY FOOLISH **DESCENDANT--**

UP UNTIL THIS MOMENT I HAVE **AVOIDED** SLAYING YOU-- PERHAPS IN SOME FOOLISH ANCESTRAL **HOPE** THAT YOU WOULD SOMEDAY WANT TO **CLAIM** YOUR TRUE NAME--

--BUT NOW **NOTHING** SHALL STOP ME ENDING YOUR PITIFUL LIFE BEFORE ANOTHER MOMENT HAS FLED,

I'M WAITING FOR YOU TO **TRY,** DRAC--I'VE BEEN WAITING FROM THE MOMENT RACHEL SAVED ME FROM **KILLING MYSELF** BECAUSE OF YOU.✱

✱ ISSUE # 3. --NOSTALGIC ROY.

...**T A SHAME** ...**WAITED** ...**AIN,** ...**NK E--**

SMAKK!

--BECAUSE YOU'RE GOING TO DIE ANYWAY.

EVEN YOUR **FATHER** WAS MORE OF A MAN THAN **YOU** TURNED OUT TO BE, DRAKE--

--AT LEAST HE WAS A **SOLDIER**-- A MAN WHO KNEW WHAT **FIGHTING** WAS ALL ABOUT--

--BUT ALL YOU KNOW IS HOW TO **COWER,** AND **CRINGE**--AND ULTIMATELY--

--**TO DIE!**

BUT IT IS **NOT** A DEATH THAT SHALL BE **EASILY** COME BY--

--FOR EVEN AS DRACULA CLOSES IN ON HIS SANDY HAIRED **DESCENDANT**, RACHEL VAN HELSING COMES **BETWEEN** THEM.

DRACULA PAUSES FOR A MOMENT, FOR HE HAS **LEARNED** SHE IS NO MERE **SNIP OF A GIRL**--

--RATHER, BEHIND HER **FRAIL FACADE**-- THERE LURKS AN EXPERIENCED **FIGHTER.**

AND SO, EVEN AS THE **GRANDDAUGHTER** OF DRACULA'S ONE TIME FOE, ABRAHAM VAN HELSING, LATCHES ONTO LORD OF VAMPIRES' **WOUNDED ARM**--

DRACULA **CHANGES** AGAIN INTO THE BAT--

--AND, WITH ONE MIGHTY **SHOVE,** THROWS THE GIRL SPRAWLING SIDEWAYS.

DRACULA KNOWS THAT **VICTORY** MIGHT BE HIS-- BUT IT WILL BE A VICTORY THAT WOULD BE **COSTLY** INDEED--

AND SO, FLEES AS A **DARKLING SILLHOUETTE** THROUGH THE CORRIDORS OF THIS SPEEDING **EXPRESS...**

...ONLY TO REGAIN HUMAN FORM WHEN **SAFETY** CAN AGAIN BE HIS--

--AND ESCAPE EASILY WITHIN HIS GRASP.

WE'LL MEET **AGAIN** SOON, MY FRIENDS-- WITHIN THE WALLS OF CASTLE DRACULA

--WHERE THEY SHALL BECOME YOUR **EVERLASTING TOMB!**

WHILE, ON THE **OTHER S** OF THE CORRIDOR...

ACH! HERR GRANET HAS **NOT RETURNED**-- AND I FEAR HE **NEVER** SHALL.

M
ENEMIES
MUST
CLOSE
IN ON H
KILLED
SO THA
VOULD
EASY P

BUT
SH
NE
GET
OR T
CASE
SEE
NEF

102

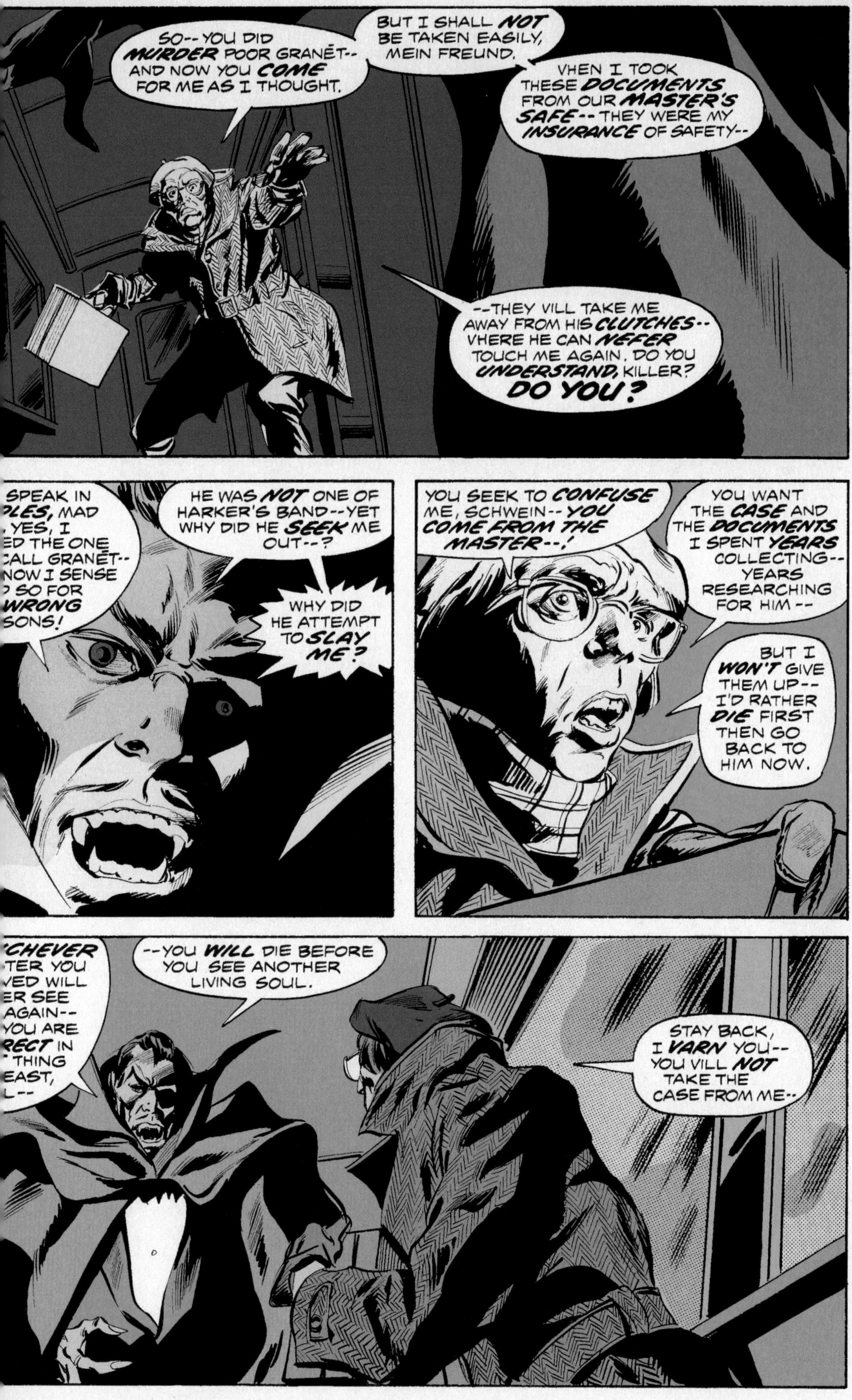
SO-- YOU DID MURDER POOR GRANÉT-- AND NOW YOU COME FOR ME AS I THOUGHT.
BUT I SHALL NOT BE TAKEN EASILY, MEIN FREUND.
VHEN I TOOK THESE DOCUMENTS FROM OUR MASTER'S SAFE-- THEY WERE MY INSURANCE OF SAFETY--
--THEY VILL TAKE ME AWAY FROM HIS CLUTCHES-- VHERE HE CAN NEFER TOUCH ME AGAIN. DO YOU UNDERSTAND, KILLER? DO YOU?
SPEAK IN PLES, MAD YES, I ED THE ONE CALL GRANÉT-- NOW I SENSE SO FOR WRONG SONS!
HE WAS NOT ONE OF HARKER'S BAND--YET WHY DID HE SEEK ME OUT--?
WHY DID HE ATTEMPT TO SLAY ME?
YOU SEEK TO CONFUSE ME, SCHWEIN-- YOU COME FROM THE MASTER--!
YOU WANT THE CASE AND THE DOCUMENTS I SPENT YEARS COLLECTING-- YEARS RESEARCHING FOR HIM --
BUT I WON'T GIVE THEM UP-- I'D RATHER DIE FIRST THEN GO BACK TO HIM NOW.
CHEVER TER YOU VED WILL ER SEE AGAIN-- YOU ARE RECT IN THING EAST, L--
--YOU WILL DIE BEFORE YOU SEE ANOTHER LIVING SOUL.
STAY BACK, I VARN YOU-- YOU VILL NOT TAKE THE CASE FROM ME--

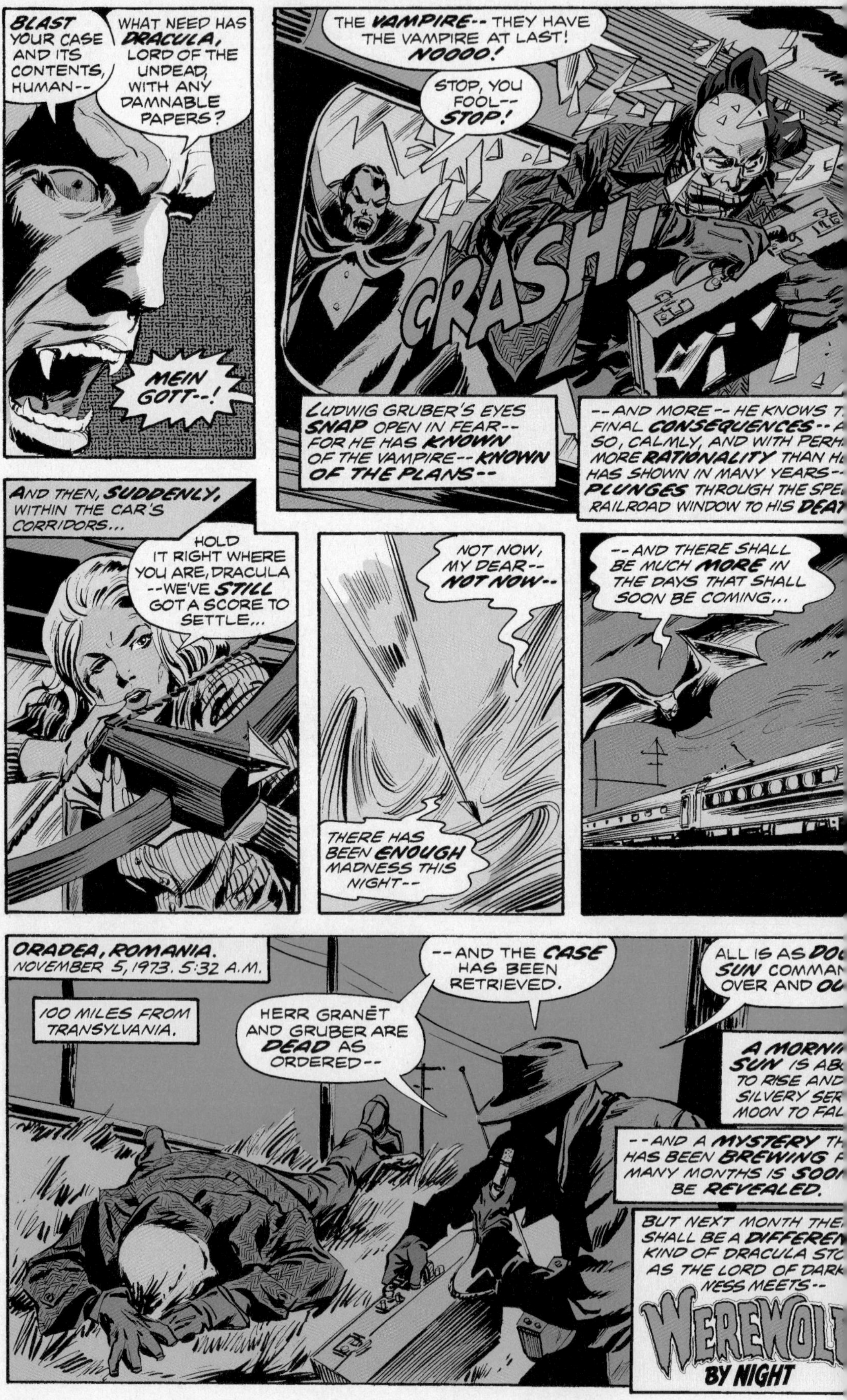
BLAST YOUR CASE AND ITS CONTENTS, HUMAN--
WHAT NEED HAS DRACULA, LORD OF THE UNDEAD, WITH ANY DAMNABLE PAPERS?
MEIN GOTT--!
THE VAMPIRE-- THEY HAVE THE VAMPIRE AT LAST! NOOOO!
STOP, YOU FOOL-- STOP!
CRASH!
LUDWIG GRUBER'S EYES SNAP OPEN IN FEAR-- FOR HE HAS KNOWN OF THE VAMPIRE-- KNOWN OF THE PLANS--
AND THEN, SUDDENLY, WITHIN THE CAR'S CORRIDORS...
HOLD IT RIGHT WHERE YOU ARE, DRACULA --WE'VE STILL GOT A SCORE TO SETTLE...
NOT NOW, MY DEAR-- NOT NOW--
THERE HAS BEEN ENOUGH MADNESS THIS NIGHT--
--AND THERE SHALL BE MUCH MORE IN THE DAYS THAT SHALL SOON BE COMING...
ORADEA, ROMANIA. NOVEMBER 5, 1973. 5:32 A.M.
100 MILES FROM TRANSYLVANIA.
HERR GRANËT AND GRUBER ARE DEAD AS ORDERED--
--AND THE CASE HAS BEEN RETRIEVED.
BY NIGHT

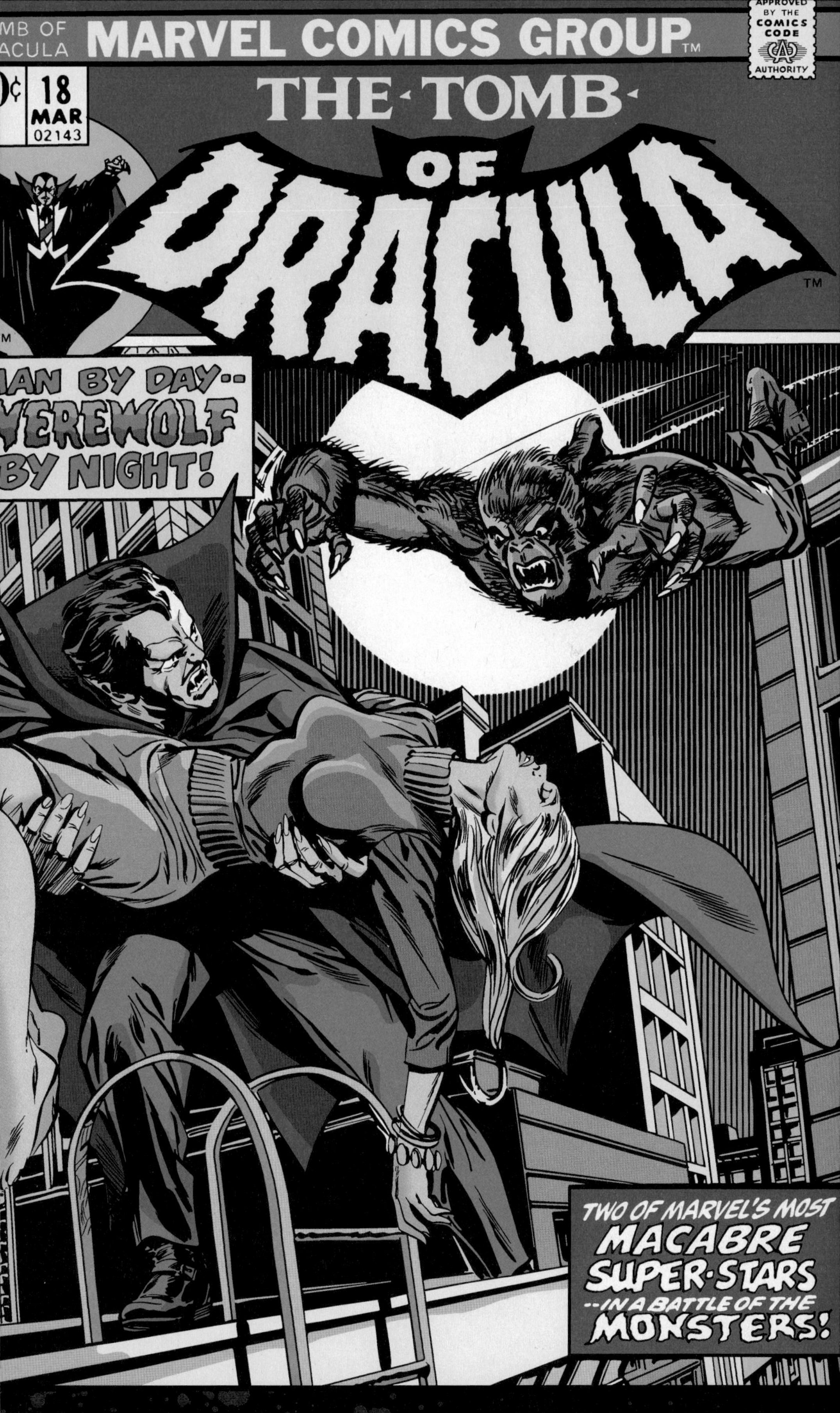
MB OF
ACULA
MARVEL COMICS GROUP™
APPROVED BY THE COMICS CODE AUTHORITY
18
MAR
02143
THE TOMB
OF
DRACULA™
IAN BY DAY--
VEREWOLF
BY NIGHT!
TWO OF MARVEL'S MOST
MACABRE
SUPER-STARS
--IN A BATTLE OF THE
MONSTERS!

STAN LEE PRESENTS: **TOMB OF DRACULA**

MARV WOLFMAN / WRITER | **GENE COLAN** / ARTIST | **TOM PALMER** / INKER | JOHN COSTANZA, letterer / L. LESSMANN, colorist | **ROY THOM** EDITOR

BECAUSE YOU DEMANDED IT:

ENTER: WEREWOLF BY NIGHT

NSYLVANIA: A TWO-DAY
RNEY IS ABOUT TO **END**
E IN THIS ANCIENT VILLAGE
EN DEEP WITHIN THE
MANIAN WASTELANDS--

FOR **JACK RUSSELL** AND
YSTERIOUS GIRL NAMED TOPAZ,
URNEY HAS YET TO **BEGIN.**

FOR THIS BLEAK
VILLAGE IS WHERE
AN **INFANT** JACOB
RUSSOFF WAS
BORN, AND AN
AMERICANIZED
JACK RUSSELL
CAME TO LIFE.

≷YAWWWNNN≷ MAN! COULDN'T
SLEEP A WINK LAST NIGHT,
TOPAZ -- SPENT THE WHOLE
NIGHT COUNTING SHEEP--

--UNTIL **THEY**
DOZED OFF ON ME.
HOW'D **YOU** DO?

I SLEPT,
JACK -- BUT MY
DREAMS WERE
PLAGUED WITH
THE THOUGHTS
OF **TABOO!** *

* WEREWOLF BY NIGHT #14.--DATA REEPER ROY.

T I CAN
HE WAS
GH TO
NIGHT-
RES TO
RIS
OFF!

FUNNY--I HAD
DREAMS, TOO
--ABOUT **MY**
FATHER--
RATHER, A
FATHER I **NEVER**
REALLY HAD!

HOW MUCH DO
YOU **KNOW**
ABOUT HIM,
JACK?

PRACTICALLY **ZILCH!** I
REMEMBER HIM AS KIND,
GENTLE, AND THAT MY
MOTHER **LOVED**
HIM...

...AND THAT HE
WAS ALSO PLAGUED
WITH THE **CURSE
OF THE
WEREWOLF!**

BLASTED
CURSE! I KEEP
THINKING OF
HOW HE BECAME
THE WEREWOLF, AND--

...AND HOW
YOU CAN
CURE
YOURSELF,
JACK?

I KNOW
THAT'S
THE REASON
YOU WERE
SO DESPER-
ATE TO **COME**
HERE.

PLEASE BELIEVE
ME -- IF THERE IS
ANY WAY I CAN
HELP YOU, I WILL. YOU
MUST BELIEVE THAT.

A MOMENT'S **TENDERNESS**
BEFORE DAYS OF **HORROR...**

...A TENDERNESS
BETWEEN TWO YOUTHS
WHO HAVE TRAVELLED A
LONG, CRUEL DISTANCE...

...AND WHO HAVE,
IN ITS WAKE,
FOUND **COVE!**

AND IT'S A JOURNEY **COMPLETED** AS RAILS SCREECH INTO AN OLD, ALMOST ABANDONED STATION, WHERE **FOUR PASSENGERS** WHO TAKE LITTLE HEED OF EACH OTHER, GO THEIR **SEPARATE** WAYS.

THEY ARE FOUR **STRANGERS** TO THESE FOREIGN SHORES OF TRANSYLVANIA, AND THEIR FOUR LIVES SHALL **SOON** BE DRASTICALLY CHANGED...

...FOR NOW THEY ARE ALL CAUGHT IN A WEB SPUN IN THE VERY DEPT. OF **HELL** ITSELF...

...BY **DRACULA**--LORD OF **DARKNESS, PRINCE OF EVIL**--

--AND NEITHER THE TWO YOUTHS, NOR THE VETERAN **VAMPIRE HUNTERS** CALLED **DRAKE** AND **VAN HELSING** SHALL LEAVE THIS TANGLED WEB UNSCATHED!

HOME! AT LAST, AFTER THREE LONG YEARS-- **I HAVE RETURNED!**

IN **ENGLAND** AND THE WORLD OVER I AM **HUNTED, ATTACKED, HOUNDED!**

BUT HERE IN THIS LAND THAT **SPAWNED** ME-- ALL **COWER** BEFORE THE SOUND OF MY VOICE--

ALL **BOW** BEFORE MY LORDLY PRESENCE.

FOR **DRACULA** IS LORD AND MASTER OF **ALL TRANSYLVANIA.!!**

ALWAYS I HAVE BEEN ITS LORD-- AS ITS COUNT AND PRINCE WHEN I **DEFEATED** THE TURKISH HORDES.

AND THE **AGAIN** AFTER BECAME THE FEA SOME VAMPIRE AN RECLAIMED CASTLE AS MI

*DRACULA LIVES #4.

...THERE ARE
MORIES
E--OF PAST
ORIES--
EVEN OF
EATS!

DEFEAT --ITS VERY
SOUND TASTES
BITTER ON MY
TONGUE--

--FOR IT WAS
THROUGH *DEFEAT*
THAT MY BELOVED
MARIA DIED.*

* DRAC LIVES #2. RT.

DIED? *NO!*
SHE WAS
MURDERED.

THE *ONLY* WOMAN
I HAVE EVER TRULY
LOVED MURDERED BY
THOSE *SELF-RIGHTEOUS*
SCUM WHO DARE CALL
THEMSELVES *HUMAN!*

WHILE, IN THE *CATACOMBS*
BENEATH PARIS...

BLADE!

AND IN THE
NAME OF GOD
IN HEAVEN--

--DRACULA'S
KILLED
HIM!!

ST MY WIFE--
DAUGHTER--
NOW *THIS!*

FORGIVE
ME, BLADE
--BUT THERE
IS *NO OTHER
WAY* TO SET
YOUR SOUL AT
REST...

...ONLY *THIS*--
THIS *STAKE* MAY GIVE
YOU THE *PEACE* YOU
WISH FOR.

*THERE IS A
MOMENT OF
SILENCE AS
THE STAKE
PLUNGES
DOWN--*

--BUT WE SHALL *NOT* SEE
ITS IMPACT-- *THAT
IS FOR THE *NEXT ISSUE*--*

HILE *NOW,* WE AGAIN
NGE OUR SCENE--BACK
AN ILL-LIT *COUNTRY
AD* IN THE CENTRAL
ARE OF TRANSYLVANIA...

EXCUSE US-- BUT WE'RE
INTERESTED IN *TWO
ROOMS* FOR THE
NIGHT.

SIR--?

YES, YES-- AH,
THE IMPATIENCE
OF YOUTH.

COME IN--
THERE ARE
MANY ROOMS
HERE TO CHOOSE
FROM-- WE
RARELY HAVE
VISITORS--

--VERY
RARELY!

'OW MANY D'YA **NEED**, OTTO-- WHEN THEY'RE AS LOVELY AS **THIS** BIRD, EH?

CUM TA SCRATCHER, BIRDEE.

YES, YOU **ARE** A LOVELY ONE, BIRDEE-- JUS' THE KIND SCRATCHER **LOVES** TO LOVE.

LET'S GET A MOVE ON TA **MY** BOAT, BIRDEE.

TOPAZ--

NO, JACK-- I CAN **HANDLE** HIM MYSELF.

NO NEED TO, LITTLE LADY--

I DON'T **MIND** SOILING MY KNUCKLES ON A CREEP LIKE HIM...

...LONG AS I DON'T HAVE TO GET A **TETANUS SHOT**, THAT IS.

Y'LANDED A GOOD ONE, PUNK-- **TOO GOOD!**

BUT SCRATCHER DO LIKE TO GIT 'IMSELF HIT--

--NOT WITHOUT GETTIN' A BIT OF **REVENGE**, UNDERSTAND, PUNK?

C'MON, TOPAZ-- THE **AIR** AROUND HERE'S STARTING TO STINK--

--OF CHEAP BOOZE AND EVEN CHEAPER **CREEPS!**

HERE'S YOUR **HOVEL** FOR BETTER OR WORSE, HONEY--AND YOU BETTER **LOCK** IT TIGHT--

--BECAUSE THIS IS THE **NIGHT OF THE FULL MOON.**

THERE IS NO REASON TO **WORRY**, JACK-- I CONTROLLED THE BEAST **BEFORE** *-- AND I CAN DO IT AGAIN IF I MUST.

BUT YOU MUST TRUST ME **YOU MUST!**

*WEREWOLF #13--

110

...GHT, AND TRANSYLVANIA
...QUIET, ALMOST
...UNDLESS...

...EXCEPT
...R THE SOFT
...YTHMIC
...TING OF
...THERY
...GS...

...NGS WHICH **SOAR**
...OUGH THE NIGHT IN
...RCH OF...**BLOOD.**

BUT...

STINKIN' TWERP--
BUT HIS BIRD'LL BE
MINE TONIGHT...

...AN' NO RUDDY
PUNK'S GONNA
STOP ME.

'LESS HE'S
TIRED
A' BREATHIN'!

...U'VE HAD **TOO MUCH** TO DRINK,
...PATCHER MARTIN-- BUT **THAT**
...ESN'T STOP YOU FROM WOBBLING
...THE
...KING
...DDEN
...RCASE...

...OR ENTERING
THROUGH AN
EASILY
UNLOCKED
DOORWAY...

...AND THEN LETS YOU
SCREAM AS YOUR VERY
LIFE FADE FROM YOUR
EYES.

...AND
...CING
...OUR
...ATH.

...N THE PAST
...U'VE SEEN
...NK ELEPHANTS,
...ANCING FROGS,
...ND EVEN
...LOBBERING
...EA WORMS
...HILE **INTOX-**
...CATED--

--BUT THE SIGHT
...WHICH **GREETS**
...YOU IN THIS DIMLY LIT
...ROOM SHAKES THE DRUNKEN
...**STUPOR** FROM YOUR EYES...

MOTHER
IN HEAVEN--
NO.!!

FIRST NIGHT:

111

STAY BACK-- WHATEVER YA ARE, YA BLASTED THING-- *BACK*, OR THE GIRL GETS *STUCK.*

DON'T ATTACK, JACK. I CAN SAVE MY--

BUT THE BEAST-- THE THING THAT IS *JACK RUSSELL* DOES NOT MOVE OFF... IT DOES *NOT* STEP ASIDE...

...*RATHER, LEAPS*, WITH TALON DRAWN

--ATTACKS

WOODEN BANNISTERS *SPLIT* AND SHATTER AS THE TWO TUMBLING FIGURES SPILL OUT OF THE ROOM AND DOWN THE ROTTING *STAIRWAY...*

THE WEREWOLF IS *SILENT* SAVE FOR A LOW GUTTERAL *GROWLING* PITTE DEEP WITHIN ITS STOMACH...

...BUT THE SAILOR CALLED SCRATCHER MARTIN *SCREAMS* AN ALMOST UNEARTHLY SCREAM.

TABLES *SPLINTER* AND BONES *CRACK* AS THE TWO FIGHT ON...

CRASH!

...BUT BE IT BECAUSE OF JACK'S *WOLFISH MIND* OR THE SAILOR'S *LUCK* CHANCE KICK--IT IS THE *WEREWOLF* WH FALLS FIRST.

ATCHER MARTIN KNOWS WHEN HE IS ATEN, AND RATHER THAN BATTLE LUPINE FOE ONCE AGAIN...

HE TURNS D FLEES.

AT LEAST **THIS** WAY HE WILL LIVE FOR OTHER FIGHTS...

BUT **LIFE** IS NOT A COMMODITY THAT SLASHER MARTIN HAS EARNED...

...AND SO, IT IS THE **WEREWOLF** WHO ONCE AGAIN **RENEWS** HIS DEADLY ATTACK.

YE OLDE BOOT INN

SHER'S SCREAMS MEAN THING TO THE BEAST-- WORDS ARE ONLY MEAN- LESS, FOOLISH **SOUNDS**...

BUT THE **FEAR** THE SAILOR'S CE...**THAT** THE EREWOLF UNDER- ANDS, AND **THAT** E RESPONDS TO...

...WITH **MORE FORCE**... WITH **MORE HATRED**.

TWICE...AND TWICE MORE HIS RAZOR- SHARP **TALONS** SLASH AT THE WRIGGLING, TERRIFIED **SAILOR**...

...AND THEN THE **SCREAMING** AND THE **WRITHING** STOPS...FOREVER.

YOU **DIDN'T** HAVE TO **KILL** HIM, JACK... I WOULD HAVE STOPPED HIM WITHOUT PAIN... **WITHOUT VIOLENCE**.

AND NOW, BECAUSE FOR ONE MOMENT YOU WERE A **MINDLESS SEETHING BEAST**, A PRECIOUS **LIFE** HAS BEEN STILLED.

113

THERE IS... THERE *MUST* BE A MIND... *YOUR MIND* HIDING SOMEWHERE INSIDE THERE, JACK... AND *YOU* COULD HAVE STOPPED THE ATTACK IF YOU WANTED TO...

WE MUST *FIND* THAT INTELLIGENCE BEFORE YOU *KILL* AGAIN...

BUT NOW, COME WITH ME -- THE *AUTHORITIES* MUST BE NOTIFIED BEFORE WE CAN DO ANYTHING ELSE.

NO, WOMAN -- NO ONE SHALL BE TOLD OF THAT *SAILOR'S* DEATH...

...NOR SHALL THE BE TOLD OF *YOURS*.

I THIR AND IT S BE *YO BLOO* WHICH QUENCH MY THIR THIS NIG

WHAT--?

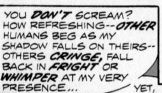

YOU *DON'T* SCREAM? HOW REFRESHING -- *OTHER* HUMANS BEG AS MY SHADOW FALLS ON THEIRS -- OTHERS *CRINGE*, FALL BACK IN *FRIGHT* OR *WHIMPER* AT MY VERY PRESENCE...

YET, IN YOUR *EYES* THERE, IS NO FEAR... NO FRIGHT...

YOUR EYES... THEY... THEY...

WAIT! WHAT ARE YOU DOING TO ME...? I FEEL YOUR *EYES* *PROBING* INTO MINE -- TEARING INTO MY BRAIN...

STOP! DRACULA COMMANDS THAT YOU *STOP!!*

BUT THE GIRL CALLED TOPAZ D NOT *STOP* -- FOR EVEN AS HER GREEN EYES *BORE* THROUGH T CONSCIOUSNESS OF THE *PRINC OF EVIL*...

...THE *BEAST*... THE WEREWOLF -- SENSING *ANOTHER EVIL* -- *ANOTHER CONFLICT*... ANOTHER ENEMY... ATTACKS ONCE MORE.

WHAT YOU CREAT *DAR* ATTAC

VERY WEL THEN, WOMA IF I CAN'T STRIKE A *YOU* --

114

--AT LEAST I CAN *DESTROY THIS BEAST* OF YOURS.

BACK, WRETCHED ONE--AND FEEL THE WRATH OF DRACULA--LORD OF EVIL--

--AND MASTER OF *ALL* WHO TREAD THE *DARKLING*

THERE IS A *BONE-CRUNCH-ING* THUD AND THE WERE-WOLF FALLS CRUMPLED IN A BLOODIED HEAP... BLOOD WHICH *BECKONS* THE HUNGRY DRACULA TOWARDS HIS FALLEN FOE...

...BUT IT IS THE *GIRL*... THE *SORCERESS TOPAZ,* WHO STEPS IN THE KING OF VAMPIRES' PATH, AND *CALMS* THE ANGER THAT BREWS IN DRACULA'S HEART.

HE *TURNS,* THIS *WARRIOR,* THIS *CONQUEROR* OF NATIONS AND MEN -- TURNS HESITANTLY BEFORE THE *POWER* OF THIS GIRL--

--AND, AS THE NIGHTWINGED *BAT,* TAKES ONCE AGAIN TO THE INDIGO SKIES.

HE KNOWS NOT *WHY* HE COULD NOT COMPLETE THE ATTACK; ALL HE DOES IS SOAR *HIGHER* AND EVER HIGHER.

...CROSS THE VILLAGE OF TRANSYLVANIA ...FLIES, AND AS THE FRIGHTENED ...POPULACE BELOW STARE AT THE ALL-...ILIAR SHROUD OF DEATH ABOVE ...EM, THEY *CLOSE* THEIR WINDOWS ...NTLY WITH GARLIC-DRENCHED ...PES, AND *PRAY* THE EVIL LEAVES.

BUT THERE ARE THOSE WHO DO *NOT* PRAY FOR SALVATION...

...AND SAMELY, THERE ARE THOSE WHO MUST *DIE.*

115

20 HOURS LATER, AND ACROSS THE LARGE EXPANSE OF *TRANSYLVANIA*...

THIS IS *IT*, TOPAZ-- RUSSOFF MANOR.

BRINGS BACK *MEMORIES* OF THOSE OLD *UNIVERSAL MOVIES*, DOESN'T IT?

NOW, IF I CAN FIND ONE LITTLE THING...

BUT WHAT? WHAT ARE YOU *SEARCHING* FOR?

GUESS WHAT I REALLY WANT IS SOMETHING-- *ANYTHING*--TO FILL IN THE MANY PIECES THAT ARE *MISPLACED* IN MY LIFE.

I KNOW SOME THINGS...SMALL DETAILS...SOME ANSWERS--BUT THERE ARE *STILL* SO MANY *MORE* QUESTIONS.

I REMEMBER MY FATHER AS A GENTLE MAN...

--AH, JACOB-- YOU'RE A *BIG* LAD, EH?

BIG LIKE YOUR *FATHER*-- BRIGHT LIKE YOUR *MOTHER*!

I REMEMBER MY MOTHER TELLING ME OF THE NIGHT MY FATHER *DIED*...

THERE-- IN THE *SHADOWS*-- SOMETHING *MOVED*!

WEREWOLF!

THOUGH SHE WASN'T THERE--MY MOTHER TOLD ME--SHE COULD *HEAR* THE SOUND OF GUNSHOTS--

BLAM

BLAM

"AND MY FATHER DIED-- THE SILVER BULLET PIERCING HIS *HEART*."

AAARRGGH

116

...AH, THOSE
...SOME OF
...E ANSWERS...
...T GOD KNOWS
...EY'RE NOT
...LL.

AND FURTHERMORE-- I KEEP WONDERING IF I REALLY WANT TO KNOW ALL THE ANSWERS.

JACK-- COME HERE. I THINK I'VE FOUND IT.

IT'S A DIARY-- BUT IT'S BEEN BOUND AND LOCKED.

DIARY

THEN I DEFINITELY WANT TO READ IT.

PERHAPS I CAN CRACK THE LOCK-- IT MUST BE HALF-CRUMBLING WITH AGE ANYHOW.

WAIT A MINUTE-- WHAT'S THIS LEATHER TAB-- IT'S NOT A BOOKMARK OR A--

JACK-- LOOK-- A DOOR IS OPENING.

DIARY

NGO!
EHOW
FATHER
ST'VE
GED UP
YSTEM
OPENING
PASSAGE
ULLING
TAB.

NEXT STEP, I GUESS, IS TO LEARN WHY.

YOU STILL WITH ME, HONEY?

ALWAYS, JACK.

MOTHER ONCE MENTIONED THAT HE'D LOCK HIMSELF IN HIS ROOM FOR HOURS AT A TIME--

--AND NOW I KNOW WHY.

THERE, TOPAZ-- THROUGH THE FOG AND MIST-- THAT'S WHAT MY FATHER WAS DOING. LOOK!

CASTLE DRACULA LAY BENEATH THE MANY-SHROUDED LAYERS OF FOGGY GLOOM, HALF SEEN BY THE LIVING SOULS OF THE FRIGHTENED VILLAGE BELOW...

I'VE SEEN PICTURES OF THAT BEFORE, TOPAZ-- IT'S CASTLE DRACULA...

...AND FOR SOME REASON... MY FATHER WAS OBSERVING IT.

WHICH MEANS, TOPAZ-- I'M GOING INSIDE-- TO EXPLORE IT!

BUT NOW... HERE IN THE LOWER DEPTHS BENEATH RUSSOFF MANOR ITS AWESOME SPECTER GLIMMERS IN THE LIGHT OF THE SINKING SUN...

BUT NOT NOW... NOT AT THIS MOMENT... FOR THE MUST STARE A WHILE LONGER AT THE GRANDEUR THAT LIES BEFORE THEM...

...AYE-- THE GRANDEUR--AND ALSO THE TERROR!

FOR INSIDE THAT DARK-KNIGHTED TEMPLE OF HELL WAITS THE MAN-BAT MEN DARE CALL DRACULA...

THIS CASTLE IS HIS HOME... HIS BIRTHPLACE ...AND AS SUCH IT HOLDS A SPECIAL PLACE IN EVEN HIS COLD HEART.

FOR IT IS ALSO HERE TH HE LEFT HIS BIRTHRIGH OF HUMANITY BEHIN AND DONNED THE CLOAK THE UNDEAD.

AT LAST MY **MISSION** HERE IS DONE-- NEW **COFFINS** FILLED WITH THE SACRED **EARTH** HAVE BEEN PREPARED...

ND SOME HAVE READY BEEN PPED TO ENGLAND.

ONE DAY MORE, AND I MAY **RETURN** TO THAT DREADED COUNTRY. *

＊ **DRACULA'S COFFINS WERE DESTROYED BY QUINCY HARKER'S VAMPIRE HUNTERS.** --ROY T.

BUT I'LL NOT RETURN TO LIVE BENEATH A **CEMETERY GROUNDS**-- FOR THAT IS **NOT** THE WAY OF A DRACULA.

I AM A **COUNT**-- A **PRINCE**-- AND AS SUCH, DIGNITY MUST BE MINE--

THUS THIS DAY I DO **SWEAR**--DRACULA SHALL **HIDE** NO MORE-- FLEE AGAIN FROM NO MORTAL MAN--

--AND, IF **ANY** HUMAN DARES DO **BATTLE** WITH ME-- THEN IT SHALL BE **HE** WHO MUST RUN 'TIL THE HEAVENS THEMSELVES **WEEP** WITH PITY FOR HIS DYING **SOUL.**

CE THERE WERE **LEGENDS** OF DRACULA'S GE, FOR IT WAS SAID THAT ON THE NIGHTS SCREAMED AT THE **HEAVENS**--

--HIS **VOICE** COULD BE HEARD THE WORLD OVER, **ROARING** WITH THE CRACKLING SHARDS OF LIGHTNING AND THUNDER.

YE OLDE BOOT INN

AND **WHEREVER** THAT MOCKING **HOWL** IS HEARD, THE HEARTS AND SOULS OF HUMANS WOULD FREEZE FOR A CHILLING MOMENT IN THE NIGHT'S COLD, CRUEL **WIND.**

SO IT HAS BEEN **DECIDED**, AND MY PLANS ARE NOW **COMPLETE**. TOMORROW I LEAVE FOR **LONDON**--

--TO RECLAIM THE BIRTHRIGHT THAT IS **MINE!**

BUT...

...AH, I SEE THOSE TWO YOUNG **FOOLS** FROM THE VILLAGE HAVE FOLLOWED ME TO MY CASTLE...

VERY WELL-- THE **GIRL** INTERESTED ME-- FOR THERE WAS **SOMETHING** IN HER...**EYES**... SOME **POWER** SHE POSSESSED THAT I WISH TO **STUDY.**

YES... I DO WISH TO LEA NOW SHE KEPT ME FR DESTROYIN HER.

AND **NO** SHE HA STUMBL DIRECTLY ME. GO **VERY GO**

HIS TONGUE CURLS AROUND AND BEHIND HIS **FANGS** AS HE **LEAPS** FROM THE TOWER ROOF--

--AND FLIES ONCE AGAIN AS THE RAVEN-WINGED **BAT.**

HIS WINGS ARE **SILENT,** BUT IT IS THE LOW SHRILL HISSING FROM HIS **LIPS** WHICH ALERTS JACK RUSSELL AND THE GIRL NAMED TOPAZ...

TOP RU

IT'S **DRAC ATTACKIN**

BUT BEFORE THE GIRL CAN **MOVE**...

...AZ--! ...D ...SEN ...R!

BUT I'LL **FOLLOW**, TOPAZ -- I'LL SEARCH THROUGHOUT **CASTLE DRACULA** UNTIL I FIND YOU.

THAT I SWEAR, TOPAZ -- **THAT I SWEAR!**

ONE HOUR JACK RUSSELL SCALES THE PEAK TO CASTLE DRACULA -- BUT AS HE REACHES THE HIGHEST **PLATEAU** HE FAILS TO SEE A SILVER-SPECKED ORB RISE INTO AN INDIGO SKY...

...AN ORB WHICH **BATHES** HIM IN THE LIGHT OF THE **FULL MOON.**

SECOND NIGHT:

...EVER, **INSIDE** CASTLE ...CULA...

...THERE ...OTHING I ...DO FOR YOU, ...ACULA--

...EN I ...NOT ...AIN ...ERS.

YOU **KNEW** WHAT I WAS ABOUT TO ASK--? **INTERESTING.**

THEN YOU **ALSO** KNOW WHAT I SHALL DO WITH YOU--

SHOULD YOU **FAIL** TO DO AS I COMMAND.

DRACULA WAITS FOR THE GIRL'S REPLY... BUT ALL HE HEARS IS **SILENCE**... AND THEN THE HARSH GUTTERAL **GROWLING**...

...OF THE **WEREWOLF!**

WHAT? YOUR BEAST ATTACKS HERE IN -- **MY CASTLE?**

HOW HE CAME HERE IS OF NO INTEREST TO ME--

--BUT IT IS **HERE** THAT HE SHALL FINALLY **PERISH!**

AS HE HAD TRIED *BEFORE* WITH THIS BEAST-- DRACULA COMMANDS IT TO STOP...TO *HALT*...

AND AS BEFORE, THE BEAST ONLY *ATTACKS*.

IT IGNORES THE ORDERS OF THIS DEMON WHO CAN CONTROL SUCH THINGS AS RATS AND BATS..., AND EVEN *WOLVES*...

...*FOR SOMEHOW*... *FOR SOME REASON* ...DRACULA'S ORDERS AFFECT IT NOT-- FOR THE WEREWOLF BITES ITS IVORY FANGS *DEEPER* AND *DEEPER* INTO DRACULA'S NECK...

RAWING THE
PIRE'S PRECIOUS
E-FLUID--
SPILLING IT
HE CASTLE'S
FLOOR.

UNTIL DRACULA *TURNS* -- HIS FACE BLAZING WITH BLOOD-THIRSTY *RAGE*...

...AND IT IS THE FALLEN *WERE-WOLF* WHO BECOMES THE *VICTIM.*

STAY AWAY FROM HIM, DRACULA. I DON'T WANT TO USE MY POWERS...
--BUT IF YOU TRY TO HARM HIM, I PROMISE YOU I WILL.
YOU THREATEN DRACULA, WOMAN? DO YOU TRULY REALIZE THE FOLLY OF YOUR ATTEMPT?
BUT, NO MATTER-- FO YOU'LL NOT HAVE TI TO DO ANYTHING--
--NOT WHI YOU'RE SPRAW UNCONSCIO AT MY FEE
FOR I HAVE OTHER PLANS FOR YOU, GIRL--
--BUT FOR NOW, DRACULA THIRSTS--
--AND HE THIRSTS THE BLOOD OF THE WEREWOLF!
CONTINUED WEREWOLF BY NI #15 WHERE WE LEA THE ORIGIN OF TH WEREWOLF, AND TH CONCLUSION OF T MOST SENSES-SHA TERING BATTLE OF THEM ALL.
NEXT
SNOWBOUN HELL!

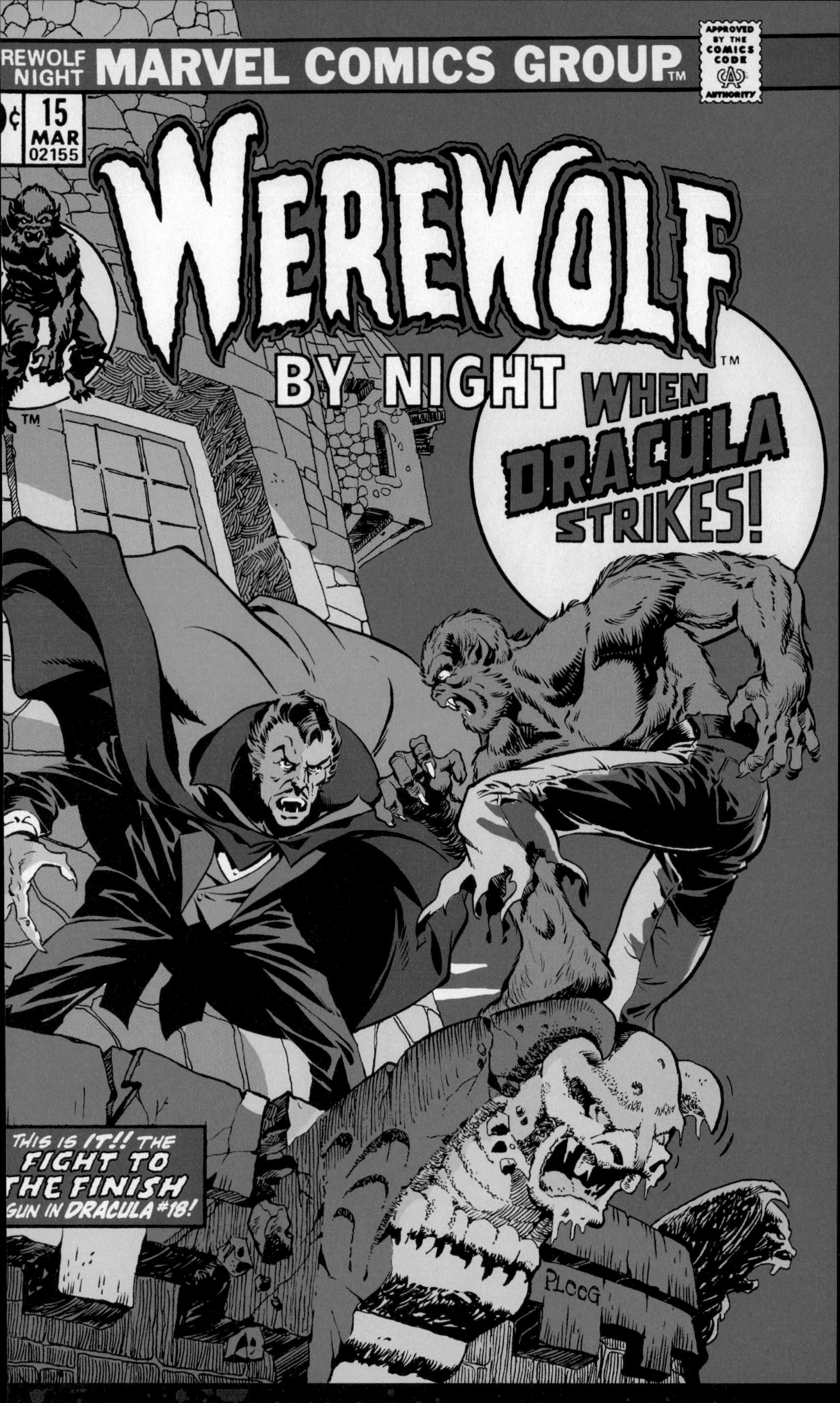

REWOLF NIGHT
MARVEL COMICS GROUP
APPROVED BY THE COMICS CODE AUTHORITY
15 MAR 02155
WEREWOLF BY NIGHT
WHEN DRACULA STRIKES!
THIS IS IT!! THE FIGHT TO THE FINISH
GUN IN DRACULA #18!
PLOOG

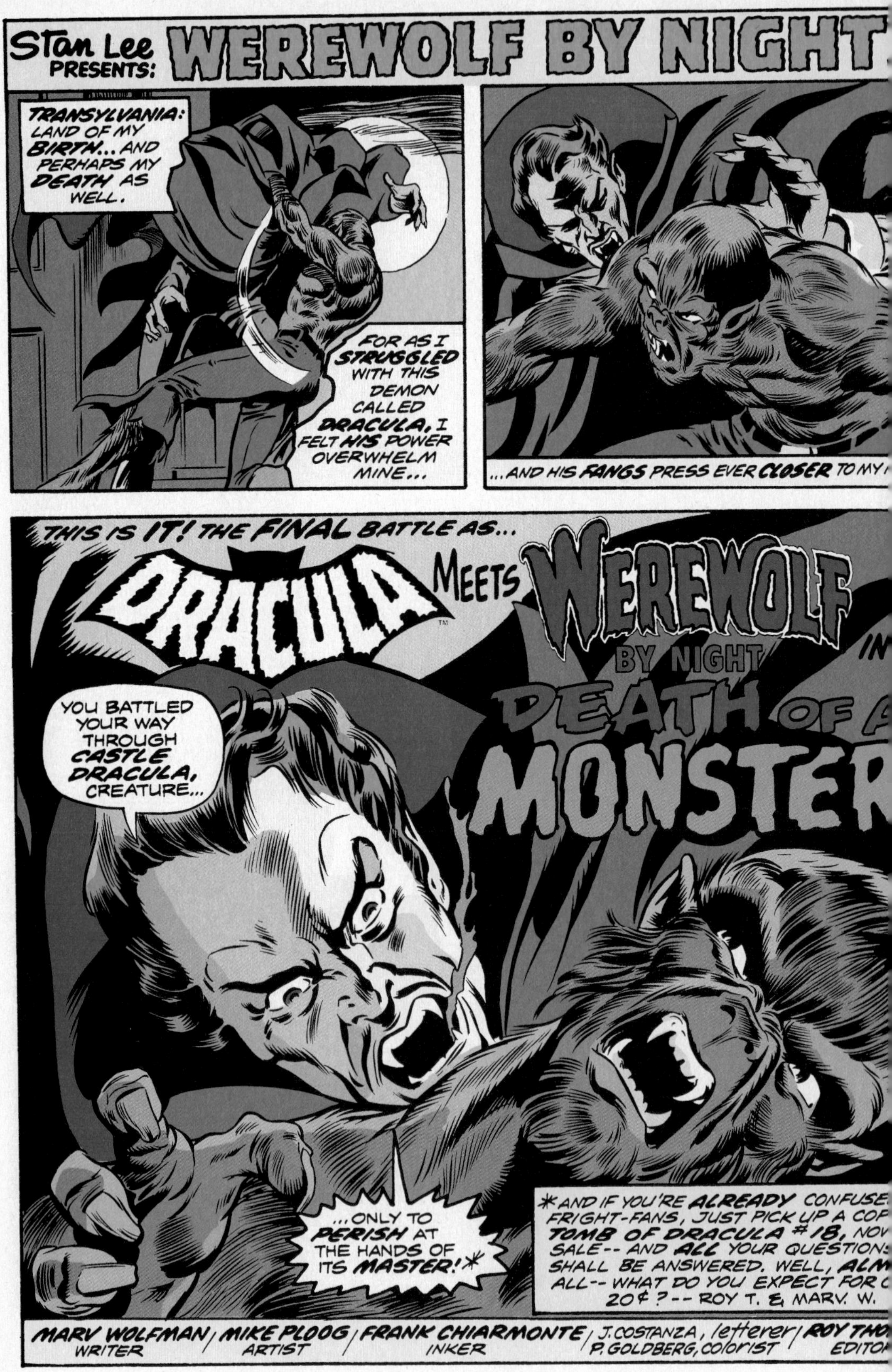
Stan Lee PRESENTS: WEREWOLF BY NIGHT
TRANSYLVANIA: LAND OF MY BIRTH... AND PERHAPS MY DEATH AS WELL.
FOR AS I STRUGGLED WITH THIS DEMON CALLED DRACULA, I FELT HIS POWER OVERWHELM MINE...
...AND HIS FANGS PRESS EVER CLOSER TO MY
THIS IS IT! THE FINAL BATTLE AS...
DRACULA MEETS WEREWOLF BY NIGHT IN
DEATH OF A MONSTER
YOU BATTLED YOUR WAY THROUGH CASTLE DRACULA, CREATURE...
...ONLY TO PERISH AT THE HANDS OF ITS MASTER!*
*AND IF YOU'RE ALREADY CONFUSE FRIGHT-FANS, JUST PICK UP A COP TOMB OF DRACULA #18, NOV SALE-- AND ALL YOUR QUESTION SHALL BE ANSWERED. WELL, ALM ALL-- WHAT DO YOU EXPECT FOR 20¢? -- ROY T. & MARV. W.
MARV WOLFMAN WRITER / MIKE PLOOG ARTIST / FRANK CHIARMONTE INKER / J. COSTANZA, letterer P. GOLDBERG, colorist / ROY THO EDITO

JACK RUSSELL WITHIN FELT *FEAR* AND ~~R~~MISSION AS THE ~~FANG~~S *SANK* DEEP INTO ~~THE~~ FLESH OF MY NECK.

BUT THE *WEREWOLF* COULD NOT UNDERSTAND THE *HORROR* THAT PRESSED UPON ME, AND INSTEAD OF *RUNNING* TO SAFETY--

--HE BATTLED ON--*TWISTING* AND *WRITHING* IN ANIMAL ANGER UNTIL THE *LORD OF VAMPIRES* COULD HOLD HIM NO LONGER.

AND MY *HEART* FROZE IN STRICKEN *TERROR* AS DRACULA WAS *FLUNG* ACROSS THE MARBLE BALCONY BY THE MINDLESS BEAST I WAS...

...FOR EVEN THOUGH I WAS *SUBMERGED* IN SOME DARK NUMBING CHAMBERS OF THE WEREWOLF'S *MIND*, I KNEW HOW HORRIBLE THE *VENGEANCE* OF DRACULA COULD BE.

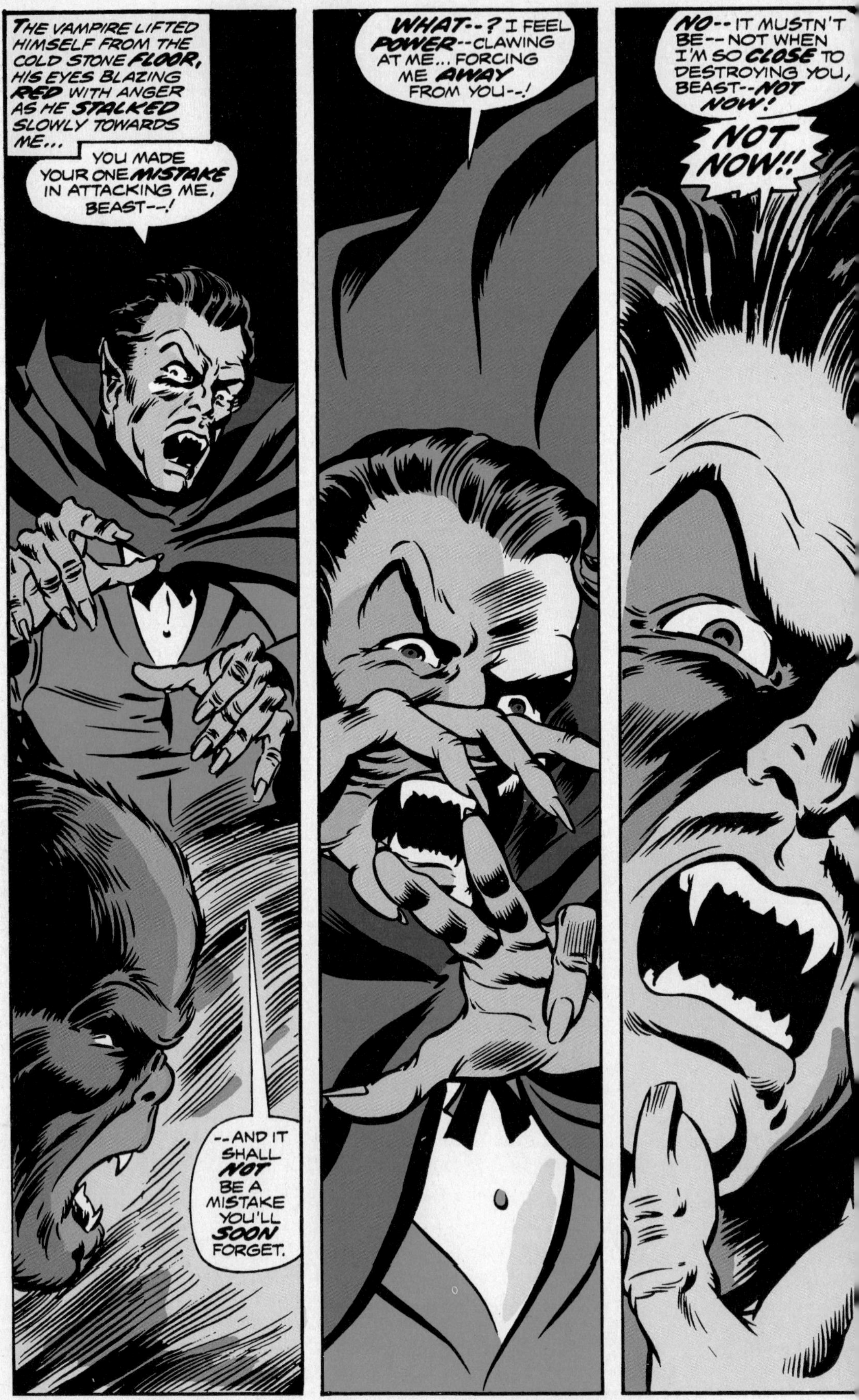
THE VAMPIRE LIFTED HIMSELF FROM THE COLD STONE FLOOR, HIS EYES BLAZING RED WITH ANGER AS HE STALKED SLOWLY TOWARDS ME...
YOU MADE YOUR ONE MISTAKE IN ATTACKING ME, BEAST--!
--AND IT SHALL NOT BE A MISTAKE YOU'LL SOON FORGET.
WHAT--? I FEEL POWER--CLAWING AT ME... FORCING ME AWAY FROM YOU--!
NO--IT MUSTN'T BE--NOT WHEN I'M SO CLOSE TO DESTROYING YOU, BEAST--NOT NOW!
NOT NOW!!

HELPLESS, ALMOST *PARALYZED* BY THE POWER THAT COURSED THROUGH HIM, DRACULA WAS UNABLE TO *RESIST* AS I LIFTED HIM HIGH INTO THE *AIR,* AND...

...*THREW HIM DOWN* TO THE WINTER-COLD EARTH BELOW...

BUT AS HE FELL HEADLONG GROUNDWARDS, HIS BODY SHIMMERED WITH AN *UNEARTHLY GLOW*...HIS ARMS *MELTED* INTO LEATHERY WINGS,...

-- AND THE MAN WAS GONE -- LEAVING A RAVEN-WINGED *BAT* IN ITS FRIGHTFUL PLACE.

FOR THIS WAS NO *ORDINARY* HUMAN THE WEREWOLF BATTLED -- THIS WAS DRACULA -- LORD OF THE UNDEAD -- *KING OF VAMPIRES!*

AND A MAN WHO COULD NOT *EASILY* BE KILLED AGAIN.

WEREWOLF SQUINTED AS THE BAT *FLEW* FROM HIM ON AN ERRATIC, WOBBLING [COUR]SE... A FLIGHT FILLED WITH A HUNGRY BLOOD-[LUS]T TO REPLACE THE *ENERGY* AND *LIFE* [THA]T WAS SO SUDDENLY DRAINED FROM HIS [BOD]Y...

[...]AND DEEP WITHIN [TH]E TRANSYLVANIAN [COU]NTRYSIDE HE FOUND [TH]E *'NOURISHMENT'* [H]E SO *DESPERATELY* REQUIRED.

COME TO ME, WOMAN -- DRACULA HAS *NEED* OF YOU THIS NIGHT...

ELIZABETH GORNIG SCREAMED AND THE SCREAMS FADED LONG BEFORE THEY COULD BE HEARD...

...AT LEAST BY ANYONE *HUMAN.*

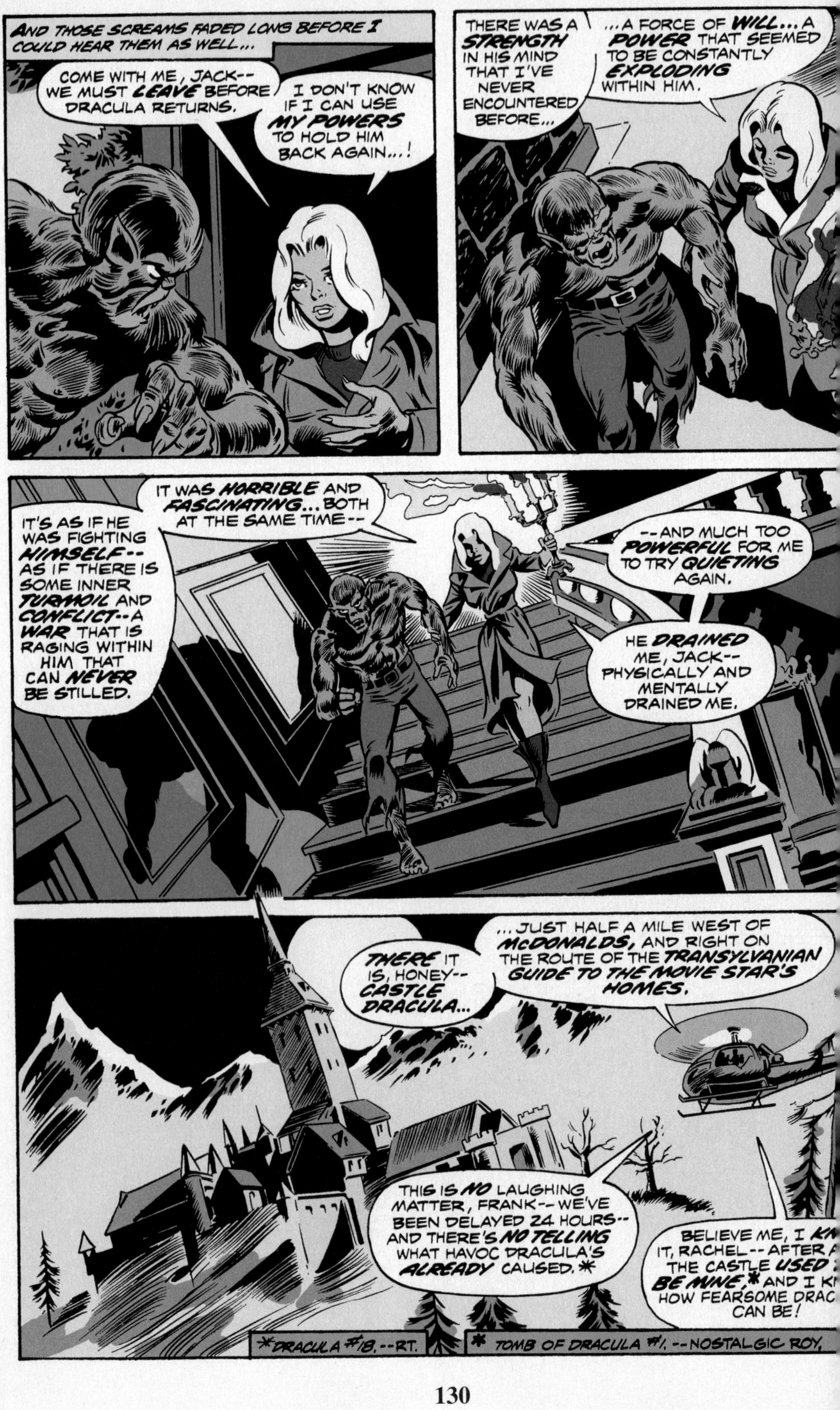
AND THOSE SCREAMS FADED LONG BEFORE I COULD HEAR THEM AS WELL...
COME WITH ME, JACK-- WE MUST LEAVE BEFORE DRACULA RETURNS.
I DON'T KNOW IF I CAN USE MY POWERS TO HOLD HIM BACK AGAIN...!
THERE WAS A STRENGTH IN HIS MIND THAT I'VE NEVER ENCOUNTERED BEFORE...
...A FORCE OF WILL... A POWER THAT SEEMED TO BE CONSTANTLY EXPLODING WITHIN HIM.
IT WAS HORRIBLE AND FASCINATING... BOTH AT THE SAME TIME--
IT'S AS IF HE WAS FIGHTING HIMSELF-- AS IF THERE IS SOME INNER TURMOIL AND CONFLICT--A WAR THAT IS RAGING WITHIN HIM THAT CAN NEVER BE STILLED.
--AND MUCH TOO POWERFUL FOR ME TO TRY QUIETING AGAIN.
HE DRAINED ME, JACK-- PHYSICALLY AND MENTALLY DRAINED ME.
THERE IT IS, HONEY-- CASTLE DRACULA...
...JUST HALF A MILE WEST OF McDONALDS, AND RIGHT ON THE ROUTE OF THE TRANSYLVANIAN GUIDE TO THE MOVIE STAR'S HOMES.
THIS IS NO LAUGHING MATTER, FRANK-- WE'VE BEEN DELAYED 24 HOURS-- AND THERE'S NO TELLING WHAT HAVOC DRACULA'S ALREADY CAUSED.*
BELIEVE ME, I K IT, RACHEL-- AFTER THE CASTLE USED BE MINE,* AND I K HOW FEARSOME DRAC CAN BE!
*DRACULA #18.--RT.
* TOMB OF DRACULA #1.--NOSTALGIC ROY.

SIDES, I **AM** A DESCENDANT OF OUR FRIENDLY COUNT, REMEMBER--? AND I'D LOVE TO SEE ME BECOME AS **MORBID** AS HE IS.

BY THE WAY, IT LOOKS **QUIET** DOWN THERE-- I'VE GOT A HUNCH DRACULA'S **OUT**...

...WHICH MEANS WE MAY BE ABLE TO LAY OUR **TRAP** WHILE HE'S **GONE**.

NO TIME, FRANK-- **COOK!**

DRACULA!

MY **GOD**-- HE'S FORMING AS **MIST**-- SEEPING INTO THE FILTER-- THE **STAKE**-- GIVE ME THE STAKE, **RACHEL**.

CAN'T--IT'S **PACKED AWAY**--! **FIGHT HIM OFF**--! YOU'VE **GOT** TO TRY!

IT'S **WRAPPING** ITSELF AROUND ME-- CLAWS DIGGING INTO MY HEAD...

NOOOO!

FRANK!!

GONE-- BUT IT'S **TOO** LATE...

CONTROL'S **STUCK**-- CAN'T PULL HER UP...

BRACE YOURSELF.

131

TRY *EASING* THE CONTROLS-- SLOWLY!

YOU MAY BE ABLE TO *TUG* IT LOOSE.

THEN HERE GOES *NOTHING*, HONEY.

TELL ME IF IT *WORKS*-- 'CAUSE I'LL BE TOO BLASTED *SCARED* TO OPEN MY EYES TO FIND OUT THAT I'M *DEAD!*

MADE IT! ONE MORE INCH AND THAT'D BE ALL SHE WROTE! YOU KNOW, RACHEL, SOMETIMES I THINK I'D LIKE A *LESS DANGEROUS* JOB THAN *HUNTING VAMPIRES*--

--YEAH, MAYBE SOME THING LIKE A *DYNAMITE JUGGLER.*

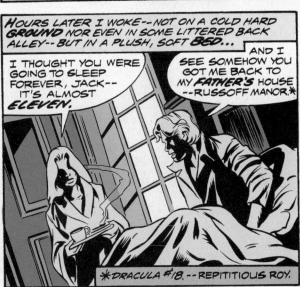

HOURS LATER I WOKE--NOT ON A COLD HARD *GROUND* NOR EVEN IN SOME LITTERED BACK ALLEY--BUT IN A PLUSH, SOFT *BED*...

I THOUGHT YOU WERE GOING TO SLEEP FOREVER, JACK-- IT'S ALMOST *ELEVEN.*

AND I SEE SOMEHOW YOU GOT ME BACK TO MY *FATHER'S* HOUSE --RUSSOFF MANOR.*

*DRACULA #18.--REPITITIOUS ROY.

WELL, I CAN'T SAY I'VE EVER HAD A MORE BEAUTIFUL *NURSEMAID.*

OR AN *ANGRIER* ONE, JACK--IF YOU *DON'T* EAT YOUR BREAKFAST QUICKLY.

Y ST HAVE PRO OF T *BOOK* SOU

MY FATHER'S *DIARY*-- SEALED WITH UNBREAKABLE *STEEL*. IN ALL THE CONFUSION WITH DRACULA, I HAD ALMOST *FORGOTTEN* ABOUT THAT.

SO FAR WE'VE LEARNED ONLY ABOUT THE *TAB*, JACK.

AND THAT IF YO *PULL* IT--IT SOMEHOW ELECTRO ALLY *OPENS* THE TOWER DOOR TO GREGORY RUSS LIBRARY!

BUT *STI* DOESN'T US HOW OPEN BOOK-- LET *READ*

132

T WHAT ABOUT *YOU*, TOPAZ-- YOU THINK YOUR *POWERS* AN BREAK AN UNBREAK- ABLE LOCK?

OO TAUGHT TO *FUNNEL* OWERS TO DO OST *ANYTHING* EEDED... THEN ERHAPS--✳

BOO AND TOPAZ WERE *FIRST* ODUCED IN WEREWOLF #13. ROSPECTIVE ROY, *AGAIN!*

I *HOPE* I CAN WORK THIS, JACK-- BUT EVER SINCE YOUR BATTLE WITH TABOO, I'VE BEEN *WEAKER*-- AS IF SOME OF MY POWER HAS DRAINED OFF...✳

✳ *WEREWOLF #14.--RT.*

HAVE TO *CONCENTRATE*-- FOCUS *THROUGH* THE CHAMBERS OF THE LOCK-- *UNBALANCE* THE DELICATE MECHANISMS...

THERE! IT IS *DONE!*

D THIS IS TLY AT I'VE EN RCHING R, Z!

HERE, READ *THIS*-- HOW MY GREAT, GREAT, GREAT GRANDFATHER, BECAME THE WEREWOLF.

IT BEGAN IN 1795-- ALMOST *180 YEARS AGO*-- AND STILL THE CURSE AFFECTS MY FAMILY-- THROUGH *ME*, AND PERHAPS EVEN LISSA, MY *SISTER*.

IT BEGAN *NOT* IN THIS SMALL MANOR, BUT IN OUR FAMILY *CASTLE*-- WHICH MY STEP-FATHER SOLD OVER A *YEAR* AGO. ✳

✳ *MARVEL SPOTLIGHT #4.--RT.*

EAD THE DIARY OST *DISBELIEVING* WORDS THAT WERE NDWRITTEN FORE ME--

FOR THESE WORDS ERE *PENNED* BY HE *FIRST* MEMBER F MY FAMILY TO BE *STRICKEN* BY THE CURSE...

"IT BEGAN ONE WEEK BEFORE-- AND WHEN IT SHALL *END*, I FEAR I WILL *NEVER* KNOW.

"BUT I PRAY TO WHICHEVER *GOD* WHO LISTENS-- PLEASE LET THIS CURSE END SWIFTLY.

"HOW I *SURVIVED* THIS PAST WEEK I SHALL NEVER KNOW," IT BEGAN, "BUT I NOW FEAR THE COMING OF EACH *NIGHT*-- EACH *FULL MOON*, FOR THE *HORRORS* THAT IT BRINGS ME...

133

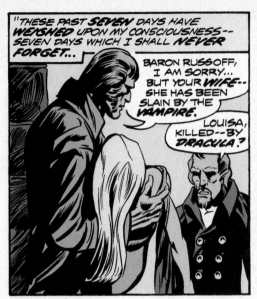

"THESE PAST *SEVEN* DAYS HAVE *WEIGHED* UPON MY CONSCIOUSNESS-- SEVEN DAYS WHICH I SHALL *NEVER FORGET*...

BARON RUSSOFF, I AM SORRY... BUT YOUR *WIFE*-- SHE HAS BEEN SLAIN BY THE *VAMPIRE*.

LOUISA, KILLED--BY *DRACULA?*

HE THREATENED IF I DID NOT *KNEEL* TO HIS POWER THAT I WOULD *SUFFER*--

--AND *I* SWORE TO *SLAY* HIM IF HE TRIED.

FOR LOUISA, I SHALL MAKE MY *PROMISE* COME TRUE.

GUSTOFF, LAY MY WIFE TO REST--

I SH RETL LATE TO MC FOR HE

BUT *NOW*, I HAVE *WORK* THAT MUST BE DONE--AND SWIFTLY--BEFORE *DARKNESS* AGAIN COVERS *TRANSYLVANIA*...

--AND THE DEMON I GO TO *KILL* HAS FLED.

"CASTLE DRACULA WAS *UNGUARDED*, FOR THERE WERE NONE IN THE VILLAGE BELOW WHO WOULD HAVE *DARED VENTURE TOWARDS* IT SAVE I--

"--AND SO, MAKING MY *ENTRANCE* TO THE FIEND'S UNDERGROUND *CHAMBERS* WAS DONE WITH EA

YOU SLEEP IN *COMFORT*, DO YOU, DRACULA? THEN SLEEP *TIGHTLY* DARK BEAST--

--FOR YOU SHALL *NEVER WAKEN* AGAIN!

"THE 'DEVIL' SCREAMED AS THE WOODEN STAKE *STABBED* THROUGH HIS *HEART*--BUT HIS SCREAM LASTED ONLY ONE SHORT-BREATHED *MOMENT*...

"...FOR IN *INSTAN.* THERE W ONLY *ASA* WHERE FL HAD ONC BEEN.

...NCASED HIM IN A **COFFIN** LINED ...BALLS OF **GARLIC**, THEN THREW HIM OVER THE BALCONY EDGE TO THE COLD **DANUBE** WATERS BELOW...

"...AND, THOUGH **REVENGE** HAD BEEN MINE, I WAS NOT SATISFIED STILL--

"BUT AS I LAY WASTE TO **ANTIQUES** MORE THAN FOUR CENTURIES OLD, I HEARD A MUFFLED SOUND... A **CRY**...

"...AND, HEAVEN HELP MY FOOLISH **CURIOSITY**, I TURNED TO ITS **SOURCE**.

"**ENRAGED** WITH THE ANGER THAT HAD WELLED WITHIN ME, I SMASHED MY WAY THROUGH HIS **VALUABLES**, DESTROYING WHATEVER HERITAGE HE COULD HAVE CLAIMED AS HIS.

...RE WAS A DOOR, ...ED WITH A WOODEN ...M-- AND, **IDIOT** ...I WAS, I OPENED ...TO FIND...

...RL--? WHO ...YOU, LASS--? ...WHY ARE YOU ...PRISONED ...HIS LIVING ...ELL?

I AM CALLED **LYDIA**, SIR...

...AND IT WAS **DRACULA** WHO PLACED ME HERE-- **AFTER** HE MURDERED MY FATHER AND MOTHER.

DAMNED DEVIL! HE DESERVED A DEATH MORE HORRIBLE THAN HE RECEIVED. HOW **LONG** HAVE YOU BEEN HERE, GIRL?

ONE MONTH, SIR... AND KEPT ALIVE ONLY AS LONG AS MY **BLOOD** PLEASED HIM.

EACH NIGHT HE WOULD **COME** TO ME-- AND EACH NIGHT HIS HORRIBLE **FANGS** WOULD DRAIN THE BLOOD FROM MY NECK.

LIVE IN **FEAR** NO LONGER, LYDIA-- THE FIEND IS **DEAD**-- AND FOR YOUR PARENTS, AND MY **LOUISA**-- MAY HE LAY IN DEATH **FOREVER**.

"WE WALKED IN **SHADOWS** BENEATH THE MOON-SPECKLED TREES, AND I TALKED, BELIEVING THE YOUNG GIRL TO BE **LISTENING**...

"...BUT MY CONVERSATION WAS THE **LAST** THING SHE CARED ABOUT...

"..., FOR, AS THE FULL SILVERED **MOON** LOOMED ABOVE US, I HEARD A FIERCE, SLAVERING **GROWL**...

"...A **WAIL** FROM A BEING NEITHER HUMAN NOR **ANIMAL**.

"AND WHEN I TURNED TOWARDS IT-- I SAW THE *FACE* OF MY *DEATH.*

HER *CLAWS* GLISTENED IN THE MOONLIGHT-- HER TEETH, SHARP AS *WOODEN NAILS,* SPARKLED THROUGH THE DARKNESS--

"BUT IT WAS HER *EYES*...THOSE FIERY, GLOWING EYES THAT CAUGHT MY OWN--*TRANSFIXED* ME HELPLESSLY ON MY SPOT...

"I TRIED TO *SCREAM* RIGHT THEN, BUT THERE WAS *NO SOUND* LEFT WITHIN ME.

"--AND *PARALYZED* ME AS MY *MURDERER* SANK HER FANGS INTO MY NECK.

"AND FOR THE NEXT TWO NIGHTS, BENEATH THE RISING FULL MOON, I UNCONTROLLABLY SHOOK OFF MY *MANTLE* OF HUMANISM--

"--AND BECAM[E] *MINDLES[S] RAMPAG[ING] WEREWOL[F.]*

THERE'S [N]... TOPAZ-- ENC[...] TO READ S[O...] *OTHER* TIME[...] BUT NOT N[OW,] NOT NOV[...]

" HER *SALIVA* MIXED WITH MY *SWEAT* AND *BLOOD,* AND FROM THAT MOMENT ON I WAS *CURSED.*

BUT WHY DID *DRACULA* KEEP A *WEREWOLF* LOCKED AWAY? WHAT COULD *HE* FEAR FROM IT?

THE DIARY SAID DRACULA COULD *NOT* CONTROL THE BEAST AS HE WAS ABLE TO CONTROL *OTHERS*--

--THAT THERE WAS *SOMETHING* ABOUT HER THAT MADE HER *IMPERVIOUS* TO HIS COMMANDS.

WHICH PROBABLY *EXPLAINS* WHY DRACULA'S *COMMAND* DIDN'T AFFECT *ME*-- AND WHY HE HAD TO FINALLY USE *FORCE* TO STOP ME.*

PERHAPS I HAD *BETTER* READ ON. THERE MAY BE SOMETHING WRITTEN IN HERE THAT COULD HELP US *FIGHT* THAT VAMPIRE.

YOU S[TILL] WANT[...] BATT[LE...] HI[M...] JAC[K?]

*DRACULA #18.--RT.

I DON'T KNOW WHAT *HAPPENED* BACK IN THAT HELICOPTER --MAYBE I REAL-IZED FOR THE *FIRST TIME* HOW POWERFUL DRACULA REALLY IS --

BETTER IEVE IT, CHEL-- *NOTHING'S* G TO STOP ME.

BUT I WANT HIM *DEAD*-- AND I WANT TO BE THE GUY WHO *KILLS HIM*.

YOU KNOW SOMETHING, RACHEL-- I'VE *FOUGHT* HIM BEFORE-- I WATCHED HIM TURN *EDITH* * INTO A VAMPIRE-- AND I SAW THE GRIEF ON QUINCY'S FACE AS HE HAD TO SLAY HIS OWN *DAUGHTER*--

--BUT UP UNTIL *NOW, I* WAS LEFT ALMOST *UN-TOUCHED*-- AND MAYBE THAT'S WHY HIS ATTACK NOW HIT ME AS *HARD* AS IT DID.

* DRACULA #12, FRIGHT-FANS. AND BY THE WAY--LOOK AT THIS BLUEISH 'MIST' HEADING TOWARDS OUR TWO VAMPIRE HUNTERS. --ROY.

ANK-- E'S RE-- IN ROOM--

--AS A *MIST!*

WHAT'S *WRONG*-- WHAT'S HE *DOING* TO YOU--?

CHOKING ME--CAN'T... BREATHE... CAN'T...

RACHEL!!

FIGHTING *ME*, ACULA--LET'S SEE AT YOU CAN DO INST A *MAN* TEAD OF ALWAYS TTLING MEN--

C'MON, *ANCESTOR*-- LET'S SEE YOU BE SO *BRAVE* WITH ME.

YOU ARE A *FOOL*, MY DESCENDANT-- A FOOL WHO *DESERVES DEATH*--

BUT FOR NOW YOU HAVE A **REPRIEVE**-- FOR I SENSE I MUST BE **ELSEWHERE**--

--WHERE **TWO OTHER FOOLS** HAVE FOUND THE **BOOK** I SEARCHED SO LONG FOR--

--THE **DIARY** OF **BARON RUSSOFF**--

--A **BOOK** FAR MORE **FEARFUL** AND **TERRIFYING** THAN THE ANCIENT DARKHOLD **SCROLLS**--

--FOR IN ITS **BOUND PAGES** LIES THE SECRET OF THE **SECOND BOOK OF SINS**--

--A BOOK THAT **THREATEN THE VE** LIFE OF THE **LOR** OF **VAMPIRE**.

--A BOOK THAT COULD MEAN T **DEATH OF DRACULA.**

I CAN ALSO **SENSE** THAT MY **ENEMIES** SHALL COME THIS WAY-- ALL **FOUR** SHALL CONVERGE ON **THIS SPOT**--

--SO IT SHALL BE **HERE** THAT I MAKE MY **STAND**--

--AND HERE WHERE I SHOW THAT **ALL** WHO OPPOSE MY WILL MUST **PERISH** BEFORE MY MIGHT.

BUT **FIRS** TO BE **SUR** VAN HELSI **AND DRAKE** CAN NO **ESCAP**

THESE **CONTROLS** GIVE FLIGHT TO THIS VEHICLE-- AND IF THEY ARE **DESTROYED**--

--THEN THERE SHALL BE **NO ESCAPE** AT ALL!

HA! HA! HA! HA! HA!

TOPAZ AND I READ FROM THE **DIARY** OF GRANDFATHER-- READ WHAT WE WERE **AB** TO, SINCE THERE WERE **SECTIONS** SCRIBL IN LATIN WHICH **NEITHER** OF US COULD DECIPHER...

SOME OF WHAT WE READ WERE ACCOUNTS OF **FAMILY**, OF NORMAL DAILY MATTERS...

...BUT EVEN THESE **INNOCENT PASSAG** WERE LACED WITH THE **HORRIBLE** CURSE THAT BEEN PASSED DOWN THROUGH THE YEARS TO **ME**

CURSE--I HAD BEEN A FOOL MYSELF--
...R IN THE HOURS THAT HAD PASSED WHILE I
...D FROM THE DIARY, DAYLIGHT HAD FADED
...M THE HEAVENS...

...NLY TO BE
...LACED BY THE
...STER LIGHT OF
...FULL MOON.

IT'S ALMOST *TIME* NOW, TOPAZ--TIME FOR THE CURSE TO TAKE EFFECT!

BUT *THIS* TIME I WANT THE CURSE TO *WORK* FOR ME.

AS JACK RUSSELL I'M *HELPLESS* AGAINST DRACULA --HE'S *STRONGER*, MORE CUNNING THAN I CAN EVER *HOPE* TO BE!

BUT THE *WEREWOLF*-- HE MIGHT STAND A CHANCE--IF *YOU* COULD HELP, TOPAZ-- ONLY IF *YOU* COULD HELP.

WHAT CAN *I* DO, JACK?

...WEREWOLF
...MINDLESS--
...EN HE FIGHTS
...S THROUGH
...STINCT
...D NOT
...WLEDGE--

--BUT *YOU* CAN SUPPLY HIM THAT KNOWLEDGE-- YOU CAN *GUIDE* HIM THROUGH HIS FIGHT.

WITH YOUR *POWERS*, YOU COULD FORCE *MY* INTELLIGENCE TO THE SURFACE-- HAVE *MY* BRAIN RULE *HIS* BODY.

THERE WILL BE A *STRAIN*, JACK--YOUR MIND AS THE WERE- WOLF IS TOO *POWERFUL* --AND I HAVE *NO* IDEA HOW LONG I'LL BE ABLE TO GIVE YOU CONTROL...

IT WON'T TAKE *LONG*, TOPAZ-- BECAUSE I COULDN'T *SURVIVE* TOO LONG AGAINST SUCH A FOE SUCH AS *DRACULA*.

...EFT RUSSOFF MANOR WITH TOPAZ
...LOWING BEHIND--BUT WITH EACH
...EP I TOOK, I BEGAN TO *CHANGE*...
...BECOME NOT WHAT I WAS--

--BUT *THE WEREWOLF.*

THIRD NIGHT:

...T FOR THE FIRST
...E SINCE MY
...GHTEENTH
...THDAY, I *KNEW*
...AT IT WAS LIKE
...LIVE INSIDE THE
...DY OF ANOTHER--

--FOR NOW IT WAS THE MIND OF *JACK RUSSELL* WHO WAS TOTALLY IN *CONTROL* OF AN OTHERWISE *MINDLESS BEAST.*

BUT I *QUIETED* THAT FEELING AS I MOVED CLOSER TO THE DEMON CALLED *DRACULA!*

--AND FOR ONLY A *MOMENT,* I REVELED IN LUST FOR THE INHUMAN ENERGY I FELT COURSING THROUGH ME.

I FELT THE POWER IN MY *LEGS,* THE STRENGTH IN MY *ARMS*--

BUT, EVEN AS I *APPROACHED...*

I'VE BEEN *WAITING* FOR YOU, CREATURE OF THE MOON--

WE HAVE *UNSETTLED* BUSINESS TO COMPLETE THIS NIGHT.

BECAUSE I COULD NOT SPEAK, I MERELY *GROWLED* MY REPLY...*

...AND THEN *GIRDED* MYSELF FOR *ACTION.*

DRACULA STOOD *UNMOVING* AS I TESTED MY *UNFAMILIAR LIMBS* AND THEN *ATTACKED...*

YOU HAVE THE *SECOND BOOK OF SINS,* BEAST --AND I MEAN TO POSSESS IT FOR MY OWN...

...AND SHOULD *YOU* NEED PERISH FOR ME TO *TAKE* IT-- THEN *DIE* BENEATH MY HANDS YOU SHALL--

--FOR *NONE* MAY HOLD WHAT DRACULA DESIRES WITHOUT FEELING HIS HORRIBLE *WRATH.*

MY CLAWS SCRAPED INTO THE *FLESH* OF THIS VAMPIRE- BEING-- THIS *UNDEAD* FORM WHO URGED ME ON!

HE WAS HOPING TO *RILE* THE BEAST WITHIN ME, UNKNOWING THAT IT WAS A *SO-DISTANT TOPAZ* WHO GUIDED MY EVERY STEP.

EVEN AS SHE TIGHTLY CLUTCHED THE VERY BO DRACULA DEMANDED,

140

YOU ARE NOT THE [SA]ME BEAST I FOUGHT [EAR]LIER--THIS TIME YOU [BAT]TLE WITH *REASON*--

[T]HIS TIME YOU [FIGH]T *KNOWING* [WH]EN TO WITHDRAW [AN]D WHEN TO [F]EINT--

BUT THIS SUDDEN *INTELLIGENCE* WILL DO YOU LITTLE GOOD, BEAST--

DRACULA IS *STILL* YOUR *MASTER*-- STILL MORE POWERFUL THAN *YOU.*

[THE] VAMPIRE [SMI]LED ON-- [SHO]UTING [CON]FIDENTLY [OF] *VICTORY* [WHI]LE I [CUR]SSED MY [B]ACK.

I HAD NO NEED FOR MEANINGLESS *WORDS* OR A MADMAN'S *RANTINGS*--

--I SOUGHT ONLY *VICTORY* AND TOTAL DEFEAT FOR THIS SELF-NAMED *'PRINCE OF EVIL.'*

[THE]N, AS IF KNOWING I WAS NO *ORDINARY* [FOE,] FRIGHTENED BY HIS CEASELESS *PRATTLING,* [THE] KING OF VAMPIRES CAME *QUIET*--

[A] GRIM [SPE]CTER [OF E]VIL [CRO]SSED [HIS F]ACE--

--AND THE *TRUE* 'LORD OF VAMPIRES' SHOWED THROUGH HIS MOCKING VENEER...

[AN]D THE *TRUE FACE* I SAW WAS *HORRIBLE* BEYOND ALL WORDS OF HORROR.

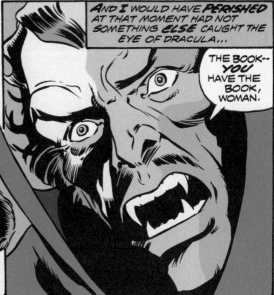

AND I WOULD HAVE *PERISHED* AT THAT MOMENT HAD NOT SOMETHING *ELSE* CAUGHT THE EYE OF DRACULA...

THE BOOK-- *YOU* HAVE THE BOOK, WOMAN.

I WANT IT-- **NOW!**

TOPAZ CLUTCHED THE BOOK A MOMENT MORE, AND THEN, AS HER POWER WAS *FOCUSED* ON ME, SHE GAVE THE ANCIENT *DIARY* TO MY FOE...

YES-- THESE **ARE** THE PAPERS.

GO, WOMAN-- FOR THE MOMEN THE BEAST'S LIFE AND YOUR ARE *UNNEEDE*

AND **YOUR'S** IS ABOUT TO BE *ENDED,* DRACULA.

WHO--?

VAN HELSING AND DRAKE-- **EXPECTED** YOU--BUT NOT SO **SOON.**

YOUR MISTAKE IS **OUR** GAIN, DRACULA. AND WE'VE A LOT TO PAY YOU **BACK** FOR!

BUT RIGHT NOW I'M **EQUALLY** AS INTERESTED IN LEARNING WHY THAT BOOK IS SO *IMPORTANT* TO YOU.

YOU LITTLE **FOOL**-- ONLY I CAN DECIPHER THE *MEANING* OF THE WORDS.

SOMEHOW I **DOUBT** THAT, COUNT --OR ELSE YOU **WOULDN'T** BE SO **FRANTIC.**

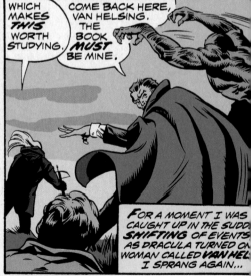

WHICH MAKES **THIS** WORTH STUDYING.

COME BACK HERE, VAN HELSING. THE BOOK **MUST** BE MINE.

FOR A MOMENT I WAS CAUGHT UP IN THE SUDD, **SHIFTING** OF EVENTS AS DRACULA TURNED ON WOMAN CALLED **VAN HEL** I SPRANG AGAIN...

BUT THIS TIME, DRACULA HAD NO TIME FOR FIGHTING...

AWAY WITH YOU, BEAST-- YOU'RE NO LONGER IMPORTANT TO ME NOW.

I MUST HAVE THE BOOK.

IN THE HANDS OF THAT WOMAN--

--IT CAN BE USED TO DESTROY ME FOREVER!

NO-- ALREADY THE HELICOPTER RISES-- I HAD NO TIME TO WRECK IT ALL--

BUT, STILL VAN HELSING MUST NOT ESCAPE.

I WATCHED AS DRACULA'S BODY SHIFTED AND CHANGED-- AND THEN ROSE ON BONY WINGS TOWARDS THE SWIFTLY FLEEING COPTER...

I WANTED TO FOLLOW THE BAT-- AND COMPLETE MY BATTLE, BUT A GENTLE HAND HELD ME BACK, AND SO ALL I DID WAS WATCH AND OBSERVE...

...AND REALIZE THAT THE ANCIENT AXIOM WAS STILL QUITE TRUE--

--FOR THERE, BUT FOR THE GRACE OF GOD-- GOES I.

AND THE HORROR OF WHAT I AM QUIETED FOR THE NIGHT.

CONTINUED in TOMB OF DRACULA #19 BUT NEXT MONTH in WEREWOLF by NIGHT: A NEW MENACE BECKONS! THE HUNCHBACK of NOTRE DAME!

143

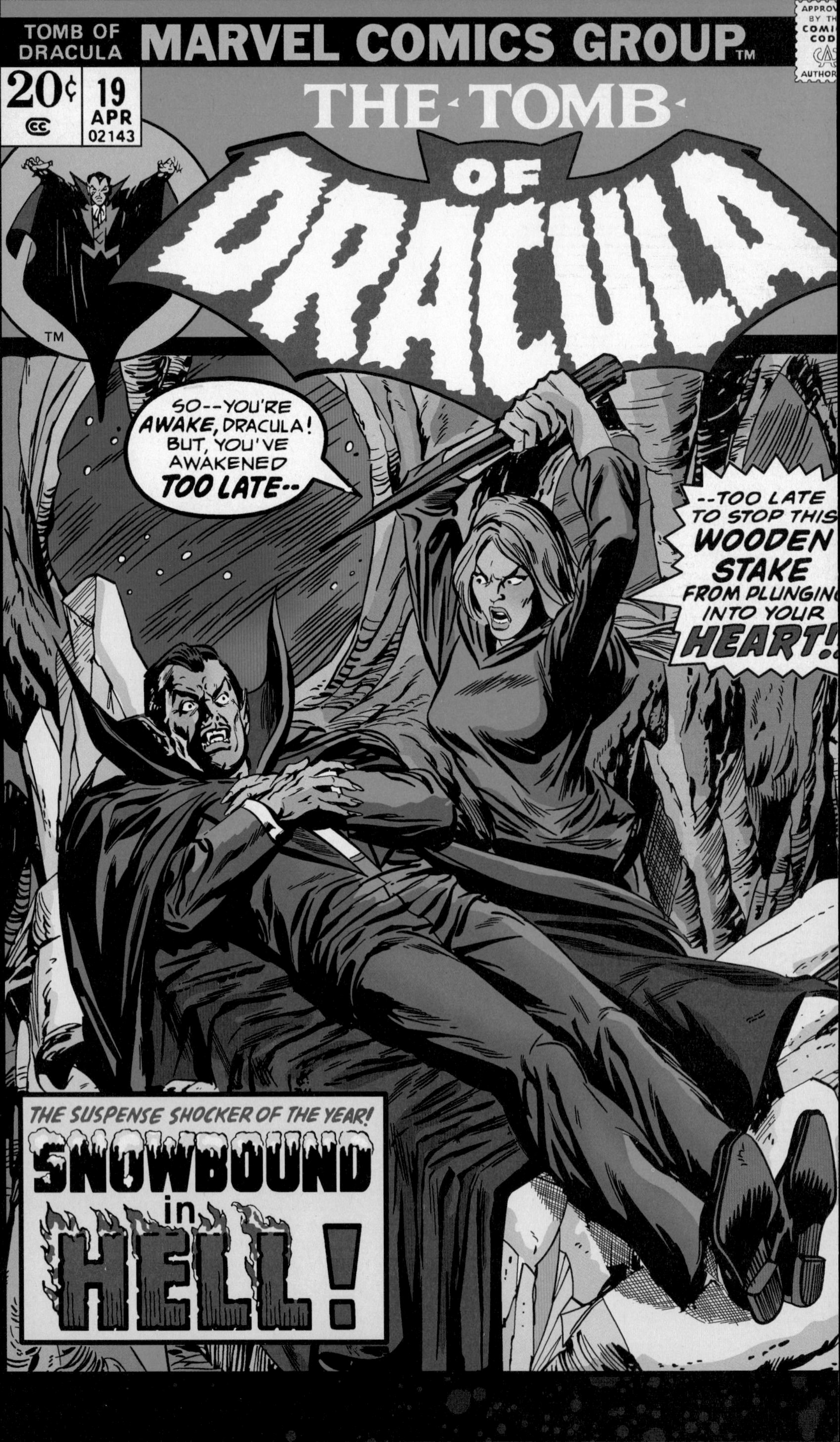
TOMB OF DRACULA
MARVEL COMICS GROUP
20¢
19 APR 02143
THE TOMB OF DRACULA
SO--YOU'RE AWAKE, DRACULA! BUT, YOU'VE AWAKENED TOO LATE--
--TOO LATE TO STOP THIS WOODEN STAKE FROM PLUNGING INTO YOUR HEART!!
THE SUSPENSE SHOCKER OF THE YEAR!
SNOWBOUND in HELL!

an Lee PRESENTS: **TOMB OF DRACULA!**

RY WOLFMAN / GENE COLAN / TOM PALMER / JOHN COSTANZA, *letterer* / ROY THOMAS
WRITER   ARTIST   INKER   GLYNIS WEIN, *colorist*   EDITOR

HE MOUNTAINS HEAVED IN **AGONY** AS A BITTER WIND **WHIPPED** AROUND AND THROUGH THEM...

FOR THIS WAS THE **FIRST** SUCH **WINTER** STORM THESE **TRANSYLVANIAN** ALPS HAD **SUFFERED** AFTER A SUMMER OF RELATIVE **CALM**...

THE DARK-OLIVE **SLOPES** WERE NOW LINED WITH AN IVORY **BLANKET** OF UNDISTURBED **SNOW** AND **ICE** AS THE STORM RAGED MORE **INTENSE** AND **FURIOUS** WITH EACH PASSING MOMENT.

THIS WINTER WOULD BE **HARSH** INDEED FOR THESE LONG-WEATHERED MOUNTAINS, BUT THEY WOULD **SURVIVE** AND VERDANT GREENS WOULD SPROUT ONCE AGAIN AFTER CALM HAD BEEN **RESTORED**.

YES, THE ALPS WOULD SURVIVE, THERE WAS NO **QUESTION** IF THEY WOULD-- BUT THE ONLY **PUZZLE** WHICH REMAINS IS-- WILL A VERY LOST **DRACULA** AND **RACHEL VAN HELSING** SURVIVE AS WELL?

AND AT THIS **MOMENT**, IT'S A QUESTION WHICH SEARCHES **DESPERATELY** FOR AN ANSWER.

SNOWBOUND IN HELL!

I CAN HARDLY **SEE**-- CAN'T WE **REST**..?

PLEASE, I'M ABOUT TO **COLLAPSE**.

WE MOVE ON, VAN HELSING, TO STAY **HERE** WOULD MEAN THE **DEATH** OF BOTH OF US.

THEN I **WON'T** GO ON ANY FURTHER. I DON'T CARE IF **I** DIE-- IF I TAKE **YOU** ALONG WITH ME.

YOU **WILL** MOVE, WOMAN-- YOU HAVE **NO** CHOICE.

WHAT..?

SLIPPED... I'M **FALLING!**

SO YOU MAY **WISH**, VAN HELSING-- BUT YOU SHALL **NOT** BE SO LUCKY TO FALL TO YOUR **DEATH**--

--**NOT** WHILE I NEED YOU MORE **ALIVE**.

FOR ALMOST **TWENTY YEARS** I HAVE SOUGHT TO **SLAY** YOU-- TO ADD YOUR NAME TO MY EVER-GROWING **LEGIONS**..

--AND NOW, **NOW** I MUST **PREVENT** YOUR DEATH-- **AT ALL COSTS!**

THUS, FOR THE **MOMENT** AT LEAST-- I MUST BE YOUR **SAVIOR**--

--AND **CURB** THE THIRST THAT GROWS EVER STRONGER ON MY **LIPS**.

SO **NOW**, MY LIFE-LONG **HUNTRESS** WE MOVE ON -- AND THOUGH IT **ACHE** US BOTH, WE **MUST** COOPERATE. OUR **SURVIVAL** DEPENDS ON IT.

N LONG THEY TREK AIMLESSLY THROUGH THE
DLESS BLIZZARD NO ONE CAN SAY--

--AND HOW MANY OPEN CAVES THEY BLUNDER BLINDLY PAST BEFORE THEY FIND THIS ONE, AGAIN ONLY A GOD OR A HELL-WROUGHT DEMON COULD KNOW...

I HAVE PREPARED A FIRE FOR YOU, VAN HELSING--REST BY IT QUIETLY, YOUR HURTS WILL SOON PASS.

L THE BROKEN MES HEAL THEMSELVES OO, DRACULA?

INJURIES YOUR FAULT, DEAR. I NDAGED EM AFTER CRASH--

--THE SPEED WITH WHICH THEY MEND THEMSELVES IS NO LONGER MY CONCERN.

I PROVIDE YOU WARMTH, COMFORT--AND SHORTLY--FOOD. WHAT ELSE COULD YOU WANT?

WHAT I'VE SOUGHT FOR ALL THESE YEARS, DRACULA-- YOUR FINAL AND EVER-LASTING DEATH.

I OWE YOU-- FOR THE COUNTLESS HORRORS YOU'VE COMMITTED AGAINST ME-- TO MY FAMILY-- TO THE WORLD!

AND EVEN IF I MUST FORFEIT MY OWN LIFE, I'LL SEE THE DAY THAT YOU'RE LONG DEAD AND BURIED.

RDLY, MY AR--YOU BARELY AND ON T FOOT, ALONE HT ME.

NO, I'D SAY FOR NOW, YOU WILL SIMPLY DO AS I COMMAND TO SAFEGUARD YOUR SELF AS LONG AS POSSIBLE.

I BELIEVE YOU MODERN HUMANS CALL THAT 'SELF-PRESERVATION'?

PARDON ME, PLEASE, WHILE I TEND TO IT.

AH, I SEE YOUR DINNER HAS FINALLY ARRIVED, MY DEAR.

THE WIND IS *TOO GREAT* FOR ME TO FLY AS THE *BAT,* YET I NEED NO TALONS AND *CLAWS* TO REND THAT BEAST HELPLESS.

REMAIN WHERE YOU ARE, GREAT *GOAT* -- TONIGHT YOU WILL FILL THE STOMACHS OF *TWO HUNGRY SOULS.*

THE GIANT *CAUCASIAN TUR* MERELY *MOOS* ITS WIDE-HORNED HEAD AND WAITS...

BUT IT *FAILS* -- FOR IT'S A *HUNGRY* DRACULA IT FACES -- A HUNGRY AND *DESPERATE* DRACULA INDEED.

...AS DEATH DESCENDS MADLY UPON IT.

AND *DESPERATE* MEN THROW CAUTION *AND* VIRTUES TO THE WIND.

*T*WIN FANGS SINK INTO THE GOAT'S HARDENED *NECK* AND BLOOD, THOUGH *FOUL* BY ALL HUMAN STANDARDS, IS DRAINED FROM THE DYING BEAST.

*T*HEN, AS TWO POWERFUL HANDS CLAMBER ABOUT IT *NECK,* THE TUR VAULTS IN THE HOARFROST SKY TO *SHA-- LOOSE* ITS UNDEAD ATTACKER...

THE TASTE IS BITTER AND *WRETCHED,* YET STILL I FEEL *STRENGTH* AGAIN FLOW THROUGH MY *BONES.*

BUT NEVER -- *NEVER* AGAIN DO I WANT TO FEED ON A BEAST NON- *HUMAN.*

...OTECT THE ...I HAVE EVER ...GHT TO *SLAY*-- ...ED UPON ...BLOOD OF ...*MPURE* ...ST--

--*YES*-- SINCE THE CRASH MUCH HAS BEEN *CHANGED*-- TOO MUCH.

AND ALL BECAUSE OF THAT *CREATURE* I BATTLED-- THE ONE CALLED *WEREWOLF.* *

WE FOUGHT FOR POSSESSION OF THE *BOOK*-- THOSE ANCIENT SCROLLS INSCRIB- ED WITH A *SPELL* TO UTTERLY DESTROY ALL VAMPIRES--

*LAST ISSUE AND WEREWOLF BY NIGHT #15. --ROY.

--INCLUDING *MYSELF.*

BUT AS WE *STRUGGLED*, RACHEL VAN HELSING GRASPED THE CRUMBLING PAGES AND MADE HER *ESCAPE.*

"HER *HELICOPTER* ROSE QUICKLY THROUGH THE *TRANSYLVANIAN* WINTER COUNTRYSIDE, AND IT WOULD HAVE *OUTDISTANCED* ME THEN HAD I *NOT* MADE A FINAL PAIN-WRACKING EFFORT--

I INSTANTLY KNEW THE *DANGERS* TO ME AND MY LEGIONS IF SHE COULD *TRANSLATE* THE SYMBOLS AND SPELLS--

"--AND SO I *FOLLOWED* HER--READY TO EXACT MY LONG-DELAYED *KILL* AT LAST.

"--AND CAUGHT ONTO THE MACHINE'S LOWER *RAILINGS.*

"NEEDLESS TO SAY, VAN HELSING COULD **NOT** BELIEVE HER EYES AS I THRUST MYSELF INTO THE CABIN."

DRACULA?
DON'T KNOW HOW YOU GOT IN HERE--BUT YOU'RE **NOT** STAYING.

IF THAT BOOK IS SO **IMPORTANT** TO YOU-- THERE'S **NO WAY** I'M GOING TO LET YOU GET IT!

WOMAN, YOU ARE EVEN **MORE** A FOOL THAN THAT CLODDISH DESCENDANT OF MINE YOU STAY WITH--

WHAT MAKES YOU BELIEVE YOU CAN KEEP **POSSESSION** OF **ANYTHING** I DESIRE?

BUT WE SHALL **DISCUSS** THE PAPERS IN A MOMENT--

--**AFTER** I RID US OF SOME **UNNEEDED BAGGAGE.**

WHAT ARE YO D-DOING--? ST. **AWAY** FROM M **STAY AWAY.**

MY **GOD**-- YOU KILLED HIM-- WITHOUT EVEN A MOMENT'S CARE--

FOR YEARS I THOUGHT YOU **MURDERED** BECAUSE OF YOUR NEED FOR **BLOOD**-- BUT IT'S **MORE** THAN THAT-- YOU'RE A **MONSTER**-- AN INHUMAN MONSTER.

THEN YOU'RE IN FOR A **RUDE** AWAKENING, DRACULA-- HE WAS THE **PILOT**-- AND I HAVEN'T THE SLIGHTEST NOTION ON HOW TO **FLY** THIS.

AN SOM THING TE ME NEITH DO **YO YOU** WE'RE **ALREA** MILES O COURS HEADING THE **TRAN** VANIAN **ALPS**

HIS LIFE IS **UNIMPORTANT** IN MY SCHEME OF THINGS, VAN HELSING --AND THEREFORE **UNNEEDED.**

AIIIEEEEEEE

I CAN SEE THAT, VAN HELSING--AS A YOUTH THERE WERE MANY **WINTERS** WHEN MY FAMILY TOOK ME HERE--

--TO ENJOY THE **EVER-SNOWING** PLAINS.

YES! ALREADY THERE IS SNOW AN ICE-- WE MUST **TUR BACK** BEFORE WE AR HOPELESSLY CAUGH IN ITS **RAGE.**

150

AND HOW ARE WE GOING TO *ACCOMPLISH* THAT, DRACULA? I TOLD YOU I'M *NOT* A PILOT!

THEN WE SHALL SIMPLY *CRASH*--

--AND THOUGH *I* SHALL SURVIVE, MY DEAR-- I DOUBT IF *YOU* WILL.

CURSES! I CAN BARELY *SEE* THROUGH THE STORM-- BUT I STILL *KNOW* WHAT LIES DIRECTLY BEFORE US--

BRACE YOURSELF, WOMAN, AND WE SHALL SEE IF THE *FATES* ARE KIND TO YOU THIS NIGHT.

...HAD FOUGHT WITH *MAN* ...BEAST FOR ALMOST ...O YEARS, BUT *ALWAYS* ...ORE I WAS FREE TO ...TLE-- TO *ATTACK*--

--BUT NOW I WAS *SLAVE*-- A ...ELPLESS *VICTIM*, ...AS THE GIANT ...ELICOPTER ...MASHED ...NTO A GREAT ...HITE PEAK ...HICH SUDDENLY ...UTTED ...EFORE IT.

...AND THOUGH ...C WAS NEARLY ...IMMORTAL, EVEN *I* ...EARED SOMEWHAT THE ...ONSEQUENCES OF ...HE COLLISION.

KREEEAMMM!

...OUGH IT WAS A NEEDLESS *FEAR*, FOR...

I *LIVE*-- AS ALWAYS BEFORE, I *SURVIVE* WHERE OTHERS PERISH.

BUT--

--THE *BOOK*-- THE CAUSE OF ALL THIS *MADNESS*...

YES, THE SPELLS ARE HERE-- BUT IT LITTLE *MATTERS* NOW IN THIS DESOLATE *WILDERNESS*...

ODD HOW THINGS THAT ONCE WERE *IMPORTANT* SUDDENLY CAN LOSE THEIR *VITALNESS*.

WE ARE SO FAR FROM *CIVILIZATION* HERE THAT NONE SHALL EVER FIND THIS.

AH, VAN HELSING *AWAKENS.* GOOD-- I WAS WONDERING WHEN THE *PAIN* WOULD SUBSIDE. I KNEW YOU TO BE ONLY *UN-CONSCIOUS.*

MY *LEG--* I CAN'T MOVE-- I THINK IT'S BROKEN.

THAT WILL NOT DO ON THE LONG *JOURNEY* BEFORE US. YOU'LL NEED A *BANDAGE.*

NO-- LEAVE IT ALONE! YOU'RE *HURTING* IT.

SILENCE, WOMAN-- UNTIL THIS HEALS YOU'LL HAVE TO LIVE WITH PAIN--

--WHICH MAY KEEP YOUR MIND OFF *ATTACKING* ME FOR AWHILE.

NOW COME WITH ME. IF WE ARE TO REACH *OTHER HUMANS,* WE MUST BEGIN.

FOR I KNOW THESE MOUNTAINS WELL, AND IT IS AT LEAST A *FOUR*-NIGHT JOURNEY TO EVEN THE SMALLEST OF VILLAGES.

WHY ARE YOU *DOING* THIS FOR ME? WHY DIDN'T YOU JUST TAKE MY *BLOOD* AND BE DONE WITH IT?

YOU'VE WANTED ME *DEAD* FOR YEARS.

I STILL DO, MY DEAR-- BUT *COMMON SENSE* TELLS ME NOT TO GIVE IN TO MY LUSTS--

--IF I WERE TO TAKE YOUR BLOOD NOW, I MAY NOT *FIND* ANY FOR DAYS--

--THUS, MY DEAR-- *YOU* ARE BEING KEPT ALIVE AS AN *EMERGENCY* MEASURE--

--TO BE READY TO *DIE* WHEN THERE IS NO OTHER *COURSE.*

TH... ON THAT DEAR V HELSING YOU SH... SEE TH *FUTILI...* OF YO SITUATI...

HA

HA

HA

HA

IF YOU'RE THINKING OF *FATTENING* ME UP FOR THE FINAL *SLAUGHTER,* DRACULA, YOU'VE GOT A LOT TO *LEARN*--

OYING UR AL, ELSING? O! I H YOU D BE LTHY EN I NEED YOU.

--I DON'T DIE EASY, VAMPIRE-- BELIEVE ME, *I DON'T DIE EASY.*

LITTLE MATTER, VAN HELSING. IF THERE'S A *STRUGGLE,* I WILL EVENTUALLY WIN. IN THE LONG VIEW, I HAVE *ALWAYS WON MY BATTLES.*

MAYBE NOT *THIS TIME,* DRACULA, THE SUN WILL BE UP SOON, AND WHEN YOU GO TO SLEEP, NOT EVEN MY *BROKEN LEG* WILL STOP ME FROM SLAYING YOU.

AND IF I *CAN'T* SLAY YOU, THEN I'LL KILL MYSELF-- IN SUCH A WAY YOU'LL GET *NO BLOOD* FROM ME.

YOU MUST TAKE ME FOR A *RAVING LUNATIC,* MY DEAR. YOU KNOW AS I DO THAT YOU'LL *NEVER* KILL YOURSELF--

--NOT UNTIL THE *FINAL* MOMENT YOU ARE POSITIVE YOUR DEATH WOULD CAUSE MY OWN.

AFTER ALL, *'DOCTOR'* VAN HELSING-- YOU'D WANT TO MAKE *ABSOLUTELY SURE* THAT I COULD NOT FIND MY OWN BLOOD SUPPLY.

DO NOT TRY *LYING* TO A *MASTER LIAR,* WOMAN. IT WILL DO YOU *NO GOOD.*

CHEL VAN HELSING *SMILES* NSWER TO DRACULA. SHE 'READ' THE VAMPIRE ..., AND *PREDICTED* HIS ARKS...

HICH NOW GIVES HER E TO PLAN HER *REAL* COURSE OF ACTION.

AND GIVES *US* TIME TO SWITCH OUR FOCUSES *ELSEWHERE*-- TO THE NOTHERN IRISH COASTLINE, AND A DARK FORBODING *PAGODA...*

VAMPIRE BRAND, YOU HAVE *PASSED* ALL THE TESTS GIVEN TO YOU BY *DOCTOR SUN*--

--NOW ONLY THE *FINAL ONE REMAINS.*

DOCTOR SUN DEMANDS YOU FLY *THROUGH* THE BURNING HOOPS, A TASK *NOT* AS EASY AS IT *SEEMS*, VAMPIRE--

--FOR THE *HOOPS* ARE LINED WITH *GARLIC*, AND SHOULD YOUR FLIGHT NOT BE *PERFECT* AND YOU MERELY *TOUCH* THE HOOP'S SIDE--

--YOU WILL BE *INSTANTLY DESTROYED.*

BEGIN NOW, VAMPIRE, YOU HAVE BUT *THREE SECONDS* TO COMPLETE THE FINAL TEST.

--I SHA OBEY DOCTO SUN

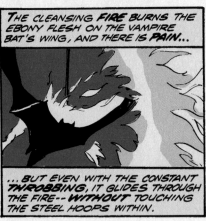

THE CLEANSING *FIRE* BURNS THE EBONY FLESH ON THE VAMPIRE BAT'S WING, AND THERE IS *PAIN*...

...BUT EVEN WITH THE CONSTANT *THROBBING*, IT GLIDES THROUGH THE FIRE-- *WITHOUT* TOUCHING THE STEEL HOOPS WITHIN.

DOCTOR SUN, THIS TIME WE HAVE PICKED *WELL.* VAMPIRE *BRAND* IS THE ONE YOU'VE *LONG* SEARCHED FOR.

YOU HAVE DONE WELL, MISTER LO. DOCTOR SUN *COMMENDS* YOU.

LET US NOW *SWITCH* OUR SCENES ONCE MORE-- THIS TIME, *BACK* TO THE *SNOWSTORM*-COVERED TRANSYLVANIAN ALPS OF ROMANIA...

STRUGGLING IS *USELESS*, VAN HELSING --WE HAVE ONLY ONE HOUR MORE TO TRAVEL BEFORE THE SUN *RISES*--

--AND I *AIM* TO HAVE TRAVELED FAR IN THAT TIME.

THEN I'LL TRY *ANYTHING* TO DELAY THAT TRIP, DRACULA.

WHAT--?

154

[RA]CHEL VAN HELSING *FLINGS* [HER]SELF FROM THE SNOW-[BOUND] PEAK, AND FALLS... [DRAG]ING A SUDDENLY *OFF-*[BAL]*ANCE* DRACULA DOWN WITH [HER]...

WITCH! [BE]CAUSE OF YOU WE [MI]GHT *BOTH* [BE] DOOMED.

[R]ACHEL DOESN'T ANSWER, [INSTE]AD, DRACULA IS *STARTLED* TO [HEAR] A HIGH PITCHED AND MOCKING [LAU]GH ECHO 'TWEEN THE JUTTING [PEAKS] OF THE TRANSYLVANIAN ALPS...

DOWN THEY CONTINUE TO *PLUNGE,* UNTIL THEY COME TO A SUDDEN AND DEADLY *HALT*--

--AS THE ROPE SNAPS *TAUT* ABOUT THE ROCK WHICH RACHEL TIED IT TO MOMENTS BEFORE--

THUNK

IS THIS *ANOTHER* LIE FROM THE PRINCE OF LIARS, DRACULA?

NO--I THINK YOU'LL *KEEP* ME ALIVE AND RISK MORE TROUBLES THAN HAVE ME *DEAD* AND PERHAPS KILL *YOURSELF* AS WELL.

REALLY, MY DEAR? I DOUBT THAT. YOU SEE, EVEN IF I AM DEAD, ONE OF MY *LEGIONS* WILL FIND ME-- AND *RESUR-RECT* ME.

--ASSURING HERSELF A *DELAY* IN THEIR TRAVELS-- BUT *NOT* A DEADLY ONE.

LAUGH IF YOU WISH, WOMAN-- BUT YOU'RE TRYING MY *PATIENCE* TOO FAR--

I MAY *YET* TASTE YOUR *BLOOD* AND TAKE MY CHANCES ALONE.

HA! HA! HA! *FRUSTRATED,* DEAR VAN HELSING? I KNEW YOU WOULD BE.

HUMANS ALWAYS FIND IT *IMPOSSIBLE* TO ACCEPT A BEING WHO CAN LIVE *FOREVER.*

IMMORTALITY *FRIGHTENS* THOSE WHO FAIL TO UNDERSTAND IT COMPLETELY-- THEY BELIEVE THERE IS *BORE-DOM, TEDIUM*-- BUT THEY FAIL TO SEE ITS *STRENGTHS*...

PERHAPS YOU SHOULD *LEARN* WHAT IT MEANS TO TASTE *ETERNITY* ON YOUR LIPS.

PERHAPS YOU SHOULD *KNOW* WHAT IT'S LIKE TO LIVE THROUGH THE AGES-- NEVER GROWING OLDER-- NEVER FEARING *AGE*.

WOULD YOU LIKE THAT, VAN HELSIN *WOULD YOU LIKE THAT?*

WELL, WORRY NOT THIS NIGHT, MY DEAR-- YOU'LL NOT BECOME A *VAMPIRE* UNTIL I CAN RESIST THE *BLOODLUST* NO MORE--

NOW, INTO THIS *CAVE*-- WE WILL SPEND THE *MORNING HOURS* HERE.

THERE SHALL BE *ANOTHER* LONG NIGHT TOMORROW, VAN HELSING-- SO PLOT NOT TO SLAY ME-- AND *REST* INSTEAD.

YOU WILL NEED YOUR SLEEP.

HER BODY ACHING WITH PAIN, RACHEL VAN HELSING CLOSES HER EYES -- BUT NOT TO *SLEEP.* SHE STILL HAS A *MISSION* TO PERFORM THIS MORNING -- AND SHE WILL NOT REST UNTIL THE DEED IS *DONE.*

AND SO, SHE VOWS, DRACULA WILL *DIE,* AND HIS AS WILL BE SCATTERED AS A SACRIFICE TO THE RAGING WINDS O

...S RACHEL VAN HELSING PREPARES
...O *SLAY* ONE VAMPIRE, HALF-WAY
...ROUND THE WORLD, IN AN UNDER-
...ROUND PARISIAN *CATACOMB,*
...UINCY HARKER SETS TO DESTROY A
...ECOND...

...A VAMPIRE NOT FULLY *BORN*--A VAMPIRE WHO WAS ONCE *BLADE,* THE VAMPIRE *SLAYER.*

...AM *SORRY*
...OR WHAT I
...UST DO, BLADE--
...T *YOU* WOULD
... THE FIRST TO
...IST ON IT--

...ACULA'S *FANGS*
...NTAMINATED YOU--
...D NOW I MUST
...D THE PLAGUE
...FORE YOU AWAKEN.*

* SEE ISSUES #17 & 18.--ROY.

THERE IS A *HEART-BEAT* BETWEEN THOSE FINAL SORROW-FILLED WORDS AND *ACTION* AS THE STAKE IS THRUST DOWN TOWARD THE RECENTLY-BITTEN BLADE--

--BUT AN *INSTANT* IS ALL IT TAKES FOR THE '*DEAD*' TO COME TO LIFE.

HOLD IT, HARKER-- I'M NOT READY TO BE MADE '*HOLY*' YET.

WHAT--?

GOD-- I STILL FEEL THE *MARKS* ON MY NECK-- THE DRIED *BLOOD* AROUND THEM. BUT I HAVEN'T CHANGED-- I HAVEN'T BECOME A *VAMPIRE.*

HOW? FOR GOD'S SAKE-- TELL ME WHY I HAVEN'T CHANGED.

IT SEEMS MOST *IMPOSSIBLE*-- YET, THE PRINCIPLE WORKS ON NORMAL HUMAN *DISEASES*--

I'M NOT SURE, BLADE-- BUT I BELIEVE YOU'RE *IMMUNE* TO VAMPIRE BITES-- TOTALLY AND COMPLETELY *IMMUNE.*

YOU MEAN BECAUSE MY *MOTHER* WAS KILLED BY A VAMPIRE WHILE SHE WAS IN *LABOR*-- WHILE I WAS BEING *BORN?*

SO THAT MEANS THERE'S SOME VAMPIRE BLOOD IN *ME*-- NOT ENOUGH TO *CHANGE* ME-- BUT JUST ENOUGH TO GIVE ME *IMMUNITY.*

OKAY, HARKER-- I DON'T GIVE A FLYING *HOOT* IF THAT'S THE REASON I'M LIVIN' OR NOT--

--BUT IF I'M *IMMUNE* THEN *NOTHIN'S* GONNA STOP ME NOW, BAB-

--NOTHIN'!

158

LAST BURNING
ERS OF THE FIRE
COLD NOW,
LED AND
NGUISHED
HE CONSTANT
LING
S...

AND ALL THE WHILE THROUGH THESE DAYLIGHT HOURS, DRACULA *SLEEPS*, HIS STRENGTH RETURNING TO HIS WEARY *BONES...*

BUT RACHEL VAN HELSING STILL *WAITS*... WAITS FOR THE MOMENT--

HE WILL FINALLY *SLAY*
DREADED *LORD OF*
PIRES.

, AT LONG LAST, THAT
OMENT IS *NOW.*

SILENTLY SHE RISES, STIFLING THE ACHING *PAIN* SHE FEELS GROW IN HER LEG--

--AND HOLDING THE *STAKE* SHE HAS KEPT *HIDDEN* IN HER PARKA SINCE *BEFORE* SHE BEGAN THIS ILL-FATED JOURNEY, SHE TREADS SOFTLY TOWARDS THE SLEEPING FIGURE.

OESN'T
F--THERE
S TO BE
WARE-
S, AND SO
STAKE IS
D
H--

--AND, WITH A *BITTER* SMILE ON HER LIPS, SHE THRUSTS *DOWN*!

--AND
MISSES!

YOU *FOOLISH FEMALE*-- I WAS *WAITING* FOR THAT MOMENT.

DID YOU TRULY *BELIEVE* YOU COULD TAKE *DRACULA* UNAWARES?

OHHHHHHH!

NOW THERE SHALL BE NO REST FOR YOU, VAN HELSING-- AND EXPECT NO *PITY* ON MY PART FOR YOUR DISCOMFITURE.

I EXPEC *NOTHING* YOU, DRAC EXCEPT TO YOU WHE CAN.

STILL YOU PERSIST, MY DEAR? YOU WASTE YOUR TIME ON *FANTASIES,* THEN.

I HAVE LIVED ALMOST *15 TIMES* YOUR AGE-- AND I SHALL LIVE LONG AFTER YOUR BEAUTIFUL FEATURES HAVE *DECAYED* INTO ASH.

NOW *MOVE,* OR BE *DRAGGED* THROUGH THE SNOW AND ICE.

--UNTIL IT IS *TOO LA* THAT IS.

WHA

PERHAPS ITS *FATIGUE,* *BLOODTHIRST*--BUT DRACULA DOES NOT *SENSE* THE HULKING FORM WHICH FOLLOWS HIS *PATH*--

--NOR DOES HE *MOVE* AS THE FIGURE *LEAPS* THROUGH THE AIR AT HIM.

GREAT BEAST ATTACKS, AND [L]IKE ITS BROTHER *TUR* WHICH [DRA]CULA HAD EARLIER FELLED, [THIS] ONE FIGHTS ON.

[...] LORD OF VAMPIRES HAS [GONE] TOO LONG WITHOUT **BLOOD**-- [TOO] LONG WITHOUT THE [STR]**ENGTH** IT GIVES, AND THE [BEA]**ST** SENSES THE WEAKNESS IN ITS PREY.

THE **GOAT** IS ALSO HUNGRY, BUT ITS HUNGER GIVES IT **MADNESS** AND **STRENGTH**-- AND SO IT IS DRACULA WHO FALLS TO THE SNOW-COVERED **MOUNTAINS**...

AND IT IS DRACULA WHO SCREAMS AS SALIVATING **TEETH** DIG THROUGH HIS FLESH.

RACHEL VAN HELSING TREMBLES AT THE SIGHT OF THE TWO **THRASHING** FORMS, ALMOST **UNSURE** OF WHAT TO DO...

AND THOUGH SHE **FIGHTS** THE URGE, HER HAND ALMOST **INVOLUNTAR-ILY** REACHES FOR HER **GUN**...

[AND SHE] [F]IRES!

[THE]RE IS A SUDDEN [AND] HORRIFYING YELL...

--AND THE GREAT WHITE **TUR** FALLS BACK--

--DEAD!

I-I **HAD** TO KILL IT, I DIDN'T WANT TO, YET I H-HAD TO.

OH GOD, I SO **DES-PERATELY** WANTED IT TO KILL YOU --BUT I COULDN'T LET IT--I JUST COULDN'T.

OF COURSE, MY DEAR-- YOU HAD NO **OTHER** CHOICE.

THEY'RE **SOMEWHERE** DOWN THERE, PILOT. KEEP **FLYING,** I'M SURE THEY CAN'T HAVE GONE FAR.

AND THE **TRACKS** I SPOTTED COMING FROM THEIR **WRECKAGE** PROVES THEY'RE BOTH STILL **WALKING.**

I DON'T KNOW HOW MUCH **LONGER** WE CAN GO, MR. DRAKE--THE WIND'S ACTING UP PRETTY **BAD.**

YOU'LL KEEP THIS CRATE FLYING UNTIL I'VE FOUND THEM.

I'M NOT ABANDONING RACHEL--NOT WHILE SHE'S WITH THAT **MANIAC.**

WAIT-- THEY DOWN THERE--RACHEL'S WAL ON HER **OW**

OKAY, PILOT-- **LOWER AWAY.**

THAT HELICOPTER--?

FRANK--?

IF YOU **FOLLOWED** ME ALL THE WAY HERE, FRANK--LEAST I CAN DO IS MAKE IT **EASY** FOR YOU TO PICK ME UP.

COME BACK HERE, WOMAN I'M NOT **DON** WITH YOU YET.

THE TIME HAS FINALLY COME FOR ME TO TASTE YOUR **BLOOD.**

DRAKE WILL NOT **HELP** YOU, WOMAN--AS SOON AS **HE** LANDS, HE'LL BE DEAD AS WELL.

NOW, MY DEAR-- YOU SHALL FINALLY LEARN THE **ECSTASY** OF **VAMPIRISM.**

NO-- YOU'LL NEVER HAVE ME, DRACULA-- **NEVER!!**

WE HAVE *CHASED* EACH OTHER FOR A LONG TIME, AND THOUGH THE FINAL *OUTCOME* WAS ALWAYS KNOWN TO ME--

I STILL SHALL DERIVE GREAT *PLEASURE* FROM THIS MOMENT.

SPUTTA SPUTTA SPUTTA

BUT--*NO!* THEY'RE FIRING *WOODEN BULLETS* AT ME--

CAN'T LET THEM GET ME-- CAN'T LET THEM *DESTROY* ME HERE.

YOU WANTED THAT SPINELESS *MILKSOP,* VAN HELSING-- NOW SEE IF HE WANTS *YOU*--

--OR IF HE'LL ABANDON YOU TO STILL HUNT *ME.*

THEY'RE SPLITTING UP, MR. DRAKE. SHOULD WE LAND OR GO AFTER THE *MAN?*

RACHEL WOULD WANT ME TO LEAVE HER--TO CHASE DRACULA AND TO FINALLY KILL HIM...

...BUT, GOD HELP ME, I CAN'T LET HER *DIE* OUT HERE OF *EXPOSURE.*

LAND THE 'COPTER, PILOT. THERE WILL BE OTHER TIMES FOR *HUNTING.*

EW MOMENTS LATER AND...

RANK--YOU'VE T-TO F-FIND --K-KILL IM...

CALM DOWN, HONEY-- AFTER YOU'VE WARMED UP A BIT WE'LL DISCUSS IT.

BUT NOW, PILOT-- HEAD BACK TO *TRANSYLVANIA*-- BOTH OF US NEED A REST.

NEXT: A *HELICOPTER CHASE* DOWN THE TRANSYLVANIAN *ALPS*-- WITH DRACULA AS THE LIVING *TARGET.* AND: THE UNVEILING OF *DOCTOR SUN!* *DON'T MISS IT.*

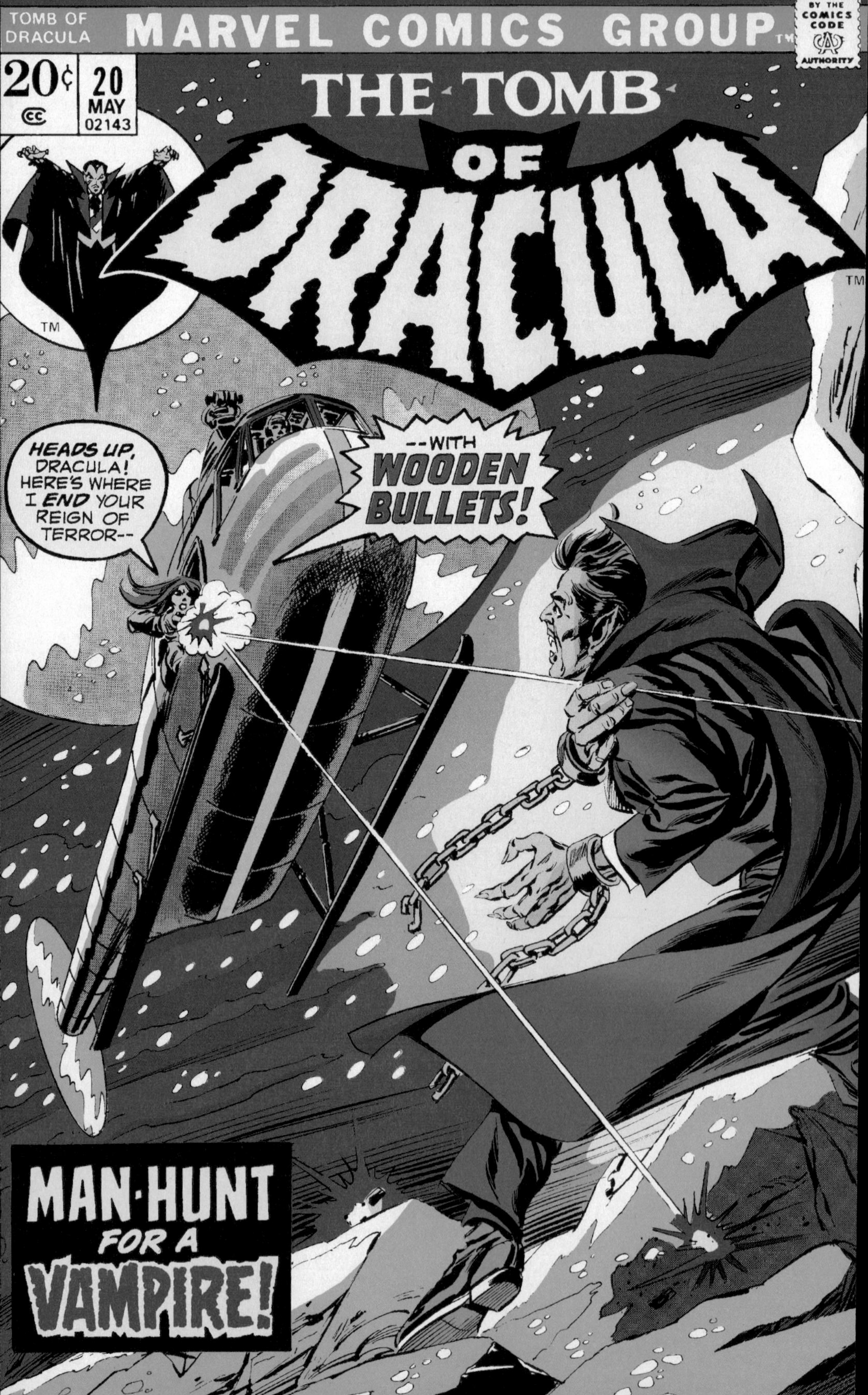
TOMB OF DRACULA
MARVEL COMICS GROUP
APPROVED BY THE COMICS CODE AUTHORITY
20¢ 20 MAY 02143
THE TOMB OF DRACULA
HEADS UP, DRACULA! HERE'S WHERE I END YOUR REIGN OF TERROR--
--WITH WOODEN BULLETS!
MAN-HUNT FOR A VAMPIRE!

V WOLFMAN / GENE COLAN / TOM PALMER / JOHN COSTANZA, letterer / ROY THOMAS
WRITER   ARTIST   INKER   GLYNIS WEIN, colorist   EDITOR

The Coming of Doctor Sun

HE'S DOWN THERE, RACHEL -- RIGHT IN OUR SIGHTS.

AND IF WE PLAY OUR CARDS RIGHT -- THIS IS THE NIGHT DRACULA WILL DIE!

WOODEN BULLETS PIERCE THE STORM-COVERED TRANSYL-VANIAN ALPS THIS BITTER-COLD NIGHT, AS DRACULA, LORD OF DARK-NESS--PRINCE OF EVIL, FINDS HIMSELF THE HUNTED PREY INSTEAD OF THE STALKING HUNTER.

AND, IT APPEARS IN THIS FRIGID HOARFROST, THAT FIVE HUNDRED YEARS OF A TWISTED, HATEFILLED UNLIFE, IS ABOUT TO END FOREVER!

165

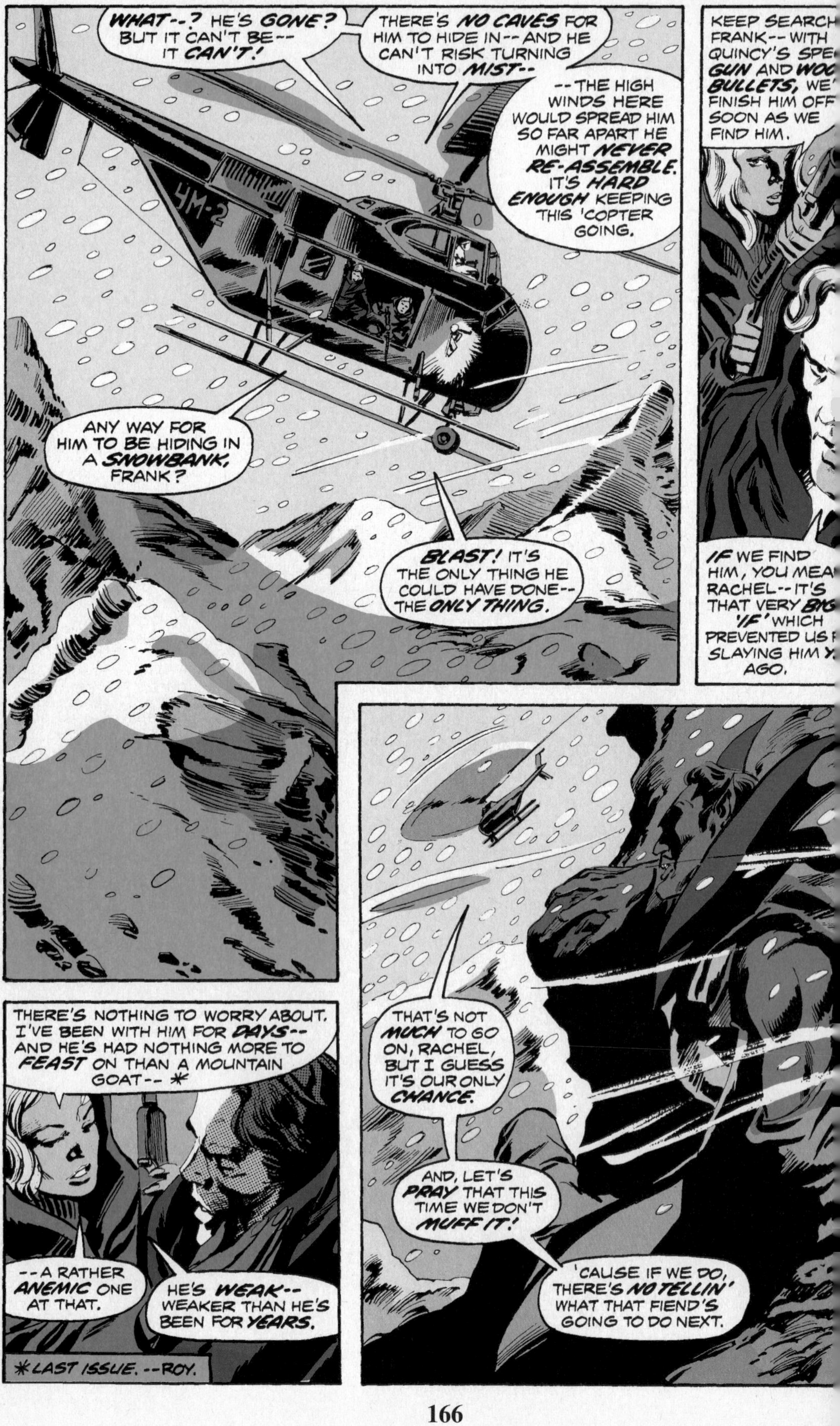

WHAT--? HE'S GONE? BUT IT CAN'T BE-- IT CAN'T!
THERE'S NO CAVES FOR HIM TO HIDE IN--AND HE CAN'T RISK TURNING INTO MIST--
--THE HIGH WINDS HERE WOULD SPREAD HIM SO FAR APART HE MIGHT NEVER RE-ASSEMBLE. IT'S HARD ENOUGH KEEPING THIS 'COPTER GOING.
ANY WAY FOR HIM TO BE HIDING IN A SNOWBANK, FRANK?
BLAST! IT'S THE ONLY THING HE COULD HAVE DONE-- THE ONLY THING.
IF WE FIND HIM, YOU MEA RACHEL--IT'S THAT VERY BIG 'IF' WHICH PREVENTED US SLAYING HIM AGO.
THERE'S NOTHING TO WORRY ABOUT. I'VE BEEN WITH HIM FOR DAYS-- AND HE'S HAD NOTHING MORE TO FEAST ON THAN A MOUNTAIN GOAT-- *
--A RATHER ANEMIC ONE AT THAT.
HE'S WEAK-- WEAKER THAN HE'S BEEN FOR YEARS.
*LAST ISSUE. --ROY.
THAT'S NOT MUCH TO GO ON, RACHEL, BUT I GUESS IT'S OUR ONLY CHANCE.
AND, LET'S PRAY THAT THIS TIME WE DON'T MUFF IT!
'CAUSE IF WE DO, THERE'S NO TELLIN' WHAT THAT FIEND'S GOING TO DO NEXT.

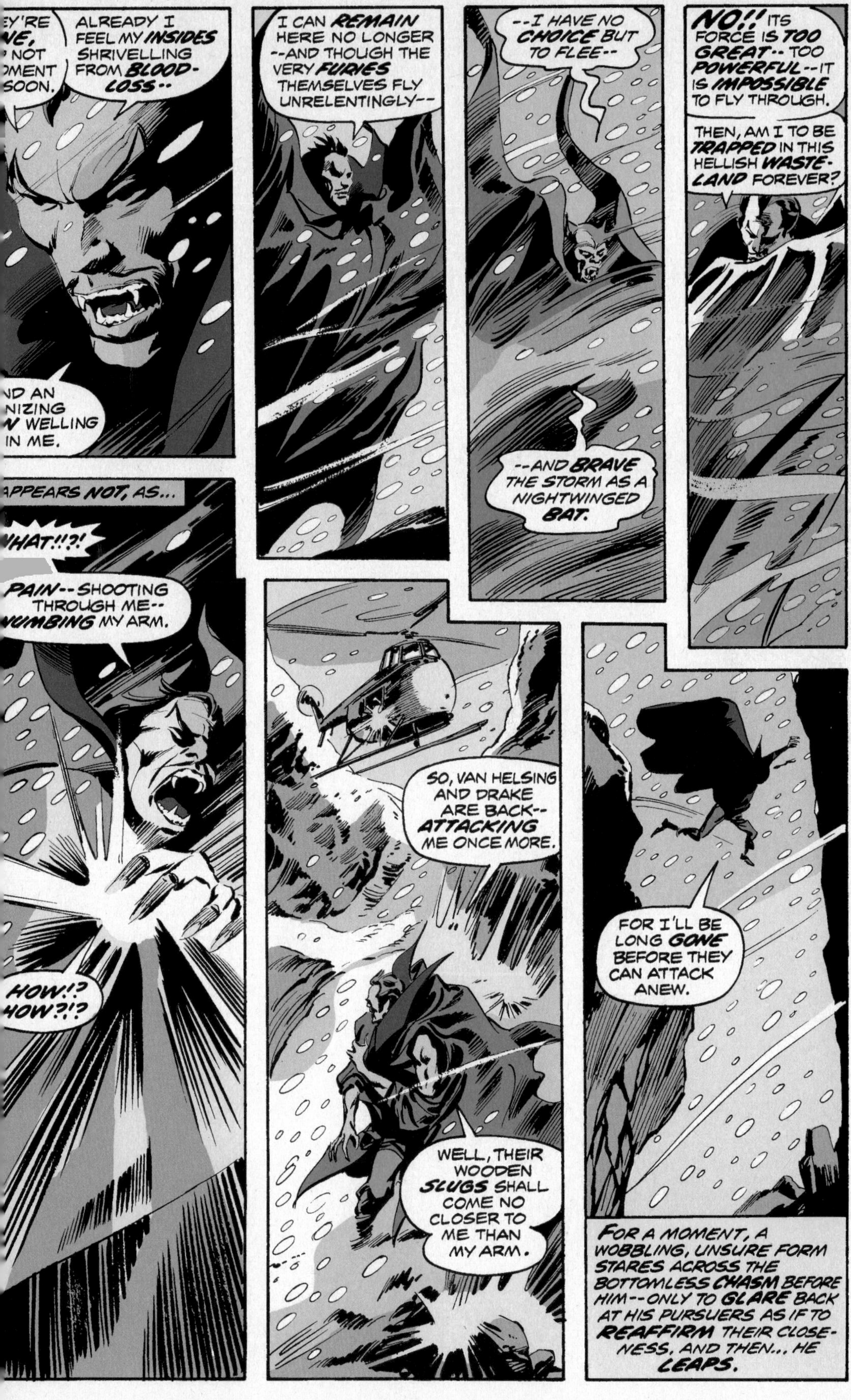
EY'RE NE. NOT MOMENT SOON.
ALREADY I FEEL MY INSIDES SHRIVELLING FROM BLOOD-LOSS--
ND AN NIZING N WELLING IN ME.
I CAN REMAIN HERE NO LONGER --AND THOUGH THE VERY FURIES THEMSELVES FLY UNRELENTINGLY--
--I HAVE NO CHOICE BUT TO FLEE--
--AND BRAVE THE STORM AS A NIGHTWINGED BAT.
NO!! ITS FORCE IS TOO GREAT--TOO POWERFUL--IT IS IMPOSSIBLE TO FLY THROUGH.
THEN, AM I TO BE TRAPPED IN THIS HELLISH WASTE-LAND FOREVER?
APPEARS NOT, AS...
WHAT!!?!
PAIN--SHOOTING THROUGH ME--NUMBING MY ARM.
HOW!? HOW?!?
SO, VAN HELSING AND DRAKE ARE BACK--ATTACKING ME ONCE MORE.
WELL, THEIR WOODEN SLUGS SHALL COME NO CLOSER TO ME THAN MY ARM.
FOR I'LL BE LONG GONE BEFORE THEY CAN ATTACK ANEW.
FOR A MOMENT, A WOBBLING, UNSURE FORM STARES ACROSS THE BOTTOMLESS CHASM BEFORE HIM--ONLY TO GLARE BACK AT HIS PURSUERS AS IF TO REAFFIRM THEIR CLOSE-NESS, AND THEN... HE LEAPS.

AND MISSES!

THE BLACK-CLOAKED BODY **STUMBLES** AND **GASHES** ITSELF AGAINST THE OUT-JUTTING STUBS OF ROCK AND STONE MOUNTAINSIDE...

BUT THIS IS NO **ORDINARY** MORTAL WHO TUMBLES HEAD OVER HEELS TOWARDS HIS APPARENTLY **UNPREVENTABLE** DESTRUCTION--

DAMNED ONES -- YOU WHO ARE BUT MINDLESS **INFANTS** COMPARED TO ME-- **HOW DARE YOU ATTACK YOUR MASTER? HOW DARE YOU?!?**

FOR A MOMENT IT **SWAYS** IN THE EMPTY EXPANSE OF FRIGID AIR-- AND THEN **DROPS**--

--HURLING **DOWNWARDS** FASTER, EVER **FASTER**, TOWARDS A VIRGIN-WHITE GRAVE BELOW.

NO, THIS IS **DRACULA**-- HE HAS LIVED FOR ALMOST **HALF** AN ETERNITY--

--AND HE SHALL **NOT** GIVE INTO **DEATH** SO EASILY.

BUT THERE IS NO ANSWE~~R~~ NO **REPLY**-- ONLY THE STEADY **GUSHING** OF WI~~ND~~ AND SNOW AND THE CONS~~TANT~~ STACCATO **BEATING** OF FADING HELICOPTER BLA~~DES~~

DRACULA'S ARM **PULSES** AND **THROBS** WITH LANCING PAIN, BUT STILL THE **LORD OF VAMPIRES** TRUDGES ON, STALKING EVER ONWARDS THROUGH THE ALMOST **BLINDING** STORM.

HIS MIND IS **ACTIVE**, PROBING CAREFULLY ITS DEEPEST RECESSES: HE FOLLOWED RACHEL VAN HELSING TO THESE MOUNTAINTOPS-- FIRST TO **RETRIEVE** A MYSTIC BOOK WHOSE SPELLS COULD UTTERLY **DESTROY** DRACULA--

BUT THE GIRL WA~~S~~ **SAVED** -- RESCUE~~D~~ BY FRANK DRAKE, DRACULA'S HAPLE~~SS~~ **DESCENDANT**-- WHILE DRACULA H~~IM~~ SELF WAS STILL A VICTIM OF THE CHU~~RN~~ ING ICE AND SNO~~W~~

--AND SECONDLY, TO **SLAY** HER. BUT INSTEAD, THEY FOUND THEMSELVES **BOTH** A CAPTIVE TO NATURE'S CRUEL **ELEMENTS**-- AND THEY WERE FORCED TO WORK AS **ONE** TO MOVE ON TO SAFETY.

ALONE, AS HE HAS FACED *FIVE HUNDRED YEARS OF LIFE*, DRACULA MOVES ON...

...EVER ONWARD... AND EVER ALONE.

I COULD *WANDER* HOPELESSLY IN THESE MOUNTAINS FOR *YEARS*-- NAY, *CENTURIES*--IF I HAD *BLOOD* ENOUGH.

BUT THERE IS *NONE.*

YET, TO *SURRENDER* IS NOT THE WAY OF A DRACULA. *NO*--! DRACULA FIGHTS ON-- AND IF HE MUST *PERISH*, IT SHALL BE A DEATH OF *VALOR*, AND NOT OF *COWARDICE.*

WAIT--! THESE *BRANCHES* WERE RECENTLY USED FOR *FIRE.* PERHAPS--

--YES! I SENSE HUMAN *FLESH*-- STILL WARM... AND YET...

BUT I SHALL *SEE* IF WHAT I SENSE IS *TRUE*-- OR MERELY THE *BLOOD-CRAZED DELUSIONS* OF THE LORD OF VAMPIRES.

WITHIN THAT ALMOST *HIDDEN* CAVE I SHOULD FIND THE *SOLUTION* TO MY PROBLEMS...

...OR THE FINAL *NAIL* TO SEAL MY COFFIN FOREVER.

169

THERE IS A MOMENT OF *SILENCE*... A MOMENT WHEN EVEN THE ANGUISHED *HOWLINGS* OF THE OUTSIDE WIND FADE FROM THE EAR...

THERE IS *SOMEONE*... *SOMETHING* IN THE CAVE, AND IT *SITS* IN A SHROUD OF SILENCE.

DRACULA REACHES OUT TOWARDS THE DARK-SHADOWED *SHAPE*...

...AND IT *FALLS*...

...*DEAD!* A HUMAN-- AND ONE *RECENTLY* DECEASED.

HE MUST HAVE BEEN *DYING*-- FREEZING TO *DEATH* ONLY TO *DRAGGED* HIMSELF IN HERE.

A *PITY* HE DID NOT LIVE LONG ENOUGH FOR *M* TO FIND HIM.

SO, AGAIN I AM *ROBBED* OF THE PRECIOUS *BLOOD* I REQUIRE--

--AND EVER *CLOSER* DO I COME TO THE MOMENT MY BODY *CONVULSES* AND THEN FINALLY *DIES*.

NO! I WILL NOT PERMIT IT-- I WILL NOT PERISH SO *IGNOBLY--!*

AND THOUGH MY ONLY *SALVATION* IS ONE WHICH STINKS OF A THOUSAND HELL-BORN *HORRORS*... SO BE IT.

I DO WHAT I *MUST*. THERE IS *NO OTHER* WAY.

DRACULA BENDS LOW TO *DEAD* MAN'S NECK, AND SHARP-POINTED *FANGS* PIERCE THE ALREADY *ROTTING* FLESH.

AT FIRST, NO *BLOOD* RIS. TO FILL THE DEEP PUNCTU. BUT, AFTER ONE LONG AGONIZING MINUTE, THE LI RED LIQUID *SWELLS* INT THE VAMPIRE'S THROAT.

CHHHHH!

HIS BLOOD IS FOUL... *STAGNANT!* ITS TASTE IS *BITTER*-- AS IF IT'S BEEN *POISONED.*

BUT BY *WHOM*... AND FOR WHAT *REASON?*

SOON, AFTER FURTHER EXPLORATION OF THE CAVE'S *INTERIOR...*

ANOTHER BODY... AND PERHAPS THE *EXPLANATION.* THIS CAVERN IS FILLED WITH *GOLD,* DIAMONDS-- *UNTOLD TREASURES... UNLIMITED WEALTH...*

...BROUGHT HERE, NO DOUBT, *CENTURIES* PAST, WHEN THE *TURKS* SACKED MY HOMELAND,

THESE TWO MUST HAVE *SEARCHED* FOR THE FORTUNES, AND THEN *TURNED* ON EACH OTHER THROUGH *GREED.*

BUT WHAT *NEED* HAVE I OF *GOLD* OR DIAMOND OR EMERALD--

HEN MY BODY EHYDRATES OM BLOODLOSS?

ALL OF THIS WORTHLESS *CLUTTER*-- *BEGONE WITH YOU!* I'VE NO NEED FOR YOU TO *MOCK* ME WITH YOUR PRESENCE.

IN A MADDENED RAGE, DRACULA SMASHES THE VALUED TREASURES...

...UNTIL HIS BLOODLOSS TAKES ITS TERRIBLE TOLL.

WHILE... THIS IS OUR *THIRD* RUNAROUND, RACHEL, AND DRAC'S *NOWHERE* TO BE SEEN.

LET'S HEAD BACK TO TRANSYLVANIA, HONEY. WE'VE *LOST* HIM.

NO. WE *SEARCH* UNTIL HE'S *FOUND.*

YOU'VE GOT A DEFINITE **STUBBORN** STREAK IN YOU, LITTLE LADY. WHY?

I DON'T WANT TO **BORE** YOU, DARLING...

CONSIDER ME A **CAPTIVE AUDIENCE.** BORE ON!

YOU KNOW OF MY **GRANDFATHER,** ABRAHAM VAN HELSING, AND OF HIS **BATTLES** WITH DRACULA*--

--AND HOW ALL BELIEV[E] THE VAMPIRE HAD BEE[N] **KILLED.**

*AS CURRENTLY BEING **SERIALIZ[ED]** IN **DRACULA LIVES!**--ROY.

"BUT HE **WASN'T.** YEARS LATER, THE **FIEND RETURNED,** AND **MURDERED** GRANDFATHER."

"BUT **STILL** HE WASN'T DONE WITH OUR FAMILY. WHEN I WAS **NINE,** HE KILLED MY **PARENTS** AS I WATCHED HELPLESS IN HORROR..."

"...EVEN AS HE THEN MO[VED] TO SLAY **ME.**"

WITH **YOUR** DEATH, YOUNG RACHEL, THE VAN HELSING NAME SHALL BE **NO MORE.**

"HIS **FANGS** STARTED FOR MY NECK AND I FELT HIS STALE, **UNDEAD** BREATH UPON ME, WHEN..."

HOLD IT, DRACULA-- DON'T EVEN **LOOK** AT THE GIRL. SHE'LL NOT BE YOUR VICTIM TONIGHT.

" **QUINCY HARKER,** MY FAMILY'S LONG-TIME FRIEND, BURST THROUGH THE DOOR..."

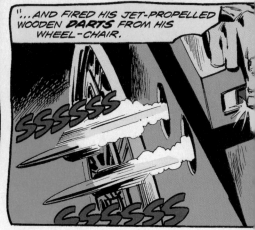

"...AND FIRED HIS JET-PROPELLED WOODEN **DARTS** FROM HIS WHEEL-CHAIR."

SSSSSS

SSSSSS

...OU'VE ADDED ...OTHER NEW ...CE TO YOUR ...SENAL, EH, ...ARKER?

WELL, THEY'LL FARE AS WELL AS YOUR OTHERS.

KEEP THE GIRL FOR NOW, OLD FRIEND, BUT BEWARE-- THERE WILL COME A TIME...

...WHEN SHE WILL BE MINE!

HA HA HA HA HA

"WHEN THE ECHO OF THAT COLD LAUGHTER FADED, THE REALITY OF WHAT HAD HAPPENED RUSHED AT ME...

COME TO ME, RACHEL-- YOU'VE GONE THROUGH FAR TOO MUCH FOR A GIRL YOUR AGE...

...AR TOO ...CH FOR ...NY ...SON.

...SAID NOTHING AS QUINCY LAID MY ...RENTS BOTH TO REST, IN THE SAME ...ETERY ALONGSIDE MY GRANDFATHER AND BROTHER.

QUINCY TOOK ME INTO HIS HOME... TAUGHT ME, TRAINED ME, RAISED ME INTO WOMANHOOD.

DOES THAT EXPLAIN WHY I'M, AS YOU SAY, "SO STUBBORN"? DOES IT, FRANK?

THERE IS NO ANSWER...NOR IS THERE A NEED FOR ONE.

...W... THEY'RE GONE AT LAST-- SEARCHING ELSEWHERE ON THIS MOUNTAINSIDE.

...O I AM ...EE ONCE ...RE...STRONG ...OUGH AGAIN, ...MAKE MY ... TO SAFETY... ...PERISH IN ...E TRYING.

THE SNOWS HAVE CALMED THEMSELVES FOR THE MOMENT. THIS MAY BE THE PERFECT TIME...

...TO FLY!

FOR ALMOST *FIVE MINUTES* THE LEATHERY FORM FLITS THROUGH THE UNDER-BREEZE...

...UNTIL, ONCE *AGAIN,* THE STORM BEGINS... AND THE SNOWS *CHURN* AND *RUMBLE* WITH A FURY ONLY *NATURE* CAN MUSTER...

...AND THE *WEAKNESS* THAT *PERMEATED* HIS EVERY FABR OF BEING CAUSES THE *LORD* DARKNESS TO COLLAPSE...

...AND PERHAPS TO SEE THE HALF-VAGUE *IMAGE* THAT FLICKERS BEFORE HIS EYES...

...CLOSE.

NORTHERN IRELAND:

DOCTOR SUN NOW PERMITS YO TO SEE HIM, VAMPIRE BRAND

AT LAST I SHALL SEE THE FACE OF MY *MASTER...* THE ONE I SERVE.

174

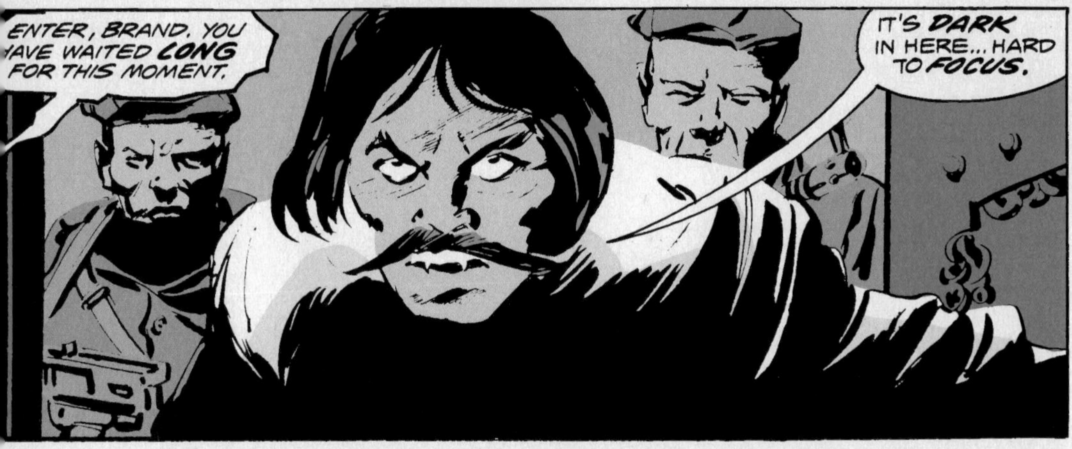
ENTER, BRAND. YOU HAVE WAITED LONG FOR THIS MOMENT.
IT'S DARK IN HERE... HARD TO FOCUS.

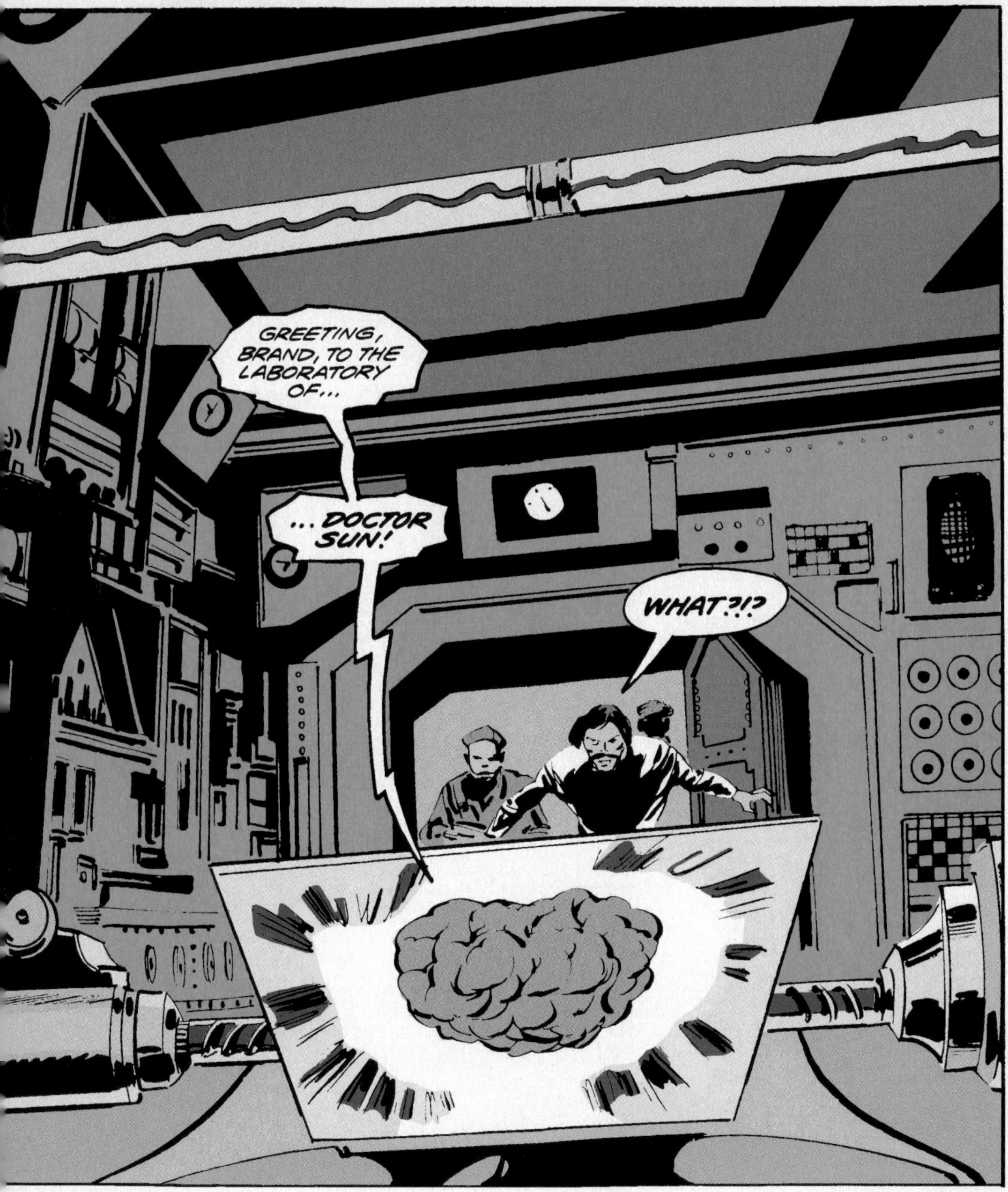
GREETING, BRAND, TO THE LABORATORY OF...
...DOCTOR SUN!
WHAT?!?

WHILE ELSEWHERE...

AHH, YOU *AWAKE,* DRACULA. THAT IS GOOD.

WHO--?

I AM PROFESSOR MORGO, A MERE HUMBLE SERVANT OF *DOCTOR SUN.*

AHHH, YOU *STRUGGLE* TO FREE YOURSELF, WHAT A *WASTE* OF YOUR REMAINING *ENERGY,* DRACULA--

--SINCE CHAIN WHICH BIND ARE LACED W CLOVES O *GARLIC*

WHO ARE YO *MADMAN,* TH YOU DARE *ATTE* CAPTURING DRACULA

WE *HAVE* CAPTURED YOU, AND WE SHALL RETAIN YOU UNTIL *DOCTOR SUN* ORDERS YOUR DEATH.

AFTER ALL, WE HAVE WAITED A *LONG* TIME FOR YOU... ALMOST *FOUR YEARS* TO BE SURE.

AND FOR THE PAST *YEAR* WE HAVE FOLLOWED YOU, AT TIMES WE HAVE EVEN CROSSED PATHS, WITH YOU ALWAYS *UNKNOWING.* *

BUT NOW OUR *PATIENCE* HAS PROVEN ITS OWN REWARD.

* DRACULA #17.
--REMEMBERIN' ROY.

OUR *TROUBLES* IN FIND YOU BEFORE NOW WAS OUR *UNCERTAINTY* O YOUR *METHODS.* BU ONCE WE FOUND O WHO *KNEW* YOU EVERY THOUGHT YOUR EVERY *INSTINCT.*

...BUT W *SPOIL* O SURPRIS SEE FO YOURS WHO YO *JUDA* WAS

176

BUT IT *CAN NOT* BE!

C'MON, EX-MASTER, IS THAT ANY WAY TO GREET AN *OLD FRIEND*--

--OR SHOULD I SAY, YOUR ONE-TIME *SLAVE*-- *CLIFTON GRAVES?*

I CAN JUST *IMAGINE* HOW MUCH YOU *MOURNED* FOR ME...

HA HA HA

[YO]U *DID* [RETU]RN FOR ME, [WAS]N'T YOU, [DR]ACULA? OR [DID] YOU JUST [GIV]E THAT [GO]ODMAN'S [LAU]GH OF [YOU]RS AND [THE]N *FORGET* [E]VER [EX]ISTED?

ANSWER ME, BLAST YOU-- *ANSWER ME!*

NO MATTER. I'VE WAITED A *LONG TIME* TO HAVE YOU *HELPLESS* LIKE THIS BEFORE ME-- TO VENT OUT MY *TRUE HATRED* FOR YOU WITH NO FEAR.

HOW DID YOU *SURVIVE* THE EXPLOSION?

SO, THE GREAT 'VAMPIRE' SPEAKS, EH?

THEN MY *ANSWER* MAY YET *SHOCK* YOU. YOU SEE, I *DIDN'T SURVIVE.*

NO, I WAS TORN TO *SHREDS*-- AS YOU CAN READILY SEE.

THINK BACK TO THE TIME WE WERE *ABOARD* THE OCEAN LINER, *MICHELE.* * YOU SET IT TO *EXPLODE...*

AND THEN *ABANDONED* ME, LEAVING ME ABOARD IT, TO CATCH THE FULL BLAST WHILE *OTHERS* SURVIVED.

* FOR THOSE WHO CAN REMEMBER-ISH #10. --NOSTALGIC ROY.

177

YES, I WAS *KILLED*, BUT SOMEHOW MY BODY FLOATED ONTO A PIECE OF *WRECKAGE*...AND I MUST HAVE DRIFTED ABOARD IT FOR HOURS...

...BEFORE I WAS *DISCOVERED*...

...BY *DOCTOR S...* HE HAD FINALLY F... A *CLUE* TO YOUR *WHEREABOUTS*, TRACED YOU TO *THE MICHELE...*

"HE WAS TOO *LATE* FOR YOU, BUT INSTEAD HE *RECOGNIZED* ME.

"*I* WAS TAKEN TO HIS BASE IN THE *PHILIPPINES* WHERE HIS *DOCTORS* PIECED TOGETHER MY FLESH...

"...AND SOMEHOW *REKINDLED* THE SPARK OF LIFE I HAD LOST.

IN RETURN, I'VE *HELPED* HIM-- TOLD HIM HOW YOU *OPERATE--* SOMETHING ONLY *I* KNEW, 'CAUSE OF ALL THOSE *MONTHS* I WORKED AS YOUR LACKEY.

AND ALL F... *REVENGE...* DRAC-- SWE... REVENGE...

SEE THIS *VIAL*, DRAC-- RECOGNIZE ITS *SMELL...?*

IT'S *BLOOD--* RICH, TASTY *BLOOD*. BUT YOU'LL HAVE *NONE* OF IT!

HERE'S TO *LIFE*, DRAC-- LIFE AND, NEED I EVEN MENTION--*DEATH!*

I *WARN* Y... GRAVES, YO... LIFE WILL... MINE.

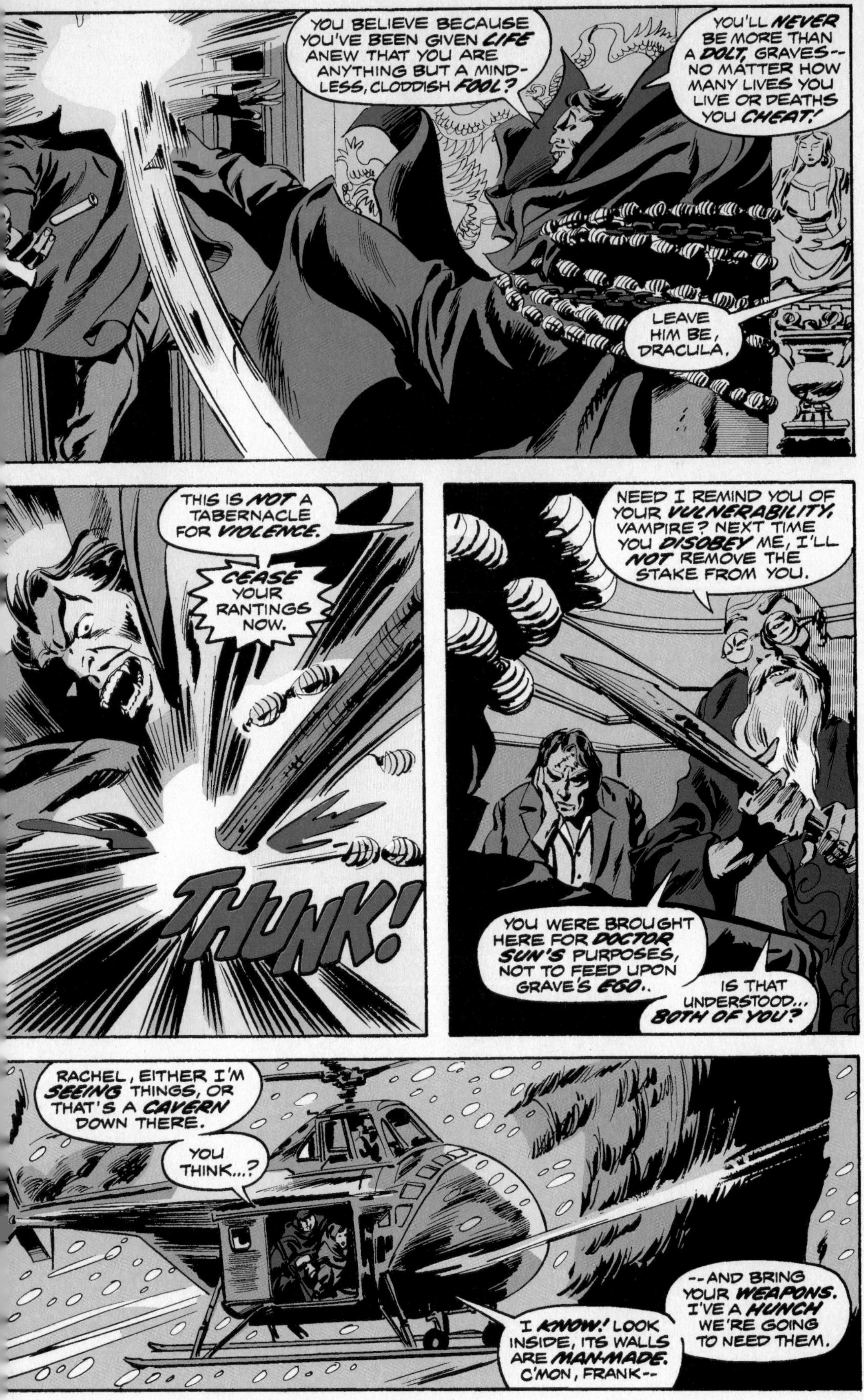
YOU BELIEVE BECAUSE YOU'VE BEEN GIVEN LIFE ANEW THAT YOU ARE ANYTHING BUT A MIND-LESS, CLODDISH FOOL?
YOU'LL NEVER BE MORE THAN A DOLT, GRAVES-- NO MATTER HOW MANY LIVES YOU LIVE OR DEATHS YOU CHEAT!
LEAVE HIM BE, DRACULA.
THIS IS NOT A TABERNACLE FOR VIOLENCE.
CEASE YOUR RANTINGS NOW.
THUNK!
NEED I REMIND YOU OF YOUR VULNERABILITY, VAMPIRE? NEXT TIME YOU DISOBEY ME, I'LL NOT REMOVE THE STAKE FROM YOU.
YOU WERE BROUGHT HERE FOR DOCTOR SUN'S PURPOSES, NOT TO FEED UPON GRAVE'S EGO..
IS THAT UNDERSTOOD... BOTH OF YOU?
RACHEL, EITHER I'M SEEING THINGS, OR THAT'S A CAVERN DOWN THERE.
YOU THINK...?
I KNOW! LOOK INSIDE, ITS WALLS ARE MAN-MADE. C'MON, FRANK--
--AND BRING YOUR WEAPONS. I'VE A HUNCH WE'RE GOING TO NEED THEM.

NO, PROFESSOR MORGO--THAT IS *NOT* UNDERSTOOD, NOR EVEN ACCEPTED.

YOU *BROUGHT* ME HERE, WHICH WAS YOUR *FIRST* MISTAKE.

YOUR *SECOND* WAS IN THINKING YOU COULD *KEEP* ME YOUR PRISONER.

YOU'LL LE[...] THE *FOLL*[...] OF THAT, ONCE I DESTROYE[...] THIS *DOL*[...]

OBVIOUSLY YOU *FAIL* TO UNDERSTAND, VAMPIRE--

--*DOCTOR SUN* GIVES YOU NO CHOICES, EITHER *OBEY* HIM OR *PERISH!*

YOU FAIL TO UNDERSTAND *ME*, MORGO--

DRACULA IS *NO ONE'S* PUPPET-- UNDER NO MORTAL'S *LAWS.*

AND THOU[...] MY STREN[...] IS BUT *HAL*[...] OF ITSELF, [...] AM STILL M[...] THAN ABLE [...] *DESTROY*[...]

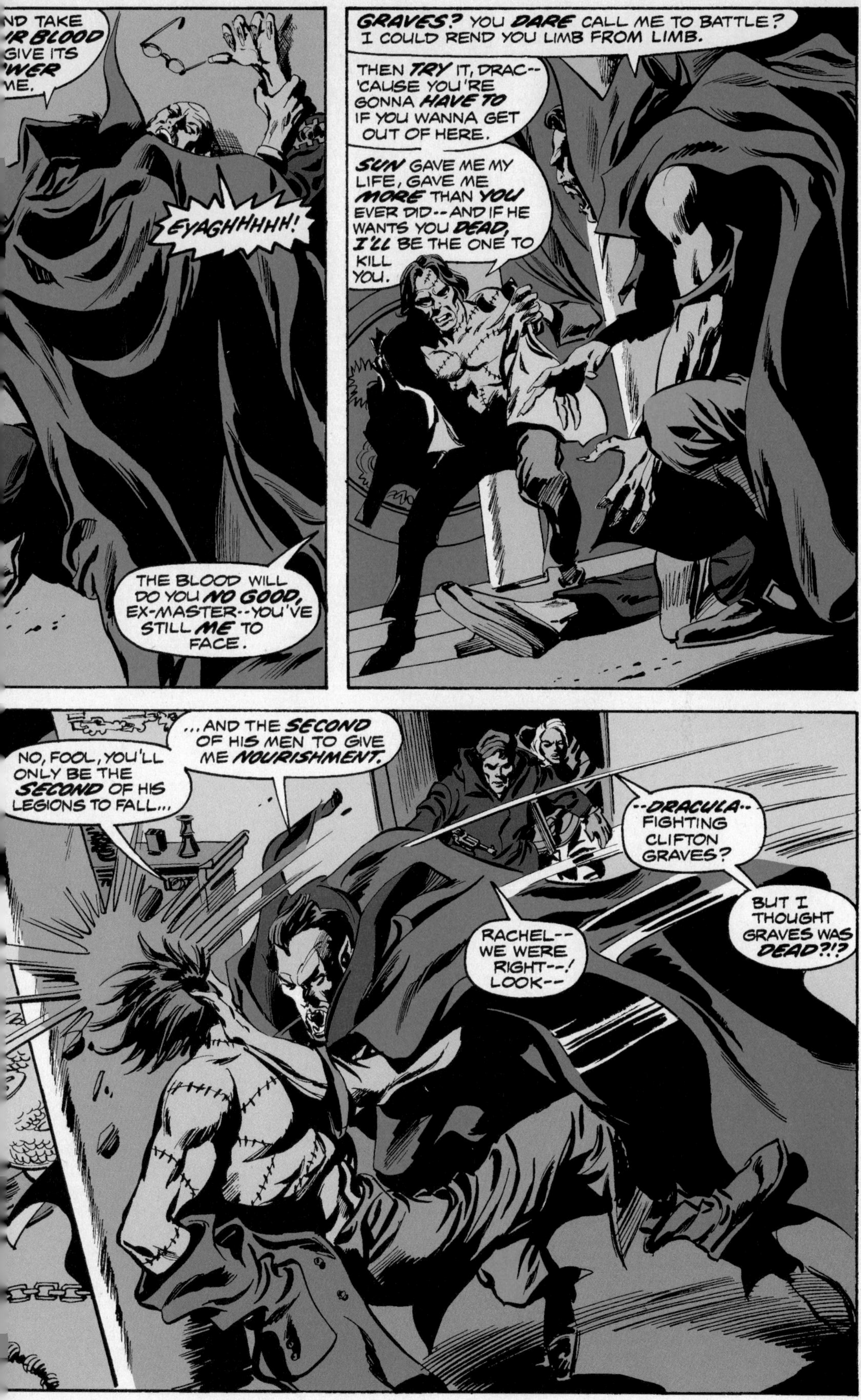
ND TAKE IR BLOOD GIVE ITS WER ME.
EYAGHHHHH!
THE BLOOD WILL DO YOU NO GOOD, EX-MASTER--YOU'VE STILL ME TO FACE.
GRAVES? YOU DARE CALL ME TO BATTLE? I COULD REND YOU LIMB FROM LIMB.
THEN TRY IT, DRAC-- 'CAUSE YOU'RE GONNA HAVE TO IF YOU WANNA GET OUT OF HERE.
SUN GAVE ME MY LIFE, GAVE ME MORE THAN YOU EVER DID--AND IF HE WANTS YOU DEAD, I'LL BE THE ONE TO KILL YOU.
NO, FOOL, YOU'LL ONLY BE THE SECOND OF HIS LEGIONS TO FALL...
...AND THE SECOND OF HIS MEN TO GIVE ME NOURISHMENT.
RACHEL-- WE WERE RIGHT--! LOOK--
--DRACULA-- FIGHTING CLIFTON GRAVES?
BUT I THOUGHT GRAVES WAS DEAD?!?

UH OH-- COMPANY'S COMING. ON YOUR GUARD, RACHEL-- THEY DON'T LOOK FRIENDLY.
KILL THEM, GUARDS-- DOCTOR SUN DEMANDS THEIR DEATH.
BAM
I'LL HOLD THEM, HONEY-- YOU GET DRACULA.
BEING FACETIOUS ISN'T NORMALLY YOUR STYLE, DRACULA-- BUT IT DOESN'T MATTER--
--AS YOU'LL BE DEAD IN A MATTER OF MOMENTS.
TWANG
AH, MY DEAR-- YOU NEED PRACTICE FIRING. YOU MISSED ME COMPLETELY--
--THOUGH POOR GRAVES HERE CAN HARDLY SAY THE SAME.
ACKKKKK

W THEN, MY
R--LET US *END*
D NIGHT WITH
D MORE SWIFT
DEATHS.

RS, AND THAT
RNAL *DESCEN-*
T'S OF MINE--
NK DRAKE.

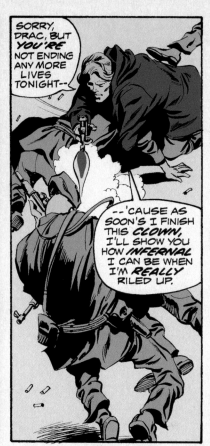

SORRY,
DRAC, BUT
YOU'RE
NOT ENDING
ANY MORE
LIVES
TONIGHT--

--'CAUSE AS
SOON'S I FINISH
THIS *CLOWN,*
I'LL SHOW YOU
HOW *INFERNAL*
I CAN BE WHEN
I'M *REALLY*
RILED UP.

ENOUGH! THE
BATTLE IS
ENDED.

WHA--?

IT'S A
VOICE...
COMING FROM
BEHIND THAT
CURTAIN.

REETINGS
MY INNER BASE.
M *DOCTOR*
N, AND *YOU*
E ALL MY
APTIVES...

...HELD IN
PLACE WITH MY
*IMMOBILITY
BEAM.*

WHILE THE MALE
AND FEMALE ARE
DISPOSED OF, DRACULA,
I SHALL *REVEAL*
WHY YOU WERE
BROUGHT HERE.

I WISH TO
DUEL WITH YOU--
FOR THE THRONE
OF THE *LORDSHIP
OF VAMPIRES!*

NEXT:
THE SINISTER SCHEME OF
DOCTOR SUN!
PLUS:
A SPECIAL SURPRISE!

183

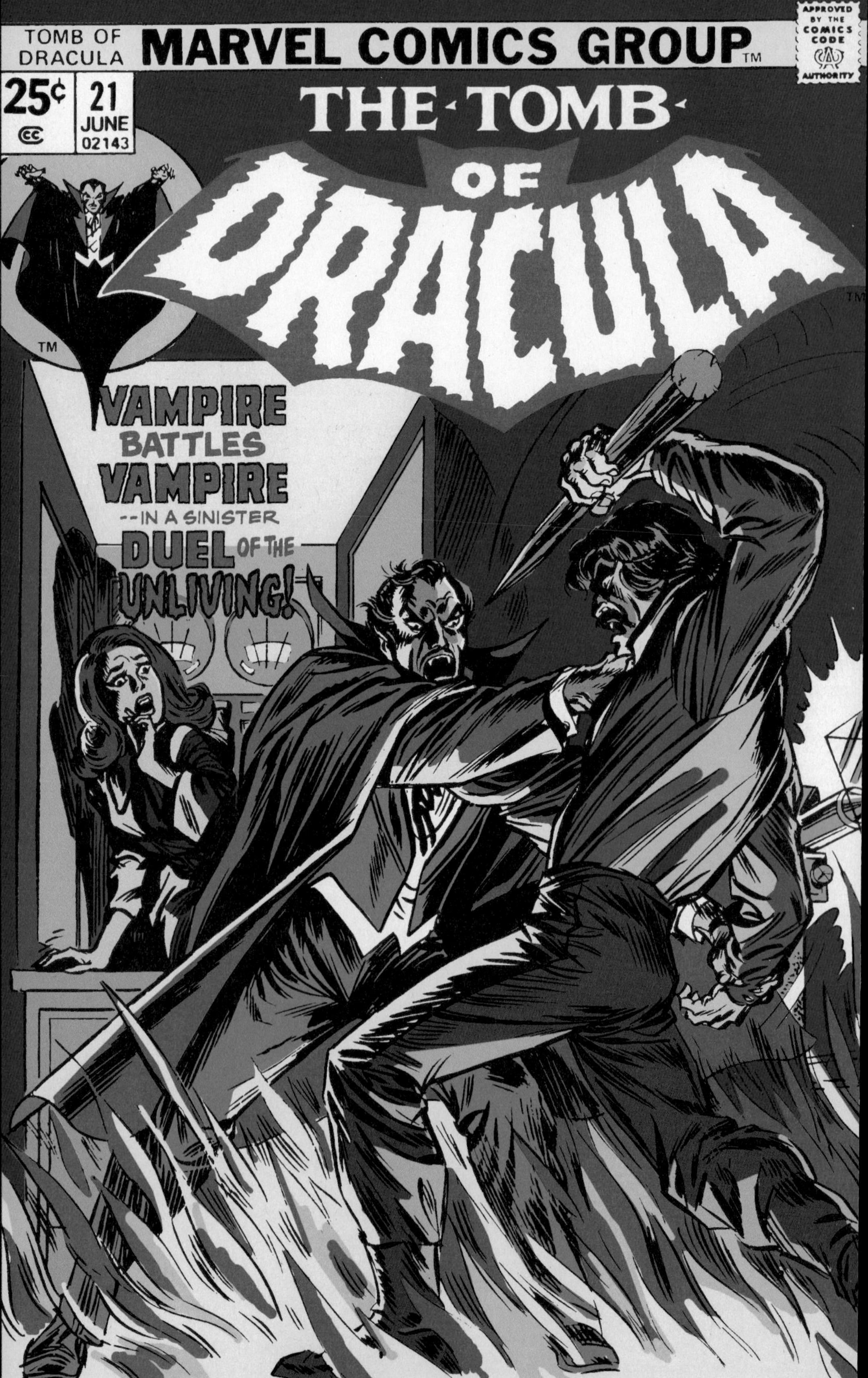
TOMB OF DRACULA
MARVEL COMICS GROUP
APPROVED BY THE COMICS CODE AUTHORITY
25¢
21 JUNE 02143
THE TOMB OF DRACULA
VAMPIRE BATTLES VAMPIRE --IN A SINISTER DUEL OF THE UNLIVING!

MARV WOLFMAN / GENE COLAN / TOM PALMER / JOHN COSTANZA / TOM PALMER / ROY THOMAS
WRITER / ARTIST / INKER / letterer / colorist / EDITOR

DEATHKNELL

ONE MOMENT BEFORE, THERE WAS SILENCE... A TURGID, UNEARTHLY QUIET WHICH QUICKLY ENDED WITH THE SNAPPED-ON DRUMMING OF MACHINERY.

AND DEEP WITHIN THE MUSKY WINDING CATACOMBS BENEATH THE TRANSYLVANIAN MOUNTAINS, THREE WRITHING FORMS FREEZE MOTIONLESS IN A BLINDING RAY OF SCARLET.

WE HAVE HUNTED YOU FOR YEARS NOW, DRACULA--

--AND NOW THAT YOU ARE PRISONER OF DOCTOR SUN...

...YOU SHALL NEVER LEAVE THESE CHAMBERS AGAIN!

185

SUDDENLY THE CHAMBER IS FILLED WITH YET ANOTHER SOUND--

--THE BONE-CHILLING PEAL OF LAUGHTER FROM ONE WHO IS ALREADY DEAD...

...LAUGHTER WHICH COMES NOT FROM HUMOR...

...BUT FROM IRONY.

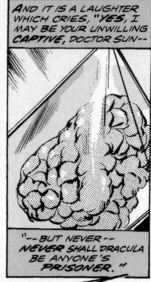

AND IT IS A LAUGHTER WHICH CRIES, "YES, I MAY BE YOUR UNWILLING CAPTIVE, DOCTOR SUN--

"-- BUT NEVER -- NEVER SHALL DRACULA BE ANYONE'S PRISONER."

AND IT IS A LAUGHTER WH CAN FREEZE THE BLOOD O SOUL--

--LIVING C UNDEAD

YOU'RE AN ARROGANT FOOL, DRACULA-- YOU CAN'T DEFEAT DOCTOR SUN--

"DOCTOR SUN IS MORE THAN HUMAN... MORE THAN A VAMPIRE, DRACULA. HE IS EVERYTHING... EVERYWHERE... LISTEN, DRACULA, AND UNDERSTAND HOW YOUR ENEMY CAME TO BE...

CHINA, 1966, DURING THE CULTURAL REVOLUTION.

YOU ARE TO COME WITH US, DOCTOR SUN. THE GENERAL DEMANDS YOUR PRESENCE.

I PITY YOU, DOCTOR SUN-- WHAT THE GENERAL HAS PLANNED FOR YOU...

...IS A FATE MORE HORRIB THAN ANY SHOULD END

AH, YOU ARE HERE. I AM SORRY, DOCTOR SUN, BUT THE GENERAL NO LONGER FEELS HE CAN TRUST YOU.

HE FEELS YOU HAVE STALLED THE TESTS TOO LONG. PERHAPS A SIGN OF WEAKNESS ON YOUR PART, HE BELIEVES

SO THE GENERAL SAY THAT YOU SHA NOW BE THE TE SUBJECT FO PROJECT: MIN

186

ALSO, AS FURTHER *PUNISHMENT*, DOCTOR SUN, THE *GENERAL* HAS ORDERED NO *ANESTHETICS*. HE WISHES YOU TO FEEL THE *PAIN*.

I DO NOT LIKE DOING THIS, DOCTOR SUN. BUT THE *GENERAL* DEMANDS *MY* SHOW OF LOYALTY.

FAREWELL, *FATHER*. I STILL LOVE YOU DEARLY.

HEART AS PPED.

QUICKLY NOW, THE INCISION.

REFUL, RE MUST NO MAGE.

IT IS *DONE*--HIS BRAIN HAS BEEN *REMOVED*...

...AND *PLACED* INTO THE *ANTI-MATTER* RECEPTACLE BEFORE IT MISSES A *CONTRACTION*.

IF ALL HAS GONE WELL, MY COLLEAGUES, THE BRAIN WILL BEGIN *FUNCTIONING* IMMEDIATELY.

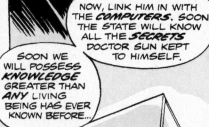

NOW, LINK HIM IN WITH THE *COMPUTERS*. SOON THE STATE WILL KNOW ALL THE *SECRETS* DOCTOR SUN KEPT TO HIMSELF.

YES, IT WORKS.

SOON WE WILL POSSESS *KNOWLEDGE* GREATER THAN *ANY* LIVING BEING HAS EVER KNOWN BEFORE...

...WHEN THE MOST *BRILLIANT* MIND IN ALL THE WORLD IS TIED IN WITH THE MOST ADVANCED *COMPUTERS* IN EXISTENCE.

FOOLS! SUFFER NOW FOR WHAT YOU'VE *DONE.* FOR WHEN YOU PLACED MY *BRAIN* IN CONTROL OF THE COMPUTERS--

YOU GAVE ME *POWER...* ABSOLUTE POWER!

POWER ENOUGH TO *DESTROY* YOU ALL!

ARRGGHHHHHHH

SO, DO YOU *UNDER-STAND* NOW, DRACULA? DO YOU SEE WHY HE IS *UNDEFEATABLE?*

AND WHY YOU WILL *DIE* IF YOU FAIL TO HEED HIS *COMMAND?*

ENOUGH RANTING, VAMPIRE BRAND. IT IS TIME TO SATISFY *YOUR* BLOOD HUNGER.

THE GIRL. *TAKE HER.* HER BLOOD IS WARM... RICH.

IF THAT IS WHAT YOU *WISH,* DOCTOR SUN... THAT IS WHAT SHALL BE *DONE.*

RACHEL VAN HELSING CAN NOT MOVE, AND WORSE, SHE *KNOWS* THIS. YET, EVEN AS THE DARKLING FORM HOVERS EVER CLOSER, SHE KNOWS SHE WILL NOT GO DOWN WITHOUT A STRUGGLE...

BUT... YOU'LL *NOT* HAVE THIS WOMAN, VAMPIRE. SHE IS MEANT FOR *ME.*

YOU'RE *FREE?* BUT THE RAY HELD YOU IN PLACE.

I HAVE FREED HIM, VAMPIRE BRAND, FOR YOUR FINAL *TEST.*

DESTROY DRACULA-- DOCTOR SUN COMMANDS IT!

YOU'RE A *MADMAN*, SUN. NO FLEDGLING VAMPIRE WILL EVER BE MY MATCH--

--ESPECIALLY NOT ONE OF MY *OWN* CREATION.*

*TOMB OF DRACULA #11. --ROY.

SO HEED YOUR *TRUE* MASTER, BRAND-- CEASE YOUR BATTLING *NOW!*

DRACULA, LORD AND MASTER OF *ALL* VAMPIRES, *COMMANDS IT!*

YOU'RE THE LORD OF *FOOLS*, DRACULA.

I'VE BEEN BRED FOR ONLY *ONE* PURPOSE-- AND THAT'S TO *HUMBLE* YOU-- TO *DEFEAT* YOU... AND FINALLY TO *DESTROY YOU!!*

AND MAN, THAT'S *JUST* WHAT I'M GONNA DO.

500 RS I'VE ENDED T IS

NST PID *ARTS* H AS ND--

500 RS I'VE ED MY WAY THE MIND- MINIONS HAVE EVER HT TO TAKE T IS *MINE.*

NEVER L MY BE EN BY SUCH OU.

AM *LORD* VIL, LITTLE --FOREVER ALWAYS!

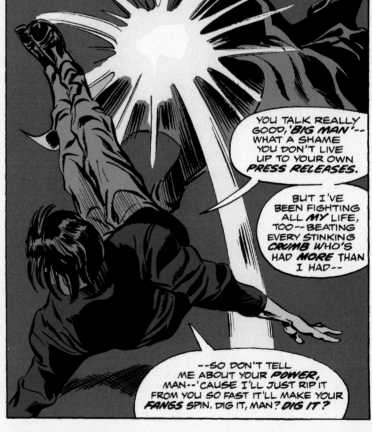

YOU TALK REALLY GOOD, *'BIG MAN'*-- WHAT A SHAME YOU DON'T LIVE UP TO YOUR OWN *PRESS RELEASES.*

BUT I'VE BEEN FIGHTING ALL *MY* LIFE, TOO-- BEATING EVERY STINKING *CRUMB* WHO'S HAD *MORE* THAN I HAD--

--SO DON'T TELL ME ABOUT YOUR *POWER*, MAN--'CAUSE I'LL JUST RIP IT FROM YOU SO FAST IT'LL MAKE YOUR *FANGS* SPIN. DIG IT, MAN? *DIG IT?*

I'M NOT *IMPRESSED* BY YOU, '*BIG MAN*'-- NOT IMPRESSED ONE LOUSY BIT. SO WHAT IF YOU'VE LIVED FIVE *MILLION* YEARS--

--YOU'RE *STILL* NOTHING, MAN--A TOTAL *NOTHING!*

'CAUSE YOU'LL HAVE NOTHING LEFT WHEN I'M *DONE* WITH YOU.

SPITZZZZ!

FINISH H BRAND. HESITA NO LONGE

I OBEY, DOCTOR SUN...

...WITH *PLEASURE!*

TWICE BEFORE WE'VE MET, VAMPIRE BRAND--*

AFTER THIS NIGHT, WE SHALL NEVER BATTLE AGAIN...

...FOR IT SHALL BE *YOUR* ASHES WHICH ARE SCATTERED TO THE FOUR WINDS.

*/ISSUE #'S 9&11. --RASCALLY,

ACKKK!

THUCK!

THEN YOU FORGET, '*BIG MAN*'-- THE *FIRST* TIME WE TANGLED, I DEFEAT- ED *YOU.*

I FORGET *NOTHING* ...NOTHING...NOTHIN...

THERE IS A SINGLE SPASM OF STRENGTH WHICH FLOODS THROUGH THE PRINCE OF EVIL...

...ONE SINGLE SPA WHICH PERMITS H *STRIKE* WITH FRE *VIOLENCE*...AND TH TO *COLLAPSE* WITH KALEIDOSCOPE O ING IMAGES AND B LUSTING ILLUSION *HORROR!*

...USIONS SPAWNED BY THE ...-PULSING BRAIN OF ...TOR SUN.

...ON, ENGLAND: FAR RE-...ED FROM THE MADNESS ...ATH THE TRANSYLVANIA ...LEX WHERE DRACULA ... SPRAWLS UNCON-SCIOUS...

...HICH IS USUALLY ...BLASTED LATE ...DO ANY GOOD.

...BUT A CITY WHICH IS UNALTERABLY ENMESHED IN THE DARKLING LORD'S BATTLEPLANS OF CON-QUEST.

AGAIN I ASK YOU, MR. BLADE. PLEASE STAY. YOUR SERVICES ARE INVALUABLE!

SORRY, HARKER-- BUT YOU PEOPLE PLAY A GAME OF WAITING. THAT'S NOT MY STYLE.

WE FIGHT WHEN WE ARE READY...

'SIDES, DRAC'S YOUR HANGUP. I'VE GOT MY OWN PROBLEMS-- NAMELY A CERTAIN KILLER OF PREGNANT WOMEN.

...IF YOU'RE ...FERRING TO ...ONE WHO ...AYED YOUR ...OTHER--

...HE IS ...DOUBTEDLY ...EAD BY NOW.

YOU FORGET, HARKER--I'VE GOT SOME OF HIS BLOOD IN ME...

...AND THAT TELLS ME HE'S STILL AROUND... STILL SKULKING IN SOME STINKIN' DARK ALLEY SOMEPLACE.

AND NOW THAT YOU TELL ME I'M IMMUNE TO VAMPIRE BITES 'CAUSE'A HIM, WELL, THERE'S NO STOPPIN' ME.*

AND, MAN, WHEN I'M DONE WITH HIM, HE'S GOING TO BE ONE BLASTED UGLY CORPSE!

* AS SHOWN LAST ISSUE. --RESEARCHING ROY.

BUT...

NO BUTS, HARKER. I'M LEAVING. AND CALL OFF TAJ.

'CAUSE IF I HAVE TO, I'LL WALK RIGHT OVER HIM TO GET OUT OF HERE.

SO TAKE IT EASY, HARKER. IT HASN'T BEEN ALL BAD.

GOODBYE, MR. BLADE. **GOD** BE WITH YOU.

AND MAY YOU FIND THE **PEACE** YOU'VE SEARCHED SO **DESPERATELY** LONG FOR.

THE **SOUNDS** BEGIN TO GROW AGAIN, AND THE IMAGES OF REALITY COALESCE AS **CONSCIOUSNE** RETURNS TO THE PRINCE OF EVIL...

HE IS **AWAKE**, DOCTOR SUN.

HIS **STAKE** WOUND IS FULLY HEALED, DOCTOR SUN!

I CAN SEE THAT FOR **MYSELF**, VAMPIRE BRAND.

HEED MY **WORDS**, DRACULA. I HAVE WAITED **LONG** TO SPEAK THEM TO YOU.

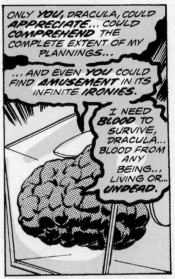

ONLY **YOU**, DRACULA, COULD **APPRECIATE**... COULD **COMPREHEND** THE COMPLETE EXTENT OF MY PLANNINGS...

...AND EVEN **YOU** COULD FIND **AMUSEMENT** IN ITS INFINITE **IRONIES**.

I NEED **BLOOD** TO SURVIVE, DRACULA... BLOOD FROM ANY BEING... LIVING OR... **UNDEAD**.

"IN ORDER FOR MY BRAIN TO CONSTANTLY FUNCTION, **BLOOD** MUST BE FOREVER PUMPED THROUGH THE MACHINERY ...BUT **HOW** ...**WHERE** DO I FIND A SUPPLY GREAT ENOUGH...? IT CAN **NOT** BE STOLEN. EVENTUALLY THE **AUTHORITIES** WOULD BECOME WISE.

"THUS TURN TO WHO KN ALL ABC BLOOD... NIGI SCAVENC YES, DRAC **THE VAMPI**

"HE HIDES IN THE **SHADOWS** UNTIL HE FINDS HIS **VICTIM**...

"...THEN HE **STRIKES** AS A DEADLY WRAITH FROM **HELL** ITSELF!

"HERE IS MY **SOURCE** OF BLOOD, DRACULA-- THE PERFECT UNDERLING-- WHO CAN LEAVE **NO TRACE**... HAVE **NO TRUE** MOTIVE OUTSIDE OF HIS OWN ALMOST **UNQUENCHABLE** BLOODTHIRST.

"BUT, WOU ATT. FOR BRING HI VICTI BODIE TAKI ENO BLO FO HIM TO SURV NOT M

FOR THAT, I NEEDED TO CONTROL THIS NEW TASK FORCE -- AND SO I BEGAN A SEARCH FOR THE CORRECT VAMPIRE.

EVENTUALLY MY MEN DISCOVERED BRAND.

"AFTER YOU KILLED HIM, HE WAS TAKEN TO THE LONDON MORGUE. MISTER LO FOUND HIM WAITING THERE ...STILL NOT FULLY REBORN. *

"HE WAS TAKEN TO MY NORTHERN IRELAND COMPLEX.

* ISSUE #15. --ROY.

ERE HE WAS TRAINED, AND EN DRUSS UNTIL HE WAS RCED TO OBEY MY EVERY RD. YOU SEE, THERE WERE YERS BEFORE HIM. ME WERE A BIT ADSTRONG, LL WE SAY?

YOU WILL LEARN MORE IN A MATTER OF MOMENTS, DRACULA, BUT NOW THE MACHINERY IS READY--

--NOW ALL I HAVE WORKED FOR IS ABOUT TO COMMENCE.

TAKE YOUR POSITION, BRAND.

THIS DEVICE WILL PROBE YOUR VERY INTELLIGENCE, DRACULA.

EVERYTHING YOU KNOW... EVERY THOUGHT YOU'VE EVER HAD -- WILL BE RECORDED BY MY COMPUTERS.

AND THAT KNOWLEDGE WILL BE GIVEN TO BRAND. HE WILL THEN KNOW ALL YOU KNOW. IN EFFECT, HE WILL BE YOU!

ARE YOU BEGINNING TO UNDERSTAND ME, DRACULA?

DOCTOR CHUNG. PRESS THE BUTTON... NOW!

THERE IS A SUDDEN **CRACKLE** AS **STATIC** FILLS THE AIR... AS **NERVE IMPULSES** ARE TORN APART AND THEN **INTEGRATED** INTO COMPLEX CIRCUITRY AND WIRES...

...AND THEN THERE IS A SUDDEN **SCREAM** AS DRACULA HAS HIS VERY **CONSCIOUSNESS** SHREDDED, RIPPED AND FINALLY PIECED TOGETHER INTO ALMOST MEANINGLESS **FRAGMENTS.**

BUT ABOVE **ALL** THE SHRIEKING SOUNDS, THERE IS AN ALMOST **MOCKING MECHANICAL LAUGHTER** WHICH FILLS IN THE FINAL **MISSING** DETAILS OF A CAREFULLY CONCEIVED **MASTERPLAN!**

HEAR IT ALL **NOW,** DRACULA-- AND UNDERSTAND AT LAST!

I KNEW **YOU** WOULD NEVER LISTEN TO MY COMMANDS, YET ONLY **YOU** CONTROLLED ALL THE **UNDEAD...**ONLY YOU WERE **MASTER OF ALL VAMPIRES!**

THUS THE VAMPIRE I HAD TO **CREATE** HAD TO BE **MORE** THAN YOUR EQUAL-- MORE **CUNNING** THAT YOU EVER WERE. HE WOULD HAVE TO KNOW ALL **YOU** KNOW AND THEN **MORE**--

--AND HE WOULD HAVE TO **TURN** YOUR KNOWLEDGE **AGAINST** YOU--

--HE WOULD HAVE TO DESTROY YOU, AND FINALLY CLAIM THE **LORDSHIP** OF VAMPIRES FOR **HIMSELF,** WITH YOUR **DEATH'S HEAD** AS HIS SCEPTRE

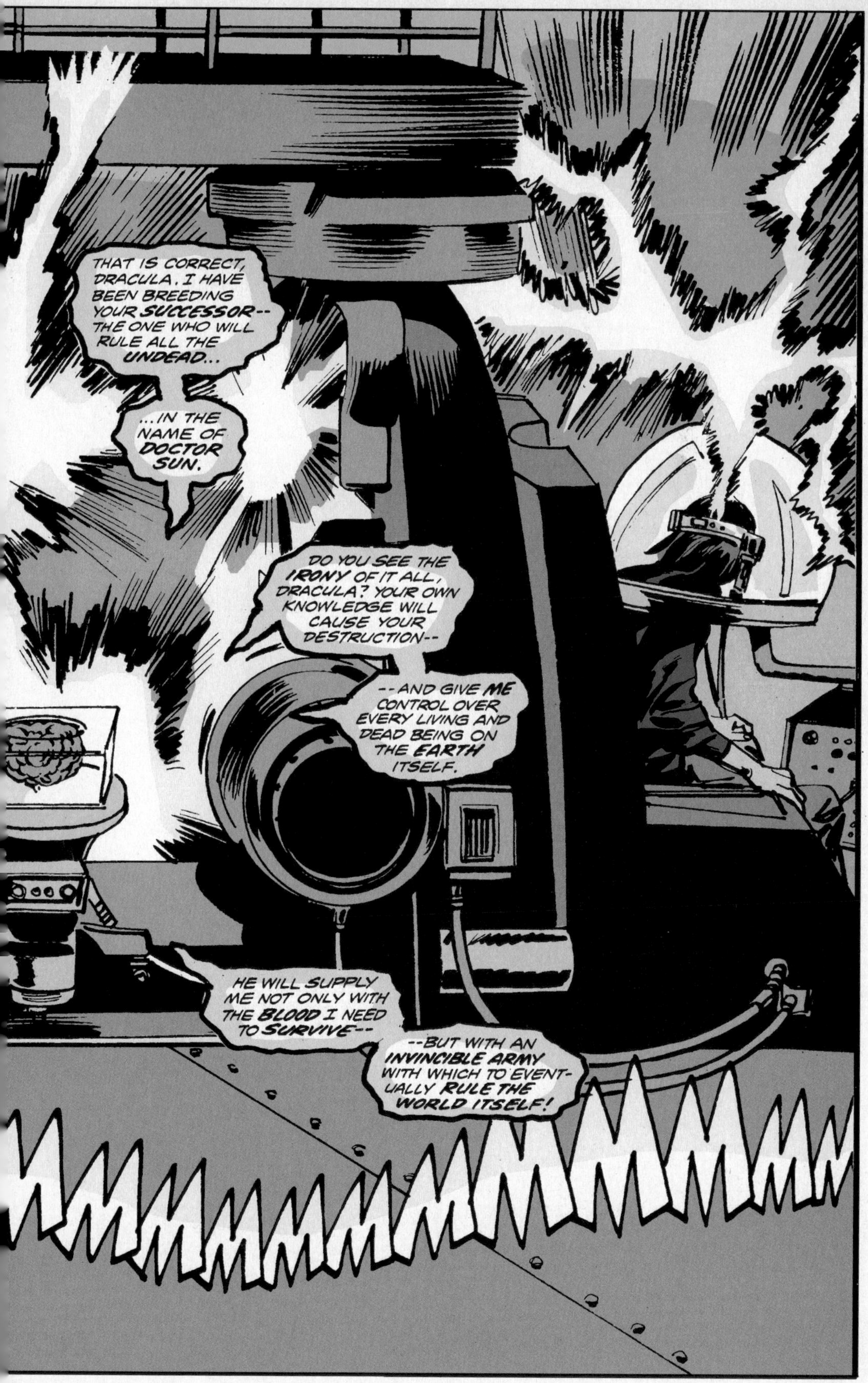
THAT IS CORRECT, DRACULA. I HAVE BEEN BREEDING YOUR SUCCESSOR-- THE ONE WHO WILL RULE ALL THE UNDEAD...
...IN THE NAME OF DOCTOR SUN.
DO YOU SEE THE IRONY OF IT ALL, DRACULA? YOUR OWN KNOWLEDGE WILL CAUSE YOUR DESTRUCTION--
--AND GIVE ME CONTROL OVER EVERY LIVING AND DEAD BEING ON THE EARTH ITSELF.
HE WILL SUPPLY ME NOT ONLY WITH THE BLOOD I NEED TO SURVIVE--
--BUT WITH AN INVINCIBLE ARMY WITH WHICH TO EVENTUALLY RULE THE WORLD ITSELF!

EVERY NERVE IMPULSE SEEMS TO *SHATTER*... EVERY SYNAPSE SEEMS TO *COLLAPSE* IN PAIN-WRACKED FURY, BUT DRACULA SWALLOWS THE *AGONY* IN SILENCE.

INSTEAD, HE FORCES HIMSELF TO *THINK*... TO *REMEMBER* WHO HE IS... WHAT HE IS, AND ABOVE ALL-- *WHY HE IS!*

"I WAS *KILLED* ON THE BATTLE-FIELD OF TRAN-SYLVANIA," HE REMEMBERS, "I *DIED* ONLY TO BE *REBORN* BY THE BITE OF A GYPSY VAMPIRE."

"BEFORE MY DEATH I WAS A *WARRIOR* AND A *RULER*, AND IN BOTH I WAS *FIERCE*... UNRELENTING... *UNFORGIVING.*

"MY *WIVES* WERE MANY, BUT ONLY *ONE* DID I EVER LOVE. MY CHILDRE[N] WERE BUT *TWO*, BUT ONLY *ONE* DID I EVER TRULY KNOW.

"*COMPASSION* IS *UNKNOW[N]* TO ME... IT IS SOMETHING I CAN NO LONGER *AFFO[RD]* COMPASSION BREEDS *WEA[K]-NESS*, AND I MUST NEVE[R] BE WEAK AGAIN.

"I AM DRACULA," THE LORD OF EVIL GASPS, "*I AM DRACULA*... AND FOR ALL THE *HERITAGE* BEFORE ME, I MUST *NEVER* BE ANYTHING LESS."

THE PAIN CHOKES ON THIS CREAT[URE] OF THE NIGHT, HE DOES SHOUT OUT. HE CAN NOT. AND MORE BELIEVES... *HE MUST NOT.*

FOR THIS IS A MAN WHO IS *PROUD*... AND TO HIM, PRIDE AND STRENGTH WILL FOREVER BE *ONE.*

BUT...

ENOUGH! I FEEL HIS POWER IN ME NOW, DOCTOR SUN.

I AM READY TO *BATTLE* HIM NOW.

THEN HE SHALL BE *FREED*, VAMPIRE BRAND.

DESTROY DRACU[LA] AND RULE THE WORLD AS MY AIDE.

T YOUR
ARDS
TTA HERE,
CTOR SUN--
ON'T NEED
ANYMORE.

T IS, I
N'T NEED
YTHING
YMORE.

IT'S AS IF THERE IS NOW *NOTHING* I CAN'T DO. *NOTHING!*

YOU'VE STILL TO BATTLE ME, BRAND. CLAIM NOTHING UNTIL I AM DEFEATED.

MIND'S
EN SUDDENLY
PENED...
PANDED
YOND BELIEF,
MAN--

IF YOU CAN DEFEAT ME, THAT IS.

CAN? MAN, I KNOW ALL YOUR *TRICKS* NOW. I KNOW THE WAY YOU MOVE... THE WAY YOU FIGHT.

I KNOW HOW YOU *THINK,* DRAC.

AND EVEN *MORE,* DRAC-- I KNOW ALL YOUR *WEAK-NESSES*... AND YOUR *FEARS.*

FEARS? YES, THERE ARE THINGS *EVERYONE* MUST FEAR.

BUT MINE NEVER ENTER INTO BATTLE, BRAND. NOW, COME FORWARD. IT IS TIME *YOU* LEARN THAT IT IS MORE THAN *KNOWLEDGE* THAT MAKES ME A DRACULA.

AND IT IS MORE THAN FIVE HUNDRED YEARS OF EXIS-TENCE WHICH HAS LET ME DEFEAT THE MULTITUDE OF *FOOLS* SUCH AS YOURSELF.

197

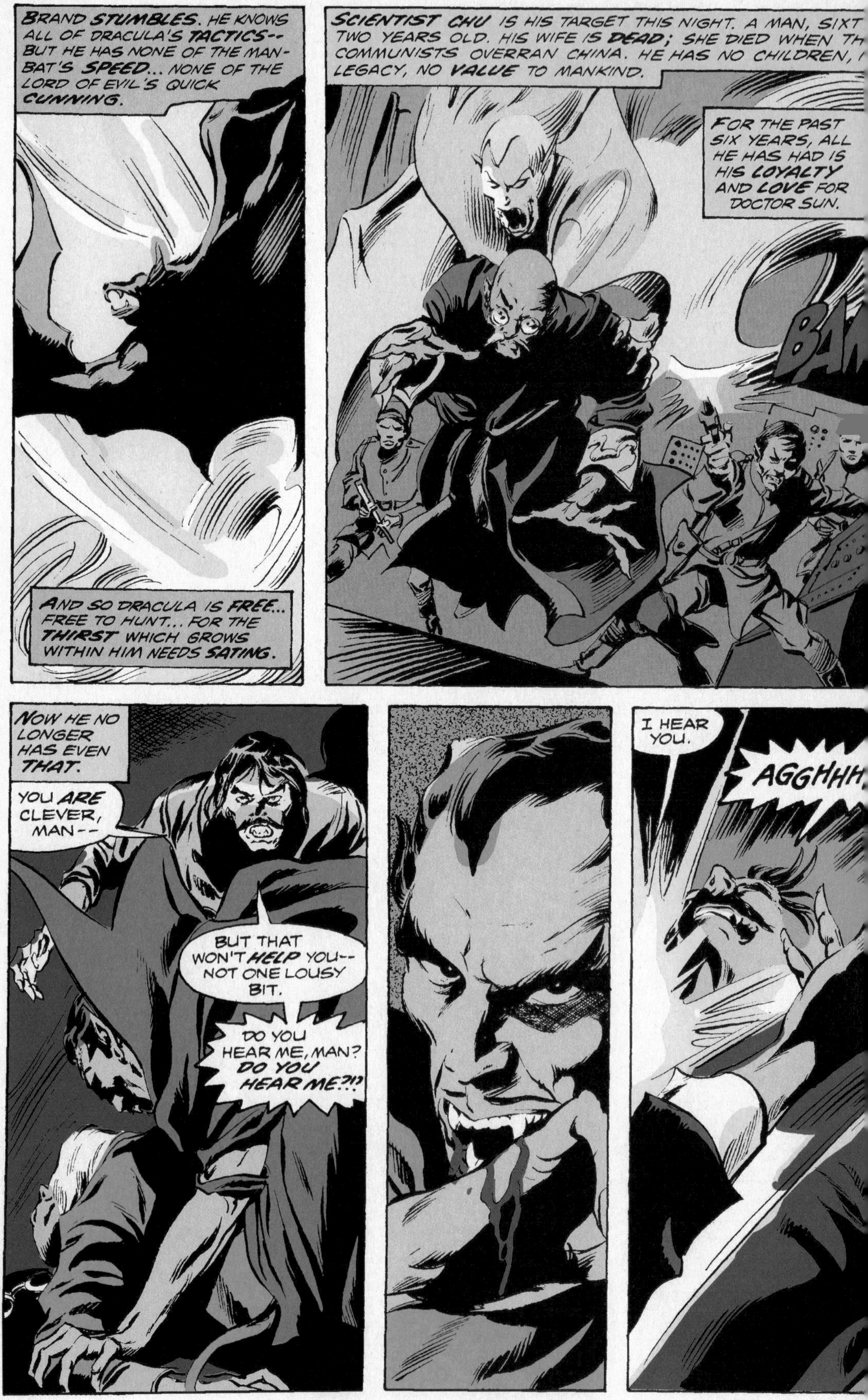

BRAND STUMBLES. HE KNOWS ALL OF DRACULA'S TACTICS-- BUT HE HAS NONE OF THE MAN-BAT'S SPEED... NONE OF THE LORD OF EVIL'S QUICK CUNNING.
AND SO DRACULA IS FREE... FREE TO HUNT... FOR THE THIRST WHICH GROWS WITHIN HIM NEEDS SATING.
SCIENTIST CHU IS HIS TARGET THIS NIGHT. A MAN, SIXT
TWO YEARS OLD. HIS WIFE IS DEAD; SHE DIED WHEN TH
COMMUNISTS OVERRAN CHINA. HE HAS NO CHILDREN,
LEGACY, NO VALUE TO MANKIND.
FOR THE PAST SIX YEARS, ALL HE HAS HAD IS HIS LOYALTY AND LOVE FOR DOCTOR SUN.
NOW HE NO LONGER HAS EVEN THAT.
YOU ARE CLEVER, MAN--
BUT THAT WON'T HELP YOU-- NOT ONE LOUSY BIT.
DO YOU HEAR ME, MAN? DO YOU HEAR ME?!?
I HEAR YOU.
AGGHHH

I IGNORE YOU, BRAND.

YOU ARE BENEATH MY *NOTICE*-- BENEATH MY *INTEREST*.

I DEALT WITH YOU ONCE BEFORE AND GAVE YOU THIS AFTER-LIFE...

...NOW I SHALL *RECTIFY* EVEN THAT.

BRAND'S BODY GIVES OFF AN *UNEARTHLY* GLOW AS IT *SHIMMERS* AND BEGINS TO *CHANGE*...TO ALTER ITSELF...

...AS IT BECOMES LIKE THE VERY *MIST* ITSELF.

DRACULA IS NOT *STARTLED*. INDEED, IT IS THE VERY TACTIC *HE* WOULD HAVE USED.

ALMOST *INVOLUNTARILY*, HE SMILES.

THE SMILE IS *SHORTENED* AS THE MIST HARDENS CHOKES AT DRACULA--HING HIM BACKWARDS...THER AND FARTHER DOWN THE *GROUND*.

THEN CULA INS TO N THAT SAME EN GLOW...

...AS HIS FORM TAKES ON THE SAME *INTANGIBLE* FORM.

WHILE...

BRAND WAS A POOR CHOICE. HE WILL *NOT* WIN THIS FIGHT.

MAKE NOTE: MISTER LO WILL HAVE TO BE *PUNISHED* FOR CHOOSING BRAND.

THERE IS NEED NOW FOR AN *EMERGENCY* PLAN.

EVENTS RUSH BY TOO *QUICKLY.* THUS VAN HELSING AND DRAKE ARE NEEDED, TO GIVE ME *TIME.*

I *FREE* THEM NOW, AND GIVE THEM THE *WEAPONS* THEY WILL NEED.

GOD, I CAN MOVE AGAIN, BUT WHERE'S MY *GUN?* HOW'D I GET THIS *STAKE?*

AND THERE'S A NEW ARROW IN MY CROSS-BOW--AS IF SOMEONE WANTS US TO ATTACK DRACULA--

--AND HAS SUPPLIED US WITH WHAT IS *NEEDED.*

BUT WE'RE *NOT* GOING TO FALL INTO WHATEVER IS *PLANNED* FOR US.

WE WAIT... AND SEE WHAT HAPPENS *BEFORE* WE MAKE OUR MOVE.

YOU WILL *NOT BE MAKING* YOUR MOVE, RACHEL VAN HELSING--BECAUSE THE VAMPIRE KNOWN AS *BRAND* LEAPS FIRST, FORCING DRACULA BACK INTO THE DELICATE ELECTRONIC *MACHINERY...*

FORCING HIM TO *UPSET* THE WIRING, THE CONTROLS...CAUSING THE MACHINE TO *SHORT CIRCUIT,* AND EVENTUALLY...

...TO EXPLODE

YOU'VE BATTLED FOR THE FINAL TIME, DRACULA--BECAUSE NOW YOU'LL BE *DESTROYED* IN THE FIRE--

--WHILE I TAKE YOUR PLACE AS *LORD OF ALL VAMPIRES!*

SO *DIE* NOW, DRACULA--BURN TO *ASHES,* OH ONCE MIGHTY *BRAGGART!*

BECAUSE NOW YOUR TIME ON EARTH IS *DONE!*

AND NOW, FRANK DRAKE-- I SHALL END *YOUR* LIFE, TOO--

--PERMITTING DRACULA AT LEAST TO HAVE ONE FINAL *PLEASANT* THOUGHT AS HE IS BURNED TO HIS ASHES.

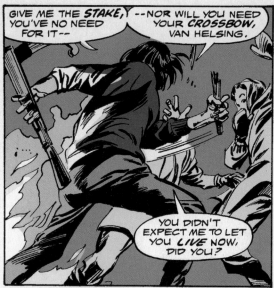

GIVE ME THE *STAKE,* YOU'VE NO NEED FOR IT--

--NOR WILL YOU NEED YOUR *CROSSBOW,* VAN HELSING.

YOU DIDN'T EXPECT ME TO LET YOU *LIVE* NOW, DID YOU?

NOW, BEFORE I *DESTROY* YOU TWO, THERE IS ONE OTHER I WISH TO SPEAK WITH.

BEEN VEN ACULA'S OWLEDGE, TOR SUN-- N GIVEN STRENGTHS, PROWESS--

--EVEN HIS *INTELLIGENCE.*

I NOW KNOW ALL I NEED TO RULE THE WORLD *MYSELF.* I'VE NO NEED OF YOU, SUN--

--AND I'VE NO *DESIRE* TO WORK FOR YOU.

WHICH MEANS, I MUST *DESTROY* YOU.

YOU ARE FAR TOO *GREAT* A RISK TO BE LEFT ALIVE.

INDEED, YOU ARE A FOOL, BRAND. DID YOU BELIEVE YOU WERE THE *ONLY* ONE TO BE GIVEN DRACULA'S THOUGHTS?

I POSSESS THEM NOW, TOO--

AND I KNEW THAT HIS *ARROGANCE* WOULD BE YOURS AS WELL--AND THAT ONCE YOU POSSESSED IT, YOU WOULD *REFUSE* TO WORK FOR ME.

BUT, AS ALWAYS, I AM PREPARED AGAINST INSUBORDINATION.

ZITT!

HAD YOU **OBEYED** ME, YOU WOULD HAVE HAD POWER BEYOND IMAGINATION.

NOW YOUR ASHES WILL **MINGLE** WITH DRACULA'S.

I'VE PROGRAMMED THIS TRANSYLVANIAN BASE TO **EXPLODE**, SO NOW IT IS TIME TO **TELEPORT** MYSELF TO ANOTHER BASE--

--FAREWELL, BRAND.

MAY MY **NEXT** CHOICE NOT BE MADE SO FOOLISHLY.

THERE IS A QUICK AND BLINDING **FLASH** OF WHITE LIGHT--

--AND THEN **NOTHING.**

WHILE...

C'MON, RACHEL-- WE'VE GOT TO **MOVE**-- BEFORE THIS WHOLE PLACE EXPLODES.

NO TELLING WHEN SUN SET THE BOMBS TO GO OFF.

MADE IT.

MORE THAN SIMPLY MADE IT FRANK, DRACULA FINALLY DEAD. **FINALLY DEAD!**

BUT, WITHIN THE STILL-BLAZING CAVERN FAR **BELOW** THE NOW DISTANT HELICOP- TER...

...A MISTY FORM BEGINS TO **RISE** OUT OF THE FLAMES... A FORM THAT SLOWLY CHANGES ONCE AGAIN INTO A RAVEN- WINGED **BAT**...

A BAT WHICH ARCS ITS WAY THROUGH THE WINDING CATA- COMBS AT AN ALMOST **BLINDING** SPEED...

...RACING TO SAVE A LIFE THAT HAS ALREADY BEEN **ENDED** MORE THAN FIVE CENTURIES PAST.

THERE IS THEN A LAUGHTER WHICH ECHOES THROUGH THE HEAVENS... A LAUGHTER WHICH DROWNS OUT THE VERY SOUNDS OF A DEEP- ROARING **EXPLOSION**--

-- WHICH TEARS APART ALMOST HALF AN ENTIRE **MOUNTAINSIDE.**

FOR THIS IS THE LAUGHTER THAT COMES FROM **BEYOND** THE GRAVE.

NEXT: BEHIND THE IRON CURTAIN

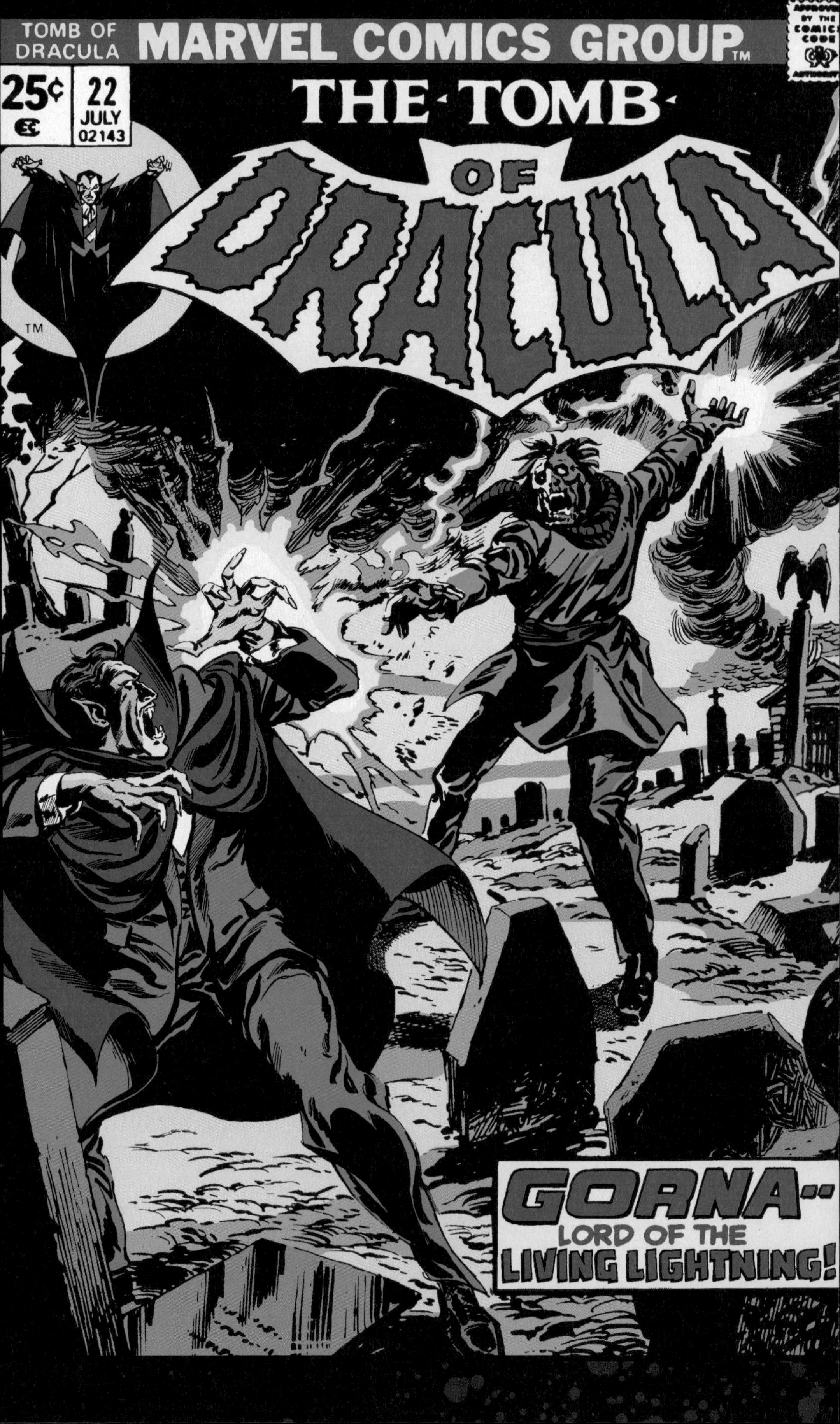
TOMB OF DRACULA
MARVEL COMICS GROUP
25¢
22
JULY
02143
THE TOMB
OF
DRACULA
GORNA--
LORD OF THE
LIVING LIGHTNING!

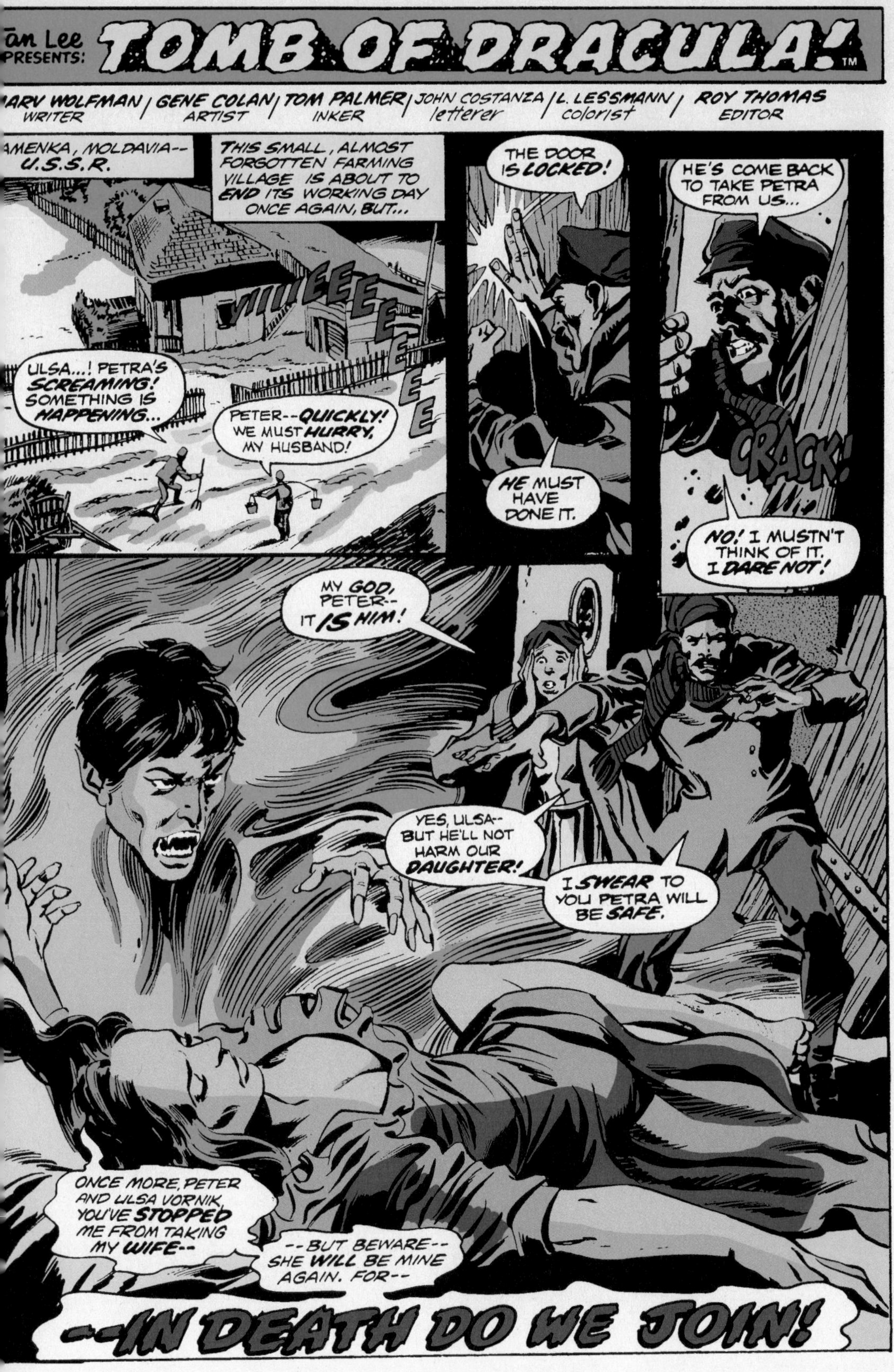

Stan Lee PRESENTS:
TOMB OF DRACULA!
MARV WOLFMAN WRITER
GENE COLAN ARTIST
TOM PALMER INKER
JOHN COSTANZA letterer
L. LESSMANN colorist
ROY THOMAS EDITOR
KAMENKA, MOLDAVIA-- U.S.S.R.
THIS SMALL, ALMOST FORGOTTEN FARMING VILLAGE IS ABOUT TO END ITS WORKING DAY ONCE AGAIN, BUT...
YIIIIEEEEEEEEE
ULSA...! PETRA'S SCREAMING! SOMETHING IS HAPPENING...
PETER--QUICKLY! WE MUST HURRY, MY HUSBAND!
THE DOOR IS LOCKED!
HE MUST HAVE DONE IT.
HE'S COME BACK TO TAKE PETRA FROM US...
CRACK!
NO! I MUSTN'T THINK OF IT. I DARE NOT!
MY GOD, PETER-- IT IS HIM!
YES, ULSA-- BUT HE'LL NOT HARM OUR DAUGHTER!
I SWEAR TO YOU PETRA WILL BE SAFE.
ONCE MORE, PETER AND ULSA VORNIK, YOU'VE STOPPED ME FROM TAKING MY WIFE--
--BUT BEWARE-- SHE WILL BE MINE AGAIN. FOR--
--IN DEATH DO WE JOIN!

PETER VORNIK **ATTACKS**, BUT IT IS ALREADY FAR **TOO LATE**. FOR, WITH EACH STEP THE BONE-WEARY FARMER TAKES, HIS **PREY CHANGES**...

...THE VAMPIRE'S **FLESH** CONTRACTS INTO A LEATHERY **HIDE**. HIS **ARMS** FOLD OUT INTO WIDE-SPREAD **WINGS**...

..., AND HE **RISES** FROM THE WINDOW INTO THE COLD **FEBRUARY** SKIES-- **NOT** AS THE MAN HE HAD **APPEARED** TO HAVE BEEN--

--BUT AS THE HELLISH **REALITY** HE TRULY IS.

AND HE LEAVES IN HIS **WAKE** A SORROW-FILLED **FATHER** CURSING ONLY HIS OWN AGONY AND GRIEF

OH LORD, ULSA. WHAT IF WE WERE TOO **LATE?** DO YOU THINK...?

WE CAN ONLY **PRAY**, MY PETER...

...AND MAY THE GOD WHO HAS BEEN **DRIVEN** FROM OUR HOMES **HEAR** OUR PRAYER AND HAVE **PITY** ON THEM.

ABOVE THE SPARSE **GRASSLANDS** OF KAMENKA, DRACULA RESTS. HIS WATCHFUL EYES TAKE IN THE TINY ANT-LIKE SPECKS FLITTING ACROSS THE VALLEY FLOOR, AND THE LORD OF EVIL **SMILES**.

THESE PEOPLE ARE **PEASANTS**, MERE WORKERS. IN OTHER TIMES THEY WOULD BE **IGNORED**, TRAMPLED OVER, AND THEN **FORGOTTEN**.

BUT THOSE TIMES ARE LONG **GONE** NOW. FOR THROUGH THEIR PEASANT VEINS FLOWS THE SAME **BLOOD** THAT COURSES THROUGH ANY PRINCE OR KING.

AND TO A THIRSTY PRINCE OF DARKNESS THAT BLOOD IS **RICH** AND **RIPE** AND WAITING FOR THE **KILL**.

S, THESE
PLE MAY BE
OR. THEIR
ALTH MAY
LY BE IN
EIR ALL-TOO-
RTAL *SOULS*...

--BUT THESE ARE PEOPLE WHO TRULY *LIVE.*

THESE ARE PEOPLE WHO KNOW HOW TO *LOVE!*

AND AS SUCH THEY ARE THE *EQUAL* OF *ANY* MAN.

NOUGH
EASURE,
AD.

THESE ARE *HARD* TIMES.

WHAT--?

AND THEY SHOULD BE SPENT IN WAYS *OTHER* THAN LOVEMAKING.

LEONID KORSAK IS FLUNG ACROSS THE BARN HE HAS TENDED SINCE HE WAS BUT *TWO.*

AND IN THAT VERY BARN HE *DIES*-- HIS HEAD SHATTERING... HIS BRAINS COMPACTING LIKE *OATMEAL.*

YOUR *FRIEND* HELD *LITTLE* INTEREST FOR ME, GIRL--

--FOR IT IS *YOUR* BLOOD I DESIRE.

KATERINA STENSKI SCREAMS. THEN...

...SHE, TOO, DIES.

DRACULA IS *SATED* ONCE AGAIN, AND SO HE RISES AND LEAVES...

...WITH TWO SILENT *CORPSES* AS THE ONLY EVIDENCE OF HIS *PASSAGE...*

207

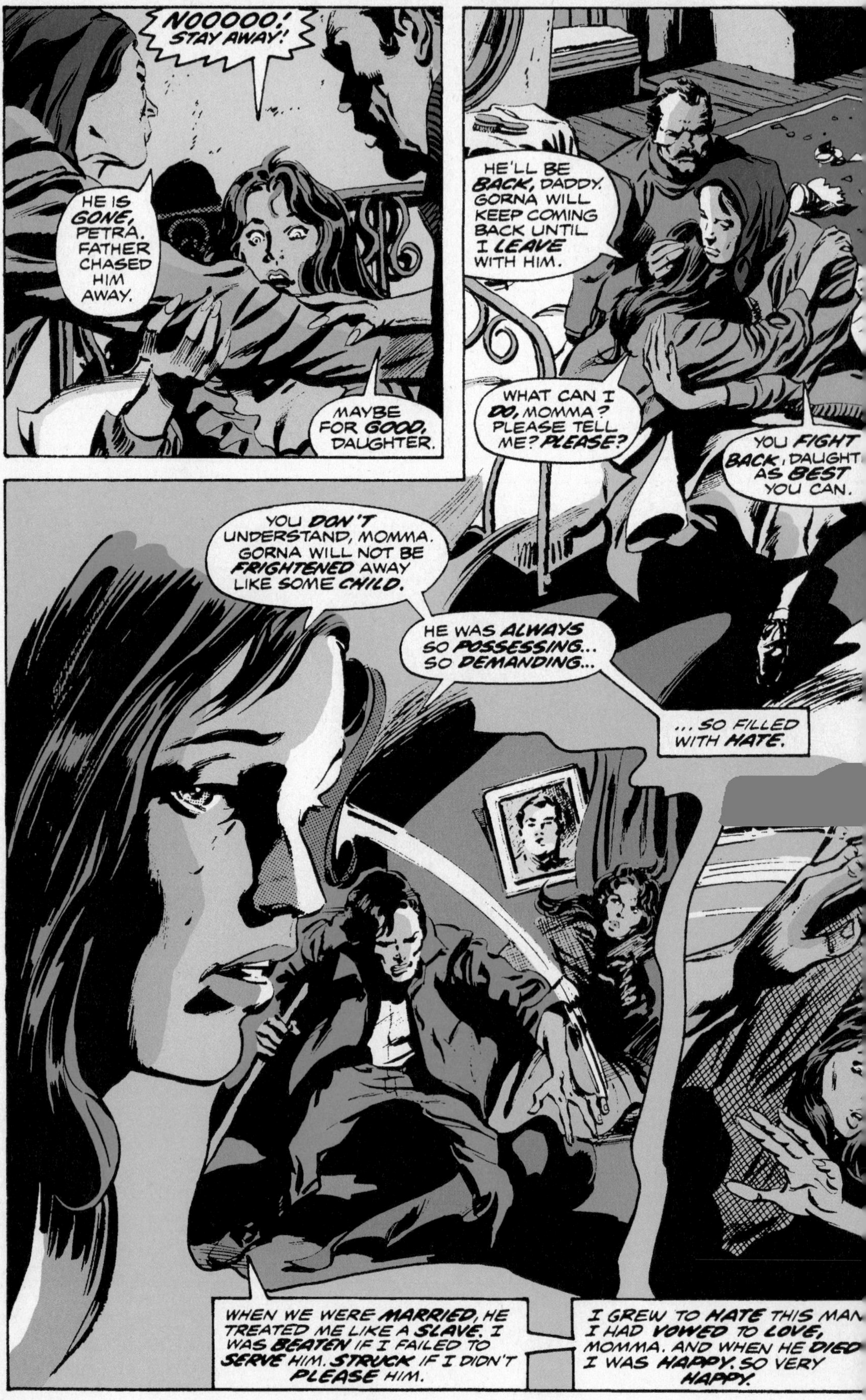
NOOOOO! STAY AWAY!
HE IS GONE, PETRA. FATHER CHASED HIM AWAY.
MAYBE FOR GOOD, DAUGHTER.
HE'LL BE BACK, DADDY. GORNA WILL KEEP COMING BACK UNTIL I LEAVE WITH HIM.
WHAT CAN I DO, MOMMA? PLEASE TELL ME? PLEASE?
YOU FIGHT BACK, DAUGHT AS BEST YOU CAN.
YOU DON'T UNDERSTAND, MOMMA. GORNA WILL NOT BE FRIGHTENED AWAY LIKE SOME CHILD.
HE WAS ALWAYS SO POSSESSING... SO DEMANDING...
...SO FILLED WITH HATE.
WHEN WE WERE MARRIED, HE TREATED ME LIKE A SLAVE. I WAS BEATEN IF I FAILED TO SERVE HIM. STRUCK IF I DIDN'T PLEASE HIM.
I GREW TO HATE THIS MAN I HAD VOWED TO LOVE, MOMMA. AND WHEN HE DIED I WAS HAPPY. SO VERY HAPPY.

"AND, MOMMA-- HE WAS SO *JEALOUS.* LAST YEAR, IN THE TOWN *CIRCLE,* A YOUNG *MAN* ASKED ME *DIRECTIONS.* GORNA GLARED AT US."

"THAT *EVENING,* GORNA *DISAPPEARED* FROM OUR *BEDROOM...*"

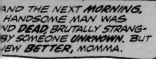

"GORNA *BRAGGED* TO ME WHAT HE DID, THEN *PUNISHED* ME FOR SPEAKING TO THE MAN."

"MOMMA, I CONFESS I *CURSED* GORNA ALL THAT WEEK. I PRAYED TO *GOD* THAT HE WOULD HAVE *HELL* SWALLOW UP THAT HATEFUL MAN."

"...AND THE NEXT *MORNING,* [THE] HANDSOME MAN WAS [FOU]ND *DEAD,* BRUTALLY STRANG[LED] BY SOMEONE *UNKNOWN.* BUT [I K]NEW *BETTER,* MOMMA."

"I WAS LOCKED AWAY IN OUR *BASEMENT* FOR ALMOST A WEEK."

"I PRAYED THAT HE WOULD *DIE* AND THAT I WOULD BE *DONE* WITH HIM."

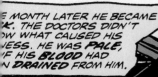

"[ON]E MONTH LATER HE BECAME [SIC]K. THE DOCTORS DIDN'T [KNO]W WHAT CAUSED HIS [ILLN]ESS. HE WAS *PALE,* [AS IF] HIS *BLOOD* HAD [BEE]N *DRAINED* FROM HIM."

"[A]S HE LAY DYING, HE [D]REW ME *CLOSE,* AND [H]E *SHOUTED,'* YOU [M]UST *NEVER* MARRY. [I] WON'T *ALLOW* IT. [N]O *OTHER* MAN MUST [N]EVER HAVE YOU."

"[DO] YOU *UNDERSTAND,* WIFE? [COU]LD YOU EVER SEE ANOTHER [MA]N, I WILL COME BACK FROM [THE] *GRAVE* TO HAUNT YOU BOTH.!"

"I LAUGHED AT HIM, AND SHOUTED TO THE WORLD THAT I WOULD BE *FREE.* BUT AS HE DIED, HE MERELY *SMILED...* KNOWINGLY.'"

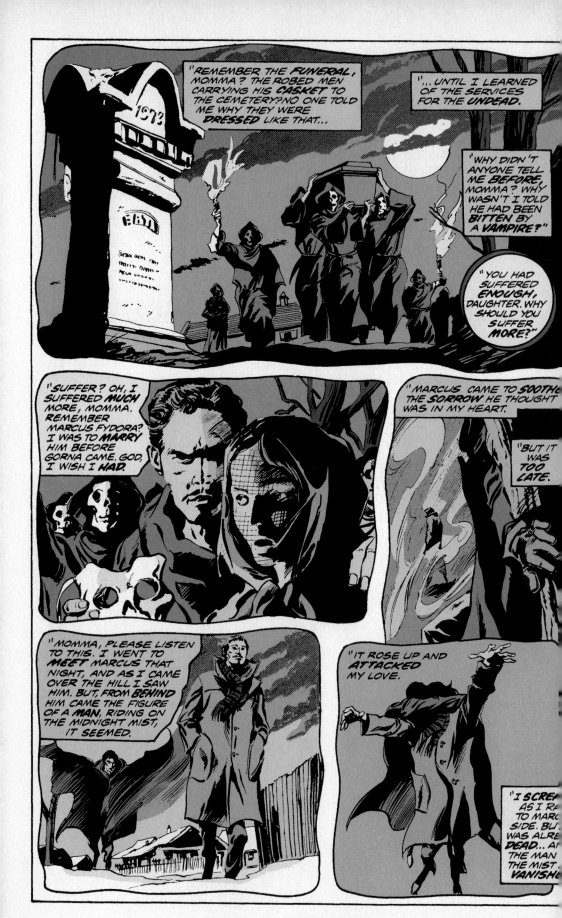

"REMEMBER THE *FUNERAL*, MOMMA? THE ROBED MEN CARRYING HIS *CASKET* TO THE CEMETERY? NO ONE TOLD ME WHY THEY WERE *DRESSED* LIKE THAT...

"...UNTIL I LEARNED OF THE SERVICES FOR THE *UNDEAD*.

"WHY DIDN'T ANYONE TELL ME *BEFORE*, MOMMA? WHY WASN'T I TOLD HE HAD BEEN *BITTEN* BY A *VAMPIRE*?"

"YOU HAD SUFFERED *ENOUGH*, DAUGHTER. WHY SHOULD YOU SUFFER *MORE*?"

"SUFFER? OH, I SUFFERED *MUCH* MORE, MOMMA. REMEMBER MARCUS FYDORA? I WAS TO *MARRY* HIM BEFORE GORNA CAME. GOD, I WISH I *HAD*.

"MARCUS CAME TO *SOOTHE* THE *SORROW* HE THOUGHT WAS IN MY HEART.

"BUT IT WAS *TOO LATE*.

"MOMMA, PLEASE LISTEN TO THIS. I WENT TO *MEET* MARCUS THAT NIGHT, AND AS I CAME OVER THE HILL I SAW HIM. BUT, FROM *BEHIND* HIM CAME THE FIGURE OF A *MAN*, RIDING ON THE MIDNIGHT MIST, IT SEEMED.

"IT ROSE UP AND *ATTACKED* MY LOVE.

"I SCRE[A]
AS I R[AN]
TO MAR[CUS']
SIDE. BU[T]
WAS ALRE[ADY]
DEAD... A[ND]
THE MAN [AND]
THE MIST [...]
VANISH[ED]

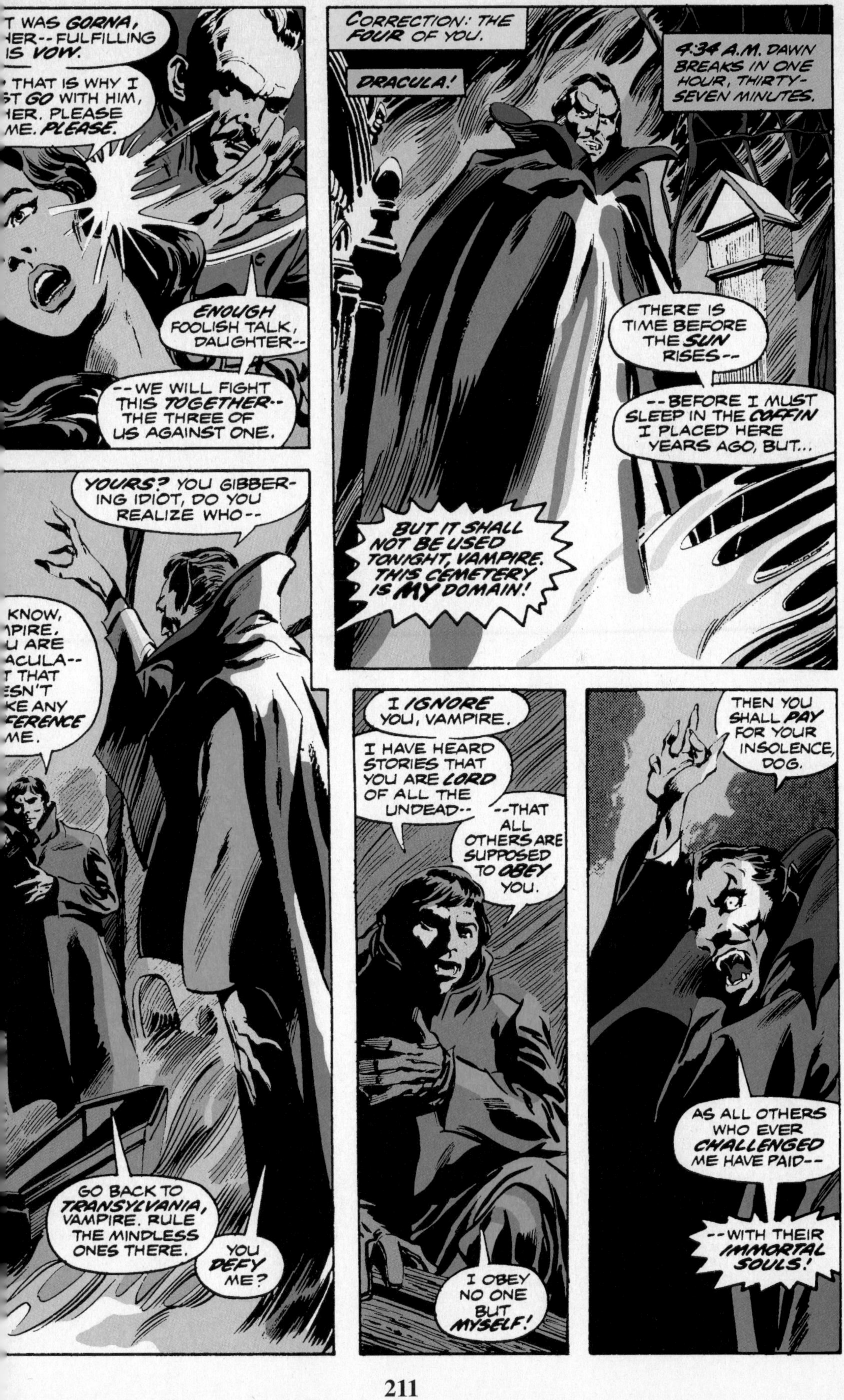

T WAS GORNA,
HER--FULFILLING
IS VOW.
THAT IS WHY I
ST GO WITH HIM,
HER. PLEASE
ME. PLEASE.
ENOUGH FOOLISH TALK, DAUGHTER--
--WE WILL FIGHT THIS TOGETHER-- THE THREE OF US AGAINST ONE.
CORRECTION: THE FOUR OF YOU.
DRACULA!
4:34 A.M. DAWN BREAKS IN ONE HOUR, THIRTY-SEVEN MINUTES.
THERE IS TIME BEFORE THE SUN RISES--
--BEFORE I MUST SLEEP IN THE COFFIN I PLACED HERE YEARS AGO, BUT...
BUT IT SHALL NOT BE USED TONIGHT, VAMPIRE. THIS CEMETERY IS MY DOMAIN!
YOURS? YOU GIBBERING IDIOT, DO YOU REALIZE WHO--
KNOW,
PIRE.
U ARE
ACULA--
T THAT
ESN'T
KE ANY
FERENCE
ME.
GO BACK TO TRANSYLVANIA, VAMPIRE. RULE THE MINDLESS ONES THERE.
YOU DEFY ME?
I IGNORE YOU, VAMPIRE.
I HAVE HEARD STORIES THAT YOU ARE LORD OF ALL THE UNDEAD--
--THAT ALL OTHERS ARE SUPPOSED TO OBEY YOU.
I OBEY NO ONE BUT MYSELF!
THEN YOU SHALL PAY FOR YOUR INSOLENCE, DOG.
AS ALL OTHERS WHO EVER CHALLENGED ME HAVE PAID--
--WITH THEIR IMMORTAL SOULS!

DRACULA'S HAND RISES TOWARDS THE EBONY-STREAKED *HEAVENS*-- HIS VOICE BECKONS THE VERY *FURIES OF NATURE,* AND THEN THE SKY *SHATTERS...*

...AND *DEATH* HURTLES DOWNWARD WITH A VENGEANCE.

IS THIS THE VERY *BEST* YOU CAN DO, VAMPIRE?

IF SO, YOUR *FAME* IS LITTLE MORE THAN A MERE *LEGEND.*

THEN *ENOU* I HAVE MY *WOMAN* TO CO CERN ME... NOT HAPLESS BRAGGAR.

NO! YOU'RE NOT TO LEAV NOT TILL I *COMMAND* IT

BUT THERE IS NO *REPLY* AS THE VAMPIRE STREAKS UPWARD... HIS LONG BLACK WINGS BEATING A PATHWAY ABOVE THE VILLAGE OF *KAMENKA...*

...FOR HIS SOUL HAS BEEN *TORTURED* BY THE INDISCRETIONS HE FEELS HIS WIFE COMMITTED, AND HE SEEKS TO SOOTHE HIS TURMOIL.

AND BY THE TIME *DRACULA* HAS TAKEN TO TH VERY SAME SKIES-- GORNA IS *GONE.*

SCOURING THE SMALL RUSSIAN VILLAGE IS *FRUITLESS,* FOR THERE ARE NO CLUES TO THE VAMPIRE'S DISAPPEARANCE. THUS DRACULA, HIS WINGS *HEAVY* WITH FAILURE, TURNS...

...AND HE PAUSES IN HIS FLIGHT TO *WONDER* HOW HIS ORDERS WERE *IGNORED.*

BUT THE QUESTION IS QUICKLY *FORGOTTE* AND WITH AN ARISTO-CRATIC ARROGANCE, THE LO OF DARKNESS FLIES ON-- SEEKING ONE MORE *VICTIM* BEFORE THE NIGHT IS DONE.

...RA VORNIK'S DREAMS LAY *UNDISTURBED* FOR HOURS, ...TING TO THOUGHTS OF HAPPY YOUTHS AND ABANDONED ...ANCES--

--AND *NOT* TO THE ENDLESS *SORROW* OF HER OWN DISMAL REALITY.

OUTSIDE HER WINDOW THE SKY SCREAMS WITH *THUNDER*...

...BRINGING WITH ITS WAIL THE *HORROR* SHE HAS *PURGED* FROM HER MIND.

AWAKEN, MY WIFE. YOUR *HUSBAND* COMMANDS YOUR OBEDIENCE.

NO, PETRA... YOU WILL NOT SCREAM. *YOU WILL NOT SCREAM!*

YOU ARE MY *WIFE,* PETRA-- AND EVEN IN *DEATH* YOU ARE MINE. *COME TO ME.*

SHE RISES AGAINST HER OWN WILL. SHE IS NAUSEOUS, SICK, BUT NOTHING COMES-- NOT EVEN AS THE VAMPIRE'S FETID *BREATH* SPILLS UPON HER.

SHE STARES AT HIS GHASTLY WHITE *PALLOR* AND IS REVOLTED BY IT, BUT SHE CAN NOT *FIGHT* HIS WILL... THERE CAN BE NO *RESISTING* HIS *HYPNOTIC* ORDERS.

...THE SOUNDS GAG ...D IN HER THROAT.

...COLD, *MAGGOT-* ...EN FINGERS CLUTCH ...NECK... HIS HARSH ...K DRY *LIPS* MEET ...R OWN AND SHE PRAYS THAT SHE MAY *FAINT.*

BUT NOTHING HAPPENS.

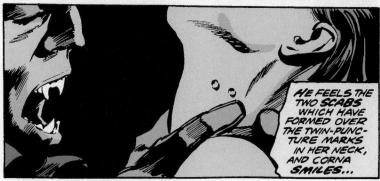

HE FEELS THE TWO *SCABS* WHICH HAVE FORMED OVER THE TWIN-PUNC- TURE MARKS IN HER NECK, AND CORNA *SMILES...*

213

...AS HE FANGS HER ONCE MORE!

RIPE BLOOD SPILLS FROM HER WOUND, BUT STILL SHE CANNOT SCREAM.

MERCIFULLY, UNCONSCIOUSNESS CLAIMS HER.

BUT THEN...

SO, I DID HEAR NOISES IN PETRA'S ROOM.

PUT DOWN MY DAUGHTER, GORNA-- OR THIS STAKE WILL END YOUR DAMNED EXISTENCE FOREVER.

I WILL NOT G HER UP S EASILY, FATHER-IN LAW...

...SHE WAS MINE IN LIFE. SHE SHALL ALWAYS BE MINE.

NO, GORNA--

VORNIK SUDDENLY THRUSTS THE WOODEN STAKE INTO THE FIREPLACE. ITS TIP IGNITES, CATCHES THE FLICKERING FLAMES, AND THEN...

--SHE WILL NEVER BE YOURS.

...HE SPINS, SHOVING THE N FLAMING STAK INTO THE ARM THE ASTONISHE VAMPIRE

FIRE! NOOOOOO!!

214

...NTICALLY, GORNA [S] TOWARDS THE [DOW], AND THEN [GE]S FORWARD, [SH]ING THROUGH SHATTERING *GLASS*...

...BUT IT IS A FLAMING *BAT* WHICH RISES INTO THE NIGHT...

...HIGHER...EVER HIGHER UNTIL IT IS SWALLOWED BY THE *DARKNESS*...

...UNTIL ONLY A FLAMING *TAIL* LIKE THAT OF A RUSHING *COMET* CAN BEEN SEEN.

[N] MANY OF THE EARLY [E]RS STARE UPWARD IN [NC]E, HARDLY COMPRE-[ND]ING THE STREAKING *FIRE*-[L] ABOVE THEM, WE WILL [ER] KNOW...

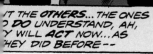

[T] THE *OTHERS*...THE ONES [O] *DO* UNDERSTAND, AH, [Y] WILL *ACT* NOW...AS [HE]Y DID BEFORE--

--WHEN THEY LAST *BURIED* THIS FLYING MAN-BAT.

A MOMENT LATER *ANOTHER* DARK-WINGED SHAPE FLITS ACROSS THE HORIZON FROM A DIFFERENT DIREC- TION...

...FOR, DRACULA HAS FINALLY *TRACED* GORNA'S PATH TO THIS WEATHERED FRAME-WOOD FARMHOUSE...

AND WITH A VENGEANCE--

--HE ENTERS, GIRDING HIMSELF FOR HIS IMPENDING *BATTLE*.

BUT... HIDE, ULSA-- GORNA'S *BACK!*

NO, PETER, IT IS NOT HIM...

AS YOUR *HUSBAND* SHOULD HAVE KNOWN, WOMAN...

I COME *SEEKING* THE ONE HE CALLED GORNA, AND HE WAS HERE, I *KNOW* THAT.

MY *SENSES* TELL ME *YOU* ARE THE FOCAL POINT OF THIS MADNESS, GIRL--

SPEAK, THEN-- TELL ME WHAT I WISH TO *KNOW.*

I...CANNOT...

YOU *WILL*, GIRL. LOOK AT ME-- *STARE* DEEPLY INTO MY EYES AND TELL ME EVERYTHING.

EVERY-THING.

THE GIRL *HESITATES,* AND THEN...

...SHE SPEAKS...SPUTTERS OUT THE *WORDS* NERVOUSLY, UNTIL...

MOST OF THE *PUZZLE* IS CLEAR NOW, AND THOUGH I STILL DO NOT UNDERSTAND *HOW* GORNA WAS ABLE TO RESIST MY COMMANDS--

--I NOW *KNOW* ENOUGH TO *BATTLE* HIM.... TO *HUMBLE* HIM.

FAREWELL NOW, GIRL, AND CONSIDER YOURSELF *FORTUNATE*--

--TO HAVE *DRACULA* DEAL WITH YOUR TROUBLES.

THE VAMPIRE LORD TURNS ONCE MORE TOWARDS THE VELVET *SKIES...*

...AND THEN HE IS *GONE.*

PETRA VORNIK *SHUDDERS* IN HIS WAKE; TWICE TONIGHT SHE HAS STARED *DEATH* IN THE FACE, AND SHE *PRAYS* SHE WILL SOON AWAKE FROM THIS *NIGHT-MARE* BEFORE IT IS *TOO LATE.*

--FROM THIS NIGHTMARE WHICH *GROWS* WITH EVERY PASSING MOMENT.

HAVE ALL LISTENED PETER VORNIK, IT IS NOW *TIME* DECIDE, MY ENDS--

--IF WE FINALLY *END* THAT WHICH WE BEGAN *MONTHS* AGO, OR IF WE ACCEPT BEING THE PLAYTHING OF THIS... THIS *WALKING DEAD.*

BY ONE A *POLL* IS TAKEN--

--A *POLL* WHICH SHALL *AFFECT* THE OUTCOME OF THIS *UNLIVING TERROR*--

--BUT FOR NOW, THE TIME AND SCENE MUST *SHIFT*-- TO LONDON, TWO EVENINGS FROM NOW--AND TO THE ESTATE OF *QUINCY HARKER.*

WHY DIDN'T YOU SEND A *TELEGRAM,* QUINCY? HAD WE KNOWN YOU WERE *ATTACKED*--

I COULD SCARCELY WRITE FROM A *HOSPITAL* BED, MY DEAR. BUT ALL IS WELL *NOW.*

* AS SHOWN IN *CHILLERS* #1. ON SALE *NOW.* --R.T.

THING BUGS QUINCY-- DRACULA DIE HE FLAMES NG HIS FIGHT * DOCTOR SUN-- THIS GIRL ATTACKED YOU...

...SAID SHE WAS DRACULA'S DAUGHTER, YES, MR. DRAKE-- SHE HAS *RETURNED* FROM THE GRAVE *I* PUT HER IN THIRTY YEARS AGO.

AND ONLY *GOD,* I FEAR, KNOWS WHAT EVIL SHE IS UP TO.

* A SOMEWHAT *DISTORTED* VIEW OF LAST ISSUE. --ROY.

THERE'S *ANOTHER* PROBLEM, QUINCY-- *TAJ HAS DISAPPEARED*...

AND ACCORDING TO THE CRUMPLED *NOTE* I FOUND ON HIS *BED*--

--HE'S RETURNING HOME... TO *INDIA.* *

* ALSO SHOWN IN *CHILLERS* #1. --R.T.

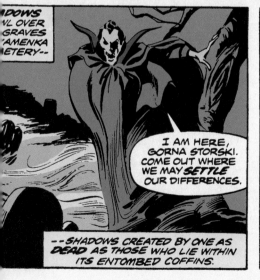

DOWS L OVER GRAVES AMENKA METERY--

I AM HERE, GORNA STORSKI. COME OUT WHERE WE MAY *SETTLE* OUR DIFFERENCES.

--SHADOWS CREATED BY ONE AS *DEAD* AS THOSE WHO LIE WITHIN ITS ENTOMBED COFFINS.

THEN SEE ME AS I *NOW* AM, PRINCE OF EVIL--

--SEE ME AND WITNESS YOUR *DESTRUCTION!*

217

DRACULA SPINS INTO THE FACE OF *DEATH* -- A SIX FOOT HORROR THAT COULD ONLY HAVE BEEN *CONCEIVED* IN THE VERY *BOWELS* OF HELL ITSELF.

HIS *FLESH* SEARED FROM HIS BONES, THE VAMPIRE GORNA STANDS, A MOCKING GHASTLY FIGURE DRAPED IN THE VERY *LIGHTNING* HE COMMANDS.

GORNA SCREAMS AS FLAMES *ERUPT* FROM HIS FINGERTIPS, AND THE SCREAM IS COLD AND EVIL, AND, MAY ALL THE *GODS* FORGIVE US, *DAMNING* WITH ITS VERY TONE.

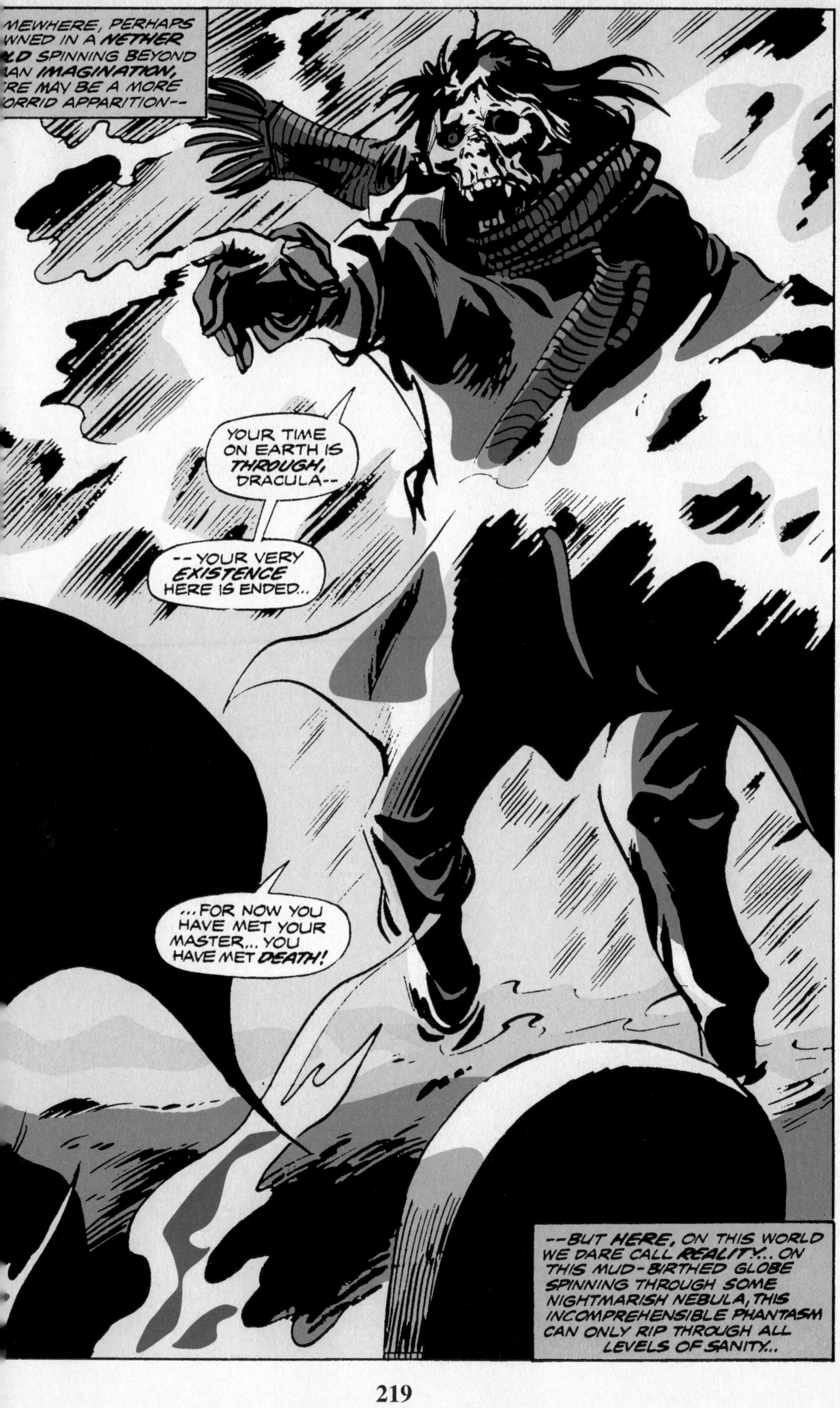
MEWHERE, PERHAPS WNED IN A NETHER LD SPINNING BEYOND MAN IMAGINATION, RE MAY BE A MORE ORRID APPARITION--
YOUR TIME ON EARTH IS THROUGH, DRACULA--
--YOUR VERY EXISTENCE HERE IS ENDED..
...FOR NOW YOU HAVE MET YOUR MASTER... YOU HAVE MET DEATH!
--BUT HERE, ON THIS WORLD WE DARE CALL REALITY... ON THIS MUD-BIRTHED GLOBE SPINNING THROUGH SOME NIGHTMARISH NEBULA, THIS INCOMPREHENSIBLE PHANTASM CAN ONLY RIP THROUGH ALL LEVELS OF SANITY...

WHILE, IN THE *TOWN* ITSELF...

WE GO NOW-- TO FIND THE *COFFIN* OF GORNA-- AND TO CAPTURE HIM IN IT.

COME WITH US, PETRA-- AND WIELD THE STAKE YOUR-SELF. WHO *DESERVES* THAT HONOR MORE?

NO, FATHER--

--YOU GO, DO WHAT YOU *MUST*, I WILL COME LATER--

--WHEN MY *HUSBAND* HAS BEEN LAID TO HIS *FINAL* REST.

THE RUSSIAN VALLEY IS BATHED IN THE COLORS OF DAWNING SUN-- THE BLUES AND BLACKS OF NIGHT MELT INTO WARM PINKS AND MORNING REDS--

--BUT EVEN IN THIS STEADILY RISING LIGHT, THE STREAM OF FLAMING *TORCHES* CARRIED ALOFT BY THE DARKLY DRESSED *VILLAGERS*, CAN BE SEEN--

--AS A SOMBERLY QUIET PARTY OF MARCHING *MOURNERS* MOVES ONWARD TO THE CEMETERY GROUNDS.

WHERE...

YOU STILL *LIVE,* DRACULA?

MY FLAMES DID NOT *STOP* YOU-- DID NOT *BURN* THE LIFE FROM YOU?

R
LL
Y,
PIRE--

THE SUN **RISES** EVEN AS WE SPEAK-- THUS THERE CAN BE **NO TIME** FOR FOOLISHNESS NOW...

NO TIME FOR PETTY **TALK.**

GORNA STORSKI, YOU HAVE **BLASPHEMED** YOUR MASTER... YOUR **LORD,** AND SO YOU MUST BE **PUNISHED.**

YOUR MADNESS HOLDS NO INTEREST FOR ME... YOUR **MISSION** ON EARTH IS OF NO IMPORT--

--FOR, IF YOU CAN NOT BE HELD AT **BAY** BY ME-- IF YOU DO NOT **NEED** AND **OBEY** MY EVERY WORD... MY EVERY **COMMAND**--

--THEN, BE **DAMNED** WITH YOU--

-- IN THE VERY FIRES OF YOUR **OWN CREATION!**

PERISH, GORNA STORSKI, AND PRAY FORGIVENESS FOR YOUR **DEEDS.**

AND KNOW-- THAT AS THE FLAMES **CONSUME** YOU-- THAT DRACULA IS YOUR **GOD**--

--AND DRACULA IS INDEED A **VENGEFUL** GOD!

AGGHHHHHH!!

221

THEY HEAR THE SCREAM--THAT HELLISH *WAIL*--AND, FOR A MOMENT, THEY FREEZE IN THEIR OWN *FEAR*.

THEN, SLOWLY-- EVER SO DESPERATELY SLOWLY, THEY MOVE ON-- THEIR STEPS WEIGHING *HEAVILY* IN THE MORNING MIST.

AND STILL THE SCREAM CONTINUES-- LONG AFTER THE REMAINING FLESH HAS BEEN *BURNED* AWAY... LONG AFT. THE ESSENCE OF *UNLIFE* HAS FLED WHATEVER *SOUL* SURVIVED--

--LONG AFTER TH. FLUTTER OF FLEEIN WINGS CAN BE HEA STILL THE SCREAM ECHOS ON... AND ON

...AND STILL C

RRAAAARRGGH

THERE, DAUGHTER-- YOUR *TERROR* IS GONE FOR GOOD NOW. FOREVER.

OH LORD, OH LORD... *OH LORD!*

NO WORDS ARE SPOKEN, BUT AS THE LAST *FLAMES* DIE, PETRA FEELS HER NECK GROW *TIGHT*...

... AND THE FINAL FATAL *BITE-MARKS* FADE.

THE SUN IS ABOUT TO RISE, AND DRACULA ABOUT TO *REST*, FOR THERE IS AN *END* NOW TO WHAT HAD *BEGUN* SO MANY MONTHS BEFORE.

PETRA VORNIK'S FINGERS SIFT THROUGH THE *ASHES* OF HER HUSBAND, AND ONE SINGLE SOLITARY *TEAR* TRICKLES DOWN FROM HER EYE.

THE *PAST* HAS FINALLY ENDED FOR HER NOW. AND A *FUTURE* BECKONS WITH THE COMING OF THE *SUN*.

222

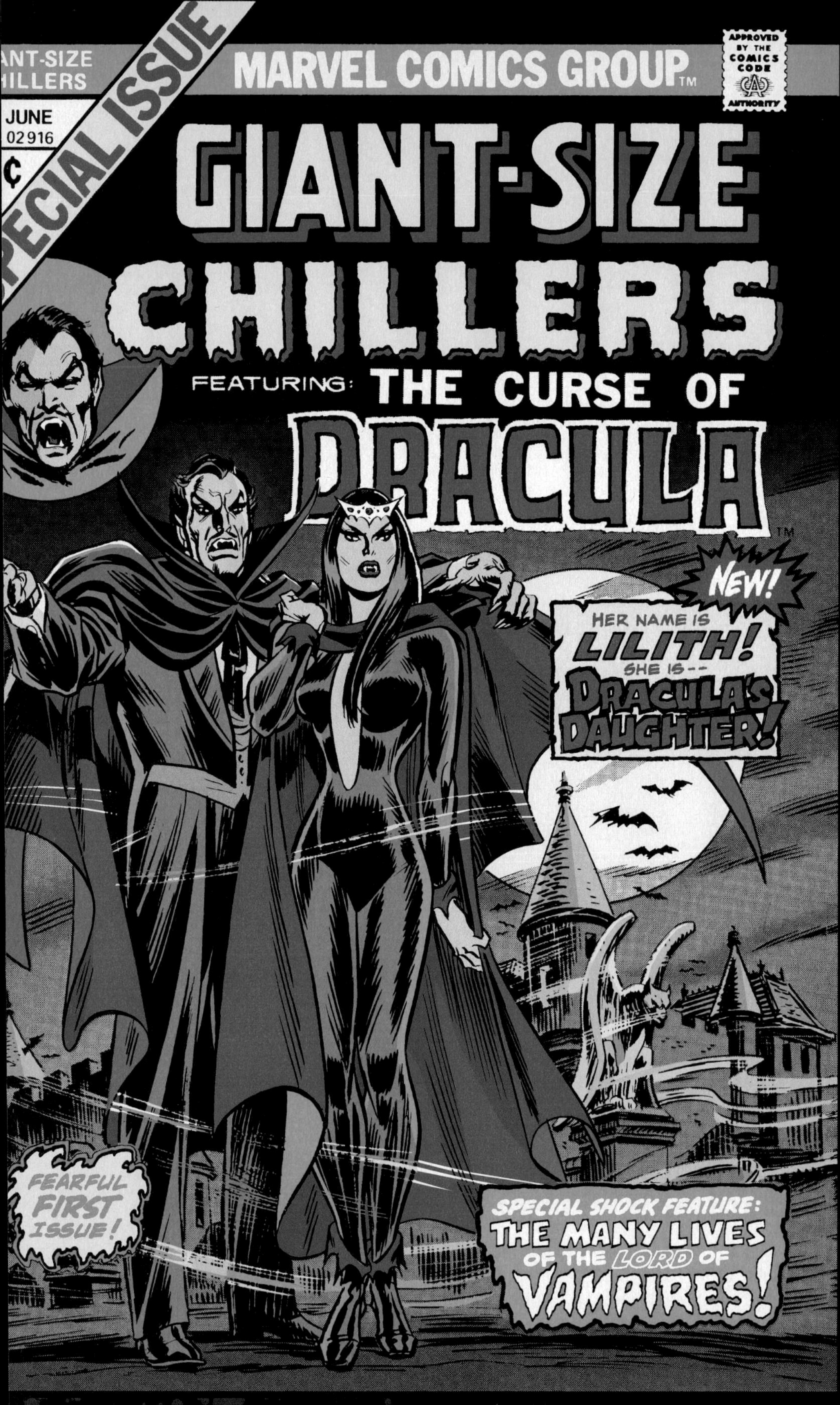
ANT-SIZE
HILLERS
JUNE
02916
¢
SPECIAL ISSUE
MARVEL COMICS GROUP
APPROVED BY THE COMICS CODE AUTHORITY
GIANT-SIZE
CHILLERS
FEATURING: THE CURSE OF
DRACULA
NEW!
HER NAME IS
LILITH!
SHE IS--
DRACULA'S
DAUGHTER!
FEARFUL
FIRST
ISSUE!
SPECIAL SHOCK FEATURE:
THE MANY LIVES
OF THE LORD OF
VAMPIRES!

STAN LEE PRESENTS: CURSE OF DRACULA!

MARV WOLFMAN *WRITER* / GENE COLAN *ARTIST* / F. CHIARAMONTE *INKER* / ARTIE SIMEK, *LETTERER* P. GOLDBERG, *COLORIST* / ROY THO... *EDITOR*

LONDON AT MIDNIGHT:

TONIGHT IT IS A QUIET, ALMOST **SULLEN** CITY, NESTLED DEEP IN MUTED LIGHTS AND SILENCED WHISPERS.

BIG BEN CHIMES SOFTLY. VOICES WAITING TO BE **REBORN** WITH THE SPRINGTIME LEAVES ARE NOW **HUSHED** IN THESE DYING DAYS OF WINTER.

TONIGHT THERE IS NO JOY, NO **GAIETY**--

--TONIGHT IS A NIGHT FOR **FEAR.**

TONIGHT IS THE NIGHT DRACULA RETURNS TO LONDON.

Night of the SHE-DEMON

...THE GUARDS DIDN'T SEE YOU... THE SERVICE EMPLOYEES NEVER HEARD THE LEATHERY FLUTTER AS YOUR WINGS RUSHED PAST THEM...

...YET, YOU'RE INSIDE NOW, WAFTING THROUGH THE ANCIENT HALLOWED HALLS OF PARLIAMENT...

...UNTIL ONE PARTICULAR OAKEN DOOR COMES WITHIN YOUR SIGHT.

YOU KNOW HE'S IN THERE, DON'T YOU, DRACULA? AND SO, YOU ENTER.

PRIVATE

THAT WILL BE ALL FOR TONIGHT, MISS RIGBY...

...AND I AM SO SORRY TO KEEP YOU HERE THIS LATE, ESPECIALLY ON A SUNDAY.

NO PROBLEM, LORD HENRY. M'GEORGE IS OFF WI' 'IS FRIENDS ANYHOW, HE IS.

WOULD'VE PROB'LY BEEN WATCHIN' THE TELLY, I GUESS. NOTHIN' ELSE.

A PLEASANT SECRETARY I HAVE, LORD HENRY. THOUGH HARDLY TOO BRIGHT. BUT I GUESS THERE ARE COMPENSATIONS, EH?

COME IN NOW, SIT DOWN. THERE ARE THINGS WE MUST DISCUSS.

UNHHHHHHH...

I WORKED LATE AS YOU DEMANDED. YOU DID SAY MIDNIGHT, MASTER?

ONE MOMENT THIS MIND SLAVE OF YOURS IS GLIB, EASY, THEN, UPON SEEING YOU, HE CHANGES...

...AND ANOTHER... A SEPARATE CONSCIOUSNESS RISES IN HIM AS HE SPEAKS TO YOU SLOWLY... PRECISELY...ORDERLY. AS YOU HAVE COMMANDED HIM THUS.

YOU LISTEN AS HE GROPES FOR HIS WORDS, AND YOU STARE AT HIS EYES...HIS GLAZED EMPTY EYES WHICH STILL MANAGE TO SHOW FEAR.

Y-YES.

AND YOU SIMPLY SMILE.

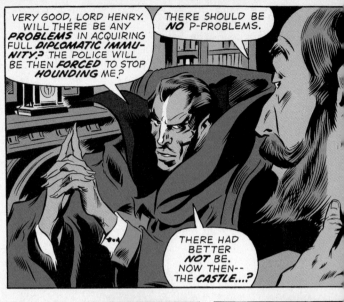

VERY GOOD, LORD HENRY. WILL THERE BE ANY PROBLEMS IN ACQUIRING FULL DIPLOMATIC IMMUNITY? THE POLICE WILL BE THEN FORCED TO STOP HOUNDING ME?

THERE SHOULD BE NO P-PROBLEMS.

THERE HAD BETTER NOT BE. NOW THEN-- THE CASTLE...?

THE ONE YOU REQUESTED IS CURRENTLY POSSESSED BY A SHIELA WHITTIER.

SHE CAN BE, UHHHHH, DISPOSED OF EASILY.

VOICES BANTER ON, REVERBERATING DOWN EMPTY CORRIDORS.

BUT ELSEWHERE, FAR TO THE NORTH, ON A COLD WINDSWEPT HILLTOP...

... A GRAVE WHICH HAS REMAINED SILENT FOR MORE THAN THIRTY YEARS BEGINS TO SHUDDER... TO QUAKE...

...AND FINALLY TO HEA

LET US NOW MOVE A BIT FURTHER TO THE EAST, TO A TINY WOODEN FARMHOUSE OWNED BY ONE MARTIN O'HARA...

SLAP

TRAMP! LOUSY STINKIN' TRAMP!

YOU'RE NO LONGER WELCOME HERE. GET OUT!

PLEASE, FATHER-- NO!

YOU'VE DISGRACED ME, DAUGHTER--

I RAISE Y MYSELF...G YOU EVER THING YO NEED--

--AND THIS IS HOW YOU REPAY ME, YOU MISERABLE FILTHY TROLLOP?

MR. O'HARA

226

BUTT **OUT**, ANNIGAN. LL GET TO OU LATER. RIGHT NOW IT'S THIS DAUGHTER OF MINE I'M **SPEAKIN'** TO.

MY **EX**-DAUGHTER THAT IS. HEAR THAT, TRAMP--MY **EX**-DAUGHTER!

AGAIN THE GRAVE HEAVES AS THE SKIES SWIFTLY **DARKEN**... AS THE LIGHTNING SPILLS DOWN, SPLINTERING THE NIGHT.

AND THEN THE GRAVE **OPENS!**

TEN ME, ARA-- NOW KNOW GEL'S NANT... T SHE'S RIED TO DO YOU ERSTAND E--SHE'S MY E. WE'VE SECRETLY RIED FOR YEAR.

I **LOVE** ANGEL, MR. O'HARA. I LOVE HER WITH ALL MY **HEART.**

LOVE?

YOU **PUNKS** DON'T GIVE ONE BLOODY **HOOT** ABOUT LOVE.

I KNOW WHAT YOU'RE INTER-ESTED IN, MISTER. DON'T TRY TO **FOOL** ME.

LUE HAZE RISES INTO THE BLACK- S OF NIGHT...AND IT **BURNS**-- BURNS WITH AN **EERIE**, GLOW- ING **LIGHT.**

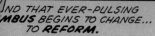

ND THAT EVER-PULSING MBUS BEGINS TO CHANGE... TO **REFORM.**

IT **RESHAPES** ITSELF, BUILDS ON ITSELF--AND THEN **COALESCES** INTO SOMETHING... **HUMAN.**

AND IT RISES, HIGHER... EVER HIGHER INTO THE MIDNIGHT SKIES.

FATHER, PLEASE **DON'T.** WE ONLY KEPT OUR MARRIAGE A **SECRET** BECAUSE WE **KNEW** YOU'D NEVER APPROVE.

BUT WE **DO** LOVE EACH OTHER, SO PLEASE DON'T MAKE IT **WORSE** THAN IT **HAS** TO BE.

WORSE? I'M JUST **BEGINNING,** DAUGHTER.

THIS MARRIAGE IS **ENDING** AS OF NOW

WHAP!

TED!

OOHHHHHHHH!!

HE'S NOT MOVING. OH GOD, FATHER-- **TED'S NOT MOVING.**

THEN HE'S **PLAYIN'.** I DIDN'T HIT HIM THAT HARD.

THOUGH I WISH TO **BLAZES** THAT I HAD.

THE LIGHT CONTINUES TO **GLOW**...CONTINU TO **RISE** OVER THE ENGLISH COUNTRYSIDE UNTIL AT LAST IT ARCS DOWNWARDS..

...TOWARDS THE PATCHED-UP **FARMHOUSE** OF MARTIN O'HARA...

YOU'VE KILLED HIM, FATHER-- HE'S **DEAD.** HIS HEAD HIT THE WALL.

GOD! OH **GOD**-- YOU'VE **KILLED** HIM.

I COULDN'T HAVE... I **SWEAR** TO YOU. I BARELY TOUCHED HIM.

BUT Y DID. Y TOOK LIFE **END** IT.

THEREFORE, DEAR DEAR FATHER-- YOU' LEFT ME ONLY **ON** COURSE OF ACTION TO TAKE. YOU **UNDERSTAND** OF COURSE...

...THAT I MUST **KILL** YOU!

WHAT?!?

THE LIGHT **FADES** NOW, TAKING WITH IT THE LOVELY GIRL NAMED ANGEL O'HARA. AND IN AN **INSTANT,** TWENTY-TWO YEARS OF LIFE **VANISH,** ONLY TO BE **REPLACED** BY A BEING WHO HAS SURVIVED ALMOST **25 TIMES** THAT AGE.

THE BRIGHT RED HAIR GIVES WAY TO **BLACKNESS** AS THE CRISP GREEN EYES FADE INTO HELLISH **RED...**

...AND THE **VOICE,** WHEN ONCE IT SPOKE WITH A GENTLE **FLUTTER** LIKE A BUTTERFLY ON WING...

...NOW IT SPEAKS IN **FROZEN PHRASES** AND SHARP, FEARSOME WORDS.

THERE IS NO **SWEETNESS** IN THE SOMBER IMAGE WHICH RISES FROM THE FLOOR--

--NOR **SHOULD** THERE BE--

--IN **LILITH,** THE DAUGHTER OF DRACULA!!

...I AM STILL YOUR **ANGEL,** DEAR, DEAR FATHER--

--BUT NOW I'M YOUR **ANGEL OF DEATH.**

SLEEP WELL AND **LONG.**

AARRGHHHH

BUT NOW THERE IS **ANOTHER** WHO MUST DIE THIS NIGHT--

--THE MAN WHO **SLEW** ME MORE THAN THIRTY YEARS AGO...

...**QUINCY HARKER!**

WITHIN THE ANCIENT HALLS OF **HARKER ESTATE**, HOWEVER, THAT CRY FOR **REVENGE** IS NOT HEARD, NOR SHALL IT BE...

...UNTIL IT IS FAR TOO **LATE**...

YES...YES. VERY GOOD. **TAJ** AND I AWAIT YOUR RETURN, RACHEL.

WE'LL SEE YOU IN **ONE WEEK** THEN, DEAR. AND PLEAS[E] CONVEY MY **BEST** [TO] MR. DRAKE. GODSP[EED], CHILD.

SOME GOOD NEWS, TAJ. RACHEL TELLS ME THAT SHE BELIEVES DRACULA TO BE FINALLY **DEAD**--

--HAVING **PERISHED** IN AN UNDERGROUND **FIRE**.*

*TOMB OF DRACULA #21--ROY.

SHE AND FRANK ARE REMAININ[G] IN TRANSYLVANIA HOPING TO FI[ND] DEFINITE **PROOF**.

LORD, TAJ--IF IT ONLY PROVES **TRUE**, AH, WE'LL **SOON** FIND OUT.

EH? YO[U] **RETIRI**[NG] EARL[Y] TONIGHT[?] TAKE C[ARE] I WISH [TO] **READ** AW[HILE] LONG[ER] JUST AW[HILE]

[T]HE SILENT **INDIAN** BOWS HIS HEAD, THEN GOES UP TOWARDS HIS SECOND FLOOR ROOM. A PACKED SUITCASE LIES UPON HIS UNMADE BED.

[A]ND ATOP THE SUIT-CASE...**THE NOTE!**

[O]NE MORE LOOK, TAJ ALLOWS HIM-SELF. YES! THERE CAN BE **NO DOUBT!** DESPITE ALL HIS WISHES, HE MUST **LEAVE** THIS SPRAWLING ESTATE...

...AND RETURN **HOME**...

...WITH NO WORD **WHERE** HE[S] GONE TO...OR EVEN **WHY**.

[A]ND IT [IS] **THIS** SECR[ET] FROM H[IS] MOST TRU[E] FRIENDS W[HICH] **ANGERS** THE[M] MOS[T.]

FEW MOMENTS LATER, A SILENT NIGHT-GLIDING [BA]T WATCHES THE TALL-TURBANED FORM SCURRY [SEC]RETLY ACROSS AN EXPANSE OF *LANDSCAPE*...

[T]HE *DAUGHTER OF DRACULA* WAITS FOR A MOMENT MORE [U]NTIL TAJ ENTERS A WAIT-ING *AUTO* AND DISAPPEARS INTO THE NIGHT...

...THEN SHE *LANDS*.

THE *DOORBELL*, THIS LATE? INSPECTOR CHELM WAS COMING OVER-- I EXPECTED HIM *MUCH EARLIER*.

R-RING R-RING

PERHAPS HE WAS *DELAYED*. HE NEVER SAID WHAT HE WANTED.

[HE]RE IS A FAMILIAR [ELE]CTRONIC *HUM*, AND THEN...

OH, THANK *GOD* YOU'RE *HOME*, MISTER. I WAS SO *WORRIED*. YOU'VE GOT TO *HELP* ME...

MY *FATHER* IS DYING. WE HAVE NO PHONE AND MY *CAR* DIED ON THE WAY TO THE *HOSPITAL*.

PLEASE SIT DOWN, MISS...

I'LL CALL FOR AN *AMBULANCE* NOW.

[IT] WILL [JU]ST BE A [MO]MENT, [M]ISS [EH]....?

THE NAME IS *LILITH*, QUINCY HARKER. *THE DAUGHTER OF DRACULA!*

[T]HERE IS NO [S]OUND AS [FA]NGS SINK [I]NTO THE [W]RINKLED [F]LESH ON [QUI]NCY'S NECK...

...AND *BLOOD* IS SWIFTLY DRAINED FROM THE WOUND.

*A*ND AS *FAST* AS THE SHE-DEMON CAME...SHE *DEPARTS* INTO THE MIST-COVERED NIGHT.

CHAPTER 2 THE GHOST ON HAUNTED HILL

IF **PLANETS** COULD CRY, THEY WOULD THIS NIGHT. IF THE **EARTH** COULD RISE IN ANGER, THERE WOULD BE **QUAKES** THE WORLD OVER.

DEATH REARS ITS FURROWED BROW AND **SNARLS**. **FEAR** HOLDS ITS FRIGHTENED **VICTIMS** TIGHTLY IN ITS FEVERED GRASP.

BUT THE WORLD MO ON, **PRETENDING**, PER NOT TO NOTICE TH MANY **BLASPHEMI** COMMITTED ON IT WELL-PAVED SURF AFTER ALL, IT CAN **FIGHT** BACK. IT CA **DEFEND** ITSELF. MUST ONLY TURN EYES **INWARD** AN CRY TO ITSELF AT **HELPLESSNES.**

MORE LIVES SHALL D THIS NIGHT. SOME JUST **MOST** UNJUSTLY. AL **FUTILEY**.

CASTLE DUNWICK BREATHES IN THIS NIGHT-COLD AIR AND SIGHS. ITS ANCIENT BALUSTRADES **SWAY** IN THE WINTER WINDS. ITS PLASTER AND STONE WALLS **MOAN** INTO THE DARKLING EVE.

THIS HOUSE IS **DYING**. IT KNOWS IT AND IT DOESN'T FIGHT BACK. IT HAS BEEN ROOTED IN THIS GROUND TOO LONG.

AND IT IS **WAITING** FOR **DEATH** TO FREE ITS SOUL FOREVER.

IT WAITS, SOMETIMES IT CRIES BUT ALWAYS IT JUST **WAIT.**

A **SUITABLE** DWELLING, JUST AS I SUPPOSED. PRIVATE AND QUITE **FITTING** MY PURPOSES,

ONLY **ONE** SMALL ITEM TO ATTEND TO, HOWEVER--

--THE GIRL... SHIELA WHITTIER.

HAS **DEATH** COME, THE CASTLE AS. YES.! IT IS **HERE** NOW. ITS COLD, FERA EYES ARE **STARING** INTO EVERY HIDD CORNER...INTO EVERY **INVISIBLE** CRE

AM I FINALLY TO BE **FREE**, THE CASTLE QUESTIONS?

DEATH MOVES SLOWLY ONWARDS...

...AND *LAUGHS.*

The CASTLE *ECHOES* DEATH'S LAUGHTER IN REPLY.

W-WHO'S THERE?

PLEASE... *ANSWER* ME. WHO IS IT?

DON'T DO THIS TO ME *AGAIN.* SPEAK TO ME.

Silence.

E GIRL S, SLIPS N HER SECOAT. E SOFT GRAZES R BACK D FOR A MENT *WELTS* E FELT GAIN.

Shiela WHITTIER WINCES. NO *WORDS* COME FROM HER TREMBLING LIPS.

She REACHES FOR A *LIGHT,* BUT IT WILL DO HER NO GOOD. SHE *KNOWS* THIS BY NOW.

She WILL *DESCEND* THE STAIRS AGAIN AND *THEY* WILL COME *UNSEEN.* THEN THEY WILL *ATTACK* HER...

S THEY E DONE RY NIGHT R *TWO* ONTHS!

But STILL SHIELA WHITTIER LIGHTS THE CANDLE. WHAT *ELSE* CAN SHE DO?

And STILL SHIELA WHITTIER MOVES ACROSS THE VELVET RUG, KNOWING THE *PAIN* THAT AWAITS HER...

...KNOWING SHE CAN NOT *FIGHT* IT.

The CASTLE *SIGHS* ONCE MORE.

THE DOOR IS **STUCK**, SO SHE PULLS ON IT HARDER.

BUT THE CASTLE HOLDS ON, **STRAINING** UNTIL IT CAN HOLD NO MORE.

AND THE DOOR IS **OPENED**.

AND **DEATH** STANDS IN THE SHADOWS, SIMPLY **SMILING**.

AND THE CASTLE **SIGHS**... STILL WAITING... **ALWAYS** WAITING.

SHIELA'S SCRE[AM] ISN'T HEARD [IN] LONDON. ITS [?] IS LONG BEF[ORE] WASHED AWAY B[Y] FLOODING RA[IN].

OVE[R] THE MA[?] TA[?] PE[?] WIL[?]

...AND THE SCREAMS OF **LAUGHTER**.

YOU FIGGER YOU CAN MAKE IT WI' 'ER? YOU MUST BE **TWICE** DAFT, MAN.

CARE TO MAKE A **WAGER**, MATE? TEN QUID, EH?

I'LL **COVER** IT, STEVEY. BUT YOU AINT GOT NO **CHANCE** WITH 'ER.

HOLD YOUR MONEY **LOOSE**.

LOOKIT 'IM, GADGER. WE'LL BE TEN QUID **RICHER** TONIGHT, EH?

THAT BIRD'S SOLID **ICE**, MAN. **UNCHIPPABLE!**

HUNH.?!?

EVE WILLINGHAM'S FLAT IS **SMALL**, AND AS UNKEMPT AS ITS MASTER.

NOT MUCH, BABE--BUT THEN I DON'T **NEED** MUCH.

GOT ALL THE **ESSENTIALS** ALREADY.

DON'T TALK, STEPHEN. **KISS** ME.

AND SUPPLY ME THE **NOURISHMENT** I CRAVE.

UNNN-GHHHHH.!!

FAREWELL, MY LOVE-- BUT IT COULD **NOT** HAVE LASTED ANY LONGER.

YOU HAD **OUTLIVED** YOUR **USEFULL-NESS,** YOU SEE.

SILENTLY SHE TURNS TOWARDS THE OPEN **WINDOW--**

--AND **VANISHES.**

STEPHEN WILLINGHAM'S DEATH WILL BE ATTRIBUTED TO CAUSES **UNKNOWN.** NO ONE WILL **CLAIM** HIS BODY AND WITHIN A **MONTH,** HE WILL BE **FORGOTTEN.**

SUCH IS THE SUM **TOTAL** OF 26 YEARS OF ONE MAN'S LIFE.

TO THE EAST AND NORTH, HOWEVER, **ANOTHER** VICTIM OF DRACULA'S DAUGHTER IS ABOUT TO BE **DISCOVERED...**

I'VE SOME NEW REPORTS ON DRACULA THAT SHOULD **INTEREST** QUINCY, WHEELING.

...BY A LONG-DELAYED INSPECTOR CHELM, AND HIS ASSISTANT, OFFICER WHEELING.

HE'S INSIDE. WHY DOESN'T HE **ANSWER?**

STAND **BACK,** WHEELING. I THINK THERE MAY HAVE BEEN...

TROUBLE!

KNOK

GOOD LORD!

WHEELER--*QUICKLY.* CALL FOR AN *AMBULANCE.*

QUINCY'S STILL *BREATHING.*

FRANK! RACHEL! TAJ? IS THERE *ANYONE* ELSE HERE?

BLAST! HE M HAVE BEEN *ALO* WHEN IT HAPPE BUT WHERE I EVERYONE ELS

Away!

*F*OR A MOMENT THE GIRL DOESN'T SEE DRACULA STANDING BEFORE HER.

OHHHHHH...

WHY DID YOU COME *BACK?* WAS IT TO *HURT* ME AGAIN?

HAVEN'T YOU DONE *ENOUGH* ALREADY?

YOU CAN'T HURT ME ANY MORE. YOU *CAN'T!* *YOU CAN'T!*

I CAN'T T IT ANY LON *PLEAS* *DON'T H* ME.

I BEG TO G PLEASE D LET *HIM* H ME ANY MO

H-HE WON'T ANSWER MY *PLEAS*, WILL HE? HE NEVER HAS BEFORE.

BUT I PROMISE YOU I WON'T *STRUGGLE* THIS TIME. I WON'T FIGHT YOU ANYMORE. I *CAN'T* FIGHT ANYMORE.

I SWEAR I WON'T IF YOU DON'T WANT ME TO.

YOU ARE *MISTAKEN*, SHIELA WHITTIER.

I AM *NOT* ONE OF YOUR TORMENTORS.

YOU AREN'T? YOU'RE NOT ONE OF THEM?

YOU'RE NOT... *LYING?*

I AM *DRACULA*, AND I HAVE *NEVER* BEEN HERE BEFORE.

YOU WON'T *HURT* ME?

*T*HE GIRL *COLLAPSES* INTO DRACULA'S ARMS. HER *TEARS* FLOOD FROM WATER-SOAKED EYES.

*S*HE IS *TIRED*. SHE HAS BEEN WAITING FOR *DEATH* TO TAKE HER FROM THIS MADNESS KNOWN AS CASTLE DUNWICK FOR *TWO MONTHS*. AND NOW SHE HAS NO *ENERGY* LEFT WITHIN HER.

*B*UT THE CASTLE CAN ONLY *SIGH*. AND WAIT.

*T*HERE WILL COME *ANOTHER* TIME.

ONE HALF HOUR LATER...

I REMEMBER EXACTLY WHEN THEY *FIRST* CAME AFTER ME. IT WAS MY *SECOND* NIGHT HERE.

YOU'VE *NEVER* SEEN THEM, THOUGH?

NO.

AND YOU DON'T *LEAVE.* WHY?

I CAN'T. ER...WOULD YOU LIKE SOME *COFFEE?*

NO. I D... DRIN... COFF...

NOW FOR A *DIFFERENT* PROBLEM. LORD HENRY OF OF PAR-LIAMENT SAID THIS CASTLE WOULD BE *AVAIL-ABLE* TO ME.

YET, WHILE *YOU* ARE HERE...

YES, YOU *ARE* HERE. WHICH MEANS THIS IS *NO* PLACE FOR ME.

I M... LEA... N... SHIE... WHITT...

YOU CAN'T LEAVE ME *ALONE* HERE. IT ISN'T *SAFE.* I NEED YOU HERE--JUST FOR *AWHILE.*

SAFE...?

I AM *SORRY,* MY DEAR. BUT FOR *YOUR* SAKE, I MUST LEAVE.

BUT BE SURE-- I *WILL* RETURN.

OUTSIDE, THE NIGHT IS STILL *COLD,* BUT THE SKY IS *CLEAR* ENOUGH FOR THE *LORD OF EVIL* TO GAZE SOLEMNLY UPWARDS...

...AND TO *SEE*--

ANOTH... BAT... VAMPI... IT OBVIOUS... *SEARCH...* ME O...

--BUT W...

NO! IT CAN-NOT BE POSSIBLE. SHE'S *DEAD.* AND YET--

--IF SOMEHOW SHE HAS BEEN *REVIVED...*

238

CHAPTER 3

DEMONS IN THE DARK!

THE **MORTAL** BODY FADES, DISSOLV- ING INTO A LEATHERY FORM WHICH FLITTERS UPWARDS INTO THE SKY, WHERE DRACULA SEES THE ONE BEFORE HIM IS DEFINITELY **HER**--

--THE ONE HE HAD THOUGHT HAD **DIED** BENEATH THE STAKE OF QUINCY HARKER ON THE NIGHT HARKER'S OWN **WIFE** WAS SLAIN.

THE TWO BATS **STARE** FOR A MOMENT...

...UNTIL THE SMALL ONE TURNS AND **FLIES.**

DRACULA **FOLLOWS.**

LONDON:

BIG BEN CHIMES THE **FIRST** HOUR OF **MORNING.**

239

LONDON SPORTS PALLADIUM.

SOON TO BE **VISITED** BY TWO BEINGS WHO HAVE LITTLE **INTEREST** IN EITHER **RUGBY** OR THE CHARITY THIS NIGHT-TIME GAME IS BEING PLAYED FOR.

SOMETIMES IT IS **FASCINATING,** DAUGHTER, TO OBSERVE **HUMANS** IN MASS.

LOOK ABOUT YOU AS WE **SPEAK.**

YOU'VE NO **INTEREST** IN HOW I **RETURNED,** FATHER? CAN IT BE YOU DON'T **CARE** ABOUT YOUR FAVORITE **DAUGHTER?**

NOR HAVE I FOR **FIVE HUNDRED YEARS.**

YOU ARE YOUR **MOTHER'S** DAUGHTER, LILITH, AND I WISH NO PART OF EITHER HER OR **YOU.**

SHE DESERVED **HER** DEATH AS YOU DID YOURS.

YES, SHE WAS MY **WIFE,** IF FOR ONLY **ONE YEAR.** BUT IT WAS A MARRIAGE I NEVER WANTED...ARRANGED FOR **COURT** PURPOSES ONLY...

"...BY MY **FATHER.**

"I **HATED** THE SIMPERING SHE-FOOL WITH ALL MY THEN-HUMAN **HEART.**

BEGONE, WENCH-- WITH MY FATHER DEAD, I NO LONGER HAVE TO **KEEP** YOU.

LEAVE BY **NIGHTF**[...] OR, SO HELP ME, I HAVE YOU **IMPALE**[...]

240

TAKE THIS
HIMPERING
HILD WITH
YOU.

BUT SHE'S OUR *DAUGHTER*, VLAD. SHE IS *BOTH* OF US.

SHE IS NOT *MINE*, WOMAN--

--ANYMORE THAN THE *LOVE* I'VE FEIGNED FOR YOU THIS YEAR WAS TRULY MINE.

I *DESPISE* YOU, WIFE. *LEAVE* NOW, AND NEVER RETURN.

I WILL GO, VLAD...AND YOU'LL NOT SEE *EITHER* OF US AGAIN.

KE CARE OF MY *DAUGHTER*, SY...MY *GOLD* WILL PAY YOU ELL FOR THAT, I PROMISE.

TCH OVER HER... NEVER, PLEASE VER LET HER OME TO HARM.

GRETCHIN MAKES THAT *PROMISE*, WIFE OF DRACULA.

AND SHE FEELS THE *SORROW* WHICH GROWS IN YOUR HEART.

GROWS? NO, GYPSY. IT IS *ENDING*.

I HAVE BEEN *STRIPPED* OF EVERY-THING DECENT BY MY HUSBAND...

AND NOW I CAN ONLY *DIE*.

GOODBYE, MY DAUGHTER. I HAVE LOVED YOU *ALWAYS*.

...GOODBYE...

"MUCH HAPPENED NEXT. WITH YOUR MOTHER'S DEATH, I MARRIED THE ONE I TRULY *LOVED*... MY DARLING, MARIA. WE HAD A SON, VLAD.

"THEN, THE GYPSY, *LIANDA*, TURNED ME INTO THE *VAMPIRE* I AM TODAY--*

"--SO, IN *REVENGE*, I SOUGHT OUT ALL GYPSYS AND *MURDERED* THEM IN TURN."

DRACULA LIVES #2. --ROY.

ARNI... MY *SON*....!

THE *DEVIL* DID IT... HE KILLED MY *ARNI*...

...HE *MURDERED* MY *CHILD!*

BUT I MAY YET HAVE MY *REVENGE*...

I AM *SORRY* WIFE OF DRAC BUT IT IS BECAUSE OF YO *HUSBAND* TH I BREAK MY V TO YOU.

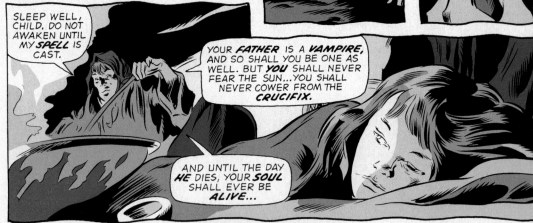

SLEEP WELL, CHILD. DO NOT AWAKEN UNTIL MY *SPELL* IS CAST.

YOUR *FATHER* IS A *VAMPIRE*, AND SO SHALL YOU BE ONE AS WELL. BUT *YOU* SHALL NEVER FEAR THE SUN...YOU SHALL NEVER COWER FROM THE *CRUCIFIX.*

AND UNTIL THE DAY *HE* DIES, YOUR *SOUL* SHALL EVER BE *ALIVE...*

SHOULD YOU PERISH, YOU WILL SEEK OUT *ANOTHER* BODY TO BE *REBORN* IN...A BODY OF AN *INNOCENT* LIKE YOURSELF WHO WISHES DEATH TO *HER* FATHER--

--AS I WISH DEATH TO *YOURS.*

AND YOU SHALL EVER *HAUNT* HIS PRESENCE... BE HIS CONSTANT *AGONY*--

--FOR YOU SHALL BECOME AN EVE LIVING *VAMPIRE*

NOW, RM LILITH *DAUGH* OF DRAC AWAKEN *QUEEN* THE UND

242

D I HAVE NOWN **ALL** HAT FOR YEARS, AUGHTER.

BUT WHY HAVE YOU SOUGHT ME OUT **AGAIN?** HADN'T WE **MENDED** OUR HATREDS OF EACH OTHER A CENTURY AGO?

WE AGREED NEVER TO **SEE** EACH OTHER AGAIN, HAD WE NOT? AND SAVE FOR THAT **EVE** AT THE HARKER ESTATE, WE KEPT OUR PROMISE.

BUT I AM BACK NOW--TO **SHARE** WITH YOU THE **THRONE** AS LORDS OF THE UNDEAD.

OUR EXISTENCE IS TOO WELL **INTERTWINED**, FATHER, TO PREVENT OUR **ALLIANCE**. WE **MUST** JOIN TOGETHER FOR **POWER**.

THIS **MEETING** IS ENDED NOW, DAUGHTER. I'VE NO WISH TO SPEAK OF **ENTENTES**--NOR OF WORLD CONQUEST.

MY AIMS NOW LIE IN **OTHER** PURSUITS.

LOOK-- OH LORD-- **LOOK!**

YOU'LL **RUE** THIS DECISION, FATHER.

DESTINIES SHALL LWAYS **LINKED**-- DAY YOU'LL BE RCED TO AC- WLEDGE THAT. SWEAR IT.

*T*HE WOMAN **RISES**, AND THE CROWD, STILL STRICKEN WITH **FEAR**, ONLY **STARES**...

*T*HIS NIGHT THEY WILL **RETURN** HOME AND SLEEP, AND NOT **ONE** WILL EVER ADMIT TO WHAT HAD HAPPENED HERE.

*F*OR THEIR OWN **SANITY**, NOT ONE WOULD EVER **DARE**.

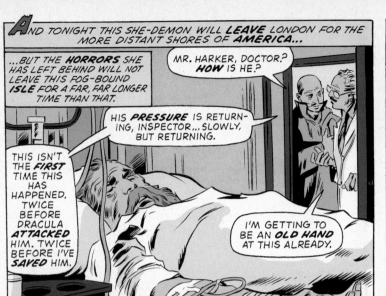

AND TONIGHT THIS SHE-DEMON WILL **LEAVE** LONDON FOR THE MORE DISTANT SHORES OF **AMERICA...**

...BUT THE **HORRORS** SHE HAS LEFT BEHIND WILL NOT LEAVE THIS FOG-BOUND **ISLE** FOR A FAR, FAR LONGER TIME THAN THAT.

MR. HARKER, DOCTOR? **HOW** IS HE?

HIS **PRESSURE** IS RETURN-ING, INSPECTOR...SLOWLY, BUT RETURNING.

THIS ISN'T THE **FIRST** TIME THIS HAS HAPPENED, TWICE BEFORE DRACULA **ATTACKED** HIM. TWICE BEFORE I'VE **SAVED** HIM.

I'M GETTING TO BE AN **OLD HAND** AT THIS ALREADY.

SO DON'T WORRY. I KNOW QUINCY--AND HE'S **TOUGH.** THIS FULL **BLOOD TRANSFUSION** WILL TAKE.

AND HE'LL PROBABLY **HOME** BEFO THE WEEK OUT.

INTENSIVE CARE

CASTLE **DUNWICK** SHUDDERS NOW; ITS **FLOORBOARDS** TREMBLE IN FRIGHTFUL ANTICIPATION; ITS MORTARED **WALLS** QUAKE IN EXPECTANT **HORROR.**

FOR SHIELA WHITTIER HAS AT LONG LAST SEEN **DEATH** FACE TO FACE...

...AND SHE RUNS.

THE **LIGHTS** FLICKER IN THIS ANCIENT MANSE. **ECHOES** REVERBERATE FROM EVERY CORNER. AND SHIELA ___ WHITTIER **RUNS.**

TO HAVE LOST ONE **LOVER,** TO HAVE POSSIBLY FOUND **ANOTHER** ONLY TO **DIE,** WOULD NOW BE A **MOCKERY.** TO SHEILA WHITTIER, IT WOULD NOT BE **FAIR.**

THOUGH **FATE** WAS N CONCEIVED WITH **FAI NESS** IN MIND.

AND SO, SHIELA WHITTIER FALLS TO HER **DEATH!**

ONLY TO HAVE CHEATED IT ONCE AGAIN.

SHE DOESN'T SEE HER SAVIOR AT THIS MOMENT. BUT SOMEHOW SHE KNOWS WHO IT IS.

JUST AS SHE FINALLY COMPREHENDS WHAT HE IS.

THOUGH SHE DOESN'T CARE.

IT IS NOT THE TIME FOR YOUR DEATH, SHIELA WHITTIER. FOR I HAVE NEED OF YOU NOW--AS MY AIDE.

WHERE THAT MINDLESS SYCOPHANT, CLIFTON GRAVES, FAILED ME, YOU SHALL NOT. SOMEHOW I KNOW THIS OF YOU.

...E SEEN HIM, DRACULA--...TAIRS. HE ...S CHASING ...TRYING TO ...ILL ME.

STAY HERE, THEN...

...WHILE I DEAL WITH YOUR TORMENTOR.

THE HALLWAY IS QUIET, TOO QUIET. BUT THROUGH THE HEAVY SHROUD OF SILENCE, DRACULA HEARS BREATHING...

SO THE VAMPIRE LORD THINKS-- THERE ARE NO GHOSTS NOR PHANTOMS HERE. THE ONE WHO HIDES IN THE SHADOWS IS AS HUMAN AS SHE.

DEATH SMILES.

AND THE CASTLE SIGHS.

245

SUDDENLY...

DIE, DRACULA. DIE, *CURSE YOU*-- *DIE!*

THE *STAKE* SLASHES THROUGH THE LORD OF EVIL...AND *BURNS* ITS WAY DEEP INTO HIS *CHEST*...

...THOUGH *NOT HIS HEART.*

THE PRINCE OF EVIL NO LONGER SMILES AS HE *RIPS* THE STAKE AWAY...

...AND HIS LONG, COLD *FINGERS* GRASP OUT-WARDS--

--SENDING HIS *ATTACKER* SPRAWLING TO THE FLOOR.

YOU HA MADE Y *FINA* MISTA HUM...

--NOW R AND L ME S THE VIS OF A M WHO ABOUT DIE

DON'T DO ANYTHING TO ME. I DIDN'T *MEAN* TO ATTACK YOU. I HAD TO, DON'T YOU UNDERSTAND--

--I JUST *HAD* TO.

WHAT? LORD HENRY! MY...

YOUR *SLAVE*, DRACULA. THAT IS WHAT YOU WERE GOING TO *SAY.*

AND I'VE BEEN YOUR *SLAVE* TOO LONG-- TOO LONG.

I'VE DONE TOO MANY THINGS... TOO MANY *HORRIBLE* THINGS TO THINK ABOUT.

AND ONLY BECAUSE I COULDN'T *RESIST*... BECAUSE I WASN'T *MAN* ENOUGH TO FIGHT YOU.

BUT THEN *SUDDENLY,* GOD KNOWS HOW-- I *WAS.* SO I TRIED TO *KILL* YOU.

YOU BRO *FREE.* IMPOSSIBL AND YET

--YOU DID. BUT DID YOU TRULY BELIEVE I'D BE *EASY* TO SLAY?

I SET IT ALL UP. I THOUGHT I WAS SO *CLEVER* LURING YOU HERE.

...THOUGH GOD KNOWS I HAD FAILED THEM ENOUGH BEFORE.

T I FAILED AIN--BOTH ELF AND MANITY...

NO MORE, DRACULA. I'LL FAIL NO MORE.

GUNFIRE CAN'T KILL ME. YOU KNOW THAT, LORD HENRY.

I KNOW IT. BLAST IT-- I KNOW IT.

BUT AT LEAST THE BULLETS IN HERE WILL TAKE ONE OF YOUR VICTIMS FROM YOU.

BAM!

I DID NOT BELIEVE HE WAS MAN ENOUGH.

H-HE SHOT HIMSELF.-- DRACULA-- HE'S KILLED HIMSELF!!

THUS ENDS YOUR MYSTERY, SHIELA WHITTIER... AND YOUR TORMENT.

RE WERE NO GHOSTS IVING IN THIS MANOR. T HIM, YOUR TORMEN- ...

...AND MY TRAITOR.

BODY LIES UNMOVING, E STILL WAFTING UPWARDS FROM HIS GUN...

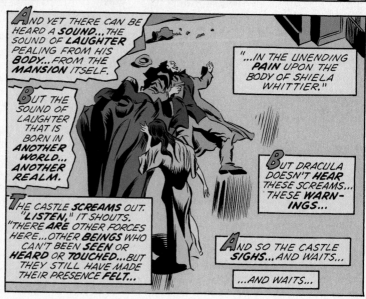

AND YET THERE CAN BE HEARD A SOUND...THE SOUND OF LAUGHTER PEALING FROM HIS BODY...FROM THE MANSION ITSELF.

BUT THE SOUND OF LAUGHTER THAT IS BORN IN ANOTHER WORLD... ANOTHER REALM.

THE CASTLE SCREAMS OUT. "LISTEN," IT SHOUTS. "THERE ARE OTHER FORCES HERE...OTHER BEINGS WHO CAN'T BEEN SEEN OR HEARD OR TOUCHED...BUT THEY STILL HAVE MADE THEIR PRESENCE FELT...

"...IN THE UNENDING PAIN UPON THE BODY OF SHIELA WHITTIER."

BUT DRACULA DOESN'T HEAR THESE SCREAMS... THESE WARN- INGS...

AND SO THE CASTLE SIGHS... AND WAITS...

...AND WAITS...

KEEPING TRACK OF DRAC!
by Marv Wolfman

In case you're wondering, no, this is not TOMB OF DRACULA. Instead, it goes under the unlikely title of GIANT SIZE CHILLERS featuring THE CURSE OF DRACULA. What's the Curse, you ask? Well, part of it is that this is one of <u>three</u> giant-sized quarterly Marvel monster mags. Next month will be CREATURES, featuring WEREWOLF BY NIGHT, followed by MONSTERS starring MAN-THING.

Now then, what about the title of this mini-article, Keeping Track Of Drac? Well, it's not an easy job, effendi. After all, the guy's lived five hundred years give or take a month. Secondly, he's been dead quite a bit of that time. Well, actually, not dead, but when he is <u>already</u> dead, how do you indicate that he is merely <u>deader</u> than usual?

I am the fourth person to write the adventures of Dracula for Marvel. Gerry Conway began it back in TOMB OF DRACULA #1. After two issues, Ger moved on to WEREWOLF BY NIGHT, leaving Drac in the capable hands of Archie Goodwin. Arch added a few characters, brought Drac from Transylvania to London full time, and began the idea that Drac had been asleep for 100 years. Gardner Fox picked up the writing reigns two issues later, didn't change too much, but had Drac return to Transylvania for the better part of an issue. I came in with issue #7. I made a few changes right off the bat, er, no pun intended. First off, Dracula had not been asleep for 100 years.

He <u>couldn't</u> have been. In the Bram Stoker novel (now being serialized in DRACULA LIVES! for completists) Dracula was slain on a country road. Had he been killed in the castle, had he been entombed where Gerry first showed him back in that fright-filled first issue, the idea that he had been asleep for all those years would have stuck. But since there was obviously one adventure between the end of the Stoker novel and the beginning

of TOMB, Marvel and I decided that it was okay to bri[ng] Count up to the present. Secondly, we had already sho[wn] DRACULA LIVES!, that Dracula, or at least his spiri[t] alive during one part of World War Two. Therefore anothe[r] that Dracula had been 'alive', note quotes around alive, [?] sometime within the past century. Lastly, there were just to[o] good story possibilities, too many problems with a cha[racter] who was out of date with today, and those reasons alone tated that the Count had to have been living or u[?] periodically at best, for the last 100 years.

In December of 1973, at the urging of Rascally Roy T[homas] I came to work for Marvel on staff. I had already been [writing] TOMB OF DRACULA for several issues, and most of S[?] and one or two highly forgettable issues of CAPTAIN MA[RVEL] by that time. Part of my job was to co-ordinate the fou[r] giant 75¢ magazines, and because I was the regular wr[iter of] TOMB OF DRACULA, I was given the task to make s[ure] the Dracula stories fit within one plausible history. If the c[harac]ter was to be believable, if Dracula was to remain con[sistent] if he was going to be a real character and not merely a car[toon] figure like some of the characters published by our D[istinguished] Competition, then everything had to fit in place. First, an [origin] had to be established. Roy asked me to write it, wi[th Neal] Adams handling the art. I handled the first chapter, then [?] a sequel drawn by John Buscema. Working with Gerry Co[nway] in a manner our senior Dracula scripter, we worked out [the] ideas to pick up where I left off. Dracula had to learn v[?] is to be a vampire, he had to grow to be the Lord of them a[ll.]

In the first issue of DRACULA LIVES! Gerry reve[aled the] arch enemy for Dracula, in the person of Cagliostro. Gerry [went] on that theme for several issues, and Tony Isabella, ne[w] for Marvel, picked up on it for another DRACULA [?] story soon to appear.

248

t enough of the past for awhile. Sometimes it is easy to fit
...ing into a past era and claim the stories follow some sort
...quence, so we will be presenting, in a future issue of
...CULA LIVES!, a timeline to Dracula's life and unlife.

...e main problem of our current stories is connecting them
...o the present Dracula legend. It is too tempting, too
...o say the stories which appear in DRACULA LIVES! happen
...to another Dracula or in another time, or in another
...sion. It may be too easy, but it would be ruinous in
...ng run. So we've taken the bull by the horns and have
...trying to give mentions of the DRACULA LIVES! stor-
...the TOMB OF DRACULA, have characters move from
...another, and connect the stories even more than they have
...without making the color series depend on the black and
...stories or vice versa.

constantly mentioned in TOMB OF DRACULA, it is not because
I'm not aware of them. As Associate Editor of the 75¢ books,
I am responsible for getting most of the stories and working
with the writers, so any reason for not mentioning them is just
for the sake of not confusing the readers. But, as any regular
reader of DRACULA LIVES! and TOMB OF DRACULA knows
constant referrals are made when possible.

It's a backbreaking job, senses shattering if you want to
use the accepted expression, but it's well worth it. If we can
keep a consistency between the half dozen or so writers of
DRACULA (Roy, Gerry, Steve G, Doug Moench, Tony Isabella,
Len Wein and myself), the character of Dracula will only
grow, rather than stagnate into mediocrity as so many of you
can think of a certain red-caped hero who hasn't _any_ personality
at all because there is no one person co-ordinating his movements. For those who spot errors, well, this is Messed-up
Marvel, and heck, I remember a little while back when a certain
smiling writer/editor called a certain other Green-skinned Goliath's
alter-ego Bob Banner instead of Bruce, then shamefacedly decided his full name is Robert Bruce Banner. So, in that pulse-
pounding tradition, errors will probably pop up now and then.
We'll just try and keep them down to a minimum. Okay, Pilgrims?

Now, before we close for another three months, remember,
next month in GIANT SIZE CREATURES, Werewolf by Night
meets— TIGRA, THE WERE-WOMAN! Be there.

...aders have asked how can Dracula appear in Paris,
...n or New York the same month he is trapped in
...lvania or battling a vampire in Russia. For an explana-
...f sorts, follow the very definite time guide that we've set
...tween issue number 16 and 17 of TOMB OF DRACULA
...is a definite break. In fact, the time set in #17 is given
...vember 5, 1973. Since his adventure in Transylvania took
...re than three nights (Werewolf having used his fourth,
...REWOLF #16), the time with Doctor Sun took no more
...wo to three nights, we can assume that this issue took
...during late November, early December, TOMB OF DRAC-
...#23, which picks up where this CHILLERS story ends,
...place about the same time. However, TOMB OF DRAC-
...#24 will probably take place in March, or early February.
...ore there is actually time between many of the stories
...e separate adventures to have taken place. If they are not

TIGRA, THE WERE-WOMAN!

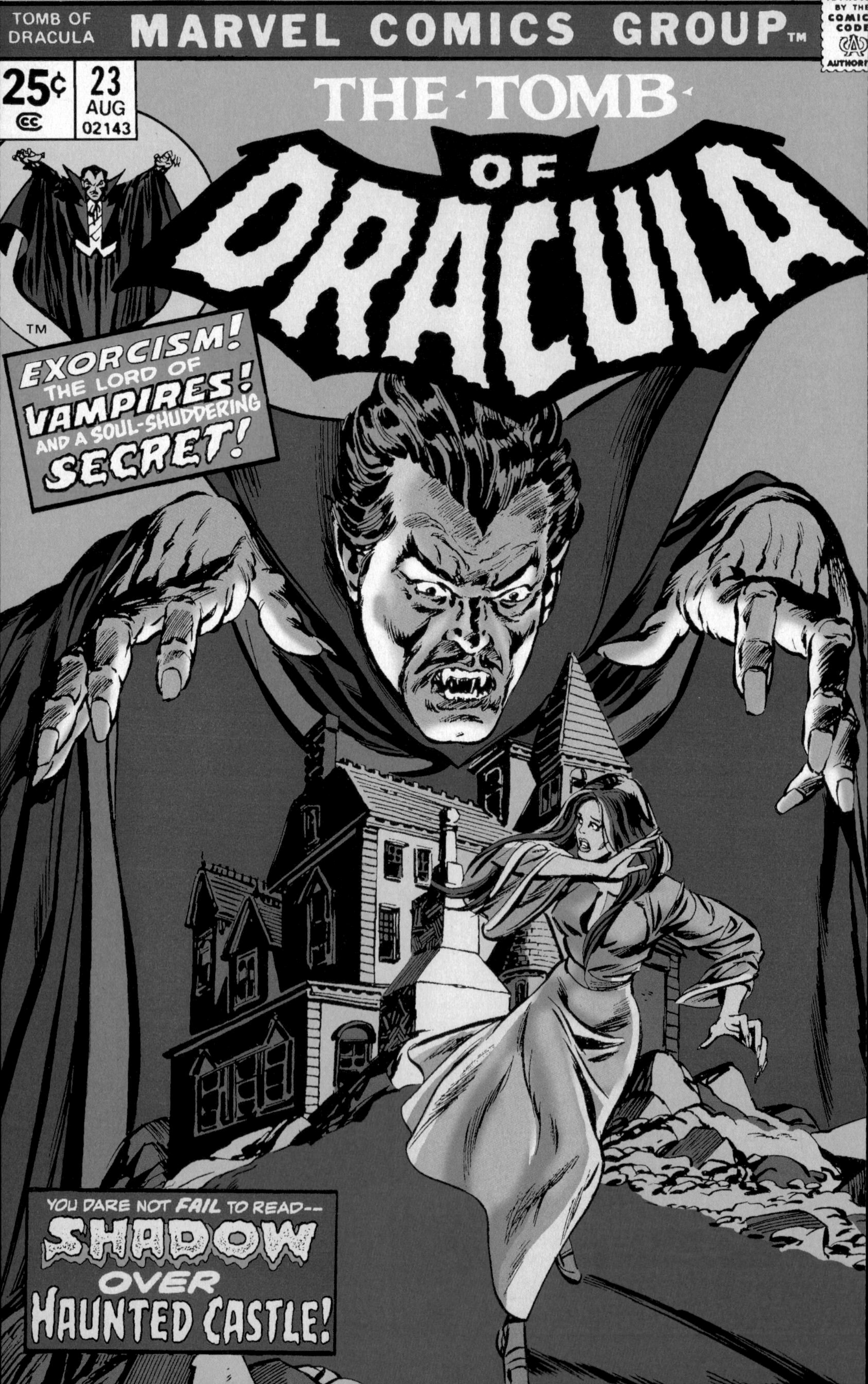
TOMB OF DRACULA
MARVEL COMICS GROUP™
APPROVED BY THE COMICS CODE AUTHORITY
25¢
23
AUG
02143
THE TOMB OF DRACULA
™
EXORCISM! THE LORD OF VAMPIRES! AND A SOUL-SHUDDERING SECRET!
YOU DARE NOT FAIL TO READ--
SHADOW OVER HAUNTED CASTLE!

Stan Lee PRESENTS: **TOMB OF DRACULA!** ™

MARV WOLFMAN WRITER / GENE COLAN PENCILER / TOM PALMER INKER / JOHN COSTANZA letterer / P. GOLDBERG colorist / ROY THOMAS EDITOR

ONLY MOMENTS HAVE PASSED SINCE HE DIED; SINCE THE FINAL SPASMS OF LIFE HAD CEASED, AND YET, RISING FROM HIS ALREADY DECAYING CORPSE COMES *LAUGHTER*... A LOW, GUTTERAL, RASPING GROWL WHICH PASSES HEAVILY THROUGH THE VISCOUS MIRE THAT IS *CASTLE DUNWICK.*

HA HA

THE GIRL SAYS NOTHING; HER VOICE IS FROZEN WITH *FEAR.*

AND *DRACULA* -- THIS *LORD OF THE UNDEAD*...THIS *DARKLING GOD* WHO WAS BORN IN *HELL* ITSELF, SPEAKS NOTHING AS WELL, FOR, HE BELIEVES, HE HAS JUST *SLAIN* THE EVIL WHICH FESTERED IN THIS ANCIENT MANSE, AND YET THERE IS *STILL* THE MOCKING LAUGHTER,...

...WITH *DRACULA* AS ITS UNCOMPRE-HENDING *VICTIM.*

Shadows IN THE NIGHT!

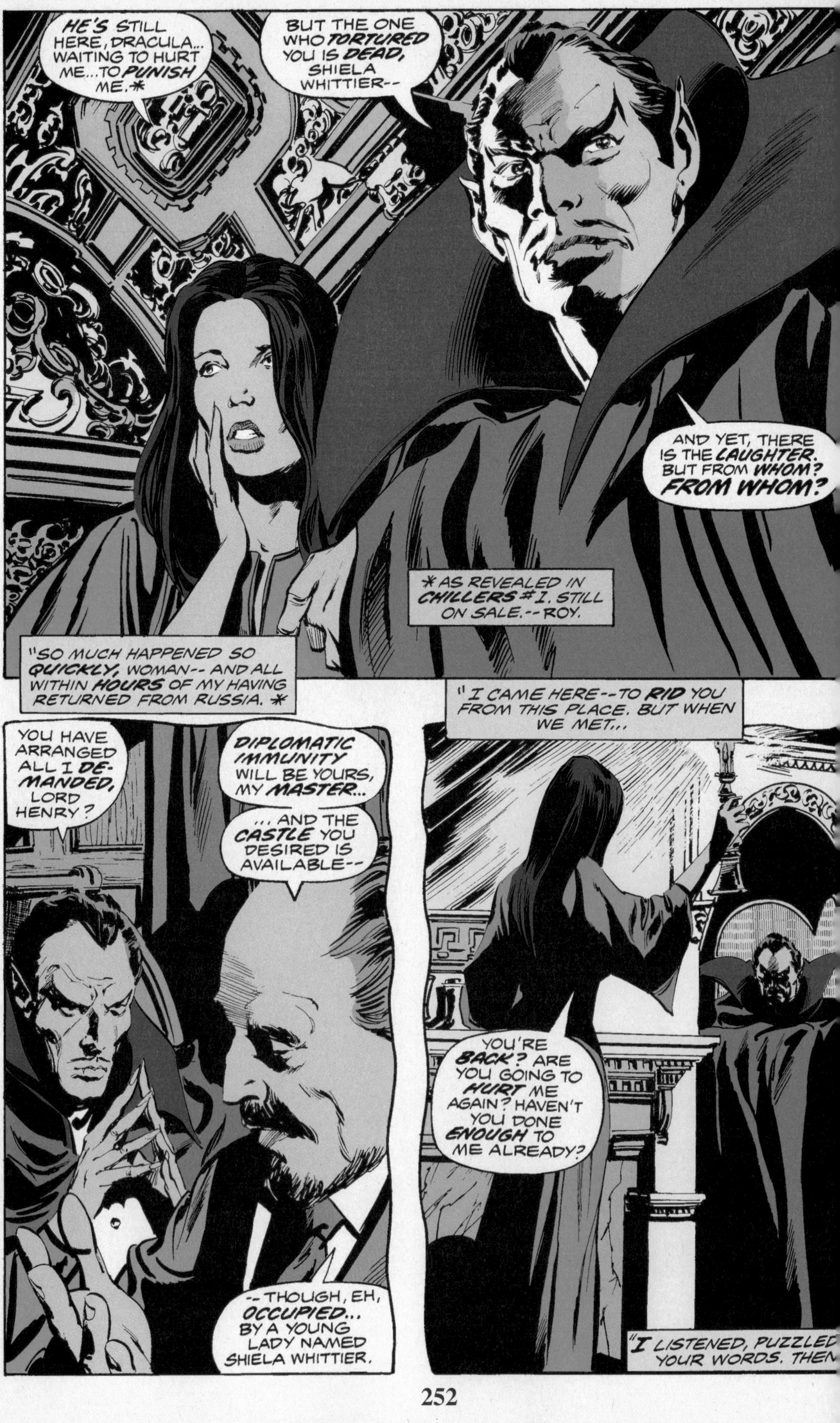
HE'S STILL HERE, DRACULA... WAITING TO HURT ME...TO PUNISH ME.*
BUT THE ONE WHO TORTURED YOU IS DEAD, SHIELA WHITTIER--
AND YET, THERE IS THE LAUGHTER. BUT FROM WHOM? FROM WHOM?
*AS REVEALED IN CHILLERS #1. STILL ON SALE.--ROY.
"SO MUCH HAPPENED SO QUICKLY, WOMAN-- AND ALL WITHIN HOURS OF MY HAVING RETURNED FROM RUSSIA.*
YOU HAVE ARRANGED ALL I DE-MANDED, LORD HENRY?
DIPLOMATIC IMMUNITY WILL BE YOURS, MY MASTER...
... AND THE CASTLE YOU DESIRED IS AVAILABLE--
-- THOUGH, EH, OCCUPIED... BY A YOUNG LADY NAMED SHIELA WHITTIER.
"I CAME HERE--TO RID YOU FROM THIS PLACE. BUT WHEN WE MET...
YOU'RE BACK? ARE YOU GOING TO HURT ME AGAIN? HAVEN'T YOU DONE ENOUGH TO ME ALREADY?
"I LISTENED, PUZZLED YOUR WORDS. THEN

HE WON'T ANSWER MY PLEAS, WILL E? WELL HEN, DO WHAT YOU MUST. I ON'T FIGHT OU ANY-MORE, I CAN'T.

YOU ARE MISTAKEN, SHIELA WHITTIER. I AM NOT ONE OF YOUR TORMENTORS.

YOU AREN'T? YOU AREN'T GOING TO HURT ME?

OH GOD... OH MY GOD.

"EXHAUSTED WITH FEAR, YOU FELL INTO MY ARMS. I KNEW THEN THAT YOU WOULD STILL BE MINE... BUT NOT NOW... NOT THE WAY I HAD ORIGIN-ALLY PLANNED.

"I HAD TO LEAVE THE MANSION THEN. BUT LATER, YOU HEARD A SOUND IN THE PARLOR...

"...YOU RUSHED DOWN THE STAIRS TO INVESTI-GATE...

AND YOU IPPED.

"THOUGH, FROM THE WAY YOU FELL, IT WAS AS IF YOU WERE VIOLENTLY PUSHED.

"BUT LUCK WAS WITH YOU THEN, FOR I HAD JUST RETURNED, AND CAUGHT YOU EVEN AS YOU TUMBLED DOWN-WARD.

"AND THEN, BOUNDING UP THE STAIRWELL, I CHASED A SMALL, DARK FIGURE WHO DARTED FROM THE SHADOWS.

"HE STOOD THERE, WAITING FOR ME-- WAITING WITH A STAKE FIRMLY HELD IN HIS HAND.

"HE TRIED TO **THRUST** THAT STAKE THROUGH MY HEART... AND THE FOOL **MISSED!**"

"...I GAVE **CHASE**, QUICKLY BRINGING HIM **DOWN**.

"BUT WHEN I SAW HIS FACE IN THE UPSTAIRS **LIGHT**, I WAS **STUNNED**.

LORD HENRY?

YES, DRACULA-- YOUR **SLAVE** IN PARLIAMENT ...THE ONE YOU'VE **ORDERED** ABOUT FOR **YEARS** BECAUSE THERE WAS **NO WAY** TO FIGHT BACK.

BUT IN SOME WAY I DON'T UNDERSTAND MYSELF, **I'M FREE NOW!**

AND **NOW** I'LL BE FREE OF YOU **FOREVER!**

"**THE BULLET** PIERCED HIS HEART, AND **INSTANTLY** HE WAS DEAD; HIS TIRED BODY FELL **HEAVILY** TO THE FLOOR EVEN AS THE **LAUGHTER** BEGAN..."

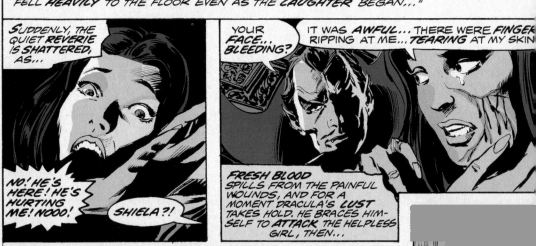

SUDDENLY, THE QUIET **REVERIE** IS **SHATTERED**, AS...

NO! HE'S **HERE!** HE'S **HURTING** ME! **NOOO!**

SHIELA?!

YOUR **FACE**... BLEEDING?

IT WAS **AWFUL**... THERE WERE FINGER[S] RIPPING AT ME... **TEARING** AT MY SKIN[?]

FRESH BLOOD SPILLS FROM THE PAINFUL WOUNDS, AND FOR A MOMENT DRACULA'S **LUST** TAKES HOLD. HE BRACES HIM- SELF TO **ATTACK** THE HELPLESS GIRL, THEN...

...HE **PAUSES**... HE FIGHTS THE OVERWHELMING LUST, AND PROMISES HIMSELF **ANOTHER** VICTIM... **SOON**... **VERY SOON**. BUT **THIS** GIRL MUST NOT BE HARMED... NOT IF SHE IS TO **SERVE** HIM LATER... DURING THE DAYLIGHT HOURS, **UNRESTRICTED** BY HYPNOTIC INFLUENCES.

WHATEVER WAS HERE IS **GONE** NOW.

...AND **TOMORROW** NIGHT WE WILL **SEARCH** THIS MANSION.

BUT YO[U] ARE **TIR**[ED] AND IT IS TIME FOR [YOU] TO **SLEE**[P].

WITHOUT AN ARGU- MENT, THE GIRL IS CARRIED UP THE CREAKING STAIRS.

SLEEP **WELL**, GIRL-- THIS MAY BE THE **LAST** PEACEFUL REST YOU'LL HAVE FOR MANY YEARS TO COME.

IT IS ALMOST **SINFUL** THAT YOU MUST BE DRAWN INTO MY **WEB**, GIRL-- BUT THE **ADVANTAGES** OF A **SLAVE** WHO CAN PROWL THE **DAYLIGHT STREETS** IS ENDLESS.

AND **YOU** SHALL DO SO MUCH **BETTER** THAN THAT MINDLESS FOOL, **CLIFTON GRAVES**.

YET--

YOU HAVE AN INNOCENCE MY **DAUGHTER** COULD NEVER HOPE TO ACHIEVE.

--AS YOU **SLEEP**, I SEE AN **INNOCENCE** WITHIN YOU THAT I **LOST** SO MANY **CENTURIES** AGO, IF, INDEED, I **EVER** POSSESSED IT AT ALL.

...**LILITH** MAY BE CRUELER THAN EVEN--

--FOR AT LEAST I LIVED MANY YEARS AS A **HUMAN**-- AT LEAST I FELT AN ENDLESS STREAM OF **EMOTIONS**...

...WHEREAS **SHE** KNOWS NOTHING OF LIFE... AND **ONLY** OF **DEATH**.

KNOCK KNOCK

BUT **ENOUGH** REFLECTION. IT IS BAD FOR THE, EH, **SOUL**. THIS GIRL WILL **LIVE** AS LONG AS SHE IS **USEFUL** TO ME, AND NOT A MOMENT MORE.

SOMEONE AT THE **DOOR**?

EH?

BUT THERE **CAN'T** BE... I WOULD HAVE **SENSED** IT.

WELL, WE SHALL SEE IF I HAVE GONE **MAD** OR NOT.

AND SHOULD THERE ACTUALLY **BE** SOMEONE BEHIND THIS **PORTAL**, THEN **THEY** SHALL REGRET HAVING HAD THE COURTESY OF KNOCKING.

--**WHAT**?

I'M BEING **PULLED** FORWARD--

--BUT THERE IS NO ONE HERE! **NO ONE!!**

*AGAIN, IN **CHILLERS #1**, RAPIDLY SELLING OUT. --ROY.

255

JAJPUR, INDIA:

THE AIR IS THICK WITH A MYRIAD OF *SMELLS:* OF SPICES, OF PEOPLE, OF UNMOVED *BEASTS* WHO SIT AS THEY PLEASE WITHIN THE MARKET PLACE.

AND ALSO NOW, THE SMELL OF *GASOLINE.*

WE ARE ALL *REJOICING* AT YOUR *RETURN,* TAJ NITALL. YOU HAVE BEEN GONE FAR *TOO LONG* FROM YOUR PEOPLE.

IT TOOK US *MANY* YEARS TO FIND YOU. WHY DID YOU NOT WRITE, *OLD FRIEND?*

SILENT AS ALWAYS, TAJ NITALL. I AM SORRY, IT HAS BEEN SO *LONG* I HAVE FORGOTTEN.

BUT THE ONE WHO AWAITS YOU IN THAT *HUT* HAS BEEN *CALLING* YOUR NAME SINCE YOU LEFT YOUR VILLAGE, TAJ.

GO, MY FRIEND. YOUR *WIFE* WAITS FOR YOU.

CASTLE DUNWICK. SIXTEEN MILE FROM LONDON:

I FELT HAN— PUSH-- YE THERE WAS *ONE* THEF

...YET *SOMEONE* WILL HAVE TO FACE MY WRATH.

...SOMEONE WILL HAVE TO *ANSWER TO DRACULA!*

AND SOMEONE WILL HAVE TO *DIE!*

WHAT? A SCREAM FROM THE GIRL'S ROOM?

STLE DUNWICK SIGHS AS WATCHES THE BAT ARC WARDS TOWARDS THE SOUNDING *SCREAM*...

FOR THIS ANCIENT MANSE HAS SEEN MANY EVILS IN ITS LONG CENTURIES OF EXISTENCE--

--MANY EVEN MORE *VILE* THAN THIS MOCKERY OF LIFE...THIS CREATURE OF THE *UNDEAD*.

D THAT INCLUDES THE L WHICH *POSSESSED* S HOUSEHOLD FOR E THAN *SEVENTY-FIVE YEARS*...

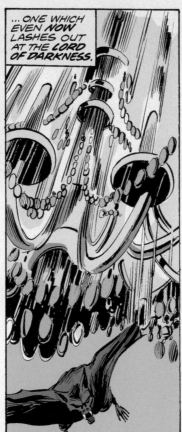

...ONE WHICH *NOW* LASHES OUT AT THE *LORD OF DARKNESS*.

THERE IS A *SOUND*...A FAINT ALMOST *INAUDIBLE* RUSTLE OF CRYSTAL SLIPPING THROUGH FOG...

BUT THAT SOUND IS *MORE* THAN ENOUGH FOR *DRACULA* TO HEAR...

CRASH

...AND THEN, TO TAKE *ACTION*.

ILE, IN THE DOWED *HALLS* SHIELA TTIER'S OM...

...A *DIFFERENT* MANIFESTATION OF *EVIL* BEGINS--

--AS THE SOUNDS OF HER *SCREAMS* ARE SILENCED BENEATH THE ROAR OF A WIND WHICH *BLOWS* THROUGH A *CLOSED* WINDOW...

HICH ERUPTS IN A FURY OF HELL-*DESTRUCTION* WITHIN A ROOM THAT LD BE QUIET...*SHOULD* BE CALM.

AND THIS PHANTOM WRAITH-LIKE *STORM* RIPS THROUGH THE SOUL OF THIS INNOCENT GIRL...

...AND *TEARS* AWAY AT THE FINAL LINGERING VESTIGES OF *SANITY*.

ONE MOMENT THERE IS A VIOLENT *HELL-STORM*...

WHAT IS WRONG, GIRL--? YOUR SCREAMS...

...AND THE NEXT, A HEAVENLY *CALM*.

OH *LORD*--HE WAS IN HERE--I FELT HIS *PRESENCE*...

HE CAME AGAIN TO *TORTURE* ME...

I THINK IT IS *TIME* YOU TELL ME WHO "HE" IS.

YOU HAVE SUFFICIENTLY ARROUS-ED MY *CURIOSITY*.

HER LIPS TREMBLING WITH FEAR, SHIELA WHITTIER SPEAKS ONE NAME...

"DUNWICK," SHE SAYS FALTERINGLY.

AND THE *SHADOWS* IN THE CASTLE... *HIS* CASTLE, GROW THICKER, AND DARKER.

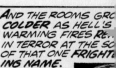

AND THE ROOMS GR... *COLDER* AS HELL'S WARMING FIRES RE... IN TERROR AT THE S... OF THAT ONE *FRIGHT*... ING NAME.

DUNWICK... ALESTAR DUNWICK.

HIS PAINTED *IMAGE* NOTE OF THE NAME, SMILES AT ITS TERR... ING *EFFECT*.

CASTLE DUNWICK *SHUDDERS*. WINDS CREATED WITHIN ITS SEALED FRAMES *HOWL* AT THE NIGHT AS IF MOCKING THE EVENING'S *DARKNESS* WITH ITS OWN HELL-BORN ETERNAL DARKNESS...

AND THEN, AFTER ALL THESE CENTURIES OF *WAITING*, THE CASTLE SCREAMS OUT...

...FOR IT *KNOWS* THE HORROR IS ONLY *BEGINNING*.

BUT THE *SCREAMS* ARE NOT HEARD, NOR SHALL THEY *EVER* BE. BUT...

SOUNDS, FROM DOWNSTAIRS. IS THERE SOMEONE...?

CRASH!

WE SHALL *INVESTIGATE*, SHIELA. COME WITH ME.

I HAVE LIVED *MANY* YEARS, GIRL-- SEEN ALMOST *EVERYTHING* THAT CAN POSSIBLY BE *IMAGINED*.

I HAVE PARTAKEN IN *HORRORS* THAT BRAVE MEN WOULD CRINGE AT--

YET, WHAT I *SENSE* HERE IN THIS MANSION IS A FILTH THAT *REPULSES* EVEN ME.

BUT THEY ALL *HIDE* NOW-- FOR THE *SOUND* WE HEARD WAS ONLY OF THIS PICTURE CRASHING TO THE *FLOOR*.

NOTHING MORE.

WRONG!

G HIM-- S IS THE TURE MY LE... STAR CAN--

--THE MAN WHO HAS BEEN *TORTURING* ME SINCE I CAME HERE TWO MONTHS AGO.

FINISH YOUR *STORY* THEN, I WISH TO HEAR THE *REST.*

YOU SAID YOU HAD NEVER *MET* DUNWICK, YET WHEN HE *DIED* HE LEFT YOU THIS MANSION.

GOD HELP ME BUT HE DID, DRACULA, AND *I* WISH I HAD NEVER GONE TO THE READING OF THE WILL.

AUNT HENRIETTA WAS GIVEN *UNCLE DUNWICK'S* EY. HIS SHIFTLESS SON, *RODNEY,* WAS GIVEN A LE ON THE ISLE OUTSIDE GREECE...

"...WITH HOPE THAT THAT *SPINELESS MILKSOP* WILL FINALLY AMOUNT TO SOMETHING."

AND THE *FINAL* PARAGRAPH READS, "TO MY NIECE, *SHIELA.* THOUGH WE HAVE NEVER MET, I HAVE OFTEN SEEN YOUR *PHOTOGRAPHS.* TO YOU I LEAVE MY *MANSION.* MAY YOU FIND IT AS *IRRESTIBLE* AS I FIND YOU."

EDDY, MY BOYFRIEND, WELL, HE I TOOK A SHORT TRIP TO IN- CT THE CASTLE. I *HATED* IT THE ENT I SAW IT.

AW, *DON'T* BE THAT WAY, SHEERY --I'LL BE WITH YOU.

BESIDES, THESE OLD CASTLES HAVE PLENTY OF OLD *ANTIQUES.* SHOULD BE RATHER *KINKY* AT THAT, LOVE.

I-I DON'T *CARE* ABOUT THEM, FRED. IT'S THIS *PLACE...*

I *CAN'T* EXPLAIN IT TO YOU... BUT IT... IT *BOTHERS* ME...

I FEEL IN MY *STOMACH* THAT IT'S *WRONG* TO BE HERE.

"'NONSENSE,' HE SAID. WE *ARGUED* A BIT, AND THEN I FOLLOWED HIM INTO THE SWELLING DARK- NESS.

"DID I TELL YOU, DRACUL THAT FREDDY DIED? DID EXPLAIN TO YOU THAT TH IS WHY I HATE THIS PLAC ABOVE EVERYTHING ELSE

"HE DIED...AND I SAW HIM DIE.

"I MUST ADMIT THERE WAS SOME BEAUTY IN WHAT I SAW. THE FURNITURE WAS MAGNIFICENT... THE HALLS WERE IMMENSE AND FILLED WITH INCRE- DIBLE STATUES. IT MUST HAVE BEEN LOVELY-ONCE.

"BUT ALL THE WHILE WE SEARCHED, I FELT I WAS BEING SPIED UPON... AND THAT FEELING NEVER LEFT ME.

"YOU SEE, WE WERE ABOUT EXPLORE THE BASEMENT.

ACCORDING TO THAT LAWYER HALEY, THERE WERE RUMORS THAT THE OLD MAN HAD A TREASURE DOWN HERE.

WE'RE GOING TO FIND IT, LOVE.

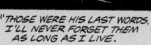

"THOSE WERE HIS LAST WORDS, I'LL NEVER FORGET THEM AS LONG AS I LIVE.

"BECAUSE, AS WE DESCENDED THE STAIRWELL, I SAW WHAT SEEMED TO BE A HAND REACHING OUT FROM THE DARK- NESS.

"AND BEFORE THE WORDS CAME TO MY LIPS...

"IT PUSHED FREDDY TO HIS DEATH.

"HIS HEAD CRACKE OPEN WHEN IT HIT BASEMENT FLOOR EYES ROLLED UP I DISGUSTING HORRO

...I FELT STOMACH AS I WATC HIS BLOO DRIP ONTC CONCR MOR

THE POLICE SAID IT WAS AN ACCIDENT, I-I COULDN'T TELL THEM DIFFERENTLY.

WE SHALL SEE... WE SHALL SEE.

4:30 A.M.

AND THE DARKNESS THAT HAS SETTLED ABOUT CASTLE DUNWICK REFUSES TO GIVE WAY TO THE DAWNING RAYS OF THE SUN.

THE **DARKNESS** DRAPES THE GIRL BEFORE YOU IN SOOTHING PATTERNS OF LIGHTS AND SHADES, AND SHE REMINDS YOU OF THE **THIRST** WHICH HAS BEEN GNAWING AT YOU THIS NIGHT.

BUT YOU CAN **NOT** KILL HER IF SHE IS TO BE YOUR **NEW SERVANT** -- IF SHE IS TO BE THE ONE YOU HAVE SOUGHT SINCE **CLIFTON GRAVES** DIED.

SO, SHE MUST **LIVE**, AND IT WILL BE **ANOTHER** WHO WILL **DIE**.

I GO NOW, SHIELA WHITTIER-- I HAVE **BUSINESS** IN TOWN THIS NIGHT.

CAN'T IT WAIT UNTIL **MORNING**?

NOTHING MUST EVER WAIT UNTIL MORNING, LASS-- **NOTHING!**

AND HE REPEATS THAT SILENT SHOUT IN HOPES THAT SOMEDAY HE MIGHT **BELIEVE** IT.

A **CURIOUS SENSATION FLOODS** OVER THE LORD OF DARKNESS AS HE RISES INTO THE COOL EVENING AIR...

...FEELING THAT SAYS [S]OME LIVES SHOULD [H]ELD **SACRED**. "BAH," [DRA]CULA RETORTS--"LIVES [EXIS]T ONLY FOR MY **SPORT**."

CAROLINE BASCOMBE HAS BEEN **TRAVELLING** ALL NIGHT, AND THE **RADIO** BESIDE HER HAS BEEN HER **ONLY** COMPANY.

IT **SINGS** TO HER, MAKING THE **HOURS** PASS MORE QUICKLY, AND, UNCONSCIOUSLY, SHE **HUMS** ALONG WITH IT.

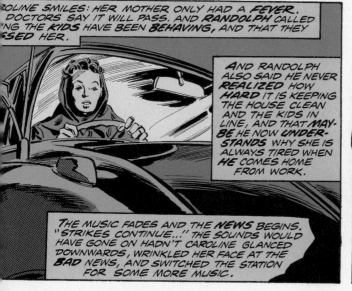

[CA]ROLINE SMILES: HER MOTHER ONLY HAD A **FEVER**. [THE] DOCTORS SAY IT WILL PASS. AND **RANDOLPH** CALLED [SAYI]NG THE **KIDS** HAVE BEEN **BEHAVING**, AND THAT THEY [MIS]SED HER.

AND RANDOLPH ALSO SAID HE NEVER **REALIZED** HOW **HARD** IT IS KEEPING THE HOUSE CLEAN AND THE KIDS IN LINE, AND THAT **MAY-BE** HE NOW **UNDER-STANDS** WHY SHE IS ALWAYS TIRED WHEN **HE** COMES HOME FROM WORK.

THE MUSIC FADES AND THE **NEWS** BEGINS. "STRIKES CONTINUE..." THE SOUNDS WOULD HAVE GONE ON HADN'T CAROLINE GLANCED DOWNWARDS, WRINKLED HER FACE AT THE **BAD** NEWS, AND SWITCHED THE STATION FOR SOME MORE MUSIC.

WHEN SHE LOOKS **UP** AGAIN, CAROLINE SEES THE **FOG** HAS CROWDED AROUND HER CAR. EVEN HER **LIGHTS** CAN'T PENETRATE IT.

"**DAMN**," SHE THINKS TO HER-SELF. SHE WANTED TO BE HOME **BY MORNING**.

261

THROUGH THE HEAVY FOG SHE SEES A *SHAPE*... HUMAN? ANIMAL? *YES* -- IT IS A *MAN*.

GOD -- IT'S A MAN STANDING IN THE *CENTER* OF THE ROAD. CAROLINE SLAMS THE *BREAK* DOWN HARD.

THE CAR JERKS SUDDENLY AND *SWERVES* TO THE LEFT.

BUT NOT *NEARLY* ENOUGH.

WHUMP

THERE IS A SICKENING *CRUNCH* AS METAL HITS FLESH.

FRANTICALLY, SHE RUNS BACK TO THE FALLEN *BO...* IT DOESN'T MOVE... ITS *CHEST* DOESN'T HEAVE.

IN SHORT: IT IS *DEAD*.

OH N... PLEAS... BE AL... PLEAS...

I CAN NOT COME *ALIVE*, WOMAN --

-- BUT I SHALL NEVER BE TRULY *DEAD*.

COME TO ME NOW, GIRL, AND *LEARN* WHAT IT MEANS TO BE --

-- A VAMPIRE!

AS THE PAIN OF HIS *FANGS* TURN TO *PLEASURE*, CAROLINE BASCOMBE'S *SCREAMS* END, AND HER BODY FALLS *LIMP*.

EEEYOOEEE!

SHE *DIES* THEN, AND IN *THREE DAYS* SHE WILL FINALLY RETURN *HOME* TO RANDOLPH. AND THEN TEDDY AND LITTLE EMILY -- YES, EVEN DARLING LITTLE EMILY -- WILL HAVE THEIR MOTHER BACK --

TWO YEARS FROM NOW RANDOLPH WILL FALL BENEATH *BLADE'S* KNIFE. CAROLINE AND TEDDY WILL SUFFER FROM *BLOODLOSS* AND PERISH. EMILY WILL LIVE *150* YEARS BEFORE SHE, TOO, DIES.

SHIELA WHITTIER HEARS *SOUNDS* AS WELL -- B... DIFFERENT SOUNDS... L... AN *OCEAN WAVE* CALLI... HER NAME AS IT *BILLOW...* ONTO A CRAGGY OUT-- JUTTING OF ISLAND ROCK...

DRACU... IS TH... YOU...

WHO'S CALLING ME? WH...

GOD-- IT [MU]ST BE *HIM* [AG]AIN-- YET, [I C]AN'T TURN [BA]CK... I [CA]N'T TURN [AW]AY.

HE'S KEPT ME HERE SO *LONG* NOW... *PREVENTED* ME FROM *LEAVING* THIS HELL HOUSE OF HIS.

BUT MAYBE NOW HE FINALLY WISHES TO *END* THE CHARADE...

FOR REASONS *UNKNOWN*, SHIELA WHITTIER CONTINUES UP THE DUST-THICK STAIRWELL.

UNCLE? IS THAT YOU, UNCLE DUNWICK?

I HAVE BEEN *CALLING* TO YOU FOR *TWO MONTHS*, SHIELA--

--BUT ONLY [NO]W HAVE I BEEN [PO]WERFUL ENOUGH [TO] *TOTALLY FORM* [M]Y ESSENCE.

WHAT YOU SEE BEFORE YOU, GIRL, IS MY *ECTOPLASM*-- THE FORCE OF MY *SOUL*... A SOUL LONG SOLD TO *SATAN*.

SOLD, MY DEAR, LONG BEFORE YOU EVER BECAME MY *DAUGHTER*.

DAUGHTER? YOU'RE *MAD!*

IF IT WERE BUT *TRUE*, LASS, THEN *YOU* WOULD NOT HAVE HAD TO *SUFFER* SO... NOR WOULD YOU HAVE TO *PERISH* NOW.

YOU *ARE* MY DAUGHTER, GIRL-- AND I AM THE MAN YOUR *MOTHER* MURDERED WHEN I TURNED OVER THIS *ESTATE* TO HER YEARS AGO.

AS I DIED, I CRIED OUT TO *HELL* FOR REVENGE. I WAS GRANTED A NEW LIFE, AND SO I CAME BACK [I]N THE *FORM* OF YOUR [M]OTHER'S *LOVER*.

SLOWLY, DIABOLICALLY, I DROVE HER *INSANE*, UNTIL SHE TOOK HER OWN LIFE.

NO! THIS IS *CRAZY!* I *REFUSE* TO BELIEVE ANY OF THIS.

YOU SEE ME HERE, THAT IS *PROOF* ENOUGH.

IN THE FORM OF HER LOVER I *CONTINUED* TO LIVE. TAKING HER *MONEY* I REMARRIED, AND FOR *YEARS* I WATCHED OVER YOU FROM AFAR.

BUT, AS YOU APPROACHED YOUR *TWENTY-FIRST* BIRTHDAY, I HAD TO KEEP THE *VOW* I SWORE ON MY *DEATH-DAY.*

I HAD TO *SACRIFICE* YOU TO THE *DARKLING* GODS.

SO, I *ABANDONED* MY MORTAL GUISE, AND WILLED YOU THIS MANSION ANEW.

I WON'T LISTEN TO ANY OF THIS. I'M LEAVING -- *YOU, THIS STINKING MANSION* -- *EVERYTHING!*

I WON'T BE *USED, DISCARDED, TAMPERED WITH,* THEN *TOSSED* ASIDE WHEN MY VALUE IS *OVER.*

FIND SOMEONE *ELSE* WHO WILL PLAY YOUR STINKING *GAMES,* UNCLE ... FATHER, OR WHATEVER YOU ARE.

BUT *NOT* ME...DON'T CHOOSE ME.

YOU HAVE MY *WILL,* DAUGHTER. VERY COMMENDABLE, BUT VERY *FOOLISH* AS WELL.

POW... SH... FORCE TO COME ME...*QUIC*

NO MO... DAUGH... IT I... TIM...

I HAVE *PLEDGED* MYSELF TO THE *DARK GODS* THAT THEY SHALL HAVE *YOU* AS THEIR *SACRIFICE.* AND SO IT SHALL BE.

FIRST YOUR *HEART* SHALL BE PLUCKED FROM YOU. YOUR *HEAD* SHALL BE THEN *SEVERED* AND USED IN THE CEREMONIAL *INCENSE* --

-- AND THE *REST* SHALL BE SENT TO *ROAST* IN HELL.

"AND THEN YOUR *BONES* WILL HANG ALONGSIDE T... *OTHERS* WHO HAVE BEEN SACRIFICED BY ME IN... PAST. I AM *SORRY,* DAUGHTER -- BUT THE GODS M... HAVE THEIR WAY."

UNKNOWING OF THE *MADNESS* WHICH BOILS BELOW...

-- DRACULA DESCENDS...LOWERING HIMSELF THR... THE PORTAL TO GAIN AN ENTRANCE WITHIN...

IDE NOW, DAUGHTER-- DE THIS SECRET AMBER AND NESS WHAT FEW N ALIVE HAVE ER SEEN BEFORE.

IS IS THE BERNACLE RE MY SOUL D FORM CAME ONE-- --THIS IS THE ENTRANCE TO THE CHURCH OF THE DAMNED!

PLEASE-- LEAVE ME ALONE--

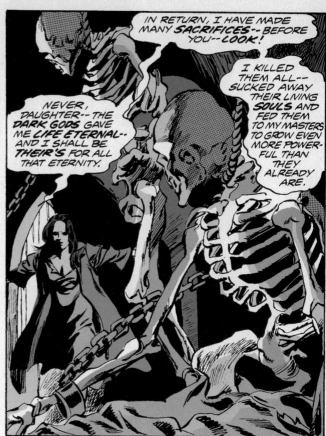

IN RETURN, I HAVE MADE MANY SACRIFICES-- BEFORE YOU-- LOOK!

I KILLED THEM ALL-- SUCKED AWAY THEIR LIVING SOULS AND FED THEM TO MY MASTERS TO GROW EVEN MORE POWER- FUL THAN THEY ALREADY ARE.

NEVER, DAUGHTER-- THE DARK GODS GAVE ME LIFE ETERNAL-- AND I SHALL BE THEIR'S FOR ALL THAT ETERNITY.

K AGAIN-- BEHIND M, UPON THE ONE-- AND SEE POWERFUL MY STERS ARE--

AND WHY THEY AND S THEIR ATTENDANT LL EVER BE PREME.

IT IS POSSIBLE-- POSSIBLE!

NOTHING IS IMPOSSIBLE TO THE DARK GODS, DAUGHTER.

BEFORE YOU SITS MY ORIGINAL BODY TURN TO GOLD-- PRESERVED FOR ALL THE AGES TO STARE AT IN AWE.

YES, THIS IS THE POWER I SERVE--

--AND THIS IS THE POWER THAT DEMANDS YOU AS SACRIFICE.

265

NO! I WON'T BE PART OF THIS **MAD-NESS.**

YOU **CAN'T** HOLD ME HERE --NO POWER ON EARTH WILL KEEP ME YOUR **PRISONER.**

"NO POWER OF **EARTH,**" MY **DEAR?**

MY POWER WASN'T GRANTED TO ME BY ANY **EARTHLY** FORCE--

NAY. MY POWERS COME FROM **SATAN** HIMSELF--

--THE **DEVIL-GOD INCARNATE!**

AS SHIELA'S **FEET** TOUCH THE WOODEN STAIRCASE **SLATS...**

...THE BOARDS COME **ALIVE--** SHOOTING APART FROM THEIR **FRAME-WORK--**

--COLLAPSING UNDER THE TERRIFIED GIRL UPON THEM.

WHAT IN **HELL'S** NAME?

HA INSA BE BO HE SIN I LE

YES, VAMPIRE-- INSANITY BORN IN **HELL...**

...SPAWNED BY THE VERY SAME MASTER THAT **YOU** MUST SERVE.

I SERVE **NO** MASTER, GHOST--

FOR ONLY **FOOLS** WORSHIP THEMSELVES.

FOOLS WHO MUST **BOW** IN SUBSERVIENCE OR PERISH.

WRONG, VAMPIRE. **ALL** MUST SERVE SOME MASTER--BE IT A GOD IN HEAVEN **OR** IN HELL.

--IT IS ALL THE **OTHERS** WHO MUST SERVE **ME.**

AND SINCE **YOU** REFUS TO LOWER YOURSELF I **WORSHIP-**

-- YOU MU. BE DESTROY.

...E ENDLESS *DEBRIS* FROM A ...TURY OF WASTE SWIRLS ...DDENINGLY AT THE *LORD* ...OF *DARKNESS*

...IRON SPIKES SPLIT ...THE AIR. *PORCELINE* ...BOWLS LONG SINCE ...CRACKED INTO JAGGED ...JUGGERNAUTS *HURL* ...THROUGH THE EMPTY SPACE.

AND *WOODEN SHARDS* FROM AGES-DECAYED *FURNITURE* SCREAM TOWARDS THE PRINCE OF EVIL IN THE FRIGHTFUL FORM OF *DEADLY STAKES.*

NO *MORTAL* MAN COULD *HOPE* TO ESCAPE THIS ENDLESS BARRAGE OF HURTLING HELL...

...BUT *DRACULA* IS NO MERE MORTAL... *DRACULA* IS *BEYOND* ALL *CONCEPTIONS* OF *MORTALITY.*

AND THUS, IT IS THIS *IMMORTAL DEMON* WHO ALTERS HIMSELF INTO AN *INTANGIBLE MIST*...

...ND *REFORMS* INTO HUMAN ...SE ONCE THE DANGER HAS ...E.

...OU HAVE ...N GRANTED ...E *ANEW,* ...OST--

--THEN *THIS* ...DEN CORPSE ...MORE THAN ...TREASURED ...MINDER OF ...R *HUMAN* ...LIFE.

INDEED, YOUR VERY *HELL-BORN* EXISTENCE IS INEXTRICABLY *TIED* TOGETHER WITH ITS *SURVIVAL.*

SATAN DEMANDS THE WORSHIPPING OF *FALSE IMAGES*...

...AND THUS WITH THIS *FETISH* DESTROYED, THEN, TOO, SHALL ITS *COUNTERPART* BE TAKEN WITH IT.

NO-- YOU *MUSTN'T TOUCH IT*-- IT MUSTN'T *BE HARMED.*

IF I AM TO SERVE THE *DARK GODS*-- I MUST BE INTACT. I *MUST BE WHOLE!*

THEN *SATAN* WILL HAVE TO DO *WITHOUT* YOU, GHOST.

YOUR TIME HERE IS *OVER.*

S M I S S H H H

HOW COULD YOU END MY LIFE SO... *HOW* COULD YOU?

YOU'RE A *CHILD OF HELL* AS I AM.

I AM *DRACULA*, GHOST...

...AND I AM A GREATER *HELL* THAN *ANY* YOU COULD EVER IMAGINE.

NEXT: BLOOD-FEAR IN TRAFALGAR

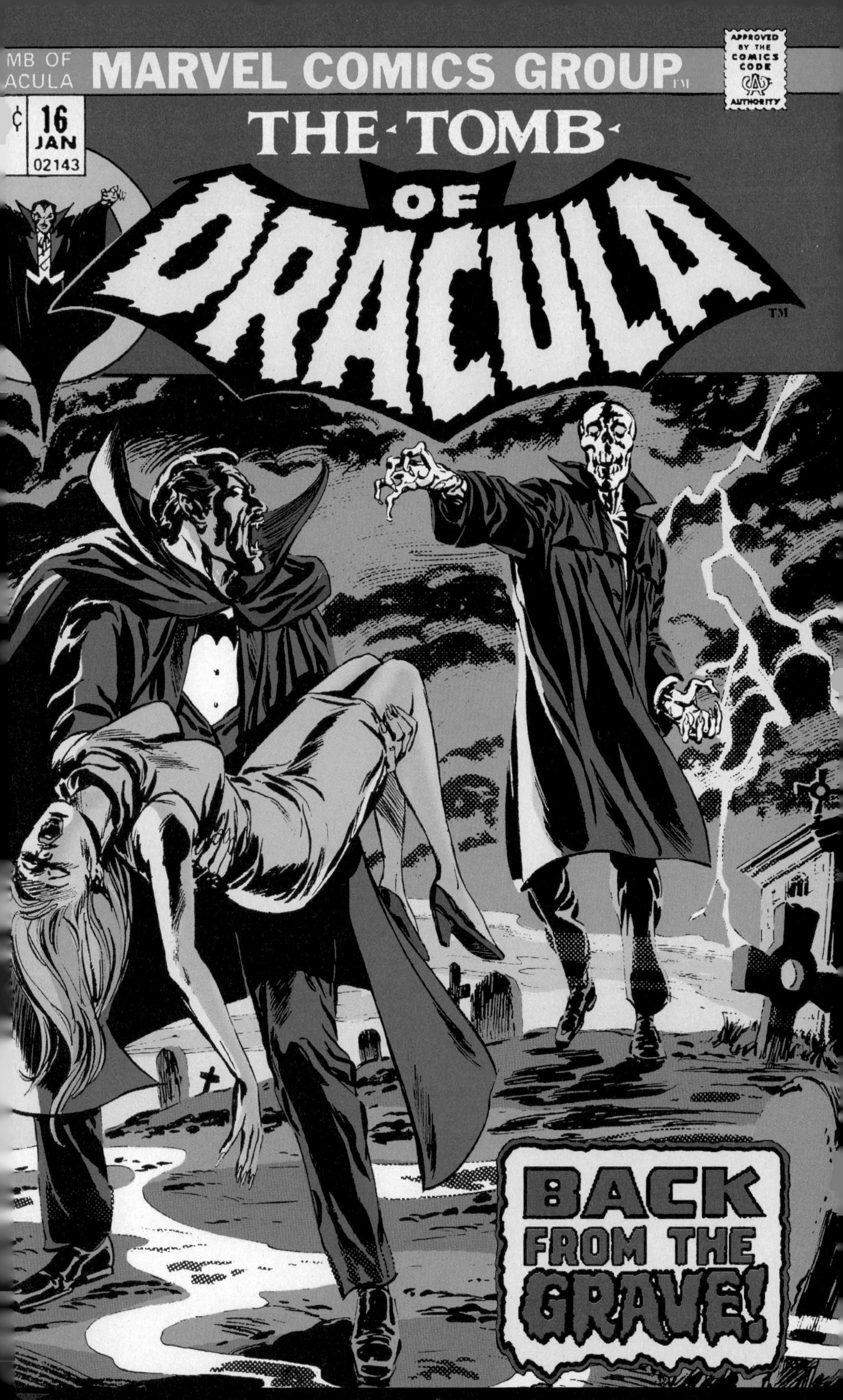
MARVEL COMICS GROUP
APPROVED BY THE COMICS CODE AUTHORITY
16 JAN 02143
THE TOMB OF DRACULA
BACK FROM THE GRAVE!

THE TOMB OF DRACULA #16 cover before art corrections

THE TOMB OF DRACULA #17 cover before art corrections

THE TOMB OF DRACULA #18 cover before art corrections

Essential Tomb of Dracula Vol. 1 back cover

Essential Werewolf by Night Vol. 1 back cover